STUDY GUIDE

MANAGERIAL FINANCE

Eighth Edition
with Tax Update

J. Fred Weston
University of California, Los Angeles

Thomas E. Copeland
University of California, Los Angeles

THE DRYDEN PRESS
Chicago Fort Worth San Francisco
Philadelphia Montreal Toronto
London Sydney Tokyo

ISBN 0-03-030732-5
Printed in the United States of America
901-066-987654321

Address orders:
6277 Sea Harbor Drive
Orlando, Florida 32821

Address editorial correspondence:
The Dryden Press
908 N. Elm St.
Hinsdale, IL 60521

The Dryden Press
Holt, Rinehart and Winston
Saunders College Publishing

Preface

Our experience in using earlier versions of the *Study Guide* for *Managerial Finance* has enabled us to make continued improvements. Since the *Study Guide* is designed mainly as an aid to students, we class-tested previous editions and the manuscript for this edition extensively, asking students for advice on how to make it most helpful to them. This trial-by-fire process has helped us improve the organization and coverage of the material. In addition, this edition of the *Study Guide* incorporates new developments in financial market theory that increase our understanding of financial decision making.

Managerial Finance is a decision-oriented textbook. Its contents reflect the present-day emphasis on decisions affecting the value of the firm. This approach has been found to be more useful than a descriptive or institutional approach. The main purpose of this *Study Guide* is to focus on the central ideas that provide the conceptual framework of *Managerial Finance*. The *Study Guide* seeks to carry out this objective by providing two kinds of assistance.

First, an outline of the subject matter of each topic is set forth. This presents the material in a stream-lined perspective. The outline should be examined prior to reading the chapter in *Managerial Finance* to obtain an overview of the material, then also should be used later for review purposes. After having studied the chapter, the student can go over the outline, recalling relatively quickly the major points that were covered.

The second major feature of the *Study Guide* is the set of problems and solutions it provides. Many instructors emphasize the problems found at the end of each chapter. Ideally, the students should be able to work the problems without an undue amount of time, and the majority of the class should be able to reach a correct solution. This reduces the necessity of devoting much classroom time to the mechanics of the problem and permits more time for discussing the basic ideas the problem illustrates. If too much time is spent reaching the solution, an insufficient amount of time remains for thinking through the principles the problem is designed to illustrate. If many students are unable to reach the correct solutions, then the instructor must devote an inordinate amount of time to explaining the mechanics of the problem.

We have attempted to forestall these pitfalls by providing a sample set of problems and solutions in the *Study Guide*. The end-of-chapter problems give examples of most of the important points covered in the text. The problems and solutions provided in the *Study Guide* illustrate most of the end-of-chapter problems. Therefore, if a person conscientiously works through the *Study Guide* problems, that person should be able to complete most of the assigned end-of-chapter problems without difficulty.

In this edition, the printing is in pica size. This enables the instructor to make transparencies of both the outline materials and the illustrative problems and solutions. Since the students will also have copies of the materials from their own Study Guide, this permits the instructor to refer to the subject matter and problem materials without having to duplicate copies for the students. Lecture and problem analysis are thereby facilitated with a minimum of expense and effort.

In summary, this Study Guide is designed to enable the user of Managerial Finance to utilize time more effectively. The subject outline can be used to show what to look for in a chapter, as well as to facilitate study when reviewing for examinations. The problems and solutions can be used to help understand the mechanics of the various arithmetic operations as well as the analytics involved. The solutions can be used as a check against the user's own solutions or as a guide to develop an efficient approach to solving a problem without excessive "wheel spinning." With the self-study guides provided, the user saves time which can be used to reflect on the concepts and general methodology for developing solutions to the key decision areas of managerial finance.

Hence this Study Guide can serve as a supplement for use with other books and reading materials for the study of finance. This edition of the Study Guide is therefore relatively more self-contained than its predecessors, including a complete set of financial and related tables in the Appendix to facilitate verification of the problem solutions set forth. Our thanks for the considerable assistance of Susan Hoag in this substantial revision. Marilyn McElroy also greatly aided in the final preparation of the materials.

August 1985

J. Fred Weston, Thomas E. Copeland
Graduate School of Management
University of California, Los Angeles
Los Angeles, California 90024

CONTENTS

PART ONE. FUNDAMENTAL CONCEPTS OF MANAGERIAL FINANCE

CHAPTER 1

THE FINANCE FUNCTION

Theme: The nature of the finance function and its significance.

I. The Finance Function.
   A. The main functions of financial managers are to plan for, acquire, and utilize funds to make the maximum contribution to the efficient operation of the organization.
   B. The key financial functions must be performed in any kind of organization.
   C. Financial markets continuously record the valuation of business firms, and in doing so, assess managerial performance.

II. Organization of the Firm's Finance Department.
   A. The four main types of financial officers are the treasurer, the controller, the vice-president of finance and the corporate secretary, with most specific finance functions divided between the treasurer and the controller.
      1. The treasurer handles the acquisition and custody of funds. Duties include:
         a. Cash budgeting
         b. Cash position
         c. Working capital position
         d. Credit management
         e. Insurance and pension management
      2. The controller is responsible for accounting, budgeting and control systems including:
         a. Financial statements
         b. Payroll
         c. Taxes
         d. Internal auditing
      3. The treasurer and controller report to the vice-president of finance who reports directly to the president and is responsible for general financial policy.
      4. Among the financial duties of the corporate secretary are:
         a. Record-keeping in connection with instruments of ownership (shares) and borrowing activities.
         b. Communications relating to financing activities.
   B. Finance committees are used in larger companies.
      1. A wider scope of knowledge and judgment may be required on major financial policy issues.
      2. Allocation of funds for capital and operating budgets may be more objectively accomplished.
      3. Other key finance committees include:
         a. Capital appropriations committee
         b. Budget committee

c. Pension committee
d. Salary and profit-sharing committee

C. The finance function is typically close to the top of the organizational structure of the firm because financial decisions are so important to the long-run well-being of the firm.

III. The Nature of the Firm.

A. The contractual theory views the firm as a network of actual and implicit contracts which specify the rights, obligations and payoffs of firm participants.

B. An agency problem arises when there is separation of ownership and control.

1. The divergence of interests between principal and agent creates an agency problem.
2. Stockholders are the owners of the firm.
3. Managers exercise control over the firm and are supposed to act as agents for the stockholders.
4. Managerialism refers to self-serving behavior by managers at the expense of stockholders.
5. Agency costs include both the costs of excessive management perquisites as well as the costs involved in limiting the potential for abuse.

C. Various market mechanisms help control the agency problem.

1. The stock market reflects its perception of management performance in higher or lower stock prices. Executive compensation plans tied to stock value help keep managers' goals tied to firm goals.
2. The managerial labor market assures that competing managers will mutually monitor performance and replace ineffective managers.
3. The market for corporate takeovers comes into play when the firm's stock price falls due to ineffective management; the corporate acquirer then replaces the ineffective management.

IV. Goals of the Firm.

A. The goal of financial management is to maximize the value of the firm.

1. Management should seek to balance the interests of owners, creditors and the other constituencies of the firm.
2. If maximization with respect to any particular interest is sought, an opportunity would be created for others to take over the firm and to increase its total value.

B. Value maximization is superior to profit maximization.

1. Maximizing value takes the time value of money into account.
2. The discount rate or capitalization rate used in seeking to maximize value reflects the risks of the flows that are capitalized, while profit maximization does not.

3. Value maximization emphasizes cash flows rather than accounting net income.

C. The goal of maximizing value through maximizing share price reflects the position of the common stockholders as claimants to the residual income of the firm.

1. This does not imply that managers should seek to improve the value of common stock at the expense of the bondholders.
    a. Riskier investments may benefit shareholders, but cause bond values to fall.
    b. Unless strong signals are given in advance to bondholders that investment and other policies will not be changed to their disadvantage, the returns promised to bondholders must compensate them for this risk.

D. Financial markets play a role in measuring performance.

1. The continuous assessment of firm value stimulates efficiency.
2. Financial markets see through accounting techniques to underlying value.

E. Social responsibility is an important aspect of the goals of the firm.

1. Successful value maximization leads to better contributions to society as a whole.
2. Effects on the external environment--pollution, job safety, product safety--must also be taken into account.
3. Responsiveness to external constituencies--consumer and other interest groups--may be required for economic survival.
4. Firms should seek to maximize shareholder wealth within legal and social constraints and to respond to the firms' changing environments and constituencies.

V. The Risk-Return Tradeoff.

A. Profitability and risk jointly determine firm value.

B. The primary policy decision is choosing the industry in which to operate.

C. Profitability and risk are then determined by decisions relating to firm size, types of equipment, debt level, liquidity position, etc.

1. In general, decisions which increase profitability also increase risk; decisions which reduce risk also tend to reduce profitability. For example:
    a. Increased cash holdings reduce risk, but since cash is not an earning asset, this also reduces profitability.
    b. Additional debt increases the rate of return to stockholders, but also increases risk.
2. The financial manager seeks to find the balance between profitability and risk that will maximize the value of the firm.

VI. The Changing Role of Financial Management.

A. Finance first emerged as a separate field of study in the early 1900's.

B. Early emphasis was descriptive, legalistic.

1. Through 1920's--focus on obtaining capital during period of industrialization and relatively primitive capital markets; emphasis on securities, mergers, formation of firms.
2. 1930's--depression shifted focus to bankruptcy, corporate liquidity, securities regulation.
3. 1940's--1950's--some attention to internal control procedures, budgeting, capital budgeting.

C. Increasing focus on internal decision-making, asset analysis, mathematical models.

D. Current issues in finance:

1. Capital budgeting and the cost of capital.
2. Innovative financing--new ways of raising funds during capital shortage.
3. Merger activity.
4. International finance.
5. Social responsibility.
6. Effect of inflation.

VII. The Impact of Inflation on Financial Management.

A. Interest rates rise; the cost of borrowing increases.

B. Costs increase; long-range planning is subject to greater uncertainties.

C. Demand for capital increases, even to merely sustain real volume of business.

D. Bond prices decline; firms shift to using more short-term debt instruments.

E. Long-term capital investment is delayed, leading to a lack of capacity or outmoded equipment when the economy turns up.

F. Reported financial data is distorted in a period of rising prices.

VIII. Organization and Structure of this Study Guide.

A. This Study Guide deals with eight major areas of managerial finance.

1. Fundamental concepts of managerial finance.
2. The time dimension in financial decisions.
3. Financial analysis, planning, and control.
4. Working capital management.
5. Decision-making under uncertainty.
6. Cost of capital and valuation.
7. The treasurer's point of view: policy decisions.
8. Integrated topics in managerial finance.

B. This Study Guide seeks to outline the material and provide problems with illustrative solution procedures for Managerial Finance, 8th edition.

CHAPTER 2

FINANCIAL STATEMENTS

Theme: Financial statements report a firm's historical performance and provide clues to its future performance.

I. The Most Basic Financial Statements are the Income Statement and the Balance Sheet.
   A. The income statement reports the flows of revenues and expenses over an interval of time.
   B. The balance sheet measures stocks of assets and liabilities at a point in time.
   C. A firm's activities during a year are fully described by three statements:
      1. Beginning-of-year balance sheet.
      2. Income statement.
      3. End-of-year balance sheet.

II. Income Statement.
   A. Format:

```
     Revenues
   - Variable costs
   - Fixed cash costs
   - Depreciation  (non-cash fixed costs)
   ----------------
     Earnings before interest and taxes (EBIT)
   - Interest payments
   ----------------
     Earnings before tax (EBT)
   - Tax
   ----------------
     Net income
   - Dividends
   ----------------
     Retained earnings
```

   B. Business risk is the combination of revenue risk and operating leverage; it refers to the variability of EBIT relative to revenue induced by operating leverage.
      1. Revenue risk varies with product line.
      2. Operating leverage varies with production technology.
         a. Technology choice is determined by the relative costs of capital and labor, the ratio of fixed to variable costs of production.
         b. Technology affects EBIT risk; fixed costs determine extent to which EBIT is more variable than revenue.
         c. The higher the ratio of fixed to total costs, the riskier the EBIT stream, the higher the operating leverage.
   C. Financial risk refers to the variability of net income relative to EBIT induced by financial leverage (fixed interest payments).
   D. Net income reflects both business and financial risk.
   E. Retained earnings is that portion of net income not paid

out to shareholders as dividends.
1. Retained earnings represent corporate savings, reinvested in the firm.
2. Thus, dividend policy impacts investment policy.

III. Balance Sheet.
A. Format: The balance sheet is arranged in order of decreasing liquidity.

ASSETS	LIABILITIES
Short-term:	Short-term:
Cash	Accounts Payable
Marketable Securities	Notes Payable
Accounts Receivable	Accruals
Inventory	Long-term:
Long-term:	Debt
Gross Property, Plant and Equipment	Preferred Stock
less Accumulated Depreciation	Equity:
Net Property, Plant and Equipment	Common at par
	Common in excess of par
	Retained earnings
	less Treasury Stock
Total Assets	Total Liabilities

B. Working capital is a measure of liquidity; it is the difference between short-term assets and short-term liabilities.
C. Long-term assets (property, plant and equipment) are the least liquid, most profitable assets for most manufacturing firms.
1. Annual depreciation of fixed assets appears as an expense on the income statement; it is an estimate of the cost of plant and equipment used in the production process.
2. Gross fixed assets are carried at original book value, reduced by the accumulated depreciation of prior and current years to arrive at net fixed assets.
a. Upon sale of an asset, its book value is removed from the gross asset account, and its accumulated depreciation is removed from that account.
b. Any gain (loss) over (under) its net book value is recorded on the income statement.
D. Short-term liabilities.
1. Accounts payable are short-term borrowings from suppliers of goods and services (also called trade credit).
2. Notes payable are short-term borrowings from banks.
3. Accruals are unpaid obligations, such as wages due.
E. Long-term liabilities form the firm's capital structure.
1. Debt--fixed interest payments, prior claim in bankruptcy.
2. Preferred stock--hybrid, with characteristics of both debt and equity; fixed dividends, but cannot force

bankruptcy.

3. Equity--included in liabilities because the firm is a legal entity which "owes" its equity to its owners, the shareholders.
   a. Common at par plus common in excess of par--the amount paid for the stock when issued.
   b. Retained earnings--the sum of each year's retained earnings; link between income statement and balance sheet.
   c. Treasury stock--cost of repurchasing shares; subtracted from the equity account; related to dividend policy.

IV. Sources and Uses of Funds Statement.

A. The sources and uses of funds statement is computed from a beginning and an ending balance sheet and the intervening income statement.

B. The statement focuses on changes in the firm's cash position.

Δ Cash = Sources of funds - Uses of funds

C. Sources of funds include:
   1. Decrease in an asset account (except Cash).
   2. Increase in a liability account.
   3. Net income plus depreciation = sources of funds from operations.
      a. Depreciation is not a cash outlay.

D. Uses of funds include:
   1. Increase in an asset account (except Cash).
   2. Decrease in a liability account.
   3. Dividends.

E. Format:

Sources of Funds	Uses of Funds
Net income	Increases in working capital
Depreciation	Increases in gross PPE
Decreases in working capital	Decreases in long-term debt
Decreases in gross PPE	Repurchase of preferred or common stock
Increases in long-term debt	Dividends paid
Sale of preferred or common stock	
Total sources	Total uses

Total sources - total uses = change in cash position

V. Reporting Requirements.

A. Data requirements of users may vary and be inconsistent.

B. Internal requirements of managers.
   1. Budgets.
   2. New project funding.
   3. Review of ongoing projects.
   4. Internal auditing.

C. External users.
   1. Shareholders--financial reports audited by independent public accounting firms facilitate raising external funds.

2. Board of Directors.
3. Public accounting firms.
4. Securities and Exchange Commission (SEC)--supervises the self-regulation of the accounting profession.
    a. 10K report--standardized, more detailed than annual report to shareholders.
    b. Registration statement for new securities issues.
5. Tax authorities--local, state, national, international.

Chapter 2 - Illustrative Problem and Solution

2.1 Construct a Sources and Uses of Funds Statement from the information provided below:

Balance Sheet	December 31, 19X0		December 31, 19X1	
Assets:				
Cash		$150		$160
Marketable securities		75		65
Accounts receivable		200		225
Inventory		350		385
Gross PPE	600		650	
less depreciation	- 125		- 150	
Net PPE		475		500
Total assets		$1,250		$1,335
Liabilities:				
Accounts payable		$ 70		$ 60
Notes payable		175		160
Long-term debt		400		485
Equity:				
Common stock		300		300
Retained earnings		400		440
less Treasury stock		- 95		- 110
Total liabilities		$1,250		$1,335

Income Statement for the year ending December 31, 19X1

Revenues	$2,025
Cost of goods sold	1,750
Selling & admin. expense	65
EBIT	210
Interest expense	60
EBT	150
Taxes (at 40%)	60
Net income	90
Dividends	50
To Retained earnings	40

Solution:

Sources and Uses of Funds Statement

Sources of Funds (excluding Cash)	
Net income	$90
Depreciation	25
Decreases in working capital:	
Sale of marketable securities	10
Increase in long-term debt	85
Total sources of funds	$210

Uses of Funds	
Increases in working capital:	
Increase in accounts receivable	$25
Increase in inventory	35
Decrease in accounts payable	10
Decrease in notes payable	15
Total	$85
Gross asset expansion	50
Purchase of Treasury stock	15
Dividends paid	50
Total uses of funds	$200

Difference in cash position = Total sources - Total uses
= $210 - $200
= $10

This firm obtained funds from operations, from selling off a portion of its marketable securities portfolio, and from issuing additional long-term debt.

The funds were used to build up inventory, to extend trade credit to the firm's customers, to repay accounts payable and outstanding short-term loans, to expand the physical plant, to repurchase stock, and to pay dividends.

CHAPTER 3

THE FINANCIAL ENVIRONMENT

Theme: An important part of the environment within which financial managers function is the financial system of the economy. The financial system consists of financial markets, financial institutions, and financial instruments. This chapter presents an overview of each of the three aspects of the financial system.

I. Financial Management.
   A. The financial manager acquires funds from financing sources via financial markets.
   B. The two major types of business financing are:
      1. Equity financing which extends ownership of the firm through the sale of common stock.
      2. Various forms of debt financing.
   C. The financial manager allocates funds among alternative uses in the firm, manages cash inflows and outflows, and returns funds to financial sources in the form of dividends, interest payments and principal repayment.

II. Financial Markets.
   A. A financial transaction results in the simultaneous creation of a financial asset and a financial liability.
      1. For savings surplus units, savings exceed investment in real assets, so they hold financial assets such as bonds, common stock, accounts receivable or deposits in financial institutions.
      2. For savings deficit units, savings are less than investment in real assets, so they issue financial liabilities such as bonds, common stock, accounts payable.
   B. Savings surplus units lend funds to savings deficit units usually through financial intermediaries.
   C. Money markets involve financial assets and liabilities with maturities of one year or less.
   D. Capital markets involve instruments with maturities of longer than one year.

III. Financing Sources and Financial Intermediation.
   A. Financial intermediaries are involved with money and capital markets. They assist in the transfer of savings from savings surplus units to savings deficit units so that savings can be redistributed into their most productive uses.
      1. Commercial banks have the ability to accept demand deposits (e.g., checking accounts).

2. Savings and loan associations (S&Ls) receive funds from passbook savings.
3. Finance companies make loans to other business firms and to households.
4. Life insurance companies sell protection against the loss of income from death or disability.
5. Pension funds collect contributions from employees and/or employers to make periodic payments upon the employee's retirement.
6. Investment funds or mutual funds sell shares to investors and use the proceeds to purchase already-existing equity securities.
7. Investment banking firms buy new issues of securities from business firms and resell the securities to other investors.
8. Investment brokers and dealers are engaged in transactions of already-issued securities.

B. Other sources of financing:
   1. Individuals and households
   2. Government and government agencies
   3. Other business firms

C. Business firms obtain funds to make investments to increase the supply of goods and services.
   1. Financial managers choose from among the financial sources listed to obtain funds.
   2. The funds are allocated to their most productive use.
   3. Financial managers seek to determine the most economical mix of financing available.

IV. Role of the Government.

A. The Federal Reserve System influences the cost and availability of funds by the following mechanisms.
   1. Reserve requirements establish the percentage of deposits that must be kept on reserve with the central bank.
   2. Open market operations are the Fed's buying and selling of treasury securities.
   3. The discount rate is the rate charged to commercial banks when they borrow from the Fed.

B. The U.S. Treasury and fiscal policy.
   1. Budget deficit generally represents a stimulating influence on the economy.
   2. Budget surplus generally represents a restraining influence.
   3. The methods used to finance deficits and the uses of fiscal surpluses influence their impacts on the financial markets.

V. Securities Markets.

A. Primary markets are involved with the initial selling of stocks and bonds (by investment banking firms).

B. Secondary markets permit trading of existing stocks and bonds.
   1. Allow resale of securities; enhance investor liquidity and lower the cost of capital to business.
   2. Foster price stability; more frequent but smaller price changes.
   3. Facilitate flotation of new security issues.
   4. Establish the market values of firms, based on the prices investors will pay for their securities.

C. Organized exchanges in the secondary markets are tangible, physical entities. The exchanges operate as auction markets conducted by specialists.
   1. New York Stock Exchange (NYSE)
   2. American Stock Exchange (AMEX)
   3. Regional exchanges

D. Over-the-counter (OTC) markets.
   1. All of the trading activity that does not take place on an exchange is OTC including almost all trading in bonds and in the stocks of most U.S. banks and insurance companies.
   2. The OTC is conducted by broker/dealers known as market makers who sometimes maintain an inventory of stocks.
   3. Brokers and dealers in the OTC market communicate through a network of private wires and telephone lines, and through NASDAQ (National Association of Securities Dealers Automated Quotation system).

E. The "third market" refers to the OTC trading in listed securities by nonmembers of an exchange.

F. The "fourth market" refers to direct transfers of blocks of stock among institutional investors without an intermediary broker.

G. Firms must meet specified requirements with respect to size, years in business, earnings record and the like in order to be listed on an exchange.
   1. Stock of new and small companies is typically traded over-the-counter until investor interest grows creating sufficient activity for use of an auction market.
   2. The increased information, liquidity and prestige which result from listing may lower a firm's cost of capital.

VI. The National Market System.

A. The Securities Acts Amendments of 1975 encouraged nationwide competition in securities trading and the development of a computerized national market system.

B. Results so far have included:
   1. Lower transactions costs due to prohibition of minimum commissions have led to the "unbundling" of investment counseling services and the rise of discount brokers.
   2. Increasing computerization has brought greater economic concentration in the brokerage industry.
   3. The major stock exchanges are linked electronically, and more information is available on OTC trading.

VII. Securities Trading.

A. Margin trading involves the buying of securities on credit.

1. Margin requirements are determined by the Federal Reserve Board.
2. The investor pays the margin requirement in cash.
3. The stockbroker lends the investor the balance needed to purchase the stock; the broker retains custody of the stock as collateral.
4. Margin buying, like other forms of leverage, magnifies the percentage gains or losses from investment activity. (See Problem 3.4.)

B. Short selling involves the "selling" of a security that is not owned by the seller.

1. To "sell short," the investor is borrowing the stock from his broker.
2. The investor hopes to buy the security subsequently at a price lower than the price at which he sold the security short. (See Problem 3.5.)
3. Short selling may also take place on margin.

C. Margin trading and short selling facilitate trading activity and may lower the costs of transacting.

VIII. Financial Instruments.

A. Government securities.

1. Treasury bills--federal government debt with less than one year to maturity; sold on a discount basis, i.e., the return is the difference between the purchase price and the amount received at maturity. (See Problem 3.6.)
2. Treasury coupon issues--notes and bonds which call for periodic interest payments prior to maturity.
3. Agency issues--the debt of government sponsored agencies which do their own financing, for example, the Federal National Mortgage Association.
4. Municipal bonds--the debt of state and local governments.

B. Business securities.

1. Federal funds are Federal Reserve member bank reserve deposits that are loaned and borrowed by banks.
2. Certificates of deposit (CD's) are negotiable savings instruments with established maturity dates.
3. A banker's acceptance is a debt instrument that is endorsed by a bank on the expectation that its customer will ultimately make the promised payment.
4. Prime rate loans are loans made by commercial banks to customers who qualify for the best rate available on short-term bank lending.
5. Commercial paper is an unsecured promissory note issued by firms to finance short-term credit needs, generally available only to firms with the highest credit ratings.

6. <u>Long-term corporate borrowing</u> includes bonds, mortgages and long-term loans.

C. International financial markets.
   1. U.S. firms often borrow funds in Europe when interest rates are lower there, or lend money in foreign countries when rates are higher.
      a. Foreign firms also trade funds in the U.S.
      b. The flow of funds between different countries tends to bring international interest rates into balance.
   2. Illustrations of international instruments.
      a. Eurodollar deposits--deposits in foreign banks denominated in dollars.
      b. Eurodollar bonds--long-term debt instruments sold in foreign countries but whose payment is promised in dollars.
      c. Eurocurrency deposits--deposits in a foreign country denominated in a currency of a different European country.
      d. Eurobonds--long-term debt instruments denominated in the currency of one European country but sold to investors in other European countries.

Chapter 3 - Illustrative Problems and Solutions

3.1 Issuing 20-year bonds creates a ____________________ for a corporation.
   a. financial liability
   b. financial asset

   Solution:
   a. financial liability. Corporate bonds are a debt instrument; the country is liable for the face value plus interest payments according to the terms of the bond.

3.2 Securities investors can increase their percentage gains or losses by ______________.
   a. short selling
   b. margin trading
   c. either short selling or margin trading

   Solution:
   b. margin trading. Margin trading allows investors to buy or sell more stock for the same investment, making greater percentage gains or losses possible.

3.3 When Federal Reserve deposits in excess of reserve requirements are traded by banks, they are called ______________.
   a. certificates of deposit
   b. banker's acceptances
   c. Federal funds

Solution:
c. Federal funds

3.4 Mr. Page purchased 150 shares of Welcon Company stock at a price of $22 3/8 per share and sold the stock after one year for $23 1/4.

a. What is Mr. Page's percentage gain or loss on his investment? (Disregard transactions costs.)

b. If Mr. Page purchased the stock on the margin when the margin requirement was 40 percent, what is his percentage gain or loss? (Page's broker charges 10 percent annual interest.)

Solution:

a. Number of shares x purchase price = 150 x $22.375 ... $3,356.25

Number of shares x sales price = 150 x $23.25 ... 3,487.50

Return on investment = $\frac{\text{Net cash inflow}}{\text{Initial cash outflow}}$

$= \frac{\$3,487.50 - 3,356.25}{\$3,356.25}$

$= \frac{\$131.25}{\$3,356.25}$

$= 3.9\%$

b.

Number of shares x purchase price = 150 x $22.375	$3,356.25
Margin requirement	x .40
Cash outlay	$1,342.50
Amount borrowed = $3,356.25 - 1,342.50	$2,013.75
Interest rate	x .10
Interest payable	$ 201.38
Net cash inflow:	
Number of shares x sales price	$3,487.50
Less initial investment	1,342.50
Less loan repayment	2,013.75
Less interest due	201.38
	$ - 70.13

Return on investment $= \frac{-\$70.13}{\$1,342.50}$

$= -5.2\%$

In the text we noted that gains and losses are magnified by margin trading. In this example we demonstrate that a small percentage gain can become a loss when the interest rate on borrowing exceeds the return on the investment.

3.5 Jane Wooden sells short 200 shares of Video Corporation at $25. She believes that industry saturation will bring Video's price down to $15 by year-end when she must buy Video stock to cover her short position.

a. Calculate Wooden's percentage gain or loss if her expectations are correct.

b. Calculate Wooden's percentage gain or loss if Video's stock price rises to $30 by year-end.

Solution:

a.

Number of shares x sales price = 200 x $25	$5,000
Number of shares x purchase price = 200 x $15	3,000
Gain	$2,000

$$\frac{\text{Gain}}{\text{Investment}} = \frac{\$2,000}{\$3,000} = 66.7\%$$

b.

Number of shares x sales price	$5,000
Number of shares x purchase price = 200 x $30	6,000
Loss	-$1,000

$$\frac{\text{Loss}}{\text{Investment}} = \frac{-\$1,000}{\$6,000} = -16.7\%$$

CHAPTER 4

THE TAX ENVIRONMENT

Theme: Most business decisions are influenced by tax factors, although the Tax Reform Act of 1986 attempts to lessen the extent of this influence. This chapter provides a summary of some of the basic elements of the new tax structure, and shows how they relate to financial decisions.

I. The Corporate Income Tax
   A. Rate structure.
      1. The corporate tax rate structure has been reduced and simplified.

Taxable Income	Rates Through 1986	Rates July 1, 1987--
First $25,000	15%	15%
Second $25,000	18	15
Third $25,000	30	25
Fourth $25,000	40	34
Over $100,000	46	34
+ 5% surtax on income from:	$1 million to $1.405 million	$100,000 to $335,000

      2. January through June 1987 was a transitional period during which blended corporate tax rates applied.
      3. The effect of the 5 percent surtax is to reduce the benefits of lower rates on the first increments of taxable income for large corporations.
         a. This provides incentives for firms to divide into one or more corporations to keep taxable income low.
         b. This practice has been essentially prohibited since the Tax Reform Act of 1969.
   B. Capital Gains and Losses.
      1. Capital gains (losses) result from the sale of capital assets (such as securities) which are not bought and sold in the ordinary course of the business.
      2. Previous tax laws distinguished between long-term and short-term capital gains (losses) based on a 6-month or 1-year holding period (under different laws).
         a. Long-term capital gains were subject to maixmum tax rates well below the maximum rate on ordinary income.
         b. Short-term capital gains were taxed as ordinary income.
      3. The Tax Reform Act of 1986 eliminates the distinction between long- and short-term capital gains; all capital gains are taxed at a maximum rate of 34 percent, the same as the maximum marginal rate on ordinary income.

C. Dividend and Interest Payments
   1. Interest payments are a tax-deductible expense.
   2. Dividend payments are not tax-deductible.
   3. To avoid multiple taxation of corporate income, 80 percent of the dividends received by one corporation from another are exempt from taxation. (The exemption had been 85 percent of dividends received under previous tax law.)

D. Firms must estimate their taxable income and pay taxes quarterly. The estimated taxes paid must be either:
   1. Equal to the previous year's actual tax liability.
   2. At least 90 percent of the actual tax liability for the current year. (Previous law required at least 80 percent of the current year's actual tax liability.)

F. Net operating loss carrybacks and carryforwards aid corporations whose income fluctuates.
   1. Losses may be carried back 3 years, then forward for 15 years to offset profits.
   2. The Tax Reform Act of 1986 tightens the restrictions on using a target company's net operating losses following a change of ownership.

G. Retained earnings in excess of $250,000 may be subject to penalty taxes as improper accumulation of earnings.
   1. Earnings retention can be justified for valid reasons--repayment of debt, financing growth, cushioning against losses.
   2. The penalty tax on improper accumulation is 27.5 percent on the first $100,000 over $250,000, and 38.5 percent beyond that.
   3. Under previous tax laws, this provision sometimes stimulated sales and mergers of closely-held firms.
      a. Owners accumulated earnings thus risking the penalty tax, to avoid receiving heavily-taxed dividends.
      b. As the risk of the penalty tax grew, the owners would sell the firm, realizing capital gains taxed at a lower rate.
      c. This capital gains tax advantage has been virtually eliminated by the new tax law.

H. Tax credits are deductions from the tax bill itself rather than deductions from taxable income to which the tax rates are applied.
   1. Among the tax credits available under the Tax Reform Act of 1986 are the following:
      a. Targeted jobs tax credit--employers may take a tax credit of 40 percent of the first year's wages (up to $6,000) paid to "disadvantaged" individuals.
      b. Research and development credit--companies may deduct from their tax bill 20 percent of their "increased" expenditures on qualifying research and development (based on a prior 3-year average).
      c. Low income housing--9 percent of the amount spent on building or rehabilitating housing to be rented to low income people, placed in service during 1987, may be taken as a credit <u>each</u> year for 10 years.

2. The investment and energy tax credits designed to stimulate investment in capital equipment and alternative energy sources are being phased out under the new tax law.

II. Depreciation and Taxation.

A. Depreciation charges are a tax-deductible non-cash expenditure which reduce taxable income and thus the cash outlay on tax payments.

B. Tax authorities can encourage investment by adjusting depreciation policy.

1. Reducing (increasing) the allowable depreciable life of an asset increases (decreases) the annual depreciation.
2. Allowing accelerated depreciation methods results in higher cash flows received sooner.
    a. More funds are made available for further investment.
    b. The rate of return on investment is increased.
3. The Accelerated Cost Recovery System (ACRS) under both the old and new tax laws specifies the allowable depreciable lives for various classes of assets.
    a. The Tax Reform Act of 1986 increases the depreciable life of assets somewhat, but allows the use of the 200 percent declining balance method (see below) as opposed to the previous 150 percent declining balance method.
    b. The new tax law requires that real estate may be depreciated only by the straight-line method over a period of 27.5 years for residential property and 31.5 years for commercial property.
4. Sale of a depreciable asset for more than its book value can result in either a capital gain or ordinary income or both.
    a. Previous tax law required that the difference between book value under straight-line depreciation and under accelerated depreciation be taxed as ordinary income (recapture of depreciation).
    b. Profit on the sale in excess of the book value under straight-line depreciation was taxed as a capital gain.
    c. Since these distinctions are almost meaningless under the new tax law, the choice of depreciation method for some types of investment is less important.

III. Depreciation Methods.

A. Straight-line method.

1. Provides a uniform annual depreciation charge:
2. $\text{Annual charge} = \dfrac{\text{Total cost - Salvage value}}{\text{Economic life}}$
3. If the estimated salvage value is not in excess of 10 percent of the original cost, it can be ignored.

B. Sum-of-years'-digits method (SYD).
   1. Calculate the sum of the years' digits using the following formula:

      $$\text{Sum} = \frac{N(N+1)}{2}$$ where N is the asset's economic life

   2. Annual depreciation charge =

      $$\left(\frac{\text{Years of life remaining}}{\text{Sum}}\right) \times (\text{Total cost} - \text{Salvage value})$$

   3. Alternative formula for annual depreciation charge:

      $$\text{Dep}_t = \frac{2(N+1-t)I}{N(N+1)}$$

C. Units of production method.
   1. Depreciation charges depend on usage.
   2. Hourly depreciation rate = $\frac{\text{Purchase price - Salvage value}}{\text{Expected useful life (in hours)}}$

      or

      Per unit depreciation rate = $\frac{\text{Purchase price - Salvage value}}{\text{Expected life capacity (in units)}}$

   3. Annual depreciation charge = Depreciation rate x hours run (or units produced) during the year

D. Declining balance methods.
   1. The annual depreciation charge is calculated by multiplying a fixed rate times the net book value (original cost less accumulated depreciation).
   2. Annual depreciation charge.
      a. 150% declining balance method:

         $$\text{Dep}_t = \frac{1.5[1-(1.5/N)]^{t-1}I}{N}$$

      b. 200% declining balance method:

         $$\text{Dep}_t = \frac{2[1-(2/N)]^{t-1}I}{N}$$

   3. The estimated salvage value is not deducted from the total purchase cost.
   4. A company switches from the declining balance method to straight-line depreciation whenever the straight-line depreciation method would exceed the declining balance amount.

IV. The Personal Income Tax.
   A. Both personal and corporate tax structures must be taken into account in the decision as to which form of business to operate since partnership and proprietorship income is taxed as personal income of the owners or partners.
   B. Effective 1988, there will be only two tax brackets -- 15 percent and 28 percent.
      1. Personal tax rates under previous tax laws ranged over 14 brackets from 11 percent to 50 percent.

2. The 15 percent rate will apply to taxable income equal to or below:
   $29,750 for married taxpayers filing joint returns
   $17,850 for single taxpayers
3. High-income taxpayers will effectively pay the maximum 28 percent rate on all of their taxable income because of a 5 percent surtax (for an effective marginal rate of 33 percent) on taxable income within certain ranges:
   $71,900--$149,250 for married taxpayers filing joint returns
   $43,150--$89,560 for single taxpayers
4. For 1987, transitional rates applied with 5 brackets reaching a maximum rate of 38.5 percent.

C. Certain exclusions, deductions and exemptions reduce gross income to arrive at taxable income. The new tax law eliminates many of these (the two-earner deduction, the $100 dividend exclusion, sales tax deduction, etc.), but some remain.
1. The personal exemption is a deduction from income for each taxpayer and his dependents.
   a. It is $2,000 for 1989, up from only $1,080 per person in 1986.
   b. Starting in 1988, the personal exemption is phased out for very high income taxpayers via a 5 percent surtax on income over $149,250 for married taxpayers filing joint returns (over $89,560 for single filers).
2. The standard deduction determines whether it will be advantageous for taxpayers to itemize deductions.
   a. By 1988, the standard deduction is raised to $5,000 for married taxpayers filing joint returns (up from $3,670 in 1986) and to $3,000 for single taxpayers (up from $2,480).
   b. The standard deduction is increased for blind and/or elderly taxpayers. (The blind/elderly tax break was previously figured into the personal exemption.)
3. State and local income and property taxes remain fully deductible.
4. Mortgage interest on first and qualifying second homes remains tax deductible, subject to certain limitations.
5. The tax deduction for other forms of personal interest is being phased out, and will be eliminated completely by the end of 1990.
6. The deduction for charitable contributions is no longer available to taxpayers who do not itemize.
7. IRA contributions are no longer fully tax-deductible for taxpayers with adjusted gross income over $25,000 per year who are covered by another retirement plan ($40,000 for married taxpayers filing jointly).
8. The Tax Reform Act of 1986 allows you to deduct 100 percent of capital losses up to $3,000 per year, regardless of whether they are short- or long-term.

D. Taxable income is determined as follows:
1. Start by adding all forms of income to get Total Income.
2. Above-the-line deductions are subtracted to arrive at adjusted gross income (AGI).
   a. Previous law included such adjustments as the two-earner couple deduction, IRAs and certain employee business expenses.
   b. Above-the-line deductions are severely curtailed under the new tax law--the two-earner deduction is eliminated; the IRA deduction is limited; and employee business expenses are deductible only for taxpayers who itemize.
3. Deduct the number of personal exemptions times $2,000.
4. Calculate itemized deductions; if this figure is less than the standard deduction, use the standard deduction to calculate Taxable Income. Otherwise, itemize deductions.
   a. Otherwise allowable travel, meals and entertainment expenses will be aggregated with miscellaneous deductions and subject to the 2-percent-of-AGI floor. As a result, the taxpayer may not be able to fully utilize the 80 percent deduction for meals and entertainment expenses.
   b. The 2-percent-of-AGI floor, and the higher standard deduction will make it less attractive to itemize under the new tax law.

V. Choice Among Alternative Forms of Business Organizations

A. Single proprietorship.
1. A proprietorship is owned by one individual.
2. Seventy percent of business firms are operated as sole proprietorships; by dollar value, they generate about 13 percent of sales.
3. The proprietorship is easily and inexpensively formed. No formal charter for operations is required; proprietorships are subject to few governmental regulations.
4. All earnings are subject to federal personal income taxes, whether they are reinvested in the business or withdrawn.
5. Disadvantages include the following:
   a. The proprietor has unlimited personal liability for business debts.
   b. Due to size, there is an inability to obtain large sums of capital.
   c. The proprietorship is limited to the life of the individual who created it.

B. Partnership.
1. When two or more persons associate to conduct a business enterprise, a partnership exists.
2. A partnership may operate under different degrees of formality, from an informal oral understanding, to a formal written agreement filed with the state government.
3. Ease and economy of formation, as well as freedom from special governmental regulations, are some advantages of a partnership.

4. A partnership makes possible a pooling of various types of resources, including skills and funds.
5. Partnership profits are taxed as personal income in proportion to the partners' claims, whether the profits are distributed to the partners or not.
6. Disadvantages include the following:
    a. Impermanence. The withdrawal or death of any one of the partners dissolves the partnership.
    b. Difficulties of transferring ownership.
    c. Unlimited liabilities. Partners risk their personal assets as well as their investment in the business. Partners are jointly and separately liable for business debts.

C. Corporation.
1. A corporation is a legal entity created by a state.
2. A corporation is a separate entity, distinct from its owners and managers.
3. It has an unlimited life.
4. It permits limited liability; stockholders are not personally liable for the debts of the firm.
5. It permits easy transferability of ownership interest in the firm.
6. The chartering of a corporation involves a complicated but routine process. A certificate of incorporation is drawn up, notarized, examined and filed with the state government.
7. The actual operations of the firm are governed by the <u>charter</u> and the <u>bylaws</u>.
8. Corporations are taxed in accordance with Congressional tax regulations. Corporate earnings paid as dividends are subject to double taxation.

VI. Tax Aspects of Forms of Organization.

A. Previous tax laws gave an edge to the corporate form of organization.
1. At low incomes, the personal income tax rate was lower than the corporate rate, making partnerships and proprietorships attractive only at quite low levels of earnings.
2. At higher incomes, the corporate tax rate was lower than the personal rate.

B. To determine whether to incorporate, a proprietorship should calculate estimated tax liabilities as a proprietorship and as a corporation over a planning horizon.

C. Factors to consider:
1. Corporate dividends are taxed twice, once to the corporation and once to the recipient.
2. Salaries paid to managers are subject only to personal taxation since they are a tax-deductible expense to the corporation.
3. A proprietor pays personal tax on the proprietorship's entire earnings, regardless of how much he keeps as his salary and how much he reinvests in the business.

D. Special tax treatment for small business (such as Subchapter S corporations and Section 1244 businesses) are less important following passage of the new tax law.

1. The divergence between corporate and personal tax rates is less.
2. There is little difference in the treatment of capital gains versus ordinary income.

VII. Tax Considerations and Financial Policy.

A. Financial managers must consider the tax effects of transactions.

B. Ways to minimize tax burden:

1. Stabilize income to avoid highest brackets.
2. Adjust timing of income and expenses in anticipation of changes in tax rates.
3. Spread income over several years to aovid highest brackets, defer tax liability.
4. Use tax-free financing wherever available.
5. Select the most appropriate organizational form.
6. Structure transactions to take advantage of tax rates, earnings potential, losses, depreciation.

Chapter 4 - Illustrative Problems and Solutions

4.1 Leisure Crafts, Inc. has just purchased industrial equipment for $13,000. The machinery has an estimated useful life of 6 years, and an estimated pattern of hourly use as shown below:

Year 1	2,660 hours
Year 2	2,400 hours
Year 3	1,850 hours
Year 4	1,350 hours
Year 5	870 hours
Year 6	750 hours
	9,880 hours

The equipment has an estimated salvage value of $650. Calculate annual depreciation under each of the following methods:

a. Straight-line
b. Units of production
c. 200% declining balance
d. Sum-of-years'-digits
e. Which method provides the greatest tax benefit during the first year? During the first 4 years?

Solution:

a. Straight-line:

$$\text{Annual depreciation} = \frac{\$13,000 - \$650}{6} = \$2,058$$

b. Units of production:

$$\text{Hourly depreciation} = \frac{\$13,000 - \$650}{9,880} = \$1.25$$

Year		Dep_t
1	2,660 x 1.25 =	$3,325.00
2	2,400 x 1.25 =	3,000.00
3	1,850 x 1.25 =	2,312.50
4	1,350 x 1.25 =	1,687.50
5	870 x 1.25 =	1,087.50
6	750 x 1.25 =	937.50
		$12,350.00

c. 200% declining balance:

$$Dep_t = \frac{2[1-(2/N)]^{t-1}I}{N} = \frac{2[1-(2/6)]^{t-1}(13,000)}{6}$$

$$= .67^{t-1}(4,333)$$

Year		Dep_t	Book Value at Year-End
1	$.67^0(4,333)$	$4,333	$8,667
2	$.67^1(4.333)$	2,903	5.764
3	$.67^2(4.333)$	1.945	3.819
4	$.67^3(4.333)$	1.303	2.516
5*		933	1.583
6		933	650
		$12,350	

*Switch to straight-line depreciation:

200% DB depreciation in year 5 = $.67^4(4,333)$ = $873
S-L depreciation in year 5 = (2,516-650)/2 = $933

d. Sum-of-years'-digits:

$$Dep_t = \frac{2(N+1-t)I}{N(N+1)}$$

$$= \frac{2(7-t)12,350}{42}$$

$$= (7-t)(588)$$

Year		
1	6(588) =	$3,528
2	5(588) =	2,940
3	4(588) =	2,352
4	3(588) =	1,764
5	2(588) =	1,176
6	1(588) =	588
		$12,348*

*Difference due to rounding

e. Year 1: 200% Declining Balance provides the greatest tax shelter in year 1 with depreciation of $4,333.

Years 1-4: Straight-line: $2,058 x 4 = $8,232
Units of production:
$3,325 + $3,000 + $2,312.5 + $1,687.5 = $10,325

200% declining balance:

$4,333 + $2,903 + $1,945 + $1,303 = $10,484

Sum-of-years'-digits:

$3,528 + $2,940 + $2,352 + $1,764 = $10,584

Sum-of-years'-digits depreciation provides the greatest tax benefits to the firm over Years 1-4. The method chosen will probably depend on the timing of expected cash flows from the investment as well as legal and tax considerations.

4.2 After using the equipment in Problem 4.1 for a very short time, Leisure Crafts realizes that its estimates were overly optimistic. It now expects the machine to last only 3 years and to have no salvage value. The expected pattern of hourly use is shown below:

Year 1	2,000 hours
Year 2	1,250 hours
Year 3	750 hours
	4,000 hours

Calculate annual depreciation under each of the following methods.

a. Straight line
b. Units of production
c. 200% declining balance
d. Sum-of-years'-digits
e. What is the effect of the shorter estimated life for the equipment?

Solution:

a. Straight line:

$$\text{Annual depreciation} = \frac{\$13{,}000}{3} = \$4{,}333.33$$

b. Units of production:

$$\text{Hourly depreciation} = \frac{\$13{,}000}{4{,}000} = \$3.25$$

Year		Dep_t
1	2,000 x 3.25 =	$6,500.00
2	1,250 x 3.25 =	4,062.50
3	750 x 3.25 =	2,437.50
		$13,000.00

c. 200% declining balance:

$$Dep_t = \frac{2[1-(2/N)]^{t-1}I}{N}$$

$$= \frac{2[1-(2/3)]^{t-1}(13{,}000)}{3}$$

$$= .33^{t-1}(8{,}667)$$

Year		Dep_t	Book Value at Year-End
1	$.33^0(8,667)$	$8,667	$4,333
2	$.33^1(8,667)$	2,860	1,473
3*		1,473	0
		$13,000	

*Switch to straight-line depreciation for year 3 since 200% declining balance depreciation for year 3 would be only $.33^2(8,667) = \$944$.

d. Sum-of-years'-digits:

$$Dep_t = \frac{2(N+1-t)I}{N(N+1)}$$

$$= (4-t)(2,166.67)$$

Year		Dep_t
1	(4-1)(2,166.67) =	$6,500.00
2	(4-2)(2,166.67) =	4,333.33
3	(4-3)(2,166.67) =	2,166.67

e. Shortening the depreciable life of the asset has greatly increased the value of the depreciation tax shelter under each method. For the facts of the case, the 200% declining balance now provides the most accelerated depreciation with the highest total depreciation for the first two years.

4.3 MCF Corporation had taxable income of $88,000 in 1984.
  a. What was the tax bill?
  b. What was the marginal tax rate?
  c. What was the average tax rate?
  d. Answer parts a--c assuming that the $88,000 of income came in 1988 (after the Tax Reform Act of 1986 is fully in place).

Solution:

a.

Income		Rate		Tax
$25,000	x	.15	=	$ 3,750
25,000	x	.18	=	4,500
25,000	x	.30	=	7,500
13,000	x	.40	=	5,200
$88,000				$20,950

b. Marginal tax rate is 40%.
c. Average tax rate = $20,950/$88,000 = 23.8%.

d. Tax bill:

Income		Rate		Tax
$50,000	x	.15	=	$7,500
25,000	x	.25	=	6,250
13,000	x	.34	=	4,420
$88,000				$18,170

Marginal tax rate = 34%
Average tax rate = $18,170/$88,000 = 20.6%

4.4 In 1984, the Pankhurst Company had income before interest, dividends and taxes of $350,000. Interest expense was $40,000, and Pankhurst paid out $70,000 in dividends to shareholders.

a. What was taxable income?
b. What was the tax bill?
c. What was the average tax rate?
d. Answer parts a--c assuming the income was earned in 1988.

Solution:

a.

Income before interest, dividends and taxes	$350,000
Less interest expense	40,000
Taxable income	$310,000

b.

$ 25,000	x .15 =	$ 3,750	
25,000	x .18 =	4,500	
25,000	x .30 =	7,500	
25,000	x .40 =	10,000	
210,000	x .46 =	96,600	
$310,000		$122,350	= Tax bill

c. Average tax rate = $122,350/$310,000 = 39.5%

Dividends paid are not a tax-deductible expense.
Net income after taxes = $310,000 - $122,350 = $187,650.
Dividends will be paid from net income, leaving
$187,650 - $70,000 = $117,650 for retained earnings.

d. Taxable income--same as in part a above.

Tax bill:

$50,000 x .15	$7,500
25,000 x .25	6,250
235,000 x .34	79,900
(310,000-100,000) x .05	10,500
	$104,150

Average tax rate = $104,150/310,000 = 33.6%

Net income after tax = $310,000 - 104,150 =	$205,850
Less dividends	- 70,000
To retained earnings	$135,850

Even with the 5 percent surtax on income over $100,000, the tax bill and average tax rates are lower under the new tax law.

4.5 The Lockhart Corporation has income from operations of $84,000 (before taxes) in 1988. In addition, Lockhart receives $8,000 in dividend income on stocks of various publicly-held corporations. How much income tax must Lockhart pay?

Solution:

$8,000	Dividend income
-6,400	80% dividend exclusion
$1,600	Taxable dividend
84,000	Income from operations
$85,600	Taxable income

Tax bill:

$50,000 x .15	=	$7,500
25,000 x .25	=	6,250
10,600 x .34	=	3,604
		$17,354

4.6 The Carrington Corporation, formed in 1984 has had the following pattern of taxable income: (Losses are shown as minuses.)

Year	Taxable income
1984	-$105,000
1985	40,000
1986	80,000
1987	70,000
1988	-90,000

What is the corporate tax liability for each year? (Use 1988 tax rates.)

Solution:

Year	Taxable income	Carry-forward	Carry-back	Taxable in current year	Tax liability
1984	(105,000)	0	0	0	0
1985	40,000	(40,000)	0	0	0
1986	80,000	(65,000)	0	15,000	2,250
1987	70,000	0	0	70,000	12,500
1988	(90,000)	(5,000)	(85,000)	0	(14,750)

The 1988 loss results in a carry-back of $85,000 to obtain a refund on taxes paid in 1986 and 1987. In addition, $5,000 can be deducted against future earnings for up to 15 years.

4.7 Robert and Sally Colson operate a vending machine business. They are trying to decide whether to incorporate or to continue to operate as a proprietorship. The Colson's have 2 children and pay themselves a combined annual salary of $54,000. Any earnings in excess of $54,000 are reinvested in the business. Their itemized deductions are $10,300 annually, and they estimate that the business will have earnings (before salary and taxes) for the next 3 years as follows:

Year	Income before salary and taxes
1987	$60,000
1988	90,000
1989	150,000

a. What will the Colson's total taxes be under:
   1. A proprietorship?
   2. A corporate form of organization?
   (Assume the Tax Reform Act of 1986 applies to all years.)

b. Should the Colson's incorporate? Discuss.

Solution:

a. Proprietorship:

	1987	1988	1989
Income	$60,000	$90,000	$150,000
Less: personal exemptions	8,000	8,000	8,000
Less: itemized deductions	10,300	10,300	10,300
Taxable income	$41,700	$71,700	$131,700

Tax bill:

1987:	29,750 x .15	= $4,463
	(41,700-29,750) x .28	= 3,346
		$7,809
1988:	29,750 x .15	= $4,463
	(71,700-29,750) x .28	= 11,746
		$16,209
1989:	29,750 x .15	= $4,463
	(131,700-29,750) x .28	= 28,546
	(131,700-71,900) x .05	= 2,990
		$35,999

2. <u>Corporation</u>

	1987	1988	1989
Income before salary and tax	$60,000	$90,000	$150,000
Less: Salary	54,000	54,000	54,000
Corporate taxable income	$6,000	$36,000	$96,000
Corporate tax bill:			
$50,000 x .15	$900	$5,400	$7,500
25,000 x .25	0	0	6,250
Balance x .34	0	0	7,140
	$900	$5,400	$20,890

Personal tax (same for all 3 years):

Salary	$54,000
Less: personal exemptions	8,000
Less: itemized deductions	10,300
Taxable income, personal	$35,700

Personal tax bill:

29,750 x .15	= $4,463
(35,700-29,750) x .28	= 1,666
	$6,129

Total combined tax bill:

	1987	1988	1989
Corporate tax bill	$900	$5,400	$20,890
Personal tax till	6,129	6,129	6,129
Combined bill	$7,029	$11,529	$27,019

b. To decide whether the Colson's should incorporate, first compare total tax liability under each form of organization:

	1987	1988	1989
Proprietorship taxes	$7,809	$16,209	$35,999
Taxes as a corporation	7,029	11,529	27,019
Advantage to corporate form	$ 780	$4,680	$8,980

The Colson's taxes will be lower under the corporate form of organization for all three years. This is because as a proprietorship, the firm's entire income is taxed as personal income, even the part of it that is reinvested in the firm. This pushes personal taxable income into its highest bracket, including the 5 percent surtax on very high income by 1989.

Under the corporate form, only the salary drawn by the Colson's is taxed at the personal rate, while the remainder is taxed at corporate rates. This income-splitting effect operates to keep both personal and corporate taxable income in lower tax brackets. Under previous tax laws, the fact that personal tax rates were often much higher than corporate rates contributed to the tax advantages of incorporation, but under the new tax law this differential is much less; in fact, at higher levels of business income, the corporate tax rate is higher than the maximum personal tax rate.

PART TWO. THE TIME DIMENSION IN FINANCIAL DECISIONS

CHAPTER 5

THE TIME VALUE OF MONEY

Theme: Most financing decisions involve commitments over extended periods. The interest factor will therefore have a crucial impact on the soundness of the decisions.

I. Future, or compound, value is defined as the sum ($FV_{r,n}$) to which a beginning amount of principal (P_o) will grow over n years when interest is earned at the rate of r percent per year. (See Problem 5.1)

   A. $FV_{r,n} = P_o(1+r)^n$

   B. Letting FVIF = future value interest factor = $(1+r)^n$, the above equation may be written as $FV_{r,n} = P_o[FVIF(r,n)]$. It is necessary only to go to an appropriate interest table to find the proper interest factor. See future value interest factors (FVIF) in Appendix Table A.1.
      1. The future value of $1,000 at 5 percent for 5 years may be found as $FV_{5\%,\ 5\ yrs}$ = $1,000(1.2763 = $1,276.
      2. The FVIF is always greater than one.

   C. The interest rate is the growth rate. Therefore, the higher the rate of interest, the faster the growth. (See Problems 5.2, 5.3 and 5.14)

II. The present value (P_o) of a future payment is the amount which, invested at a specified interest rate (r) today, would equal the future payment ($FV_{r,n}$).

   A. Finding present values (or discounting) is simply the reverse of finding future values (or compounding).

   B. The present value of $1,276 at 5 percent is found by

$$P_0 = FV_{r,n}\left[\frac{1}{(1+r)^n}\right] = \$1,276(.7835) = \$1,000$$

   The term in brackets is called the present value interest factor (PVIF): $P_o = FV_{r,n}[PVIF(r,n)]$. See present value interest factors (PVIF) in Appendix Table A.2.

   C. The PVIF is the reciprocal of the future value interest factor for any given r,n combination. Therefore, it is always less than one. (See Problem 5.6)

D. The present value of a future sum decreases as n and r increase. Therefore, higher discount rates imply lower present values for a given maturity date, and longer maturity dates imply lower present values for a given interest rate. (See Problems 5.5 and 5.14)

III. An annuity is defined as a series of payments of a fixed amount (a) for a specified number of years. The first payment is assumed to occur at the end of the first year. The future value of an annuity is the total amount one would have at the end of the annuity period if each payment was invested at a given interest rate and held to the end of the annuity period.

A. $FVA_{r,t}$ = future value of an annuity
   a = the periodic receipt
   r = the interest rate
   n = the terminal period
   t = the number of payment periods

   $FVA_{r,t}$ = a(FVIFA) where FVIFA is the interest factor shown in brackets in the following equation. See future value of an annuity interest factors (FVIFA) in Appendix Table A.3.

$$FVA_{r,t} = a\left[\frac{(1+r)^n-1}{r}\right]$$

B. The future value of a $1,000 annuity invested at 5 percent for 3 years is equal to FVIFA x annual receipt = 3.1525 x $1,000 = $3,152.50. (See Problem 5.9)

C. The FVIFA is always larger than the number of years the annuity runs.

IV. The present value of an annuity is the required lump sum on hand today to permit withdrawals of equal amounts (a) at the end of each year for t years.

A. $PVA_{r,t}$ = present value of an annuity

$$PVA_{r,t} = a\left[\frac{1-(1+r)^{-n}}{r}\right]$$

   $PVA_{r,t}$ = a(PVIFA) where PVIFA is the interest factor shown in brackets above and found in the present value of an annuity interest factor (PVIFA), Appendix Table A.4.

B. To withdraw $1,000 a year for 3 years when the interest rate is 5 percent, for example, requires:

$$PVA_{r,t} = a(PVIFA)$$

$$= \$1,000 \times 2.7232 = \$2,723.20$$

(See Problem 5.8)

C. The PVIFA is always smaller than the number of years the annuity runs.

V. Other Uses of the Basic Equations.

A. To determine annual payments required to accumulate a future sum: (See Problem 5.9)

1. $a = \frac{FVA}{FVIFA}$

2. What amount of money must be deposited at 5 percent for each of the next 5 years in order to have $10,000 at the end of the fifth year?

$$a = \frac{\$10,000}{5.5256} = \$1,810$$

B. To find the annual receipts from a specified annuity:

1. Beginning with a fixed amount of money, earning a fixed interest rate, you plan to make a series of equal withdrawals. You wish to know the size of the withdrawals that will leave a balance of zero after the last one has been made.

2. $a = \frac{PVA}{PVIFA}$

3. You have $7,000 earning 5 percent interest and you plan to make 3 equal yearly withdrawals starting in one year.

$$a = \frac{\$7,000}{2.7232} = \$2,571$$

4. This method is often used to calculate the annual payments necessary to amortize a loan.

C. <u>Interest rates</u> may be calculated.

1. Frequently one knows the present value and cash flows associated with a payment stream but not the interest rate involved. (See Problem 5.12)

2. $FVIF = \frac{FV_{r,n}}{P_o}$

3. A bank offers to lend $1,000 today upon agreement to repay $1,469 at the end of 5 years. What is the rate of interest involved?

$$FVIF = \frac{\$1,469}{\$1,000} = 1.469, \text{ the FVIF for } 8\%$$

See (FVIF) Table A.1 for 5 years.

4. The same approach may be used to determine the interest rate implicit in an annuity:

$$PVIFA = \frac{PVA}{a}$$

D. Many financial decisions involve uneven cash flows. Therefore it is important to be able to deal with varying payment streams.

1. To calculate the <u>present value (PV) of a series of uneven annual payments</u>, use the following formula (subscripts refer to time periods, X's refer to payments):

$$PV = X_1(PVIF_1) + X_2(PVIF_2) + \ldots + X_t(PVIF_t)$$

2. To calculate the present value of a series of uneven payments followed by a stream of equal payments:
   a. Calculate the present value of the unequal payments, as shown above.
   b. Calculate the present value of the stream of equal payments (an annuity), using the number of payments for t. Then find the present value of this figure.
   c. Add the present values found for the unequal and equal payment streams.
3. To calculate the <u>present value of a payments stream composed of one lump sum plus a stream of equal payments</u>, use the formula: PV = PV of lump sum + PV of series.

E. The interest factors for fractional interest rates can be calculated using the formulas for each interest factor.
1. For example, using a 9 3/4% interest rate for 7 periods:

$$FVIF = (1+r)^n = (1.0975)^7 = 1.9179$$

$$PVIF = 1/(1+r)^n = 1/1.0975^7 = 0.5214$$

$$FVIFA = [(1+r)^n-1]/r = (1.0975^7-1)/.0975 = 9.4144$$

$$PVIFA = [1-(1+r)^{-n}]/r = (1-1.0975^{-7})/.0975 = 4.9087$$

2. These equations can also be solved for the interest rate given the interest factor.

F. <u>Semiannual and other compounding periods</u> are often used.
1. Semiannual compounding means that interest is actually paid each six months.
   a. The interest rate is divided by two.
   b. The number of compounding periods is twice the number of years.
2. The results of more frequent compounding may also be calculated.
   a. Divide the nominal, or stated, interest rate by the number of times compounding occurs each year.
   b. Multiply the number of years by the number of compounding periods per year.

3. The general formula for this type of compounding is

$$FV_{r,n} = P_o\left(1+\frac{r}{q}\right)^{qn}$$

where:

q = Number of compounding periods per year
n = Number of years

4. If $1,000 is invested for 10 years with a stated 6 percent interest rate compounded semiannually:

$$\begin{aligned} FV_{6\%,10\ yrs} &= \$1,000[FVIF(3\%,\ 20\ yrs)] \\ &= \$1,000(1.8061) \\ &= \$1,806 \end{aligned}$$

5. The special case of continuous compounding occurs when q approaches infinity.

VI. The Annual Percentage Rate (APR).

A. When interest is compounded more frequently, the effective rate of interest, or APR, is greater than the nominal rate of interest.

1. Calculating the APR enables comparison of financial contracts which use different compounding periods.
2. Formula:

$$APR = r_e = \left(1+\frac{r}{q}\right)^q-1$$

where:
r = the nominal interest rate
q = the number of compounding periods per year

B. Equivalent results may be obtained in two ways. For example, what will be the value of a $1,000 investment compounded quarterly for 3 years when the nominal interest rate is 16 percent?

1. $APR = r_e = \left(1+\frac{.16}{4}\right)^4-1 = .17$

$$\begin{aligned} FV_{r,n} = FV_{17\%,\ 3\ yrs} &= P_o[FVIF(17\%,\ 3\ yrs)] \\ &= (\$1,000)(1.17)^3 \\ &= \$1,000(1.6016) = \$1,601.60 \end{aligned}$$

2. $FV_{r,n} = P_o\left[1+\frac{r}{q}\right]^{qn}$

$$\begin{aligned} &= \$1,000\left(1+\frac{.16}{4}\right)^{(4)(3)} \\ &= \$1,000(1.04)^{12} \\ &= \$1,000(1.6010) = \$1,601.00 \end{aligned}$$

(Difference due to rounding)

C. Amortized loans provide for repayment of a portion of principal as well as interest with each periodic loan payment.

1. With annual compounding, the amount of each annual payment is found using the formula:

$$a = \frac{PVA_{r,t}}{PVIFA(r,t)}$$

   a. Each annual payment is then broken down into principal and interest components in the form of an amortization table.
   b. The interest component is calculated by multiplying the interest rate times the principal balance remaining at the end of the previous period.
   c. The remainder of the annual payment is allocated to principal repayment.

2. With more frequent compounding, both the interest rate and the number of periods must be adjusted to find the appropriate PVIFA which determines the amount of each periodic payment. For example, consider a 12 percent interest rate on a 5-year loan:
   a. Semiannual compounding:

$$PVIFA = \frac{1-(1+r)^{-n}}{r} \qquad r = .12/2 = .06$$

$$n = 5 \times 2 = 10$$

$$= \frac{1-(1.06)^{-10}}{.06}$$

$$= 7.3601$$

   b. Monthly compounding: $r = .12/12 = .01$

$$n = 5 \times 12 = 60$$

$$PVIFA = \frac{1-(1.01)^{-60}}{.01}$$

$$= 44.9550$$

   c. Daily compounding: $r = .12/360 = .0003333$

$$n = 5 \times 360 = 1800$$

$$PVIFA = \frac{1-(1.0003333)^{-1800}}{.0003333}$$

$$= 1,353.4371$$

VII. Determining the Appropriate Compounding or Discounting Rates Involves Several Factors.
   A. General interest rate patterns in the economy as a whole.
   B. Differences in risk among investments.
   C. The opportunity cost of making one investment rather than another.

VIII. Continuous Compounding.

A. When the number of compounding periods per year approaches infinity, the compound value $FV_{r,n} = P_o e^{rn}$

1. In the notation of continuous compounding, this equation is generally written as $V_t = P_o e^{kt}$, where k = interest rate or cost of capital
   t = number of years
2. The equation can be restated $\ln V_t = kt$.

B. To find the continuous compounding interest factor, find the antilog of the product kt in a table of natural logarithms.

1. Alternatively, use the e^x or lnx key on a hand calculator.
2. Example: Find V_t for \$500 invested at 8 percent compounded continuously for 10 years.
   a. kt = (.08)(10) = .8.
   b. In a table of natural logarithms, .8 lies between .7951 and .80200 whose antilogs are 2.22 and 2.23; by interpolation, the antilog of .8 = 2.226.
   c. On a hand calculator, $e^{.8} = 2.22554$. Calculators without an e^x key usually have an INV key; simply push .8, INV, lnx to get 2.2255.
   d. Thus, V_t = \$500(2.226) = 1,113.

IX. Continuous Discounting.

A. To find the present value of a continuously compounded amount, use $PV = \frac{V_t}{e^{kt}} = V_t e^{-kt}$.

B. The present value of \$800 to be received in 5 years, using a continuous discount rate of 12 percent is found:

1. kt = (.12)(5) = .6.
2. $e^{-.6} = .549$.
3. PV = \$800(.549) = \$439.20.

X. Continuous Compounding and Discounting of Annuities.

A. Finding the compound and present values of a stream of payments received continuously requires the use of integral calculus.

B. The compound sum S_t of a continuous annuity is found by:

$$S_t = a_o \int_{t=o}^{N} e^{gt}\,dt$$

where a_o = initial receipt

g = growth rate

C. The present value of a continuous annuity is found by:

$$PV = \int_{t=o}^{N} a_t e^{-kt}\,dt$$

D. The continuous compounding and discounting formulas can be combined to find the present value of a stream of payments, beginning at t_o, growing at rate g, and discounted at rate k:

$$PV = \frac{a_o}{k-g}$$

XI. The Relationship between Discrete and Continuous Interest Rates.

A. Discrete interest rates can be converted into equivalent continuous interest rates, and vice versa.

1. $\ln(1+d) = c$
2. $d = e^c - 1$

   where d = the discrete interest rate

   c = the equivalent continuous interest rate
3. The continuous rate will in general be lower than the discrete rate.

B. When a nominal interest rate is compounded continuously, the equivalent discrete interest rate represents the annual percentage rate (APR).

Chapter 5 - Illustrative Problems and Solutions

5.1 You deposit $3,000 in a bank that pays 6 percent interest, compounded annually.

a. What is the total dollar amount of interest earned in the first year? How much will you have at the end of one year? (Do not use tables.)

b. How much will you have at the end of three years? (Do not use tables.)

Solution:

a. Total dollar amount of interest earned = $P_o(r)$ = \$3,000(.06) = \$180.

$FV_{6\%,1\ yr} = P_o + P_o(r) = \$3{,}000 + \$180 = \$3{,}180$

b. $FV_{6\%,3yrs} = P_o(1+r)^3$

$= \$3{,}000(1.06)^3$

$= \$3{,}573.05$

5.2 At an annual growth rate of 8 percent, how long will it take to quadruple a sum of money?

Solution:
Refer to Table A.1 in the Appendix; 3.9960($\cong$4) appears in the 18th year in the 8 percent column; therefore it requires 18 years for a sum of money to quadruple at an 8 percent rate of growth.

5.3 If you bought a nondividend paying stock 8 years ago for \$26 and the stock is now selling for \$51 7/8, at what rate of interest has your capital grown?

Solution:
(Refer to Table A.1.)
\$51.875/26 = 1.9952

In the 8th year, 1.9926($\cong$ 1.9952) appears in the 9 percent column. The interest rate is just over 9 percent.

5.4 If earnings in 1985 are \$1.18 per share, while five years earlier, in 1980, they were \$0.57, what has been the growth rate in earnings?

Solution:

$FVIF = \frac{\$1.18}{\$0.57} = 2.0702 = (1+r)^5$

$2.0702^{(.20)} = 1+r$

$1.15665 = 1+r$

$r = 15.665\%$

5.5 Robert Donne is offered the alternative of receiving \$4,000 today or \$6,700 at the end of 10 years. If he accepts the \$4,000 today, he will deposit it in a savings bank.

a. If the savings bank pays 5 percent interest, which alternative will Donne prefer?

b. Which would he prefer if the savings bank pays 6 1/4 percent interest?(Use the formula to calculate the PVIF.)

Solution:

a. Mr. Donne's opportunity cost is 5 percent:

$$P_o = FV_{r,n}PVIF(5\%, 10 \text{ yrs})$$

$$= \$6,700(.6139)$$

$$= \$4,113.13$$

Since the present value of \$6,700 is greater than \$4,000, Mr. Donne will prefer the \$6,700 at the end of 10 years.

Alternatively,

$$FV_{r,n} = P_o[FVIF(5\%, 10 \text{ yrs})]$$
$$= \$4,000(1.6289)$$
$$= \$6,515.60$$

Since the future value of the \$4,000 at the end of 10 years is less than \$6,700, Mr. Donne will prefer the \$6,700 at the end of 10 years.

b. Mr. Donne's opportunity cost is 6.25 percent:

$$PVIF(6.25\%, 10 \text{ yrs}) = 1/(1+r)^n$$

$$= 1/(1.0625)^{10}$$

$$= 1/1.83354$$

$$= .5454$$

$$P_o = \$6,700(.5454) = \$3,654.18$$

At the higher opportunity cost, \$6,700 in 10 years is worth less than \$4,000 today, so Donne will choose the \$4,000.

5.6 Given the FVIF of 3.4259, what is the PVIF for the same r,n combination? (Do not use the interest tables.)

Solution:
The PVIF is the reciprocal of the FVIF; therefore it is possible to compute the PVIF for a given FVIF even if r and n are unknown.

PVIF = 1/ FVIF = 1/3.4259 = .2919

(r = 8 percent
n = 16 years)

5.7 Henry Lithgow has just become a father. He decides to open a savings account for the child's college education. He will deposit $500 each year on the child's birthday. If the annual interest rate is 9 percent, what will be the balance in the account immediately after the child's 18th birthday?

Solution:

$FVA_{r,t} = a[FVIFA(r,t)]$

From Appendix Table A.3, FVIFA(9%, 18 years) = 41.301

$FVA_{r,t} = \$500(41.301)$

$= \$20,650.50$

By making deposits totalling only $9,000, Lithgow will accumulate over $20,000 by his child's 18th birthday.

5.8 You will receive $1,000 at the end of each year for the next 6 years. You will deposit the money in a certificate account at a savings association paying 10 percent interest. How large would a lump-sum payment have to be today to be equivalent to the annuity?

Solution:

$P_o = \$1,000 PVIFA(10\%, 6 \text{ yrs})$

$P_o = \$1,000(4.3553)$

$P_o = \$4,355.30$

5.9 The Viewpoint School is establishing a fund to make a down payment on a new gymnasium. They must accumulate $200,000 at the end of 5 years.

a. The school plans to put a fixed amount into the fund each year for 5 years, the first payment to be made in one year. Assume that the fund will earn 12 percent annual interest. What yearly contribution must be made to accumulate $200,000 at the end of 5 years?

b. A wealthy benefactor has offered to donate a lump sum today, instead of the annual payments approach. How large must the lump sum be to grow to $200,000 by the end of 5 years?

Solution:

a. The answer is found as the sum of an annuity at the end of 5 years.

From Table A.3, FVIFA(12%, 5 yrs) = 6.3528

Annual payment x 6.3528 = $200,000

Annual payment = $200,000/6.3528

= $31,482

b. $FV_{r,n} = P_oFVIF(12\%, 5\text{ yrs})$

$\$200,000 = P_o(1.7623)$

$P_o = \$113,488$

5.10 The Watson Company has outstanding $1,000 bonds which pay $65 in interest semiannually. The bonds have 10 years remaining to maturity. If an investor requires a yield of 10 percent, compounded semiannually, how much will he be willing to pay for the Watson Company bonds?

Solution:
Bond values are a special case of semiannual compounding. The value of a bond is the sum of the present value of the interest payments plus the present value of the face value that will be received at maturity.

Use r = 5%, n = 20 periods to adjust for semiannual compounding.

Present value of maturity value of bond:

$$\$1,000 \times PVIF(5\%, 20 \text{ periods}) = \$1,000(.3769)$$
$$= \$376.90$$

Present value of semiannual payments:

$$\$65 \times PVIFA(5\%, 20 \text{ periods}) = \$65(12.4622)$$
$$= \$810.04$$

Total present value of bond:

$$\$376.90 + \$810.04 = \$1,186.94$$

The bond is worth more than the $1,000 maturity value because the investor's required return (10 percent) is lower than the coupon rate (13 percent).

5.11 You have just borrowed $14,000, which must be repaid in three equal annual installments. The annual interest rate is 9.5 percent.
a. What are the annual installments?
b. Prepare an amortization table for the loan repayment.
c. If interest is compounded semiannually, what is the amount of each semiannual payment?
d. Prepare an amortization table for the loan repayment under semiannual compounding.

Solution:
a.
$$a = \frac{P_{r,t}}{PVIFA(r,t)}$$

$$PVIFA(9.5\%, 3 \text{ yrs}) = \frac{1-\frac{1}{1+r^n}}{r} = \frac{1-\frac{1}{1.095^3}}{.095} = 2.5089$$

$$a = \frac{\$14,000}{2.5089} = \$5,580$$

b. Amortization Table:

Year	(1) Payment	(2) .095 x (4) Interest	(3) (1) - (2) Principal Repayment	(4) End-of-Year Balance
0	---	---	---	$14,000
1	$5,580	$1,330	$4,250	9,750
2	5,580	926	4,654	5,096
3	5,580	484	5,096	0
	$16,740	$2,740	$14,000	

c.

$$\text{PVIFA} = \frac{1-\frac{1}{(1+r)^n}}{r} \qquad r = .095/2 = .0475$$

$$n = 3 \times 2 = 6$$

$$= \frac{1-\frac{1}{1.0475^6}}{.0475}$$

$$= 5.1165$$

$$a = \frac{\$14,000}{5.1165} = \$2,736 = \text{semiannual payment}$$

d. Amortization Table:

Period	(1) Payment	(2) .0475 x (4) Interest	(3) (1) - (2) Principal Repayment	(4) End-of-Period Balance
0	---	---	---	$14,000
1	$2,736	$ 665	$ 2,071	11,929
2	2,736	567	2,169	9,760
3	2,736	464	2,272	7,488
4	2,736	356	2,380	5,108
5	2,736	243	2,493	2,615
6	2,736	124	2,612	0*
	$16,416	$2,419	$13,997*	

*Discrepancies caused by rounding

Note that total interest payments are less by $321 in the case of semiannual compounding. This is because the loan is being paid off more quickly, and thus the principal on which interest is calculated is being reduced more quickly.

5.12 You pay $1,000 for a bond which pays no interest during its 12-year life, but which will pay $3,896 at maturity. What rate of interest will you earn if you hold the bond until it matures?

Solution:

$$\text{FVIF} = \frac{FV_{r,n}}{P_o} = \frac{\$3,896}{\$1,000} = 3.8960\text{, the FVIF for 12\% for 12 years}$$

5.13 Two investment opportunities are available to you. Project X is expected to pay $500 a year for the first 4 years, $300 a year for the next 8 years and nothing thereafter. Project Y is expected to pay $700 a year for 11 years and nothing thereafter. Risk considerations make appropriate an 8 percent yield for Project X, and a 10 percent yield for Project Y.

a. Which project has the higher present value?
b. Which project is riskier? Why?

Solution:

a. Project X:

$500 x PVIFA(8%, 4 yrs) = $500(3.3121)

= $1,656

$300 x PVIFA(8%, 8 yrs) x PVIF(8%, 4 yrs) =

$300(5.7466)(.7350) = $1,267

PV of Project X = $1,656 + $1,267 = $2,923

Project Y:

PV = $700 x PVIFA(10%, 11 yrs) = $700(6.4951)

= $4,547

The present value of Project Y is higher.

b. Project Y is the riskier investment since the problem statement indicates that risk considerations require a higher yield for Project Y than for Project X.

5.14 The Peterson Corporation paid a dividend of $1.20 per share last year. Dividends are expected to grow at a 16 percent rate for each of the next 5 years.

a. Calculate the expected dividend for each of the next 5 years.

b. Assuming that the first of these 5 dividends will be paid one year from now, what is the present value of the dividend stream if the required yield on investments of the same risk as Peterson Corporation stock is 14 percent?

c. Assume that the price of the stock at the end of 5 years will be $19.25. What is the present value of this "terminal value" using a 14 percent discount rate?

d. Assume that you will buy the stock, receive the dividends and then sell the stock, how much should you be willing to pay for it?

Solution:

a.

Year		Dividend
1	$\$1.20(1.16)$	$1.39
2	$1.20(1.16)^2$	1.61
3	$1.20(1.16)^3$	1.87
4	$1.20(1.16)^4$	2.17
5	$1.20(1.16)^5$	2.52

b.

Dividend	PVIF@14%	PV
$1.39	.8772	$1.22
1.61	.7695	1.24
1.87	.6750	1.26
2.17	.5921	1.28
2.52	.5194	1.31
		$6.31

c. $\$19.25[\text{PVIF}(14\%, 5 \text{ years})] = 19.25(.5194)$

$= \$10$

d. You would be willing to pay a maximum of $16.31 (that is, the sum of the present values of the dividend stream and the terminal value). If the stock's risk were to increase, the appropriate discount rate would also increase, and the value of the stock would be less, since the present values would be lowered by discounting at a higher rate.

5.15 If you invest \$907 in a security issued by Arabesque Corporation you are promised 25 annual payments of \$100, the first to be received one year from today. What is the yield, or rate of return, on the security?

Solution:

$$PVA = a[PVIFA(r,t)]$$

$$\$907 = 100[PVIFA(r, 25\text{ yrs})]$$

$$PVIFA(r, 25\text{ yrs}) = 9.07$$

Looking in Appendix Table A.4 in the 25-year row, we find the PVIFA 9.077 in the 10 percent column. Therefore, the rate of return is very close to 10 percent.

5.16 Sally Carlson has \$2,500 in a savings account. The account's stated interest rate is 10.5 percent.

a. Calculate the account balance after one year if interest is paid (1) annually, (2) semiannually, (3) quarterly, (4) monthly, and (5) daily.

b. Calculate the account balance after two years for each of the compounding intervals in part a.

Solution:

a. (1) Annual compounding:

$$FV_{r,n} = P_o(1+r)^n = P_o[FVIF(r,n)]$$

$$= 2,500(1.105)^1$$

$$= \$2,762.50$$

(2) Semiannual compounding:

$r = .105/2 = .0525$
$n = 2$

$$FV_{r,n} = 2,500(1.0525)^2$$

$$= \$2,769.39$$

(3) Quarterly compounding:

$r = .105/4 = .02625$
$n = 4$

$$FV_{r,n} - 2,500(1.02625)^4$$

$$= \$2,773.02$$

(4) Monthly compounding:

$r = .105/12 = .00875$
$n = 12$

$$FV_{r,n} = 2,500(1.00875)^{12}$$

$$= \$2,775.51$$

(5) Daily compounding:

$r = .105/365 = .0002877$
$n = 365$

$$FV_{r,n} = 2,500(1.0002877)^{365}$$
$$= \$2,776.73$$

b. (1) Annual compounding:

$r = .105$
$n = 2$

$$FV_{r,n} = 2,500(1.105)^{2}$$
$$= \$3,052.56$$

(2) Semiannual compounding:

$r = .105/2 = .0525$
$n = 2 \times 2 = 4$

$$FV_{r,n} = 2,500(1.0525)^{4}$$
$$= 3,067.81$$

(3) Quarterly compounding:

$r = .105/4 = .02625$
$n = 4 \times 2 = 8$

$$FV_{r,n} = 2,500(1.02625)^{8}$$
$$= \$3,075.85$$

(4) Monthly compounding:

$r = .105/12 = .00875$
$n = 12 \times 2 = 24$

$$FV_{r,n} = 2,500(1.00875)^{24}$$
$$= \$3,081.38$$

(5) Daily compounding:

$r = .105/365 = .0002877$
$n = 365 \times 2 = 730$

$$FV_{r,n} = 2,500(1.0002877)^{730}$$
$$= \$3,084.10$$

5.17 You want to borrow $18,000 from your credit union to buy a new car. The quoted interest rate is 15 percent compounded monthly for a 5-year amortized loan.

a. What annual percentage rate is equal to 15 percent compounded monthly?

b. What will your monthly car payments be (assuming they are paid at the end of each month)?

Solution:

a. $APR = r_e = \left(1+\frac{r}{q}\right)^q - 1$

$$= \left(1+\frac{.15}{12}\right)^{12} - 1$$

$$= 1.16075 - 1$$

$$= .16075 = 16.075 \text{ percent}$$

b. $a = \frac{PVA}{PVIFA(r,t)}$

$$r = .15/12 = .0125$$
$$n = 12 \times 5 = 60$$

$$PVIFA = \frac{1-(1+r)^{-n}}{r} = \frac{1-(1.0125)^{-60}}{.0125} = \frac{.4745676}{.0125} = 42.03459$$

$$a = \frac{18,000}{42.03459}$$

$$= \$428.22 = \text{monthly payment}$$

5.18 Peter Wesley, a recent medical school graduate, has received letters from two banks offering loans to start up practice. Bank A offers an effective annual rate of 16.5 percent, while Bank B offers a rate of 15 percent compounded daily. Which loan should Wesley accept?

Solution:
Find the APR of 15 percent compounded daily:

$$APR = r_e = \left(1+\frac{r}{q}\right)^q - 1$$

$$= \left(1+\frac{.15}{365}\right)^{365} - 1$$

$$= (1.000411)^{365} - 1$$

$$= .1618 = 16.18 \text{ percent}$$

Wesley should accept the loan from Bank B; even with daily compounding, its rate is still below the rate of Bank A.

5.19 Bank A offers an interest rate of 8 percent compounded annually. Bank B offers 7 percent compounded continuously. In which bank would you prefer to open a savings account?

Solution:

Find the effective annual yield of 7 percent compounded continuously.

$(1+d)^n = e^{cn}$

where d = effective annual yield
c = the continuously compounded rate = .07
n = number of periods; assume n = 1

$(1+d) = e^{.07}$

$(1+d) = 1.0725$

$d = .0725$

You would prefer to open an account in Bank A.

5.20 Bank C promises an effective annual yield of 12.75 percent due to its use of continuous compounding. What is the stated interest rate?

Solution:

In this case we know d, the effective annual yield, and want to find c.

$(1+d)^n = e^{cn}$

$(1.1275)^1 = e^c$

$\ln(1.1275) = c$

$c = .1200 = 12$ percent

5.21 At age 25 you receive an inheritance of $100,000. You want to set aside enough of the inheritance to provide $400,000 for your retirement 40 years later. You can earn a 10 percent nominal rate of interest compounded continuously. How much of the inheritance will you have left to enjoy now?

Solution:

$FV = PVe^{cn}$

$\$400,000 = PVe^{(.10)(40)}$

$\$400,000 = PVe^4$

$\$400,000 = PV(54.598)$

$$PV = \$7,326$$

If you deposit \$7,326 now at 10 percent interest compounded continuously, you will accumulate \$400,000 by the end of 40 years. You will be left with \$100,000 - \$7,326 = \$92,674 to enjoy now.

5.22 What rate of interest compounded semiannually will produce the same rate of return as 12 percent compounded continuously?

Solution:

$$\left(1+\frac{d}{m}\right)^{mn} = e^{cn}$$ where m = the number of times per year compounding occurs

$$\left(1+\frac{d}{2}\right)^2 = e^{.12}$$

$$\left(1+\frac{d}{2}\right)^2 = 1.1275$$

$$\left(1+\frac{d}{2}\right) = (1.1275)^{1/2}$$

$$1+\frac{d}{2} = 1.0618$$

$$\frac{d}{2} = .0618$$

$$d = .1236 = 12.36 \text{ percent}$$

CHAPTER 6

CAPITAL BUDGETING TECHNIQUES

Theme: Capital budgeting is of major significance because it involves commitments for large outlays whose benefits (or harmful effects) extend over a long period of years. The optimal capital budget maximizes the present value of the firm.

I. The Capital Budget is a Plan of Expenditures for Fixed Assets. It is significant for these reasons:
   A. It represents a decision whose consequences continue over an extended period, involving a loss of flexibility.
   B. It represents an implicit sales forecast. Inaccurate forecasts will result in over-investment or under-investment in fixed assets.
   C. Good capital budgeting will improve the timing of asset acquisitions and the quality of assets purchased.
   D. Asset expansion involves substantial expenditures. The requisite financing must be arranged in advance.
   E. Failure occurs both because of too much capital investment and because of undue delay in replacing old equipment with modern equipment.

II. Overall View of Capital Budgeting.
   A. It is an application of the classic economic theory that marginal revenue should be equated to marginal cost.
   B. Marginal revenue is the percentage return on an investment.
   C. Marginal cost is the firm's marginal cost of capital.
   D. The optimal investment policy can be found graphically. (See Figure 6.1)
      1. Plot the percentage rates of return of a firm's potential investment opportunities in descending order to form an investment opportunity schedule (IRR).
      2. On the same graph, chart the firm's marginal cost of capital schedule (MCC), an upward sloping line since the firm's cost of capital will rise as it must raise more funds within a particular time period.
      3. The optimal investment policy is where the IRR and MCC curves cross.

III. Investment Proposals are Assembled in Categories.
   A. Replacements.
      1. Assets wear out or become obsolete.
      2. Estimates of cost savings in replacing an old asset can be made with a relatively high degree of confidence.
   B. Expansion investments.
      1. Additional capacity is provided in existing product lines.

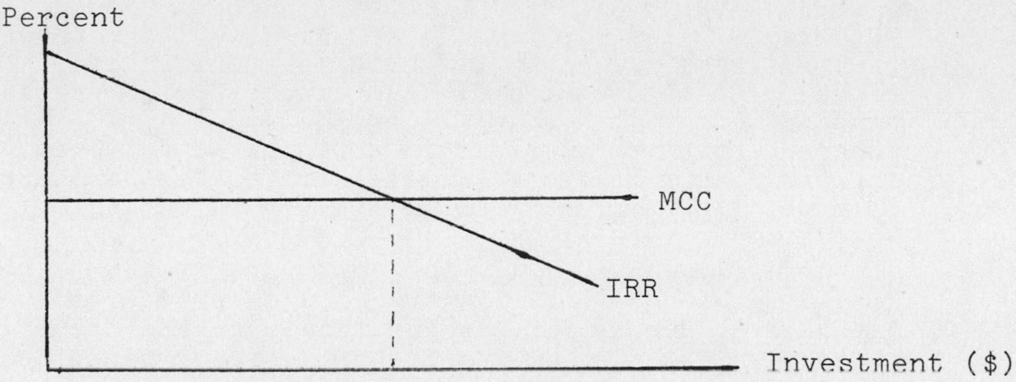

Figure 6.1 Capital Budgeting Decision Process

2. Estimates are based on prior experience.
3. Expansion and replacement decisions are often treated congruently.

C. New product activities.
   1. This represents a form of expansion and possibly diversification.
   2. Estimates are subject to a wider margin of error.

D. Others, including intangible items.
   1. Pollution control equipment
   2. Safety requirements
   3. Social and environmental considerations

IV. Administration of Capital Budgeting.

A. Approvals.
   1. Typically, larger dollar amounts require higher levels of approval.
   2. Review and approval of major outlays is an important function of boards of directors.

B. Planning horizon.
   1. It varies with the nature of the industry.
   2. When future sales can be forecast accurately, or when product technology developments require a long period before the introduction of a new product, the planning horizon will be correspondingly long.

C. Payment schedule and post-audits.
   1. Finance department works with other departments to compile systematic records on the uses of funds.
   2. Data are also compiled on equipment purchased.
   3. Feedback data on actual savings should be compiled.
   4. Comparisons between earlier estimates and actual data provide a basis for review of past decisions and the formulation of new decisions.

V. Choosing Among Alternative Proposals.

A. There are two basic types of proposals:

1. Mutually exclusive proposals are alternative methods of performing the same job, such as a choice of conveyor belts versus fork-lift trucks for materials handling.
2. Independent items are capital equipment considered for performing different tasks, such as the purchase of materials handling equipment versus a packaging machine.
3. Contingent proposals must be considered together. For example, the decision to build an office building may have to be made in conjunction with the decision on parking facilities if rooftop or subterranean parking are among the options.

B. Since there are often more proposals for projects than the firm is able or willing to finance, the capital budgeting process:

1. Ranks proposals to determine which of several investments should be accepted.
2. Calculates a cutoff point to determine how many projects should be selected.

VI. Measures of Cash Flows.

A. Focus on the change in after-tax cash flows as a result of the investment.

B. Two equivalent formulations:

1. Top-down approach:

$$\Delta\text{Cash Flow} = (1-T)\Delta\text{EBIT} + \Delta\text{Dep}$$

a. EBIT must be put on an after-tax basis, since taxes are a cash outflow.
b. Depreciation must be added back because it is a non-cash expense.

2. Bottom-up approach:

$$\Delta\text{Cash Flow} = \Delta\text{Net Income} + \Delta\text{Dep} + (1-T)\Delta rD$$

where rD = interest expense

C. Note that both definitions are independent of financing costs, which are considered in the cost of capital phase of capital budgeting.

D. Good data are important.

1. Reliable estimates of cost savings or revenue increases are critical.
2. Effective record keeping for meaningful post-audits is essential.
3. Good data require competent individuals to make the estimates.

VII. A Procedure to Rank Investments is Developed.

A. The optimal investment decision rule should meet the following four criteria:
   1. It selects the projects which maximize shareholder wealth.
   2. It considers all cash flows.
   3. It discounts cash flows at the market-determined opportunity cost of capital.
   4. It adheres to the Value-Additivity principle: Decisions on combinations of projects cannot contradict the decisions that would be made viewing projects independently.

B. Four ranking methods are discussed.
   1. Payback.
   2. Return on Assets (ROA) or Return on Investment (ROI).
   3. Net Present Value (NPV).
   4. Internal Rate of Return (IRR).

C. The payback method calculates the number of years required to return the initial investment.
   1. Payback violates all four decision rule criteria.
   2. In spite of its weaknesses, the payback method is sometimes used because it is so easy to apply.

D. ROA is calculated by dividing the average annual cash flow by the initial investment outlay.
   1. Sometimes the denominator is the gross or net investment balance.
   2. Its major deficiency is that it ignores the time value of money.

E. Both the NPV and IRR methods are discounted cash flow techniques which consider the time value of money.
   1. The NPV is the present value of expected net cash flows from an investment discounted at the cost of capital, minus the initial cost of the investment.

$$NPV = \sum_{t=1}^{n} \frac{CF_t}{(1+k)^t} - I_0$$

      a. Projects with a positive NPV should be accepted.
      b. If projects are mutually exclusive, choose the one with the highest NPV.
   2. The internal rate of return is the interest rate which equates the present value of cash flows to the initial outlay.
      a. The NPV equation is solved for the interest rate which causes the NPV to equal zero.
      b. Select those projects for which the IRR is greater than the cost of capital; with mutually exclusive projects, choose the one with the highest IRR.

VIII. The NPV Method is the Only Capital Budgeting Technique which is Always Appropriate.

A. The net present value of a project is exactly the same as the change in shareholder wealth caused by the project.

1. Cash flows are discounted at the weighted average cost of capital, which is the after-tax, market-determined opportunity cost of funds.
2. The weighted average cost of capital provides the cash flow to satisfy the required risk-adjusted rates of return to creditors and shareholders.
3. Any excess cash flows beyond these required returns result in a positive net present value.
4. Shareholders, as residual claimants, receive the benefit of the positive NPV.

B. Discounting cash flows at the weighted average cost of capital separates investment decisions from financing decisions.
  1. Cash flows are defined as the after-tax cash flows the firm would have if it had no debt.
  2. Financing considerations affect only the applicable cost of capital, not cash flows.

C. Comparison of the NPV and IRR methods.
  1. The IRR method makes a faulty reinvestment rate assumption, or opportunity cost assumption; it assumes that funds invested in a project have an opportunity cost equal to the IRR of the project.
     a. Projects of equal risk should have the same opportunity cost, but may have different IRRs; therefore, discounting at the IRR is inappropriate.
     b. The NPV method discounts at the market-determined cost of capital appropriate to the risk of the project; projects of equal risk are discounted at the same rate.
  2. The IRR criterion can violate the value-additivity principle.
     a. The NPV rule always obeys value additivity.
     b. Using NPV, the value of the firm is the sum of the values of the separate projects which comprise the firm.
  3. The IRR results in meaningless multiple rates of return whenever cash flows change direction more than once.

IX. Calculation Procedures

A. The NPV is calculated using five basic steps:
  1. Estimate the net initial cash outlay: Payment for the new equipment, proceeds from sale of the old machine, tax effects, and changes in working capital requirements should be considered.
  2. Determine the incremental cash flows (ΔF) generated by the project using the following equation:

$$\Delta F = (\Delta S - \Delta O)(1-T) + T\Delta Dep$$

where: ΔS = Change in sales
ΔO = Change in operating cost
T = Marginal corporate income tax rate
ΔDep = Change in depreciation

3. Using the firm's cost of capital, calculate the present value of the incremental cash flows.
4. The present value of the machine's expected salvage value is added as a positive cash inflow. Similarly, the present value of the recovery at the end of the project life of the incremental working capital investment is an additional positive cash flow.
5. Compare the present value of the cash inflows to the present value of cash outlays to determine whether the NPV is positive or negative.

B. The effects of accelerated depreciation on incremental cash flows can be included in the capital budgeting analysis by preparing a worksheet for each year, or by using a table of present value factors for accelerated depreciation.

X. Special Cases of Capital Budgeting.

A. Projects with different lives.
1. Make projects comparable by assuming replication at a constant scale forever.
2. Compute the NPV to infinity for each project.

$$NPV(n,\infty) = NPV(n)\left[\frac{(1+k)^n}{(1+k)^n-1}\right]$$

where $NPV(n,\infty)$ = NPV of the n-year project replicated to infinity
$NPV(n)$ = NPV of the n-year project

B. Projects of different scale (different initial outlay).
1. Different scale creates a problem only in conditions of capital rationing.
   a. Firm value is not maximized under capital rationing.
   b. All positive NPV projects should be accepted regardless of initial outlay.
   c. All projects which result in a positive NPV at the appropriate weighted average cost of capital can, by definition, be financed.
2. Use linear (or integer) programming methods to maximize firm value subject to an artificial capital constraint.
3. The Profitability Index (PI) is also used for projects of different scale.
   a. $PI = \text{benefit/cost ratio} = \frac{\text{PV of benefits}}{\text{Cost}}$

   $$= \frac{\text{Gross Present Value}}{I_0}$$

   b. PI indicates relative profitability, or the PV of benefits per each dollar of cost.

c. Select the combination of projects which maximizes the weighted average PI assuming any excess funds will be invested in cash and marketable securities with a PI of 1.
d. The PI method gives the same results as the NPV method.

Chapter 6 - Illustrative Problems and Solutions

6.1 Your firm has an opportunity to invest in a new piece of machinery at a cost of $135,750. The machine is expected to last 7 years and to produce annual cash flows of $45,000. The applicable cost of capital for this project is 16 percent.
a. What is the net present value of the investment?
b. What is the internal rate of return for the investment?
c. Should you purchase the machine?

Solution:

a. $NPV = -135,750 + \sum_{t=1}^{7} \frac{45,000}{(1.16)^t}$

$= -135,750 + 45,000(PVIFA_{16\%,\ 7\ years})$

$= -135,750 + 45,000(4.0386)$

$= -135,750 + 181,737$

$= \$45,987$

b. $0 = NPV = -135,750 + \sum_{t=1}^{7} \frac{45,000}{(1+IRR)^t}$

$= -135,750 + 45,000(PVIFA_{IRR,\ 7\ years})$

$135,750/45,000 = PVIFA = 3.0166667$

In the 7-year row, the PVIFA 3.0167 falls between 24 and 28 percent. By linear interpolation IRR = 26.96 percent.

c. The machine should be purchased by both the NPV criteria (NPV is positive) and the IRR criteria (IRR > cost of capital).

6.2 A firm is considering two mutually exclusive investments, each requiring an initial outlay of $5,000 with the following net cash flows:

Year	Project A	Project B
1	$2,000	$3,000
2	3,000	2,000
3	1,500	1,500

The firm's cost of capital is 10 percent. Calculate the payback period and net present value for each project. Comment on the results.

Solution:
Both projects have a 2-year payback.
NPV of Project A = -5,000 + 2,000(.909) + 3,000(.826) + 1,500(.751)
= $422.50
NPV of Project B = -5,000 + 3,000(.909) + 2,000(.826) + 1,500(.751)
= $505.50

Using the payback method, both projects seem equally desirable. This is because the payback method does not consider the time value of money. Using the NPV method, Project B is more desirable since it has a faster cash flow.

6.3 Ruffin Manufacturing has a plan, Mod 1, to update its assembly line with new industrial equipment at a cost of $240,000. The equipment is expected to last 11 years and to have a salvage value of $20,000. Mod 1 is expected to result in savings of $60,000 per year over the life of the equipment. Ruffin's corporate tax rate is 40 percent; it uses straight line depreciation; and the applicable cost of capital for the project is 14 percent. A pro forma income statement for Mod 1 is shown below:

Sales	$210,000
Operating costs	150,000
Earnings before depreciation, interest and taxes (EBDIT)	60,000
Depreciation	20,000
Earnings before interest and taxes (EBIT, NOI, X)	40,000
Taxes @ 40%	16,000
Net income [X(1-T)]	$ 24,000

a. Present two formulations of the tax-adjusted net cash flows from Mod 1.
b. Use the worksheet method to calculate the project's NPV.
c. Should Ruffin modernize?

Solution:

a. (1) (1-T)EBIT + Dep = (.6)($40,000) + $20,000
= $24,000 + $20,000
= $44,000 per year

(2) Net income + Dep = $24,000 + $20,000
= $44,000

b.

Outflows	Amount Before Tax	Amount After Tax	Year	Present Value Factor @14%	Present Value
Investment in Equipment	240,000	240,000	0	1.0	240,000
Inflows					
Savings (1-T)	60,000	36,000	1-11	5.4527	196,297
Depreciation (T)	20,000	8,000	1-11	5.4527	43,622
Salvage value	20,000	20,000	11	.2366	4,732
Present Value of Inflows					$244,651

NPV = Present value of inflows - outflows.
= $244,651 - 240,000
= $4,651

c. Since the NPV is positive, Ruffin should go ahead with Mod 1.

6.4 Assume that Ruffin did go ahead with Mod 1. Six years have now passed, and technological innovations in Ruffin's industry have made the Mod 1 equipment largely obsolete. A new plan, Mod 2, is now under consideration whereby Ruffin would sell the Mod 1 equipment for a scrap value of $10,000, and purchase the most modern equipment available. The Mod 2 equipment will cost $170,000, and has a life of five years with $20,000 expected salvage value. Under Mod 2 sales are expected to increase to $235,000 per year, and operating costs will be reduced by $20,000 over Mod 1.

a. Present the pro forma income statements for Mod 1, Mod 2 and for the difference between them.
b. Calculate the NPV of Mod 2.
c. Which has a larger NPV? Should Mod 2 be undertaken?

Solution:

a.

	Mod 1	Mod 2	Mod 2 - Mod 1
Sales	$210,000	$235,000	$25,000
Operating costs	150,000	130,000	(20,000)
EBDIT	60,000	105,000	45,000
Depreciation	20,000	30,000	10,000
EBIT, NOI, X	40,000	75,000	35,000
Taxes @ 40%	16,000	30,000	14,000
Net income	$ 24,000	$ 45,000	$21,000
Cash flow = NI + Dep	$ 44,000	$ 75,000	$ 31,000

b. NPV of Mod 2

Outflows (at t=0)	Amount Before Tax	Amount After Tax	Year	Present Value Factor @14%	Present Value
Investment in Mod 2	170,000	170,000	0	1.0	170,000
Salvage value of Mod 1	(10,000)	(10,000)	0	1.0	(10,000)
Tax savings from loss on Mod 1*	(110,000)	(44,000)	0	1.0	(44,000)
Net Investment					116,000
Inflows (years 1-5)					
Savings (1-T)	45,000	27,000	1-5	3.4331	92,694
Depreciation (T)	10,000	4,000	1-5	3.4331	13,732
Salvage value of Mod 2	20,000	20,000	5	.5194	10,388
Gross Present Value					116,814

NPV = GPV - I
= 116,814 - 116,000
= $814

*Calculation of tax loss on Mod 1:

Depreciable value of Mod 1	$220,000
Less accumulated depreciation	120,000
	$100,000
Plus estimated salvage value	20,000
	$120,000
Less actual salvage value	10,000
Tax loss	$110,000

c. Since Mod 2 has a positive net present value it should be undertaken. The fact that Mod 1's NPV is almost six times that of Mod 2 is irrelevant. The investments in Mod 1 were made six years ago and are sunk costs. Only the incremental investment and cash flows from Mod 2 matter at this time, and since the NPV is positive, Mod 2 will be advantageous to Ruffin.

6.5 The Lindblad Company must choose between two mutually exclusive investment opportunities. Both require an initial outlay of $10,000. Project A has expected cash flows of $4,000 per year for 5 years, and a 12 percent cost of capital. Project B is riskier and has a required return of 14 percent; Project B's expected cash flows are $6,000 per year for 3 years. Which project should Lindblad choose?

Solution:

Project A:

$$NPV(5) = \$4{,}000\ (PVIFA,\ 12\%,\ 5\ yrs) - \$10{,}000$$
$$= \$4{,}000(3.6048) - \$10{,}000$$
$$= \$14{,}419.20 - \$10{,}000$$
$$= \$4{,}419.20$$

$$NPV(5,\infty) = NPV(5)\left[\frac{(1+k)^n}{(1+k)^n-1}\right]$$
$$= \$4{,}419.20\left(\frac{1.12^5}{1.12^5-1}\right)$$
$$= \$4{,}419.20\left(\frac{1.7623}{.7623}\right)$$
$$= \$4{,}419.20(2.312)$$
$$= \$10{,}217.19$$

Project B:

$$NPV(3) = \$6{,}000\ (PVIFA,\ 14\%,\ 3\ years) - \$10{,}000$$
$$= \$6{,}000(2.3216) - \$10{,}000$$
$$= \$13{,}929.60 - \$10{,}000$$
$$= \$3{,}929.60$$

$$NPV(3,\infty) = NPV(3)\left(\frac{1.14^3}{1.14^3-1}\right)$$
$$= \$3{,}929.60\left(\frac{1.4815}{.4815}\right)$$
$$= \$3{,}929.60(3.077)$$
$$= \$12{,}091.38$$

On the basis of simple NPVs, Project A appears superior. However, when we calculate the NPV(∞) for each project to adjust for their different lives, Project B should be chosen.

6.6 A company is faced with four independent investment projects. Each project has a 4-year life and a 14 percent cost of capital. Additional information is given below:

Project	Initial Outlay	Expected Annual Cash Flow
W	$50,000	$20,000
X	35,000	15,000
Y	20,000	8,000
Z	15,000	5,000

a. Calculate the NPV for each project. Which projects should be selected?

b. Suppose that management has imposed capital rationing and that the capital budget is restricted to $70,000. Which projects should be selected?

c. Calculate the profitability index for each project. Use the weighted average profitability index method to select projects under the capital constraint.

Solution:

a. NPV_W = \$20,000(PVIFA, 14%, 4 years) - \$50,000
= \$20,000(2.9137) - \$50,000
= \$58,274 - \$50,000
= \$8,274

NPV_X = \$15,000(2.9137) - \$35,000
= \$43,705 - \$35,000
= \$8,705

NPV_Y = \$8,000(2.9137) - \$20,000
= \$23,310 - \$20,000
= \$3,310

NPV_Z = \$5,000(2.9137) - \$15,000
= \$14,568 - \$15,000
= -\$432

Projects W, X and Y have positive NPVs and should all be undertaken. Project Z has a negative NPV and should be rejected.

b. Since Project Z has a negative NPV, we must choose among Projects W, X and Y. Because the combined initial outlays for Projects W and X exceed the allowable capital budget (\$50,000 + \$35,000 = \$85,000), our choice is restricted to W + Y and X + Y.

NPVs are additive. Choose the combination with the higher total NPV.
NPV(W) + NPV(Y) = \$8,274 + \$3,310 = \$11,584
NPV(X) + NPV(Y) = \$8,705 + \$3,310 = \$12,015

The optimal capital budget subject to the constraint will involve Projects X and Y, for a combined outlay of \$55,000. The \$15,000 left over will be invested in cash and marketable securities.

Note that firm value is not being maximized in this situation since Project W would add \$8,274 to shareholder wealth.

c. Project W: $PI = \frac{\text{PV of benefits}}{\text{Cost}} = \frac{\$58,274}{\$50,000} = 1.165$

Project X: $PI = \frac{\$43,705}{\$35,000} = 1.249$

Project Y: $PI = \frac{\$23,310}{\$20,000} = 1.166$

Project Z: $PI = \frac{\$14,568}{\$15,000} = .971$

Projects W + Y:
Weighted average PI $= \frac{50}{70}(1.165) + \frac{20}{70}(1.166)$
$= .832 + .333$
$= 1.165$

Projects X + Y:
Weighted average PI $= \frac{35}{70}(1.249) + \frac{20}{70}(1.166) + \frac{15}{70}(1)$
$= .625 + .333 + .214$
$= 1.172$

The weighted average PI method gives that same results as the NPV method. Projects X and Y have the higher weighted average PI as well as the higher combined NPV.

6.7 The Carline Company is evaluating two mutually exclusive investment projects. Each involves an initial outlay of $16,000, and the projects have the following cash flow patterns:

Year	Project A	Project B
1	$8,000	$1,000
2	8,000	3,000
3	2,000	4,000
4	2,000	7,000
5	1,000	9,000

a. Calculate the gross present value and net present value of each project at costs of capital of 0, 6, 10, and 20 percent.
b. Calculate each project's IRR.
c. Graph the results of part (a) with cost of capital on the horizontal axis and net present value on the vertical axis.
d. If Carline's cost of capital is 13 percent, which project should be chosen?

Solution:

a.

Year	IF at 0%	A	B	IF at 6%	A	B
1	1.0	8,000	1,000	.9434	7,547	943
2	1.0	8,000	3,000	.8900	7,120	2,670
3	1.0	2,000	4,000	.8396	1,679	3,358
4	1.0	2,000	7,000	.7921	1,584	5,545
5	1.0	1,000	9,000	.7473	747	6,726
GPV		21,000	24,000		18,677	19,242
NPV		5,000	8,000		2,677	3,242

Year	IF at 10%	A	B	IF at 20%	A	B
1	.9091	7,273	909	.8333	6,666	833
2	.8264	6,611	2,478	.6944	5,555	2,083
3	.7513	1,503	3,005	.5787	1,157	2,315
4	.6830	1,366	4,781	.4823	965	3,376
5	.6209	621	5,588	.4019	402	3,617
GPV		17,374	16,761		14,745	12,224
NPV		1,374	761		(1,255)	(3,776)

b.

IRR_A:

$$NPV = 0 = -16,000 + \frac{8,000}{(1+r)^1} + \frac{8,000}{(1+r)^2} + \frac{2,000}{(1+r)^3} + \frac{2,000}{(1+r)^4} + \frac{1,000}{(1+r)^5}$$

$IRR_A = 14.9\%$

IRR_B:

$$NPV = 0 = -16,000 + \frac{1,000}{(1+r)^1} + \frac{3,000}{(1+r)^2} + \frac{4,000}{(1+r)^3} + \frac{7,000}{(1+r)^4} + \frac{9,000}{(1+r)^5}$$

$IRR_B = 11.4\%$

c. See next page.

d. At a cost of capital of 13 percent, Project A would be chosen, with an NPV of approximately $500 reading from the graph in part (c). At 13 percent, Project B has a negative net present value.

The significance of the findings: The different methods result in different rankings. The IRR of A is higher than that of B. At a cost of capital of 6 percent, B has a higher NPV than A. At a rate of 8 percent Carline should be

c.

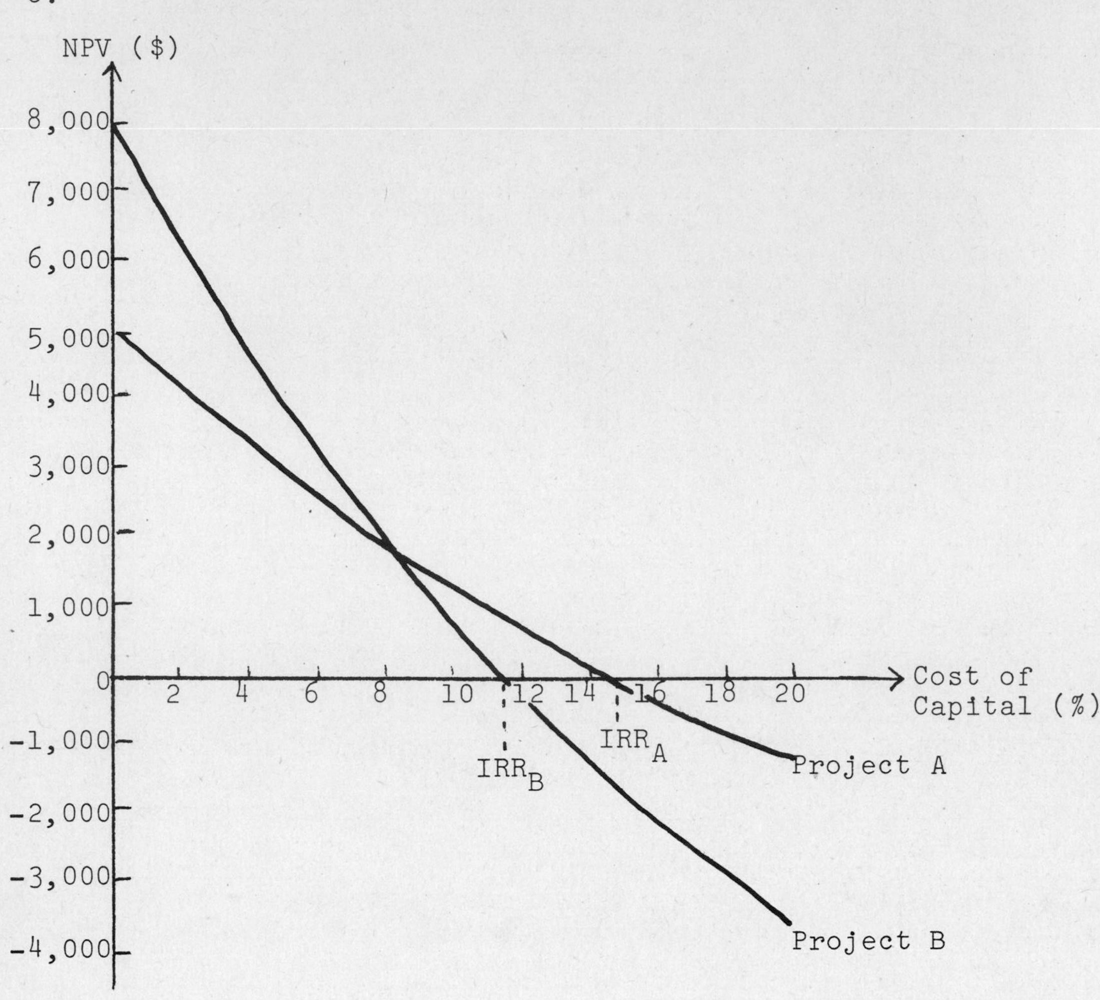

NPV ($)
8,000
7,000
6,000
5,000
4,000
3,000
2,000
1,000
0
-1,000
-2,000
-3,000
-4,000
2
4
6
8
10
12
14
16
18
20
Cost of Capital (%)
IRR$_B$
IRR$_A$
Project A
Project B

indifferent between the two investment alternatives. At rates above 8 percent, there is no conflict. Project A has a higher IRR and a higher NPV than B. This is due to the difference in timing of cash flows.

Beyond the internal rates of return (A: 14.9 percent; B: 11.4 percent) both investments have negative net present values; thus, at costs of capital higher than these levels, the projects would not be accepted. This indicates that projects cannot be ranked without taking the cost of capital into account; otherwise, errors may result.

Also note that projects that have higher returns in early years and lower returns in later years (for example, mining enterprises in which yields may drop off) are penalized less by higher costs of capital. Conversely, projects with lower returns in early years and higher returns in later years (such as fruit orchards where the trees require time to mature) have higher present values at lower rates of interest. Project A is the mining type, while Project B is the orchard type. Note that at low costs of capital, the present value of Project B is higher than A. At higher costs of capital, the present value of Project A is higher than B.

In general, a firm with a high cost of capital will tend to make short-term investments in the sense that most of the returns are realized in the early years of the life of the project. If the firm has a low cost of capital, it will tend to make longer-term investments in the sense that higher returns in later years will not be penalized by high discount factors--low present value multipliers.

6.8 Bunyan Lumber Company is considering the purchase of a lease of federal forest service lands for \$500,000. They expect cash flows from logging operations to total \$1,500,000, all coming at the end of one year. The land must be replanted at a cost of \$800,000, payable after 2 years.

a. What is the IRR of the logging project?
b. If the cost of capital appropriate to the risk of the project is 12 percent, should Bunyan purchase the lease?

Solution:

a. $$\$500{,}000 = \frac{\$1{,}500{,}000}{(1+IRR)^1} - \frac{\$800{,}000}{(1+IRR)^2}$$

By trial and error, we find two IRRs for the project.

$IRR_1 = 131\%$: $$\$500{,}000 = \frac{\$1{,}500{,}000}{2.31} - \frac{\$800{,}000}{2.31^2}$$

$$\$500{,}000 \cong \$649{,}351 - \$149{,}922 \cong \$499{,}429$$

IRR_2 = -30.6%: $$\$500,000 = \frac{\$1,500,000}{.694} - \frac{\$800,000}{(.694)^2}$$

$$500,000 \cong 2,161,383 - 1,661,005 \cong 500,377$$

Based on the IRR criterion, it would be impossible to decide whether this project will be a great success or a huge failure.

b.

$$NPV = -500,000 + \frac{1,500,000}{1.12} - \frac{800,000}{(1.12)^2}$$

$$= -500,000 + 1,339,286 - 637,755$$

$$= \$201,531$$

Since the NPV is positive at the appropriate risk-adjusted discount rate, the project should be accepted as it will add $201,531 to the company's value.

6.9 The Porteous Company is considering a project which has a 6-year life and costs $150,000. It would save $20,000 per year in operating costs and increase revenue by $27,000 per year. It would be financed with a 6-year loan with an annual interest rate of 10 percent; see the loan repayment schedule below. The project is expected to have no salvage value at the end of its life.

Payment	Interest	Repayment of Principal	Balance
$34,441	$15,000	$19,441	$130,559
34,441	13,056	21,385	109,174
34,441	10,917	23,524	85,650
34,441	8,565	25,876	59,774
34,441	5,977	28,464	31,310
34,441	3,131	31,310	0
	$56,646	$150,000	

If Porteous has a 14 percent after-tax cost of capital and a 40 percent tax rate, what is the net present value of the project using

a. Straight line depreciation?
b. Double declining balance depreciation in years 1-4, switching to straight line depreciation in years 5 and 6.

Solution:

First, note that the material given on project financing and loan repayment is irrelevant. All financing costs are reflected in the discount rate, which is the firm's after-tax cost of capital.

a. Straight line depreciation:

$$\text{Cash flows} = (\Delta\text{Sales} - \Delta\text{O})(1-\text{T}) + \text{T}\Delta\text{Dep}$$

$$= [27{,}000 - (-20{,}000)](1-.4) + .4\left(\frac{150{,}000}{6}\right)$$

$$= 47{,}000(.6) + .4(25{,}000)$$

$$= 28{,}200 + 10{,}000$$

$$= 38{,}200$$

$$\text{NPV} = -150{,}000 + 38{,}200[\text{PVIFA}(14\%, 6 \text{ yrs})]$$

$$= -150{,}000 + 38{,}200(3.8887)$$

$$= -150{,}000 + 148{,}548$$

$$= -\$1{,}452$$

Since the NPV is negative, the project should be rejected.

b. Double declining balance depreciation:
We use the table of interest factors for the present value of double declining balance depreciation. The present value tables for accelerated depreciation already take into account the switch to straight line depreciation that occurs whenever an accelerated method is used.

$$\text{NPV} = -\text{I} + (\Delta\text{Sales} - \Delta\text{O})(1-\text{T})[\text{PVIFA}(14\%, 6 \text{ yrs})]$$

$$+ \text{TDep}(\text{PVIF of DDBD at } 14\%, 6 \text{ yrs})$$

$$= -150{,}000 + 28{,}200(3.8887) + .4(150{,}000)(.718)$$

$$= -150{,}000 + 109{,}661 + 43{,}080$$

$$= \$2{,}741$$

With the use of double declining balance depreciation, the project has a positive NPV and should be accepted.

6.10 The Lahana Resort and Country Club is considering the purchase of solar-powered golf carts to replace gasoline-powered carts currently in use. The company would realize a 10 percent investment tax credit on the $200,000 purchase price of the new carts. The gas-powered carts are expected to last for 10 more years, and currently have a net book value of $75,000. The solar carts have a useful life of 10 years. At the end of 10 years both types of carts would be expected to have zero salvage value.

The gas-powered carts use 18,000 gallons of gas per year, at a cost of $1.25 per gallon. The annual operating and maintenance costs on the new carts are expected to be $10,000 less than on the old. The old carts have a current market value of $30,000.

The required rate of return on investment for Lahana is 14 percent, the tax rate is 40 percent, and the firm uses straight line depreciation.

a. Should the solar-powered carts be purchased?
b. Suppose that gas prices are expected to rise at an annual rate of 18 percent. How will this affect the investment decision?

Solution:

a. Using a worksheet methodology, and assuming that the price of gas remains at its current level over the next 10 years, we have:

Net Cash Outflows:	Amount Before Tax	Amount After Tax	Year	PV Factor @14%	Present Value
Investment in new carts	$200,000	$200,000	0	1	$200,000
Investment tax credit	(20,000)	(20,000)	0	1	(20,000)
Sale of old carts	(30,000)	(30,000)	0	1	(30,000)
Tax effect of sale**	45,000	(18,000)	0	1	(18,000)
Net investment					$132,000
Annual Inflows:					
Energy savings 18,000(1.25)	22,500	13,500	1-10	5.2161	70,417
Operating and maintenance cost savings	10,000	6,000	1-10	5.2161	31,297
Depreciation on new carts	20,000	8,000	1-10	5.2161	41,729
Lost depreciation on old carts	(7,500)	(3,000)	1-10	5.2161	(15,648)
Net inflows					$127,795

**The carts are sold for $30,000, when they have a net book value of $75,000. This is a paper loss of $45,000. However, this loss reduces the cash outflow on taxes, and therefore, the net effect of the sale is to reduce the cash outflow necessary to purchase the new carts.

NPV = PV of inflows - PV of outflows
= 127,795 - 132,000
= -$4,205

Based on this analysis, the NPV is negative, therefore, the solar-powered carts should not be purchased.

b. The present value of the energy savings must be recalculated to reflect the very plausible assumption that gas prices will increase. In terms of a compact formula, this may be written:

$$PV = 22{,}500(1-.4) \sum_{t=1}^{10} \frac{(1.18)^{t-1}}{(1.14)^{t}}$$

In table form:

Year	Before-Tax Savings	After-Tax Savings	PV Factor @ 14%	Present Value
1	22,500	13,500	.8772	11,842
2	26,550	15,930	.7695	12,258
3	31,329	18,797	.6750	12,688
4	36,968	22,181	.5921	13,133
5	43,622	26,173	.5194	13,594
6	51,475	30,885	.4556	14,071
7	60,740	36,444	.3996	14,563
8	71,673	43,004	.3506	15,077
9	84,574	50,745	.3075	15,604
10	99,798	59,879	.2697	16,149
Present value of energy savings				$138,979

PV of inflows = 70,417 + 138,979 + 41,729 - 15,648
= 235,477

NPV = 235,477 - 132,000
= 103,477

When inflation is considered, the NPV is highly positive and the carts should be purchased. Thus, the impact of inflation has been to reverse the decision. Of course, operating and maintenance costs may also rise over time with inflation, and this would have to be taken into account as well.

CHAPTER 7

HOW THE MARKET DETERMINES DISCOUNT RATES

Theme: The appropriate cost of capital (or discount rate) for use in capital budgeting is determined by the market's assessment of productivity, expected inflation, liquidity and risk.

I. Nominal Interest Rates Consist of Four Components.
   A. The expected real rate of return in the economy.
   B. The expected inflation rate over the life of the asset.
   C. The liquidity of the asset.
   D. The riskiness of the asset.
      1. Default risk.
      2. Return risk, or covariance risk.

II. The Real Rate of Interest in the Absence of Inflation and Risk.
   A. The real rate of return is the price of money across time.
      1. It is determined by the aggregate supply and demand for funds.
      2. It is the equilibrium rate which equates borrowing and lending in the economy.
   B. The Fisher separation principle says that all individuals will maximize their wealth using the market-determined interest rate as a guide.
      1. Individuals will borrow or lend according to the relationship between their subjective rate for investment versus consumption and the market rate.
      2. Projects are undertaken until the marginal rate of return on the last project just equals the market rate.
   C. There is a direct relationship between the real interest rate and productivity in the economy.
      1. The real rate rises in response to increased productivity.
         a. Greater number of profitable investment opportunities leads to greater competition for funds.
         b. As interest rates rise, average return on investment must rise; that is, investments that had been profitable when rates were lower are no longer acceptable.
      2. Government spending may weaken the relationship between the real interest rate and the real return on investment.
         a. Government deficit spending on unprofitable projects with no net benefit to the economy increases competition for funds with no increase in productive investment opportunities.
         b. Interest rates rise; private sector investment falls.

III. The Term Structure of Interest Rates.

A. The term structure describes the relationship between interest rates and maturity.

1. Yields on government securities are usually used to avoid the influence of default risk.
2. An upward-sloping yield curve indicates higher yields on longer-term securities; a downward slope indicates higher yields on shorter-term securities.
3. Comparison of yield curves from different periods can indicate a change in the general level of rates regardless of maturity.

B. The expectations theory asserts that expected future interest rates are equal to the forward rates implicit in current long-term security prices.

1. A forward interest rate is the current rate on an instrument which begins in the future. For example, in 1984, the forward rate for 1-year securities from January 1987-December 1987 might be 12 percent. (The actual 1-year rate in January 1987 may be different.)
2. Capital market competition forces the equality of implicit forward rates and expected future rates.
   a. If expected future short-term rates are higher than the forward rates implicit in long-term securities, no one would lend (or be able to borrow) on a long-term basis.
   b. If expected future short-term rates are lower than implicit forward rates, no one would lend (or be able to borrow) short-term.
3. The implicit short-term forward rates can be calculated from the yield to maturity on long-term securities.
   a. The long-term yield to maturity is the geometric average of the forward rates over its life.

   $$(1+{}_oR_t)^t = (1+{}_or_1)(1+{}_1f_2)\ldots(1+{}_{t-1}f_t)$$

   where ${}_oR_t$ = long-term yield on a t-year security

   ${}_or_1$ = current 1-year rate

   ${}_1f_2$ = 1-year forward rate for year 2 (i.e., from the end of year 1 to the end of year 2)

   ${}_{t-1}f_t$ = 1-year forward rate for year t (i.e., from the end of year t-1 to the end of year t)

   b. If we have the long-term yields on securities of t and t+1 years, the implicit forward rate for a 1-year security for year t+1 is found:

   $$1+{}_tf_{t+1} = \frac{(1+{}_oR_{t+1})^{t+1}}{(1+{}_oR_t)^t}$$

4. Transactions costs can cause a divergence between the returns on a long-term security versus an equivalent series of short-term securities.
5. Uncertainty about future 1-year rates can also cause returns to differ from the predictions of the expectations theory.

C. The liquidity preference theory says that long-term bonds will yield more than short-term bonds.
   1. Supply-side: Investors prefer to lend short term for greater liquidity, and thus will accept lower yields on short-term securities.
   2. Demand side: Borrowers prefer to borrow long term to avoid the risk of having to refund under adverse conditions.
   3. These factors lend an upward bias to the yield curve relative to the expectations theory alone.

D. The market segmentation hypothesis characterizes market participants as having strong maturity preferences.
   1. Some lenders may prefer to lend long term to achieve certainty of income or to balance debt and asset maturity.
   2. Some borrowers may prefer to borrow short term.
   3. Interest rates depend on supply and demand conditions within each maturity range.
   4. This theory is also called the institutional, or hedging-pressure theory.

E. Empirical studies have found some support for each of these interest rate theories.

IV. Interest Rates and Inflation.

A. The nominal interest rate is the product of the real interest rate and the expected inflation rate; usually simplified to the sum of the real interest rate and the inflation rate.

B. Expected inflation is thus the difference between the nominal rate and the real rate.

C. Actual inflation should equal expected inflation plus a random error term if the market forecast of inflation is unbiased.

D. Empirical results have confirmed that changes in current nominal rates are fairly good forecasts of inflation.

E. Thus, the term structure contains useful information about expected inflation.
   1. Downward-sloping: Near-term inflation expected to be higher than long term.
   2. Upward-sloping: Long-term inflation expected to be higher.

V. Capital Budgeting.

A. The correct discount rate for each year's cash flows is the risk-adjusted interest rate for that year, not the long-term rate over the life of the project.

B. Inflation impacts capital budgeting in several ways.
   1. The effect of inflation on revenues and costs in a specific line of business may differ from the economy-wide inflation rate.
   2. The discount rate must be adjusted for inflation.
   3. The depreciation tax shelter is a fixed amount, thus it becomes less valuable with inflation.

4. If a project's cash flows are expected to be affected by inflation at the same rate as the economy, equivalent results may be obtained in two ways.
   a. Discount current dollar cash flows at the real interest rate.
   b. Discount nominal dollar cash flows at the nominal interest rate.

VI. Interest Rates and Risk.
  A. Default risk refers to the probability of bankruptcy.
    1. Bond ratings indicate the default risk of corporate long-term debt.
    2. Ratings changes generally follow changes in required yields, rather than cause them.
    3. The market's reaction to a fundamental change in bond quality is what changes its required yield.
    4. Differences in yields on bonds of different risk represent differences in promised yields.
       a. High risk bonds must promise higher yields.
       b. Expected yields are likely to be very similar regardless of risk.
  B. Covariance risk, or return risk, refers to the sensitivity of security prices to changes in general economic conditions.
    1. Default risk can be diversified away at relatively low cost by holding a portfolio of risky debt.
    2. Covariance risk cannot be diversified away, thus investors require higher expected returns.
  C. The risk-return trade-off involves expected returns versus non-diversifiable risk.
    1. Treasury bills--risk-free.
    2. Long-term corporate bonds--riskier; probability of default is affected to some extent by the state of the economy.
    3. Common stock--very sensitive to state of economy; higher non-diversifiable risk; higher expected returns.
    4. Options--very risky; highest expected returns.

VII. Forward Rates and Futures Rates.
  A. The forward rate represents a return that will be realized over a future time period if the expectations of the current term structure are correct.
  B. Interest rate futures are contracts that call for transactions in specified instruments to take place on stated future dates.
  C. In the absence of market imperfections, yields on futures contracts should be the same as current implied forward rates. Institutional differences may cause divergence.
    1. Profits or losses on forward contracts accumulate until the contract matures.
    2. Profits or losses on futures contracts are transferred between traders on a daily basis.
    3. Futures contracts are traded in a well-organized market; forward contracts are on a more ad hoc basis.

D. Interest rate futures contracts were first established in the fall of 1975.
   1. Contracts have been developed for Government National Mortgage Association Securities (GNMA's), Treasury bills and bonds, and various major currencies.
   2. Major markets include the International Monetary Market (IMM) of the Chicago Mercantile Exchange, The Chicago Board of Trade (CBT) and the New York Futures Exchange (part of the New York Stock Exchange).

E. Empirical studies of the opportunities for arbitrage profits in the relationship between forward and futures rates have yielded the following results.
   1. Futures rates are generally below forward rates near the maturity date of the futures contract, probably due to lower transactions costs on futures contracts.
   2. For longer maturities, futures rates are persistently higher than forward rates, because of the risk premium above the risk-free T-bill rate introduced by the futures contract.

F. Interest rate futures markets perform socially useful economic functions.
   1. The relationship between forward and futures rates provides opportunities for reducing risk by hedging and bearing risk by speculating.
   2. The futures markets develop appropriate relations between spot and futures prices.
   3. They offer additional alternative portfolio opportunities for investors.

VIII. Riding the Yield Curve.

A. Rising interest rates raise the opportunity cost of holding idle cash.
   1. Cash managers seek to earn a return on temporarily idle funds by investing in highly liquid U.S. Treasury securities.
   2. The interest rate futures market has expanded the alternatives for investment.

B. Riding the yield curve refers to the practice of buying bills of maturities longer than the planned holding period and selling them prior to maturity.
   1. If the term structure of interest rates is positive, longer maturity bills will have higher yields.
   2. Because interest rates fluctuate, the cash manager must evaluate the risks of various strategies, among them:
      a. Match the maturity of the Treasury bill to the period during which the cash is available.
      b. Ride the yield curve on an unhedged basis by buying a T-bill of a longer maturity than needed and selling it when the cash is required.
      c. Ride the yield curve in a hedged position through a combination of T-bills and futures contracts.

C. Example of Riding the Yield Curve

1. Pattern of rates to illustrate riding the yield curve.

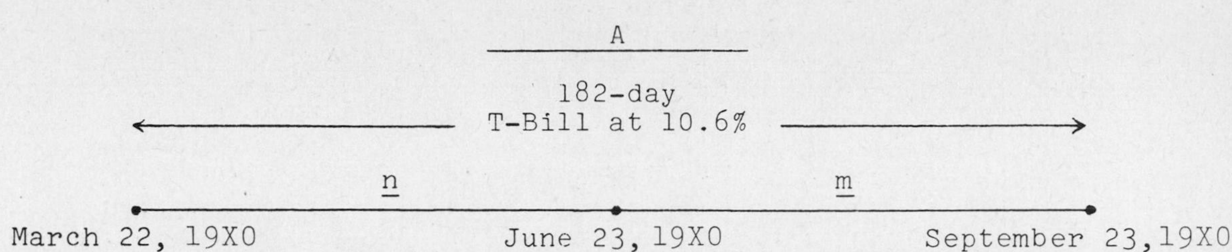

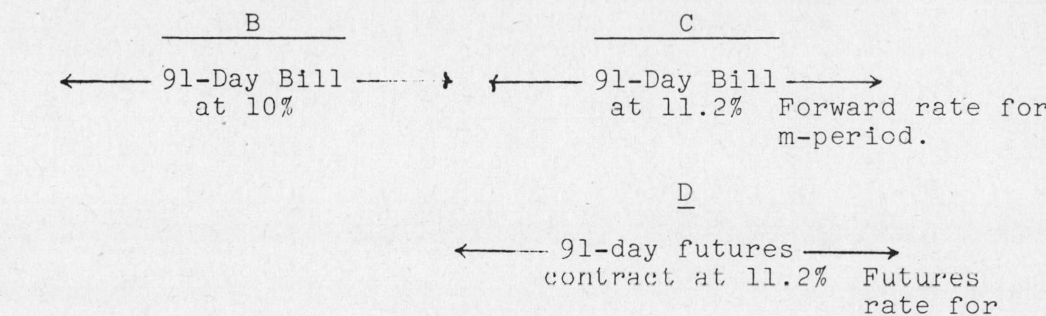

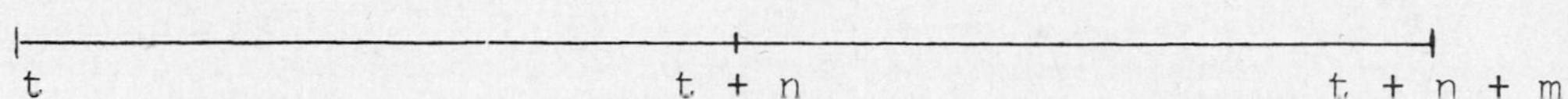

2. Description of riding the yield curve in a hedged position.
   a. Now have $10 million to meet a commitment in 90 days.
   b. Buy 182-day T-bill on 10.6% basis at a price of $948.38.
   c. Sell 91-day Futures contract on 11.2% basis at a price of $972.39.
   d. Gain is $972.39 - $948.38 = $24.01 on $ investment of $948.38 or 2.53168561% which is 10.1267% on an annual basis. This compares with 10% yield by buying 91-day T-bill for the n period.
   e. With positive term structure, buying the longer maturity provides partial participation in higher long rates.

Chapter 7 - Illustrative Problems and Solutions

7.1 Suppose that expected future short-term interest rates have the following alternative patterns:

Year	A	B	C	D
1	7%	13	8	14
2	9	12	16	9
3	11	11	15	10
4	12	9	9	12
5	13	7	7	13

a. Using a simple arithmetic average, what is the current rate on a 5-year note for each of the four patterns?
b. Using a geometric average, answer the same question as for part a. (Hint: Multiply one plus each of the five rates, then take their fifth root.)

Solution:

a. A: (7 + 9 + 11 + 12 + 13)/5 10.4%

B: (13 + 12 + 11 + 9 + 7)/5 10.4%

C: (8 + 16 + 15 + 9 + 7)/5 11%

D: (14 + 9 + 10 + 12 + 13)/5 11.6%

b. A: $\sqrt[5]{(1.07)(1.09)(1.11)(1.12)(1.13)} = 1.10379$

$r = 10.4\%$

B: $\sqrt[5]{(1.13)(1.12)(1.11)(1.09)(1.07)} = 1.10379$

$r = 10.4\%$

C: $\sqrt[5]{(1.08)(1.16)(1.15)(1.09)(1.07)} = 1.10937$

$r = 10.9\%$

D: $\sqrt[5]{(1.14)(1.09)(1.10)(1.12)(1.13)} = 1.11585$

$r = 11.6\%$

7.2 Alice Abel has a subjective rate of interest of 15 percent. Bill Bly has a subjective rate of 7.5 percent. Formulas representing their investment opportunity schedules are as follows:

$$r_A = 21 - 3I_A \qquad r_B = 24 - 6I_B \quad (\$\text{ millions})$$

a. How much will Abel and Bly each invest if they cannot borrow or lend?
b. If they can borrow and lend, what will be the market equilibrium rate?
c. How much will each borrow or lend?

Solution:

a. $r_A = 15 = 21 - 3I_A$ $\qquad$ $r_B = 7.5 = 24 - 6I_B$

$-6 = -3I_A$ $\qquad$ $-16.5 = -6I_B$

$\underline{I_A^* = \$2 \text{ million}}$ $\qquad$ $\underline{I_B^* = \$2.75 \text{ million}}$

Abel's higher subjective rate indicates a greater preference for current consumption versus investment. This is confirmed by Abel's lower optimal investment.

b. $I_A = 7 - (1/3)r_A$ $\qquad$ $I_B = 4 - (1/6)r_B$

$B_A = I_A - I_A^*$ $\qquad$ $B_B = I_B - I_B^*$

$B_A = 7 - (1/3)r - 2$ $\qquad$ $B_B = 4 - (1/6)r - 2.75$

$= 5 - (1/3)r$ $\qquad$ $= 1.25 - (1/6)r$

Since in equilibrium aggregate borrowing must equal aggregate lending, the $B_A + B_B = 0$:

$$5 - (1/3)r + 1.25 - (1/6)r = 0$$
$$6.25 - .5r = 0$$
$$.5r = 6.25$$
$$\underline{r = 12.5\% = \text{market rate}}$$

c. $B_A = I_A - I_A^*$ $\qquad$ $B_B = I_B - B_B^*$

$= 5 - (1/3)r$ $\qquad$ $= 1.25 - (1/6)r$

$= 5 - (1/3)(12.5)$ $\qquad$ $= 1.25 - (1/6)(12.5)$

$= \underline{\$.8333 \text{ million}}$ $\qquad$ $= \underline{\$-.8333 \text{ million}}$

Alice Abel will borrow, since for her the market rate is below the subjective rate. Bly will lend because the market rate is above his subjective rate. Both individuals will be better off than in the no borrowing or lending situation.

7.3 Under the terms of their grandfather's will, each of 10 grandchildren will receive, in order of their birth, his entire fortune of $5 million to invest in government securities for one year. After 10 years, the $5 million principal is to be used to establish bird sanctuaries throughout the United States. The youngest grandchild wants to know how much money he can expect to earn when his turn comes around. The current long-term rates for U.S. government securities are 14 percent for a 10-year maturity, and 13 percent for a 9-year maturity.

Solution:

$$1 + {}_9f_{10} = \frac{(1 + {}_0R_{10})^{10}}{(1 + {}_0R_9)^9} = \frac{1.14^{10}}{1.13^9}$$

$$= \frac{3.707}{3.004}$$

$$= 1.234$$

The forward rate is 23.4%.

$5,000,000(.234) = $1,170,000 = one-year earnings to be expected

7.4 The Kenyon Corporation is evaluating an investment decision. The project will cost $200,000 and have a life of 5 years. Kenyon uses straight line depreciation, and has an opportunity cost of capital of 14 percent. An incremental income statement is provided below:

Revenues	$420,000
Operating costs	350,000
EBDIT	70,000
Depreciation	40,000
EBIT	30,000
Taxes @ 40%	12,000
Net income	$18,000

a. Should the project be accepted?
b. In reviewing the project evaluation, Kenyon's treasurer notes that no adjustment has been made for anticipated inflation. The data is correct for the first year, but increasing demand for Kenyon's product calls for an annual inflation rate of 5 percent for revenues. The inflation rate for the economy as a whole is expected to be 4 percent; operating costs and the cost of capital are expected to rise at the overall inflation rate. Re-evaluate the investment decision.

Solution:

a. Cash flow = NI + Depreciation = $18,000 + $40,000
= $58,000

$$\begin{aligned} NPV &= -\$200,000 + (\$58,000)(PVIFA, 14\%, 5 \text{ yrs}) \\ &= -\$200,000 + (\$58,000)(3.4331) \\ &= -\$200,000 + \$199,120 \\ &= -\$880 \end{aligned}$$

The project should be rejected.

b.

	Year 1	Year 2	Year 3	Year 4	Year 5
Revenues (i=5%)	420,000	441,000	463,050	486,203	510,513
Op. costs (i=4%)	350,000	364,000	378,560	393,702	409,450
EBDIT	70,000	77,000	84,490	92,501	101,063
Depreciation	40,000	40,000	40,000	40,000	40,000
EBIT	30,000	37,000	44,490	52,501	61,063
Taxes @ 40%	12,000	14,800	17,796	21,000	24,425
NI	18,000	22,200	26,694	31,501	36,638
Cash flow	58,000	62,200	66,694	71,501	76,638

Discount rate = .14 + .04 = .18

$$\begin{aligned} NPV &= -200,000 + \frac{58,000}{1.18} + \frac{62,200}{1.18^2} + \frac{66,694}{1.18^3} + \frac{71,501}{1.18^4} + \frac{76,638}{1.18^5} \\ &= -200,000 + 49,153 + 44,671 + 40,592 + 36,879 + 33,499 \\ &= -200,000 + 204,794 \\ &= \$4,794 \end{aligned}$$

After adjusting for anticipated inflation, the project is acceptable.

7.5 The table below gives the yields to maturity and implied forward rates for bonds with approximately the same risk as Project A and Project B for which cash flows are also given.

			Cash flows	
Year	Yield to maturity	Forward rate	A	B
0	---	---	-1,000	-1,000
1	16%	16%	400	700
2	17	18	450	400
3	18	20	500	190

a. Find the NPV of each project using the 3-year yield to maturity.

b. Find the NPV of each project using the annual forward rates to discount cash flows.

Solution:

a. $$\begin{aligned} NPV_A &= -1,000 + 400(.8475) + 450(.7182) + 500(.6086) \\ &= -1,000 + 339 + 323 + 304 \\ &= -34 \end{aligned}$$

$NPV_B = -1,000 + 700(.8475) + 400(.7182) + 190(.6086)$
$= -1,000 + 593 + 287 + 116$
$= -4$

Neither project is acceptable using the 3-year yield to maturity as the discount factor.

b. Discount factors for cash flows:

Year 1 $1/1.16 = .8621$

Year 2 $1/[(1.16)(1.18)] = 1/1.17^2 = .7305$

Year 3 $1/[(1.16)(1.18)(1.20)] = 1/1.18^3 = .6086$

$NPV_A = -1,000 + 400(.8621) + 450(.7305) + 500(.6086)$
$= -1,000 + 345 + 329 + 304$
$= -22$

$NPV_B = -1,000 + 700(.8621) + 400(.7305) + 190(.6086)$
$= -1,000 + 603 + 292 + 116$
$= 11$

When the term structure is upward-sloping, using the 3-year rate tends to underestimate the present value of cash flows--both projects were unacceptable. Using the appropriate forward rates as the discount rates, Project B becomes acceptable.

7.6 You are offered two 10-year discount bonds. Bond A sells for \$385.54; bond B sells for \$269.74. Both bonds pay \$1,000 at maturity

a. What is the yield to maturity on bond A? On bond B?

b. Assume that the risk of default is uncorrelated with the economy as a whole, and that the expected yield on bond B is the same as on bond A. If a bond pays nothing in default, what is the expected probability of default on bond B?

Solution:

a. $B_A = \$385.54 = \frac{\$1,000}{(1+r_A)^{10}}$

$(1+r_A)^{10} = \$1,000/\$385.54$
$= 2.5938$

$1+r_A = 1.10$

$r_A = 10$ percent = promised yield

$$B_B = \$269.74 = \frac{\$1,000}{(1+r_B)^{10}}$$

$$(1+r_B)^{10} = \$1,000/\$269.74$$
$$= 3.7073$$
$$1+r_B = 1.14$$
$$r_B = 14 \text{ percent} = \text{promised yield}$$

b. Return to bond B in default = $\frac{0 - \$269.74}{\$269.74} = -100\%$

Non-default return to bond B = $\left(\frac{\$1,000}{\$269.74}\right)^{.10} - 1 = 14\%$

Expected return_B = Expected return_A = 10%

$$(1.10)^{10} = p(0\%) + (1-p)(1.14)^{10}$$
$$2.59374 = 3.70722 - 3.70722p$$
$$3.70722p = 1.1135$$
$$p = 30\% = \text{probability of default}$$

PART THREE. FINANCIAL ANALYSIS, PLANNING, AND CONTROL

CHAPTER 8

FINANCIAL RATIO ANALYSIS

Theme: Financial ratio analysis is basic to understanding and evaluating the results of business operations. It also provides a framework for financial planning and control.

I. Basic Financial Statements Include.

A. Balance sheet--shows the firm's financial position at a point in time.

Assets	Claims on Assets
Cash	Accounts payable
Marketable securities	Notes and loans payable
	Current maturities of long-term debt
Accounts receivable	Taxes payable
Inventories	Other accrued expenses
Total Current Assets	Total Current Liabilities
Investments in Affiliated Cos.	Long-Term Debt
	Obligations under Capital Leases
Gross fixed assets	Deferred Credits
Less: Res. for depreciation	Reserves--Employee Annuity Plans
	Total Liabilities and Deferred Credits
Net fixed assets	Preferred Stock
Prepaid and Deferred Charges	Common Stock
	Capital in Excess of Par Value
TOTAL ASSETS	Retained Earnings
	Stockholders' Equity
	TOTAL CLAIMS ON ASSETS

B. Income Statement

Revenues (Sales)
Cost of goods sold
Gross profit
Less operating expenses:
  Selling
  General and administrative
  Lease payment on office building
Gross operating revenue
Depreciation
Net operating income (NOI)
Other income and expense (except interest expense)
Earnings before interest and taxes (EBIT)
Less interest expense:
  Interest on notes payable
  Interest on first mortgage
  Interest on debentures
Income before income taxes (IBT)
Federal income tax
Net income (NI)

Earnings per share (EPS)

C. Statement of retained earnings shows the amount of net income reinvested in the business.
   1. Retained earnings represents funds reinvested in the business over a period of years.
   2. Retained earnings do not represent available cash but are usually invested in other assets of the company.

II. Basic Financial Ratios.
   A. Liquidity ratios measure the firm's ability to meet its maturing short-term obligations.
      1. The current ratio (current assets divided by current liabilities) is a generally accepted measure of short-term solvency.
         a. Current assets include cash, marketable securities, accounts receivable, and inventories.
         b. Current liabilities consist of accounts payable, short-term notes payable, current maturities of long-term debt, accrued income taxes, and other accrued expenses.
      2. The quick ratio, or acid test, is calculated by deducting inventories from current assets and dividing the remainder by current liabilities. This ratio measures short-term solvency but removes inventories from the calculation because inventories are the least liquid of a firm's current assets, and their liquidation frequently results in losses.
   B. Leverage ratios measure the extent to which the firm has been financed by debt. Creditors look to the equity to provide a margin of safety, but by raising funds through debt, owners gain the benefits of maintaining control of the firm with a limited investment. If a firm earns more on borrowed funds than it pays in interest, the return to the owners is magnified.
      1. The debt-to-total-assets ratio measures the percentage of total funds that have been provided by creditors.
         a. The lower the ratio, the greater the protection against creditors' losses in the event of liquidation.
         b. Owners may seek high leverage either to magnify earnings or because raising new equity means giving up some degree of control.
      2. The times-interest-earned ratio (net income before interest and taxes divided by interest charges) measures the extent to which earnings can decline without resultant financial embarrassment to the firm because of inability to meet annual interest costs.
      3. Fixed charge coverage (net income before interest, taxes and lease obligations divided by interest charges plus

lease obligations) generalizes the preceding ratio by adding fixed charges such as long-term lease payments to recognize the increasing use of lease arrangements.

4. Cash flow coverage [cash inflows divided by fixed charges plus (preferred stock dividends and debt principal repayment on a before-tax basis)] measures a firm's ability to meet cash obligations. Depreciation, a non-cash expense, is added to the numerator, and the non-tax-deductible expenses in the denominator are adjusted by dividing by (1-T).

C. Activity ratios measure how effectively a firm is using its resources.

1. Inventory turnover (sales or cost of goods sold divided by average inventory) measures the efficiency of inventory utilization.
   a. A high inventory turnover demonstrates that a company does not hold excessive stocks of inventory.
   b. The average figure should be adjusted if the firm's business is highly seasonal or if there has been a strong upward or downward sales trend during the year.
2. The average collection period (receivables divided by sales per day) is compared to the terms on which the firm sells its goods. This measures efficiency in collection of accounts receivable.
   a. Sales per day equals annual sales divided by 360 days.
   b. The average collection period should be supplemented with the aging schedule. This groups accounts receivable according to how long they have been outstanding.
3. Fixed asset turnover (sales divided by fixed assets) measures the turnover of capital assets or the efficiency of fixed assets; a low ratio indicates idle capacity of assets.
4. Total asset turnover (sales divided by total assets) measures the overall utilization of assets. A low ratio indicates that the company is not generating an adequate volume of business for the size of its asset investment.

D. Profitability ratios measure management's overall effectiveness as shown by the returns generated on sales and investment.

1. The profit margin (net profit after taxes divided by sales) gives the profit per dollar of sales. A profit margin somewhat below the industry average indicates that the firm's sales prices are relatively low or that its costs are relatively high, or both.
2. Return on total assets measures the return on the firm's total investment, or the ROI.
   a. After-tax interest costs should be added to net profits after taxes to form the numerator of

the ratio because assets are financed by both stockholders and creditors.

b. A low ratio can result from a low profit margin on sales, or from a low turnover of total assets, or both.

3. The return on net worth ratio represents the relationship of net income to the stockholders' investment.

E. Growth ratios measure how well the firm is maintaining its economic position in the general economy and in its own industry.
   1. Growth rate analysis must separate real growth from nominal growth which includes the influence of inflation.
   2. To find the growth rate over a period of time, divide the last period figure by the first period figure to obtain a compound sum interest factor. The percent growth rate can then be determined from the compound interest tables.

F. Valuation ratios reflect the combined influence of risk ratios and return ratios.
   1. The price to earnings ratio is an indication of the financial market's assessment of a firm's future earning potential.
   2. The market to book ratio indicates the value that financial markets attach to the management and organization of the company as a going concern.

III. Major financial ratios:

A. Liquidity ratios.

1. Current ratio $= \dfrac{\text{Current assets}}{\text{Current liabilities}}$

2. Quick ratio $= \dfrac{\text{Current assets} - \text{Inventories}}{\text{Current liabilities}}$

B. Leverage ratios

1. Debt-to-total-assets $= \dfrac{\text{Total debt}}{\text{Total assets}}$

2. Times interest earned $= \dfrac{\text{Net income before interest and taxes}}{\text{Interest charges}}$

3. Fixed charge coverage

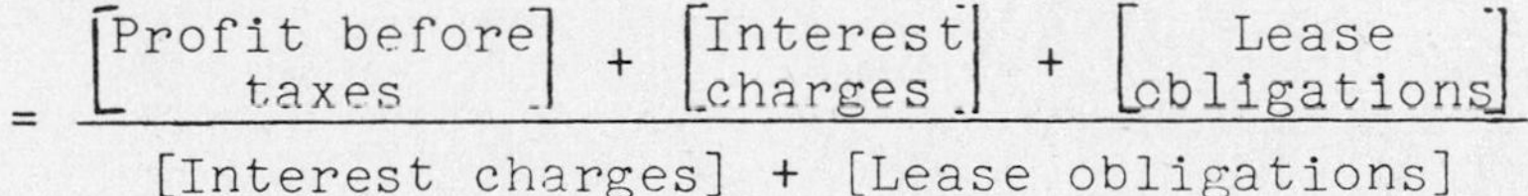

$$= \frac{\left[\text{Profit before taxes}\right] + \left[\text{Interest charges}\right] + \left[\text{Lease obligations}\right]}{[\text{Interest charges}] + [\text{Lease obligations}]}$$

4. Cash flow coverage

$$= \frac{\text{Cash inflows}}{\text{Fixed charges} + \frac{\text{Preferred Stock Dividends}}{1 - T} + \frac{\text{Debt repayment}}{1 - T}}$$

C. Activity ratios.

1. Inventory turnover

$$= \frac{\text{Sales}}{\text{Average inventory}} \text{ or } \frac{\text{Cost of goods sold}}{\text{Average inventory}}$$

2. Average collection period $= \frac{\text{Receivables}}{\text{Sales per day}}$

3. Total asset turnover $= \frac{\text{Sales}}{\text{Total assets}}$

D. Profitability ratios

1. Profit margin $= \frac{\text{Net profits after taxes}}{\text{Sales}}$

2. Return on total assets (ROI)

$$= \frac{\text{Net profit after taxes + (1-T)interest}}{\text{Total assets}}$$

3. Return on net worth $= \frac{\text{Net profit after taxes}}{\text{Net worth}}$

E. Growth ratios

1. Sales
2. Net income
3. Earnings per share
4. Dividends per share
5. Market price per share
6. Book value per share

$$\frac{\text{Ending value}}{\text{Beginning value}} = FVIF_{r,N}$$

F. Valuation ratios

1. Price to earnings ratio $= \frac{\text{Price}}{\text{Earnings}}$

2. Market to book ratio $= \frac{\text{Market value}}{\text{Book value}}$

IV. Methods of Ratio Analysis.

A. Trend analysis involves computing the ratios of a particular firm for several years and comparing the ratios over time to see whether the firm is improving or deteriorating.

B. Comparative analysis is comparing the key ratios of the firm with those of other similar firms in the industry or with an industry average. Industry ratios for comparative analysis may be found in sources such as Dun & Bradstreet, Robert Morris Associates, the Department of Commerce's *Quarterly Financial Report*, trade association reports, public accounting firms, and others.

V. The Emphasis of Financial Ratio Analysis Varies with the Requirements of the Analysis.
   A. The emphasis in credit analysis is on the ability to repay short-term debts.
   B. Abbreviated analysis is used in credit decisions involving a large number of transactions per day.
      1. The current ratio is calculated to determine the degree of pressing burdens of short-term debt.
      2. The total debt-to-assets ratio is calculated to determine the extent of debt financing.
      3. Inadequate equity often results in a current ratio that is too low.
      4. Excessive debt usually results in slow payments.
      5. The decision to grant credit to a marginal credit risk rests heavily on whether the profitability ratio is high enough to bring the customer to a current payment position in the foreseeable future.
   C. Among the qualitative factors considered by the credit manager are the economic position of the customer firm and its managerial qualities, as well as his own firm's profit margin.
   D. The principal emphasis in security analysis is on the long-run profit potential of the firm.
      1. The focus is, therefore, on activity and profitability ratios.
      2. Leverage ratios will influence the firm's solvency in the longer run.

VI. Financial Ratios have Limitations.
   A. Ratios are based on accounting data, so the bases upon which the data are developed must be considered.
   B. Conformance with industry standards is no guarantee that the firm is performing satisfactorily and is managed well.
   C. When a company's ratios depart from the industry norm, there is a need to question and analyze further to determine whether there is a sound explanation for the variance or whether changes in policies or correction of management practices are required.
      1. Inventory (thus cost of goods sold) and depreciation expense are likely to increase, reducing net operating income.

2. Gains will result from the decline in the purchasing power of net monetary amounts owed and from the increased value of inventory and fixed assets.
3. Inflation-adjusted income is usually below reported corporate earnings in a period of rising inflation, although the effect will vary among industries.
4. The levels of reported profits affect the amounts of tax paid and therefore cash flows since income taxes are still based on accounting income before inflation adjustments.
5. Conventional accounting reporting based on historical cost postulates when inflation rates are high can be misleading, and financial reports based on current values become desirable as a check.

VII. The Need for Adjustments for Changes in Price Levels

A. Ratios may be distorted during a period of inflation.

1. Assets are recorded at cost while cash revenue and expense flows are in current dollars of a different purchasing power.
2. Balance sheets cannot accurately reflect the firm's current financial position since assets are not recorded at their current values.
3. Gains or losses resulting from the sale of assets are reported in the period of sale, although the amount of the gain or loss depends upon the historical cost; thus income is distorted.

B. The choice of inventory valuation method can have a major impact on profitability during an inflationary period.

1. FIFO (first-in-first-out) understates Cost of goods sold, thus overstating Net income, but the Inventory account of the balance sheet is closer to current costs.
2. LIFO (last-in-first-out) Cost of goods sold is closer to current costs, but Inventory investment on the balance sheet is understated.

VIII. FASB Statement No. 33, September 1979, Addresses the Problem of a Non-stable Measuring Unit.

A. Effects of both general inflation (purchasing power) and specific price changes (current costs) must be disclosed in annual reports for firms over a certain size.

1. The general inflation, purchasing power adjustment retains the historical basis of accounting for the value of non-monetary assets, but adjusts it through the use of a general price index.
2. The adjustment for specific price changes reflects the fact that inflation is not the only influence on asset value changes and inflation does not affect all assets equally.

B. The effects of the adjustments
   1. Generally, adjusted net income is lower.
   2. Income taxes are presently applied to an overstated figure.

IX. Discriminant Analysis can be Used to Develop an Equation which Allows the Classification of an Observation into Groups.
   A. One use of discriminant analysis is to construct an index based on financial ratios, then to use this index to classify a firm as likely to be bankrupt or to receive a tender offer, etc.
   B. Basically three steps are involved.
      1. Establish mutually exclusive group classifications such as bankrupt or non-bankrupt, for example.
      2. Collect data for each group (the relevant financial ratios).
      3. Derive linear combinations of the ratios which best discriminate between the groups, i.e., which minimize the probability of misclassification.
   C. The end result of the discriminant analysis will be an equation of the form:

$$Z = V_1X_1 + V_2X_2$$

   where X_1 and X_2 are different financial ratios and V_1 and V_2 are multiples of these ratios, determined by past data, which will result in a Z which has value as a predictor of group membership.
      1. If Z is above a certain point, one can say that a firm is most likely to be in one group. If Z is below a certain point, the firm is most likely to be in the other group.
      2. There may be a region of overlap of Z values in which the firm's group classification will have a greater likelihood of error.

X. Applications.
   A. Edward I. Altman identified five ratios useful in the prediction of bankruptcy.
      1. Working capital/total assets = X_1
      2. Retained earnings/total assets = X_2
      3. EBIT/total assets = X_3
      4. Market value of equity/book value of debt = X_4
      5. Sales/total assets = X_5
   B. The Z equation was
   $Z = .012X_1 + .014X_2 + .033X_3 + .006X_4 + 1.0X_5$
   The average values of the five financial ratios for the two groups of firms was:

	Bankrupt (br)	Nonbankrupt (nbr)
X_1	-6.1%	41.4%
X_2	-62.6%	35.5%
X_3	-31.8%	15.4%
X_4	40.1%	247.7%
X_5	1.5X	1.9X

The resulting Z values are as follows:

		X_1		X_2		X_3		X_4		X_5		Z
Z_{br}	= -	.0732	-	.8764	-	1.0494	+	.2406	+	1.4985	=	- 0.2599
Z_{nbr}	= +	.4968	+	.4970	+	.5082	+	1.4862	+	1.8981	=	+ 4.8863

C. An application to an industrial firm would be Chrysler for 1979.

X_1 = Working capital/total assets = (110)/6,653 = -1.65%

X_2 = Retained earnings/total assets = 496/6,653 = 7.46%

X_3 = EBIT/total assets = (-887)6,653 = -13.3%

X_4 = Market value of equity/book value of debt = 563/5,048 = 11.15%

X_5 = Sales/total assets = 12,004/6,653 = 1.80 Times

Chrysler's Z = .012(-1.65) + .014(7.46) + .033(-13.3) + .006(11.15) + 1.8
= -.0198 + .1044 - .4389 + .0669 + 1.8
= 1.5126

For Altman's study, the critical Z value was 2.675 and the zone of uncertainty was between 1.81 and 2.67. Chrysler's Z value of 1.51 for 1979 indicates a fairly high probability of bankruptcy without the government loan guarantee.

Chapter 8 - Illustrative Problems and Solutions

8.1 Complete the balance sheet and sales data (fill in the blanks) using the following data from the Cornelius Co.:

Debt/Net worth	41.8%
Acid test ratio	2.3
Days sales outstanding	40 days
Gross profit margin	22%
Inventory turnover	6.5 times
Asset turnover	1.3

Balance Sheet, Cornelius Company, December 31, 19X0

Cash	______	Accounts payable	______
Accounts receivable	______	Common stock	20,000
Inventories	______	Retained earnings	35,000
Plant and equipment	______		
Total assets	______	Total liabilities and capital	______

Sales	______
Cost of goods sold	______

Solution:

a. Debt/Net worth $= \frac{\text{Debt}}{\text{CS + RE}} = \frac{\text{Debt}}{55{,}000} = 41.8\%$

Debt = \$22,990 = Accounts payable

b. \$55,000
  22,990
\$77,990 = Total liabilities = Total assets

c. Acid test $= 2.3 = \frac{\text{Cash + Accounts receivable}}{\text{Current liabilities}} = \frac{\text{Cash + AR}}{22{,}990}$

Cash + AR = \$52,877

d. Asset turnover $= 1.3 = \frac{\text{Sales}}{\text{Assets}}$

$1.3 = \frac{\text{Sales}}{77{,}990}$

Sales = \$101,387

e. Days sales outstanding in accounts receivable = 40

$\frac{40}{360} \times 101{,}387 = 11{,}265 = \text{AR}$

f. Cash = (Cash+AR) - AR
= 52,877 - 11,265
= $41,612

g. Gross profit margin = 22%
Cost of goods sold = (1-GPM) x Sales = .78 x 101,387
CGS = $79,082

h. Inventory turnover = 6.5 times

$$\frac{101,387}{\text{Inventory}} = 6.5$$

Inventory = $15,598

i. Cash 41,612
+ A/R 11,265
+ Inventory 15,598
68,475

Total assets = 77,990
-68,475
$ 9,515 Plant and equipment

Therefore,

Cash	41,612	Accounts payable	22,990
Accounts receivable	11,265	Common stock	20,000
Inventories	15,598	Retained earnings	35,000
Plant and equipment	9,515		
Total assets	77,990	Total liabilities and capital	77,990

Sales	101,387
Cost of goods sold	79,082

8.2 The following data were taken from the financial statements for Bethel Brewers for calendar year 19X0 . The industry norms are based on averages for "malt beverages."

a. Fill in the ratios for Bethel Brewers.
b. Indicate by comparison with industry norms the possible errors in management policies reflected in these financial statements.

Bethel Brewers Balance Sheet as of Dec. 31, 19X0 (in thousands)

Assets			Liabilities		
Cash	5,000		Accounts payable	2,000	
Receivables	40,000		Notes payable (at 12%)	8,000	
Inventory	15,000		Other current liabilities	5,000	
Total current assets		60,000	Total current liabilities		15,000
Net fixed assets		50,000	Long-term debt (at 10%)		28,000
			Net worth		67,000
Total assets		110,000	Total claims on assets		110,000

Bethel Brewers Income Statement for year ended Dec. 31, 19X0
(in thousands)

Sales			220,000
Cost of goods sold			
Materials	80,000		
Labor	75,000		
Heat, light and power	22,000		
Depreciation	8,000		185,000
Gross profit			35,000
Selling expense		12,000	
General and administrative expense		15,500	27,500
Net operating profit (EBIT)			7,500
Less interest expense			3,760
Net profit before tax			3,740
Less federal income tax			1,108
Net Income			2,632

Ratio	Industry Norm
Current assets/current liabilities	1.51 times
Debt/total assets	39%
Times interest earned	4.2 times
Average collection period	26 days
Sales/inventory	17.6 times
Sales/total assets	2.8 times
Net profit/sales	1.90%
Return on total assets	7%
Net profit/net worth	8.31%

Solution:

a.

	Industry Norm	Bethel	Comment
Current assets/current liabilities	1.51 times	4 times	High
Debt/total assets	39%	39%	
Times interest earned (EBIT/Int.)	4.2 times	2.0 times	Poor
Average collection period (Receivables/ Daily sales)	26 days	65 days	Poor
Sales inventory	17.6 times	14.7 times	Poor
Sales/total assets	2.8 times	2 times	Poor
Net profit/sales	1.90%	1.20%	Poor
Return on total assets	7%	4.79%	Poor
Net profit/net worth	8.31%	3.9%	Poor

b. Most of Bethel's ratios are poor, especially the average collection period. The excessive investment in accounts receivable causes total assets to be higher than the norm, and thus the turnover ratio, sales/total assets, and the profitability ratio, return on total assets, also suffer. The reason for the high accounts receivable may be longer credit terms than the industry average, inadequate investigation before extension of credit, poor collection procedures, or a combination of all three.

Since the debt/total assets ratio is normal, the excess receivables must be financed by a combination of debt and equity. This causes both the times interest earned and the net profit/net worth ratio to be lower than the industry standards.

Another effect of the large investment in receivables is to inflate the current ratio. While a low current ratio may be cause for alarm, so may too high a ratio indicate that management is not using current assets efficiently. Further it is possible that some of the receivables may be uncollectible.

8.3 The following financial statements of the Craft Company are of the years 19X0, 19X1, and 19X2. The norms for the financial ratios given below for the industry are from industry composites.

a. Fill in the blanks to show Craft's financial ratios.

b. What management problems are reflected in these financial data during each of the years?

The Craft Company--Comparative Balance Sheets for Years 19X0-X2

Assets	19X0	19X1	19X2
Cash	6,000	7,000	12,000
Receivables, net	22,000	16,000	27,000
Inventories	16,000	21,000	26,000
Total current assets	44,000	44,000	65,000
Net property	28,000	28,000	30,000
Other assets	1,000	1,000	1,000
Total assets	73,000	73,000	96,000
Liabilities and Capital			
Accounts payable	9,000	12,000	14,000
Notes payable (10 percent)	5,000	5,000	5,000
Other current liabilities	4,000	2,000	8,000
Total current liabilities	18,000	19,000	27,000
Long-term debt (10 percent)	20,000	20,000	20,000
Net worth	35,000	34,000	49,000
Total claims on assets	73,000	73,000	96,000

The Craft Company--Comparative Income Statements for Years 19X0-X2

	19X0		19X1		19X2	
Sales		110,000		120,000		135,000
Material	35,000		33,000		45,000	
Labor	40,500		41,500		42,000	
Heat, light, and power	9,000		9,600		9,800	
Depreciation	1,500	86,000	1,500	85,600	1,500	98,300
Gross profit		24,000		34,400		36,700
Selling expenses	8,000		10,000		15,000	
General and administrative expenses	6,700	14,700	7,800	17,800	8,000	23,000
Operating profit		9,300		16,600		13,700
Less: Interest expenses		2,500		2,500		2,500
Net profit before taxes		6,800		14,100		11,200
Federal income taxes		2,760		6,000		4,480
Net income		4,040		8,100		6,720

The Craft Company--Financial Ratios

	19X0		19X1		19X2	
	Company Ratio	Average Ratio	Company Ratio	Average Ratio	Company Ratio	Average Ratio
1. Current assets / Current liabilities	______	2.5	______	2.5	______	2.6
2. Sales / Inventories(at book)	______	5.3	______	5.1	______	4.9
3. Receivables / Sales per day	______	56.0	______	54.3	______	53.0
4. Net profit / Sales	______	5%	______	6%	______	6%
5. Net profit / Net worth	______	18%	______	20%	______	18%
6. Return on total assets	______	12%	______	13%	______	13%

Solution:

a. The Craft Company--Financial Ratios

	19X0	Norm	19X1	Norm	19X2	Norm
1. Current ratios	2.4	2.5	2.3	2.5	2.4	2.6
2. Inventory turnover	6.9	5.3	5.7	5.1	5.2	4.9
3. Collection period	72	56.0	48.0	54.3	72	53.0
4. Net profit to sales	3.7%	5%	6.8%	6%	5.0%	6%
5. Net profit to net worth	11.5%	18%	23.8%	20%	13.7%	18%
6. Return on total assets	7.6%	12%	13.0%	13%	8.6%	13%

b. During 19X0 the Craft Company had a poor collection policy. This was evident in that the collection period was almost one and one-half times the norm for the industry. Because of this poor collection policy, profit ratios were also low. In 19X1 all ratios were very close to the norm for the industry, showing a much improved collection policy. But, in 19X2, the collection period again went way out of line with the industry norm, and profits once again dipped below the industry average.

CHAPTER 9

FINANCIAL PLANNING AND CONTROL

Theme: The planning framework is continued and expanded in this chapter to include profitability analysis both in broad terms and in connection with the shorter-term budgeting process. The use of the cash budget is emphasized.

I. The Framework of Financial Planning and Control.
   A. Financial planning involves the use of projections based on standards of performance.
   B. The development of a mechanism for feedback and adjustment to performance standards is the basis of financial control.
   C. A budget system encompasses planning and control aspects, by comparing plans with results.
      1. Budgets analyze costs for every major area of a firm's activities.
      2. Projections in pro forma budgets for each department lead to forecasted income statements, balance sheets, and other financial statements.
      3. Projections of financing requirements give a firm the lead time necessary to arrange for such financing with greater flexibility.

II. Break-even Analysis is an Important Tool for Profit Planning.
   A. It is an analytical technique for studying the relations among fixed costs, variable costs, and profits.
   B. It provides information on the volume of sales at which total revenues begin to cover total costs fully.
   C. The practical significance is that break-even analysis guides the manager in the comparison of prices, expected volume, and the required volume to cover total costs.
   D. Figure 9.1 illustrates break-even analysis, as do the tables and related materials that follow it.

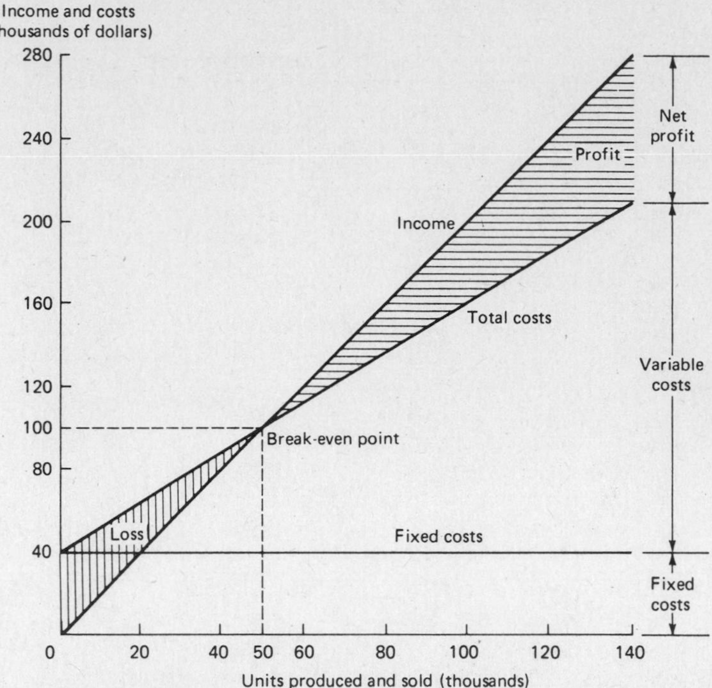

Figure 9.1 Break-even Chart

1. Relations between volume and profits.

Table 9.1

(1) Units Sold	(2) Total Sales	(3) Total Variable Costs	(4) Contri-bution Margin	(5) Fixed Costs	(6) Total Costs	(7) Net Profit (Loss)
0	$ 0	$ 0	$ 0	$40,000	$ 40,000	$(40,000)
20,000	40,000	24,000	16,000	40,000	64,000	(24,000)
40,000	80,000	48,000	32,000	40,000	88,000	(8,000)
50,000	100,000	60,000	40,000	40,000	100,000	--
60,000	120,000	72,000	48,000	40,000	112,000	8,000
80,000	160,000	96,000	64,000	40,000	136,000	24,000
100,000	200,000	120,000	80,000	40,000	160,000	40,000
120,000	240,000	144,000	96,000	40,000	184,000	56,000
140,000	280,000	168,000	112,000	40,000	208,000	72,000

2. Formula using sales volume:

a. $$\frac{\text{Total fixed costs}}{1 - \dfrac{\text{Total variable costs}}{\text{Total sales volume}}} = \text{Break-even sales}$$

b. Let:

TR^* = Break-even revenues = PQ
Q^* = Break-even quantity of units sold
P = Sales price per unit
F = Total fixed costs
V = Total variable costs
v = Variable cost per unit
c = Contribution margin per unit = $P - v$
C = Contribution margin = $Q(P-v) = cQ$
CR = Contribution Ratio = $1 - \frac{V}{PQ}$

Then

$$TR^* = \frac{F}{CR} \qquad (9.1)$$

c. Illustration from preceding table.
(1) For 20,000 sales volume shown in table:

$$\frac{\$40,000}{1 - \dfrac{24,000}{40,000}} = \frac{\$40,000}{.4} = \$100,000$$

(2) For highest volume shown in table:

$$\frac{\$40,000}{1 - \dfrac{168,000}{280,000}} = \frac{\$40,000}{.4} = \$100,000$$

3. Formula using units of output.
a. The break-even quantity is defined as that volume of output at which revenue is just equal to total costs (fixed costs plus variable costs).

b. $P \cdot Q^* = vQ^* + F$
$P \cdot Q^* - vQ^* = F$

$$Q^* = \frac{F}{P - v}$$

$$Q^* = \frac{F}{c} \qquad (9.2)$$

c. Illustration:

$$Q^* = \frac{\$40,000}{\$0.80}$$

$$= 50,000 \text{ units}$$

4. See also Problems 9.1 and 9.2.

III. Limitations of Break-even Analysis.
   A. Constant sales price assumption--profit possibilities under different prices would require a whole series of break-even charts.
   B. Cost assumptions--variable costs per unit may rise as capacity limits are approached. Increasing levels of output may require additional fixed costs in plant and equipment.
   C. Product mix changes over time may influence the level and slope of the cost function.

IV. Applications of Break-even Analysis.
   A. New product decisions--break-even analysis helps determine the sales volume required on a new product to realize a profit.
   B. General expansion of operations--break-even points are calculated on the basis of total sales (in dollar amounts rather than in units of output) and total costs.
   C. Automation and modernization decisions--break-even analysis helps determine the consequences of substituting fixed costs for variable costs, and the effects of volume changes on profitability at varying relationships of fixed and variable costs.

V. <u>Operating leverage</u> is defined as the extent to which fixed costs are used in operations. High fixed costs arise from employing larger amounts of capital, thus permitting the firm to operate with reduced labor and smaller variable costs.
   A. A high degree of operating leverage implies that a relatively small change in sales results in a large change in net operating income.
      1. The break-even point is higher with higher operating leverage.
      2. Once past the break-even point, profits rise at a faster rate with higher operating leverage.
   B. The degree of operating leverage (DOL) is defined as the percentage change in operating income that results from a percentage change in units sold.

$$\text{DOL} = \frac{\text{Percentage change in net operating income}}{\text{Percentage change in units sold}}$$

$$= \frac{\frac{\Delta X}{X}}{\frac{\Delta Q}{Q}}$$

C. This can also be expressed in a formula developed for calculating the degree of operating leverage at any level of output Q.

$$DOL = \frac{\frac{\Delta X}{X}}{\frac{\Delta Q}{Q}} = \frac{\frac{c\Delta Q}{cQ-F}}{\frac{\Delta Q}{Q}} = \frac{Qc\Delta Q}{\Delta Q(cQ-F)} = \frac{cQ}{X} = \frac{C}{X} \qquad (9.3)$$

D. Figure 9.2 illustrates the effects of variations in operating leverage.

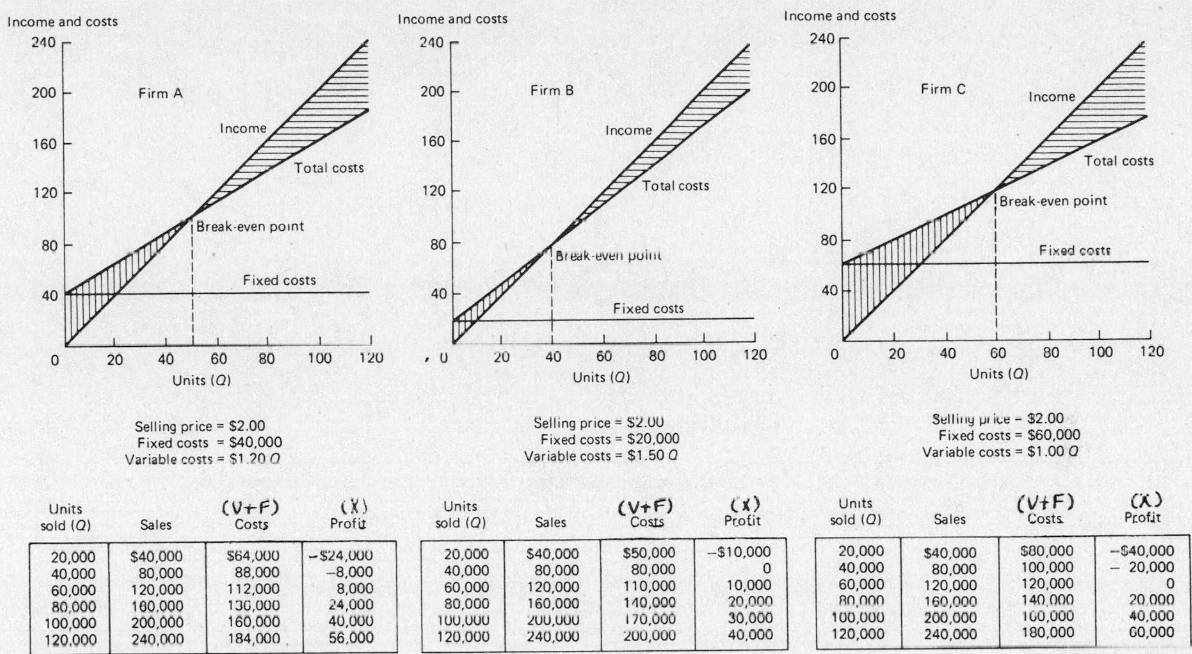

Units sold (Q)	Sales	(V+F) Costs	(X) Profit
20,000	$40,000	$64,000	–$24,000
40,000	80,000	88,000	–8,000
60,000	120,000	112,000	8,000
80,000	160,000	136,000	24,000
100,000	200,000	160,000	40,000
120,000	240,000	184,000	56,000

Units sold (Q)	Sales	(V+F) Costs	(X) Profit
20,000	$40,000	$50,000	–$10,000
40,000	80,000	80,000	0
60,000	120,000	110,000	10,000
80,000	160,000	140,000	20,000
100,000	200,000	170,000	30,000
120,000	240,000	200,000	40,000

Units sold (Q)	Sales	(V+F) Costs	(X) Profit
20,000	$40,000	$80,000	–$40,000
40,000	80,000	100,000	– 20,000
60,000	120,000	120,000	0
80,000	160,000	140,000	20,000
100,000	200,000	160,000	40,000
120,000	240,000	180,000	60,000

Figure 9.2 Operating Leverage

E. Calculations for the degree of operating leverage involve the following steps:

1. Operating leverage is measured by the ratio of the percentage change in profit to the percentage change in output (quantity sold). DOL is calculated for the three firms shown in Figure 9.2, as units sold increase 25 percent, from 80,000 to 100,000 units.
2. Operating leverage at 80,000 units of output is measured by the DOL formula.

$$DOL = \frac{C}{X}$$

Table 9.2

	Firm A	Firm B	Firm C
Profit at 80,000 units	$24,000	$20,000	$20,000
Profit at 100,000 units	$40,000	$30,000	$40,000
Percent change in profit	67%	50%	100%
Percent change in output	25%	25%	25%
Degree of operating leverage (DOL)	2.7	2.0	4.0

$$\text{Firm A} = \text{DOL} = \frac{C}{X} = \frac{64{,}000}{24{,}000} = 2.7$$

$$\text{Firm B} = \text{DOL} = \frac{40{,}000}{20{,}000} = 2.0$$

$$\text{Firm C} = \text{DOL} = \frac{80{,}000}{20{,}000} = 4.0$$

3. This is significant for the following reasons:
   a. The relative influence of fixed costs in operations is affected by (1) price changes, (2) changes in variable costs, and (3) changes in the relative importance of fixed costs.
   b. The higher the degree of operating leverage, the greater the impact of a given percentage change in output on profit in both directions.
   c. The degree of operating leverage (DOL) influences decisions on the amount of financial leverage the firm employs because financial and operating leverage jointly affect the variability of the firm's net income.
4. See Problem 9.3.

VI. Cash Break-even Analysis as illustrated in Figure 9.3 can be used to analyze the firm's situation on a cash basis.
   A. The formulas for break-even quantity and sales level must be adjusted for noncash outlays:

$$TR^* = \frac{F - \text{noncash outlays}}{CR}$$

$$Q^* = \frac{F - \text{noncash outlays}}{c}$$

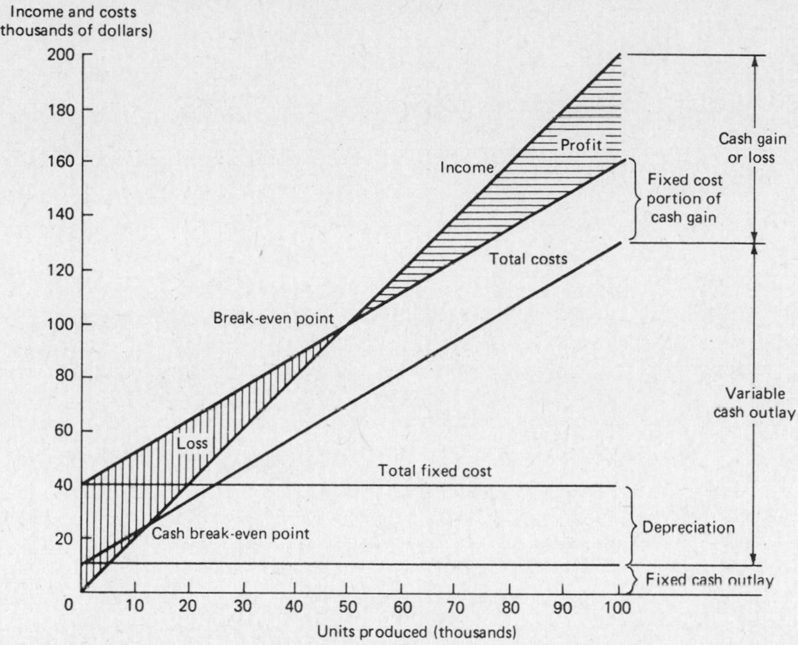

Figure 9.3 Cash Break-even Analysis

B. Cash break-even analysis provides a picture of the flow of funds from operations.
   1. A firm may utilize a high degree of operating leverage (high fixed costs) to achieve high profits.
   2. If cash outlays are low, such a firm will be able to continue to operate during periods of loss, as long as it remains above the cash break-even point.

VII. The Cash Budget.
   A. A cash budget reflects the effects of future operations on a firm's cash flow.
   B. It provides the financial manager with an overview of probable patterns of cash receipts and disbursements so that he can attempt to maximize net cash flows.
   C. It provides the necessary lead time to prepare for future external financing that may be needed, or to plan for short-term investment of excess cash that may temporarily become available.
   D. Preparing a cash budget.
      1. The sales forecast, by product line and for the firm as a whole, is the critical element.
         a. The top-down approach is based on the relationship between the state of the economy and industry sales.
         b. The bottom-up approach consolidates the sales estimates of individual sales representatives to arrive at an estimate for the entire firm.

2. If a firm sells on credit, there is a lag between sales and cash collections.
3. Similarly, a firm buying on credit benefits from a waiting period before having to disburse cash.
4. In expenditures, some cash payments are made in lumps at irregular intervals, while some expenses occur on a uniform monthly basis, and similarly with cash receipts.
5. It is important to take into account debt service requirements, both interest and principal, as cash outflows.
6. Since most of the estimates in the cash budget are subject to uncertainty and variability, computer analysis may help financial managers to prepare "what-if" scenarios.

VIII. The du Pont System of Financial Analysis reveals the manner in which activity ratios and profit margins on sales interact to determine the profitability of assets.

A. Profit planning depends to a great extent upon control of costs and turnover of investment.

1. The calculation of ROI in the du Pont system illustrates the importance of turnover in determining the return on total investment.

$$\frac{\text{NOI}}{\text{Sales}} \times \frac{\text{Sales}}{\text{Investment}} = \text{ROI}$$

a. This definition of ROI differs from that given in Chapter 8 on financial ratios.
b. The du Pont system is most often used for divisional control in large firms.
c. Since financial leverage and corporate tax decisions are made at the corporate rather than the divisional level, the numerator consists of net operating income before interest expense and taxes.

2. The nature of the industry determines to a large extent the level of assets required, and turnover is largely determined by the nature of the product.

a. Firms with low asset turnover tend to have higher profit margins on sales, e.g. shipbuilders.
b. Firms with high asset turnover tend to have lower profit margins on sales, e.g. wholesalers.

B. When the du Pont system is used for divisional control, it is often called ROI control.

1. Each division is defined as a profit center with its own investments and is expected to earn an appropriate return on them.
2. If a division's ROI falls below a target figure, the central corporate staff traces back through the du Pont system to locate the cause.
3. Division managers are judged by their division's ROI, and therefore are motivated to keep ROI up to target level.

4. Divisional ROI performance is also used to allocate corporate resources.
5. ROI may be influenced by factors other than managerial competence:
   a. Depreciation policy
   b. Book value versus current values
   c. Transfer pricing methods
   d. Short-term versus long-term perspectives
   e. Industry conditions
6. These factors necessitate supplementing the performance evaluation with other criteria, including:
   a. The division's growth rate in sales
   b. The division's equipment modernization and replacement policies
   c. The division's market share as compared with other firms in the industry

C. Figure 9.4 below is an illustrative du Pont chart for divisional control.

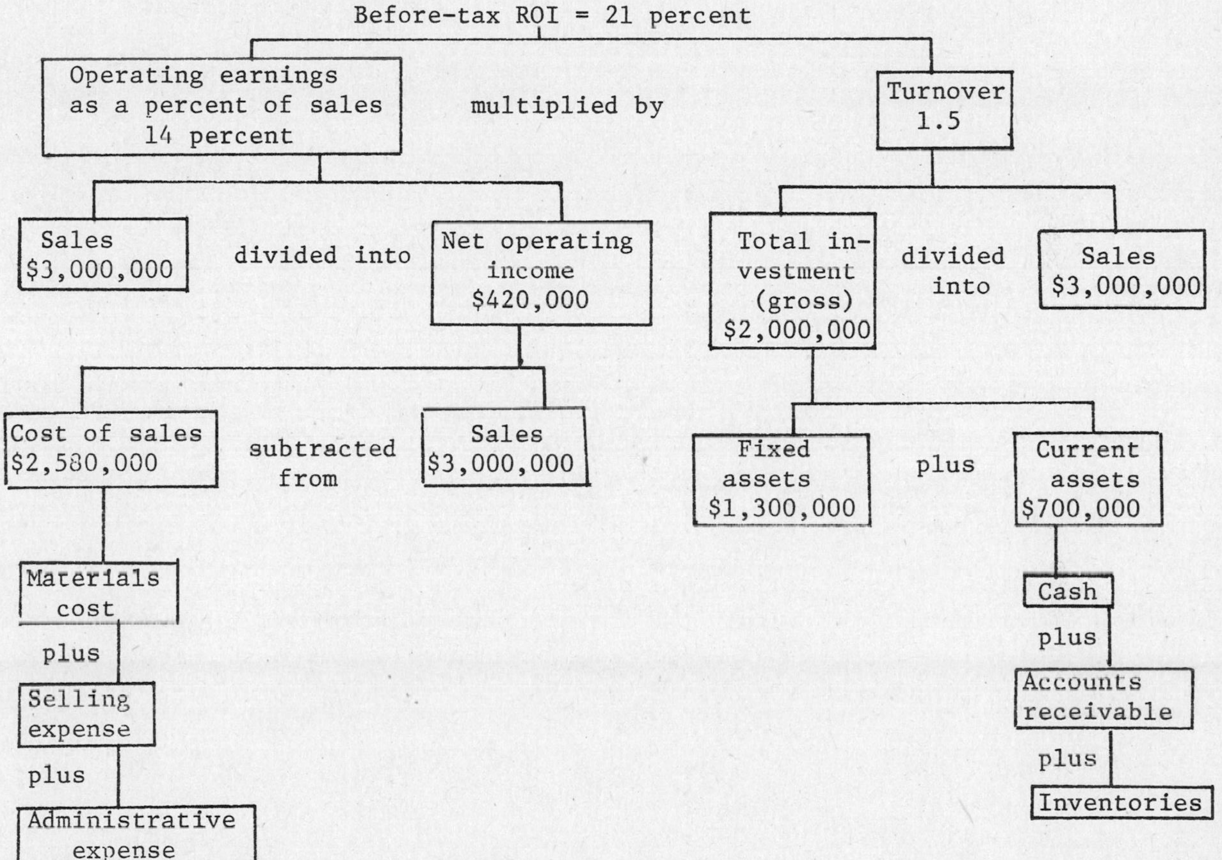

Figure 9.4 Illustrative du Pont Chart for Divisional Control

IX. Overall Planning Models Focus on the Firm Rather than Divisional Performance.

A. Symbols used in this literature are listed below:

T = asset turnover
m = profit margin on sales
L = financial leverage = total assets/equity
b = retention rate = 1 - dividend payout rate
BV = book value (BVS = book value per share)
EPS = earnings per share
DPS = dividends per share
G = sustainable growth

B. The return on equity is a function of asset turnover, profit margin and leverage.

$$ROE = \frac{\text{Sales}}{\text{Total assets}} \times \frac{\text{Net income}}{\text{Sales}} \times \frac{\text{Total assets}}{\text{Equity}} = \frac{\text{Net income}}{\text{Equity}}$$

ROE = TmL

C. Earnings per share are a function of return on equity and book value per share.

$$EPS = \frac{\text{Net income}}{\text{Equity}} \times \frac{\text{Equity}}{\text{Number of shares}} = \frac{\text{Net income}}{\text{Number of shares}}$$

EPS = ROE x BVS

D. Dividends per share are a function of earnings per share and the dividend payout ratio.

$$DPS = \frac{\text{Net income}}{\text{Number of shares}} \times \frac{\text{Dividends}}{\text{Net income}} = \frac{\text{Dividends}}{\text{Number of shares}}$$

DPS = EPS x (1-b)

E. The concept of sustainable dividends brings together all the preceding factors.

$$DPS = \frac{\text{Sales}}{\text{TA}} \times \frac{\text{NI}}{\text{Sales}} \times \frac{\text{TA}}{\text{Equity}} \times \frac{\text{Equity}}{\text{\# of shares}} \times \frac{\text{Dividends}}{\text{NI}}$$

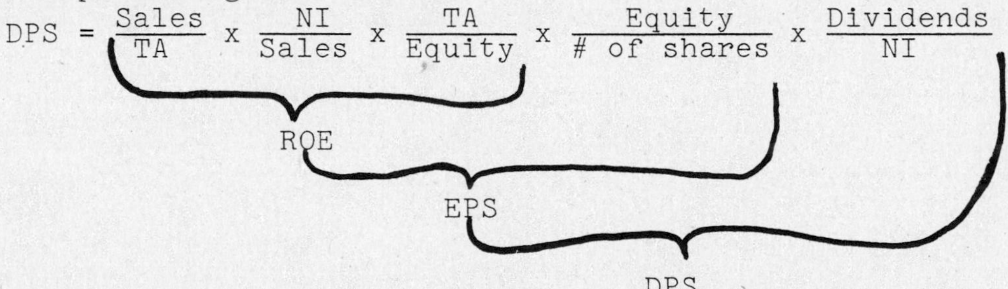

Alternatively, DPS = T x m x L x BVS x (1-b)

F. Sustainable growth may be expressed as the return on equity times the retention rate.

G = ROE(b) = T x m x L x b

G. Each factor represents an important area of business decision-making.

Chapter 9 - Illustrative Problems and Solutions

9.1 The Mart Corporation makes jackhammers, which it sells at P = \$1,200. Variable cost per unit (V) is \$800, and fixed costs for annual production of up to 1,500 units are \$200,000.

a. Make a contribution statement for Mart Corporation at sales levels of 400 and 800 units.
b. What is the break-even quantity of sales?
c. What is the break-even dollar sales?
d. What price must Mart Corporation charge to break even at 400 units?

Solution:

a. Contribution statement:

	400	800
Units sold (Q)	400	800
Sales revenue (TR = PQ)	\$480,000	\$960,000
Total variable cost (V=vQ)	320,000	640,000
Contribution margin (C=TR-V)	\$160,000	\$320,000
Fixed operating costs (F)	200,000	200,000
Net operating income (X=C-F)	\$(40,000)	\$120,000

b. $Q^* = \frac{F}{c} = \frac{F}{P - v} = \frac{\$200,000}{\$400} = 500$ units

Alternatively:

$PQ^* = F + vQ^*$
$1,200Q^* = 200,000 + 800Q^*$
$400Q^* = 200,000$
$Q^* = 500$ units

c. $TR^* = \frac{F}{CR} = \frac{\$200,000}{1 - .6667} = \frac{\$200,000}{.3333} = \$600,000$

Check: 500 x \$1,200 = \$600,000

d. $Q^* = \frac{F}{P - v} = 400$

$\frac{200,000}{P - 800} = 400$

$400P = 200,000 + 320,000 = 520,000$

$P = \$1,300$

9.2 Amboy Corporation also produces jack-hammers which it sells at $1,000 per unit. Amboy uses more modern production equipment and has fixed costs of $400,000 at output of up to 1,500 units and variable costs of $600 per unit.

a. Make a contribution statement for Amboy Corporation at sales levels of 800 and 1,200 units.
b. What is the break-even quantity of sales?
c. What is the break-even dollar sales?
d. What price must Amboy charge to break even at 400 units.

Solution:

a. Contribution statement

Units sold (Q)	800	1,200
Sales revenue (TR=PQ)	$800,000	$1,200,000
Total variable cost (V=vQ)	480,000	720,000
Contribution margin (C=TR-V)	320,000	480,000
Fixed operating cost (F)	400,000	400,000
Net operating income (X=C-F)	$(80,000)	$ 80,000

b. $Q^* = \frac{F}{c} = \frac{F}{P - v} = \frac{\$400,000}{\$400} = 1,000 \text{ units}$

Alternatively:

$PQ^* = F + vQ^*$
$1,000Q^* = 400,000 + 600Q^*$
$400Q^* = 400,000$
$Q^* = 1,000 \text{ units}$

c. $TR^* = \frac{F}{CR} = \frac{\$400,000}{1 - .60} = \frac{\$400,000}{.4} = \$1,000,000$

Check: 1,000 x $1,000 = $1,000,000

d. $Q^* = \frac{F}{P - v} = 400$

$\frac{400,000}{P - 600} = 400$

$400P = 400,000 + 240,000 = 640,000$

$P = \$1,600$

9.3 Under normal conditions, Mart and Amboy, in Problems 9.1 and 9.2, each sell 1,100 jackhammers per year at a price of $1,200.

a. Calculate the degree of operating leverage for both companies at sales of 1,100 units.

b. If sales for both companies rise to 1,200 units at the same price, what will be the percentage increase in profit for each firm?

c. If sales drop to 900 units at the same price, what will be the percentage decrease in profit for each firm?

Solution:

a.

	Mart	Amboy
Q	1,100	1,100
S	$1,320,000	$1,320,000
V	880,000	660,000
C	$ 440,000	$ 660,000
F	200,000	400,000
X	$ 240,000	$ 260,000

$DOL_{1,100} = \frac{C}{X} = 1.8333$ 2.5385

b. $\frac{1,200}{1,100} = 1.09 = 9\%$ increase in units sold

Mart's profit will increase by
9% x 1.8333 = .165 = 16.5%

Amboy's profit will increase by
9% x 2.5385 = .2285 = 22.85%

c. $\frac{1,100 - 900}{1,100} = .1818 = 18\%$ decrease in units sold.

Mart's profit will decrease by
18% x 1.8333 = .3299 = 33%
Amboy's profit will decrease by
18% x 2.5385 = .4569 = 45.7%

9.4 George Cash, the owner of the Cashflow Company, has concluded that he can reduce the amount of idle cash in his bank account by accurately forecasting his cash needs for the next six months. Mr. Cash makes all sales on credit with 60 percent collected in the first month following the sale and 40 percent in the second month. Monthly expenses are 50 percent of the current month's sales. Purchases are 40 percent of the following month's sales and are paid in the current month. Mr. Cash does not want the cash balance to fall below the beginning level of $1,000. Any cash over

$1,000 will be used to pay any outstanding loans. The six-month sales forecast is as follows:

Actual Sales, 19X1		Sales Forecast, 19X2	
November	$8,000	January	$12,000
December	$9,000	February	14,000
		March	16,000
		April	15,000
		May	12,000
		June	10,000
		July	8,000

Prepare Cashflow Company's cash budget for January through June, 19X2.

Solution:
See following page.

9.5 Narragansett Corporation has been in the manufacturing business for over 100 years. The descendents of the founder manage the company and still hold a majority of the common stock; they seem content and comfortable with the returns of the firm. Young Jane Wood, the great-great granddaughter of the founder has just received her MBA and believes that Narragansett can and should be doing better. She sets out to prove to the family how poorly the firm is doing relative to other companies in the industry. Narragansett's most recent financial statements are reproduced below, along with industry data.

a. Calculate the indicated financial ratios.
b. Apply a duPont chart analysis to Narragansett.
c. Do you agree with Jane on the level of the firm's performance?

Industry Average Ratios

Current ratio: 2.2
Quick ratio: 1.1
Debt to total assets: 53.1%
Times interest earned: 8.5 times
Inventory turnover: 6.3 times
Average collection period: 43 days
Fixed assets turnover: 8.1 times
Total assets turnover: 2.2 times
Net profit on sales: 4.9%
Return on investment (ROI--duPont): 20.46%
Return on net worth: 23.0%

Solution: (Problem 9.4)

Cashflow Company

Cash Budget for January to June 19X2

	Cash Inflows	Nov.	Dec.	Jan.	Feb.	Mar.	Apr.	May	June
1.	Sales	$8,000	$9,000	$12,000	$14,000	$16,000	$15,000	$12,000	$10,000
2.	Collections from last month's sales			5,400	7,200	8,400	9,600	9,000	7,200
3.	Collections from previous two months' sales			3,200	3,600	4,800	5,600	6,400	6,000
4.	Total cash inflow (2)+(3)			$ 8,600	$10,800	$13,200	$15,200	$15,400	$13,200
5.	Payment for purchases			$ 5,600	6,400	6,000	4,800	4,000	3,200
6.	Cash expenses			6,000	7,000	8,000	7,500	6,000	5,000
7.	Total cash outflows (5)+(6)			$11,600	$13,400	$14,000	$12,300	$10,000	$ 8,200
8.	Beginning cash balance			$ 1,000	1,000	1,000	1,000	1,000	2,900
9.	Net cash change (4)-(7)			(3,000)	(2,600)	(800)	2,900	5,400	5,000
10.	Unadjusted cash balance			$(2,000)	(1,600)	200	3,900	6,400	7,900
11.	Bank borrowing required			3,000	2,600	800	0	0	0
12.	Cumulative bank borrowing			3,000	5,600	6,400	3,500	0	0
13.	Ending cash balance			$ 1,000	1,000	1,000	1,000	2,900	7,900
14.	Excess cash available for investment (cumulative)			$ 0	0	0	0	1,900	6,900

Common Size Balance Sheet
for firms in Narragansett's Industry
(in percentages)

Assets		Liabilities	
Cash	6.1%	Due to Banks - short-term	8.3%
Marketable securities	3.2	Accounts payable	11.6
Receivables, net	26.3	Income taxes	2.6
Inventory, net	35.1	Current maturities, long-term debt	2.5
All other current	1.2	All other current	7.6
Total current	71.9%	Total current debt	32.6%
Fixed assets, net	27.2	Long-term debt	20.5
All other non-current	0.9	Tangible net worth	46.9
Total Assets	100.0%	Total Claims on Assets	100.0%

Common Size Income Statement
for firms in Narragansett's Industry
(in percentages)

Net sales	100.0%	
Cost of sales	74.6	
Gross Profit		25.4%
Selling and delivery expenses	3.8%	
Officer's salaries	2.6	
Other general and administrative expenses	8.9	
All other expenses, net	0.8	
Operating expenses		16.1
Net income before interest and tax (NOI)		9.3%
Interest expense		1.1
Net income before tax		8.2%
Taxes at 40%		3.3
Net Income		4.9%

Narragansett Corporation
Balance Sheet as of Dec. 31, 19X0
(in thousands)

Assets			Liabilities		
Cash	1,500		Accounts payable	1,350	
Marketable securities	500		Notes payable(@8%)	800	
Receivables	3,000		Other current liabilities	500	
Inventory	5,000				
Total current assets		10,000	Total current liabilities		2,650
Net fixed assets		2,000	Long-term debt(@6%)		2,480
Total assets		12,000	Net worth		6,870
			Total Claims on Assets		12,000

Narragansett Corporation
Income Statement for year
ended Dec. 31, 19X0
(in thousands)

Sales			17,750
Cost of goods sold:			
Materials	4,500		
Labor	7,000		
Heat, light, power	2,000		
Depreciation	500		14,000
Gross Profit			3,750
Selling expenses		600	
General and administrative expenses		1,800	2,400
Earnings before interest and taxes (NOI)			1,350
Less interest expense			213
Income before taxes			1,137
Less income tax (@40%)			455
Net Income			682

Solution:

a.

Ratios	Industry	Narragansett
Current	2.2	3.8
Quick	1.1	1.9
Debt/Assets	53.1%	43%
Times interest earned	8.5 times	6.3 times
Inventory turnover	6.3 times	3.6 times
Average collection period	43 days	61 days
Fixed asset turnover	8.1 times	8.9 times
Total asset turnover	2.2 times	1.5 times
Net profit on sales	4.9%	3.8%
Return on investment (ROI)	20.46%	11.25%
Return on net worth	23.0%	9.9%

b. See next page.

c. Narragansett's profitability ratios are well below the industry norms. Except for fixed assets, the turnover ratios are also low. This may indicate that the firm is operating with somewhat old, depreciated plant and equipment since older fixed assets would have been depreciated to lower values making the turnover of net fixed assets more favorable than with new, less-depreciated assets. The average collection period is too long, and times interest earned is below average. Liquidity ratios, conversely, are high, perhaps too high, indicating perhaps too conservative a policy regarding current asset management. Cash, inventory and marketable securities are kept at too high a level to be optimal. Notice also the low debt ratio in relation to the industry norm.

Thus, while the company does not appear to be in any danger, Jane Wood has a valid point in stating that it could be doing better.

b.

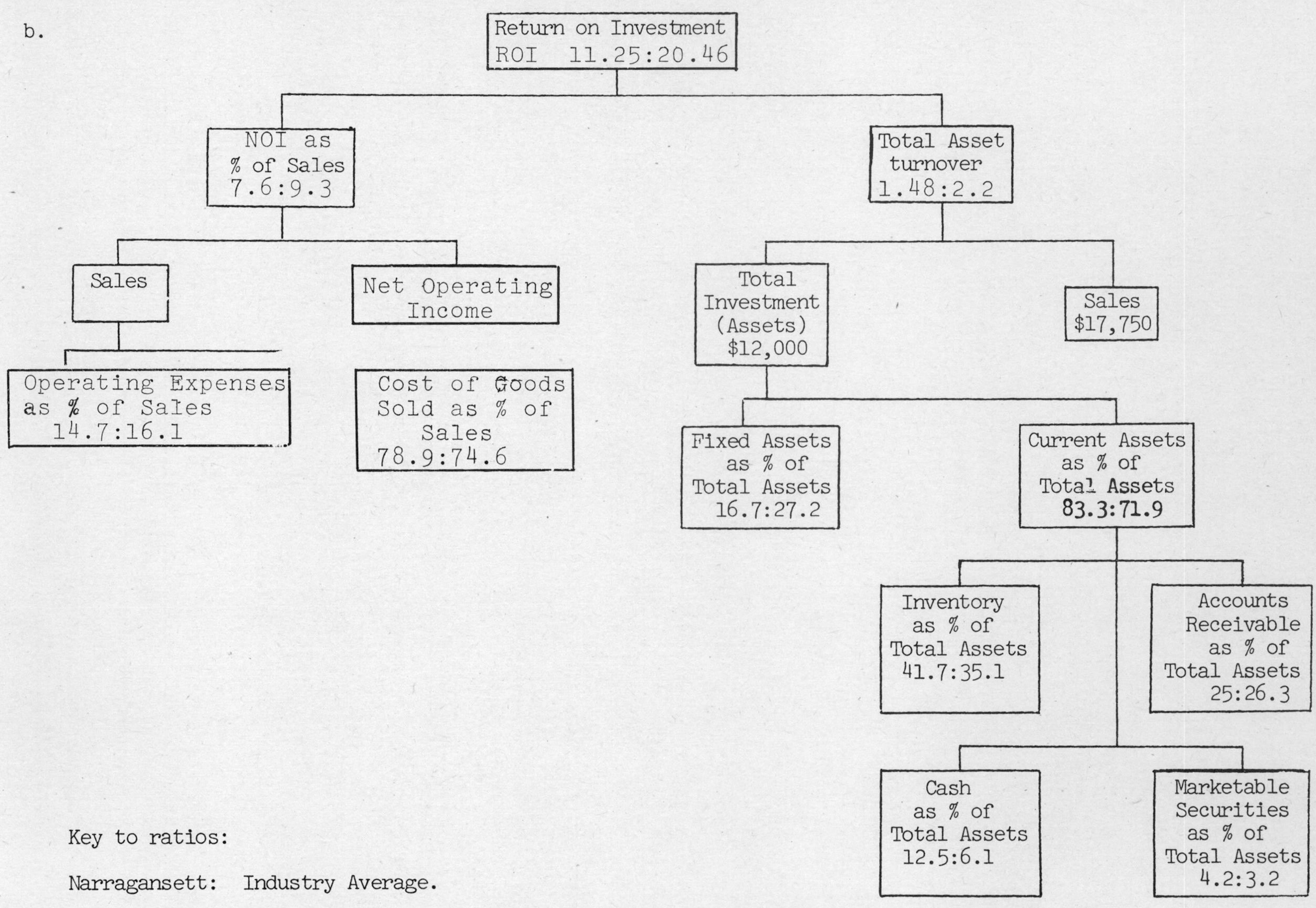

Key to ratios:

Narragansett: Industry Average.

CHAPTER 10

FINANCIAL FORECASTING

Theme: Growing firms constantly require new investment to finance sales growth. Because of cost considerations new debt and equity funding is typically raised in large increments at long intervals. To avoid cash flow problems, financial managers must use the forecasting techniques presented in this chapter to estimate the need for funds during the planning period.

I. The Cash Flow Cycle.
   A. Sales are the causal variable motivating investment in assets and their financing.
      1. An order is received.
      2. Raw materials are purchased on credit; accounts payable arise.
      3. Labor is applied.
         a. Wages payable accrue.
         b. Work-in-process inventories build up.
      4. Furnished goods inventories are sold on credit; accounts receivable arise.
      5. Accounts receivable are collected and become cash.
      6. The cash is used to begin the next cycle.
         a. For a growing firm, the cash will generally not be sufficient to complete the cycle.
         b. External financing must be planned for on the basis of projected sales.
   B. Asset financing should be related to the permanence of assets.
      1. Permanent assets consist of both current and fixed assets.
         a. Short-term sales fluctuations result in temporary changes in current assets.
         b. A rising long-term trend in sales results is a steady increase in current assets (and fixed assets as well).
         c. Thus, a certain level of current assets become, in effect, permanent.
      2. Permanent assets should be financed by permanent liabilities.
         a. Permanent liabilities include both current liabilities (for example, the permanent level of accrued wages, accounts payable, etc) and long-term liabilities and owners' equity.

3. Financing long-term needs (whether classified as current or fixed assets) with short-term financing can result in cash flow problems even for a profitable firm.

C. Basic methods of forecasting include the percent-of-sales method and linear regression.

1. The percent-of-sales method expresses balance sheet items in terms of their percentage of sales. For example, if sales were $1,000,000 and accounts receivable were $200,000, the percent-of-sales relation for accounts receivable would be 20 percent.
2. Linear regression is a more accurate forecasting technique which does not presuppose direct proportionality between the dependent and independent variables.

D. The most important variable influencing a firm's financing requirements is its project dollar volume of sales. Therefore a good sales forecast is essential. For purposes of illustrating the percent-of-sales method, however, we assume that a sales forecast has been made. Later we will illustrate how the regression method can be used in forecasting sales.

II. Percent-of-Sales Method.

A. Determine those balance sheet items that vary directly with sales.

B. Tabulate those items as a percentage of sales, in balance sheet form.

C. Increases in assets represent financing requirements; some liabilities grow spontaneously with sales and provide a spontaneous source of funds.

D. The difference between the required growth in assets and the spontaneously generated funds from liability increases represents the firm's total financing requirements. This is normally first met by internally generated increases in retained earnings (profit margin on total sales less dividend payout). Financing needs in excess of this must be obtained externally, such as through borrowing or by selling new common stock.

E. In equation form:

$$\text{External funds needed} = \text{EFN} = \frac{A}{TR}(\Delta TR) - \frac{L}{TR}(\Delta TR) - cb(TR_2)$$

where

$\frac{A}{TR}$ = assets that increase spontaneously with total revenues or sales, as a percent of revenues or sales

$\frac{L}{TR}$ = liabilities that increase spontaneously with total revenues as a percent of total revenues or sales

ΔTR = change in total revenues

c = profit margin on sales

b = earnings retention ratio

TR_2 = total revenues projected for next year

F. Table 10.1 provides an illustration.

Table 10.1 The Barnum Company--Balance Sheet Expressed as a Percent of Sales, December 31, 19X1

Cash	3.0%	Accounts payable	9.0%
Receivables	15.0	Accrued taxes and wages	4.0
Inventories	18.0	Mortgage bonds	*
Fixed assets (net)	25.0	Common stock	*
		Retained earnings	**
Total	61.0%	Total	13.0%

Assets as a percent of sales	61.0%
Less spontaneous increase in liabilities	13.0
Percent of each additional dollar of sales that must be financed	48.0%

*The account does not automatically vary with sales.
**The relationship to sales depends on profit margin and payout rate as shown below.

Suppose sales increase from $500,000 to $800,000; profit margin on sales of $800,000 is 4 percent; the dividend payout is 50 percent.

External funds required = .61(300,000) - .13(300,000)
- .04(.5)(800,000)
= .48(300,000) - .02(800,000)
= $128,000

However, if sales increase by only $15,000, to $515,000:

External funds required = .48(15,000) - .02(515,000)
= ($3,100)

This means no external funds are required. The company in fact has $3,100 in excess of its requirements. This could be used to increase dividends, retire debt, or seek additional investment opportunities.

G. This example highlights two points:
1. Higher levels of sales bring about greater needs for funds.
2. While small rates of growth can be financed by internal sources (through retained earnings), higher rates of growth are more likely to require external financing.

H. It should also be noted:

1. Increase in sales can also be written gS_1.
2. The percentage of the increase in sales that will have to be financed externally (PEFR) can be expressed:

$$PEFR = I - cb(1+g)/g$$

where

$$I = \frac{A}{TR} - \frac{L}{TR}$$

For the first example under F above:

$$PEFR = .48 - (.04)(.5)(1.6)/.6$$
$$= .48 - .0533 = 42.67\%$$

Check: \$128,000/\$300,000 = 42.67%

3. External financing has become more important to firms because of the increasing inflation rate, which causes a firm that is not growing at all in real terms to require external financing for its growth in sales in inflated dollars.

I. The percent-of-sales method of forecasting is neither simple nor mechanical.

1. It is important to understand the basic technology of the firm and the logic of the relationship between its sales and assets.
2. The percent-of-sales method is most useful in forecasting relatively short-term changes in financing needs.

III. Mean and Variance are Discussed as an Introduction to Linear Regression.

A. The mean and variance of the dependent variable, sales in the illustrative data below, are first explained unconditionally, that is, without reference to the independent variables, GNP and an inflation index in the example below.

Year	Sales ($ millions)	GNP ($ billions)	Inflation
19X0	550.3	1,116.2	100.0
19X1	587.6	1,000.7	112.4
19X2	524.0	985.4	108.7
19X3	478.3	974.3	110.9
19X4	475.1	962.8	113.4
19X5	500.8	971.5	113.2

1. The mean, or average, is the expected value.

$$E(Y) = \overline{Y} = \sum_{i=1}^{N} p_i Y_i = \frac{1}{N} \sum_{i=1}^{N} Y_i$$

where Y = the dependent variable
N = the number of observations
p_i = the probability of each observation = 1/N

For the data above, the unconditional mean of Sales, Y, is calculated:

$$E(Y) = \frac{3,116.1}{6} = 519.35$$

2. The variance is the expected value (or average or mean) of the deviations from the mean squared.

$$Var(Y) = E\{[Y_i - E(Y)]^2\}$$

a. When working with sample data, as above, the sum of mean deviations squared is divided by N-1 rather than by N.

$$\sigma_Y^2 = Var(Y) = \sum_{i=1}^{N} [Y_i - E(Y)]^2/(N-1)$$

The unconditional variance of Sales for the data above is calculated below:

Year	Sales (Y)	Y-E(Y)	$[Y-E(Y)]^2$
19X0	550.3	30.95	957.90
19X1	587.6	68.25	4,658.06
19X2	524.0	4.65	21.62
19X3	478.3	-41.05	1,685.10
19X4	475.1	-44.25	1,958.06
19X5	500.8	-18.55	344.10
			9,624.84

$$Var(Y) = 9,624.84/5 = 1,924.97$$

b. Variance is very sensitive to observations which depart widely from the mean.

c. The standard deviation is the square root of the variance; for the data above, the standard deviation is 43.87.

C. The extra information provided by the independent variables enables the computation of a <u>conditional</u> distribution with a lower standard deviation than the unconditional distribution.

IV. Linear Regression Refers to the Development of an Equation Based on Past Relationships Among Variables which may be Used to Predict One of the Variables in the Future.

A. Linear regression is based on a graphic scatter diagram of the relationship between the variables.

1. The independent variable is plotted on the x-axis.
2. The dependent variable (that which we want to predict or are trying to explain) is plotted on the y-axis.

3. Figure 10.1 is a scatter diagram for the data above, with the linear regression line also illustrated.

B. The equation of a linear regression line can be written as

$$Y = a + bX$$

where Y = the dependent variable
a = the y-axis intercept of the regression line
b = the slope of the regression line
X = the independent variable

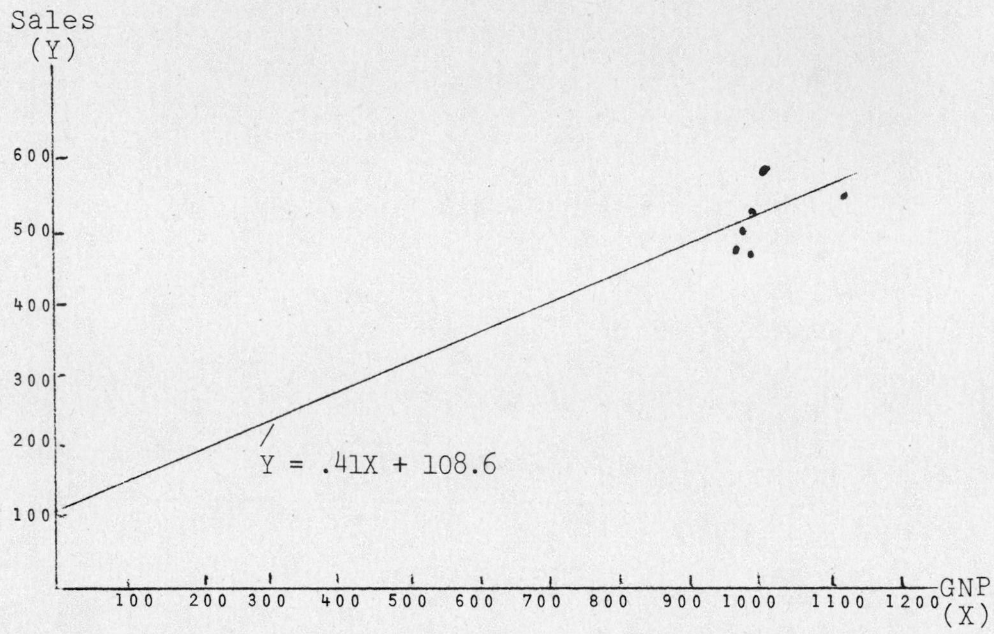

Figure 10.1 Scatter Diagram and Linear Regression Line

1. Since forecasts can be expected to have some error, the linear regression line can be written as

$$Y = a + bX + \varepsilon$$

where ε = a random error term

2. The object of linear regression is to find the intercept, a, and slope, b, which best fit the data, that is, which minimize the sum of squared error terms (the variance of the error terms).

3. $Var_{\varepsilon} = \sigma^2_{\varepsilon} = \sigma^2_Y + 2bCOV(Y,X) + b^2\sigma^2_X$

   a. Taking the derivative with respect to b, and setting the result equal to zero, we find the value of b (the slope of the linear regression line) which minimizes the variance of the error terms:

$$\hat{b} = \frac{COV(Y,X)}{\sigma^2_X}$$

   b. Substitute the value of b into the linear regression equation to find

$$\hat{a} = \overline{Y} - \hat{b}X$$

C. The <u>coefficient of determination</u>, r^2, measures the extent of increased explanatory power over the unconditional distribution of Y which is introduced by including the independent variable, X.

1. Residual errors, ε, are the difference between the actual value of Y and the value of Y predicted by the regression equation, given the value of X.
2. Residual errors indicate the extent of movement in the dependent variable not explained by the independent variable.
3. The coefficient of determination is found as:

$$r^2 = \frac{\Sigma(Y-\overline{Y})^2 - \Sigma(\varepsilon-\overline{\varepsilon})^2}{\Sigma(Y-\overline{Y})^2}$$

= the percent of the unconditional variance of the dependent variable explained by the independent variable

   a. Since the expected value of ε, $\overline{\varepsilon}$, is equal to zero,

$$\Sigma(\varepsilon-\overline{\varepsilon})^2 = \Sigma(\varepsilon)^2$$

   b. $0 < r^2 < 1$.

      i. $r^2 = 1$: All variance is explained in the regression equation.

      ii. $r^2 = 0$: The regression equation does nothing to reduce the variance of the dependent variable.

D. Table 10.1 on the following page represents a complete computation of the linear regression for the data above. The independent variable explains 29 percent of the unconditional variance of the dependent variable.

1. Many pocket calculators are preprogrammed to calculate the slope and intercept of a linear regression equation.

Table 10.1 Linear Regression Computations

Year	Sales Y	GNP X	$Y-\overline{Y}$	$(Y-\overline{Y})^2$	$X-\overline{X}$	$(X-\overline{X})^2$	$(Y-\overline{Y})(X-\overline{X})$	$\hat{Y}$	$\varepsilon=Y-\hat{Y}$	ε^2
19X0	550.3	1116.2	30.95	957.90	114.38	13082.78	3540.06	566.24	-15.94	254.15
19X1	587.6	1000.7	68.25	4658.06	- 1.12	1.25	-76.44	518.89	68.71	4721.48
19X2	524.0	985.4	4.65	21.62	-16.42	269.62	-76.35	512.61	11.38	129.64
19X3	478.3	974.3	-41.05	1685.10	-27.52	757.35	1129.70	508.06	-29.76	885.84
19X4	475.1	962.8	-44.25	1958.06	-39.02	1522.56	1726.64	503.35	-28.25	797.95
19X5	500.8	971.5	-18.55	344.10	-30.32	919.30	562.44	506.92	-6.12	37.39
	3116.1	6010.9		9624.84		16552.86	6806.05			6826.45

$\overline{Y} = 3116.1/6 = 519.35$

$\overline{X} = 6010.9/6 = 1001.82$

$Var(Y) = \sigma_Y^2 = \Sigma(Y-\overline{Y})^2/(N-1)$

$= 9624.84/5 = 1924.97$

$\sigma_Y = 43.87$

$Var(X) = \sigma_X^2 = \Sigma(X-\overline{X})^2/(N-1)$

$= 16552.86/5 = 3310.57$

$\sigma_X = 57.54$

$COV(Y,X) = \Sigma[(Y-\overline{Y})(X-\overline{X})]/(N-1)$

$= 6806.05/5 = 1361.21$

$\hat{b} = COV(Y,X)/\sigma_X^2$

$= 1361.21/3310.57 = .41$

$\hat{a} = \overline{Y} - \hat{b}\overline{X}$

$= 519.35 - .41(1001.82) = 108.60$

$Var(\varepsilon) = \sigma_\varepsilon^2 = \Sigma\varepsilon^2/(N-1)$

$= 6826.45/5 = 1365.29$

$r^2 = (\sigma_Y^2-\sigma_\varepsilon^2)/\sigma_Y^2 = (1924.97-1365.29)/1924.97$

$= .29$

$r = .29^{1/2} = .54$

D. The significance of the intercept and slope is determined by t-tests.
   1. The t-statistics of the intercept, a, and slope, b, terms are defined as their estimates divided by their respective standard errors of estimate:

$$t(a) = \frac{\hat{a}}{se(\hat{a})} \qquad t(b) = \frac{\hat{b}}{se(\hat{b})}$$

   2. Comparing these results to a table of t-statistics allows one to determine whether the slope and intercept terms are significantly different from zero at various levels of confidence.
   2. The significance of the coefficient of determination (r^2) is tested using the F-statistic.
   3. These significance tests are included in most computerized statistical packages.

E. A multiple regression uses two or more independent variables to explain the dependent variable.
   1. Prediction accuracy can be improved by multiple regression.
   2. The slope coefficients can be interpreted as measures of the sensitivity of the dependent variable to each of the independent variables; however, the absolute value of the independent variable can mean a large impact on the dependent variable even if the slope coefficient is relatively small, or vice versa.
   3. Multiple regression can be a powerful tool, but there may be problems with its use.
      a. It is complicated.
      b. Estimates of the slope and intercept terms may be biased.
      c. Over- or under-estimates of significance tests may cause problems.

V. Comparison of Forecasting Techniques.

A. Just as linear regression can be used to forecast sales based on external independent variables, it can also be used to project individual asset account requirements (such as inventory) using sales as the independent variable, and thus can be compared to the percent-of-sales method.

B. The percent-of-sales method assumes that balance sheet items which vary with sales have a direct linear relation with sales which passes through the origin.
   1. For example, Inventory = .20 Sales.
   2. The slope of this relationship is .20, and the intercept is 0; that is, the line passes through the origin.

C. In linear regression, the line which graphs the relationship between variables does not assume that the line must pass through the origin.

1. The intercept in the linear regression equation may be thought of as a base stock of the account to which additional amounts are added as sales change.
2. Mathematically, a non-zero intercept indicates a changing percentage, in which case the percent-of-sales method would result in faulty forecasting.

D. For short-term forecasts, such as month-to-month, either the percent-of-sales method or the regression method may be employed.

E. For longer-term forecasts, it is best to use the regression method to avoid major errors that might result from systematic shifts in the ratios.

VI. Linear Regression Assumes an Approximately <u>Normal Distribution</u> of Returns.

A. When a probability distribution (of, for example, returns from an investment) is normal, it is described completely by its mean and variance (or standard deviation), thus facilitating comparison with other normal distributions.

B. By calculating the area under the normal curve, we can find the probability that an outcome will be between any two points.

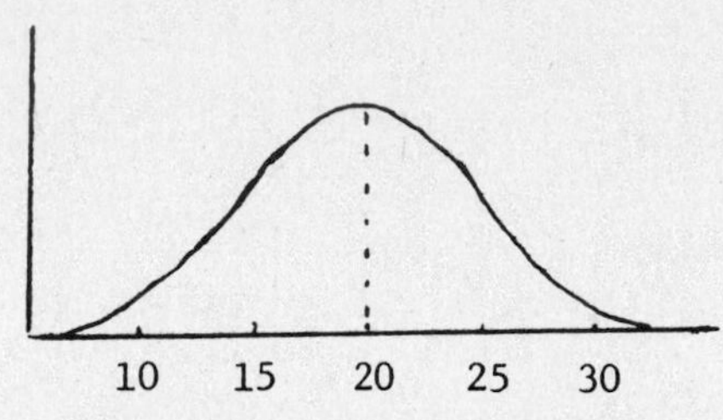

Outcomes (X values)

1. Standardized statistical tables are available to calculate this area without tedious integration.
2. To use the tables, the probability distribution to be investigated must first be standardized as

$$Z = \frac{X - \mu}{\sigma}$$

where

μ = the mean of the distribution
σ = the standard deviation of the distribution
X = the point in question
Z = the number of standardized standard deviations an observation lies from the mean of the normal curve.

3. 68.26% of all observations fall within $\pm$ 1 standard deviation of the mean; 95.46% fall within $\pm$ 2 standard deviations; and 99.74% fall within $\pm$ 3 standard deviations.

C. The assumption of normality also permits us to calculate the probability that an outcome will be greater or less than a certain amount through use of <u>cumulative probability distributions</u>.

D. The normal distribution is widely assumed because many distributions do fit this pattern and because it is easy to work with.

1. Other possible distributions are skewed to the right or left.
2. An investor would prefer a right skewed distribution for its chance of very high returns.
3. Right Skewed

Probability

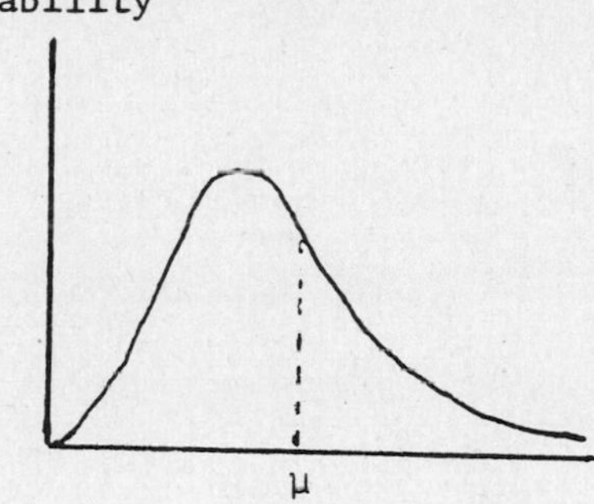

Left Skewed

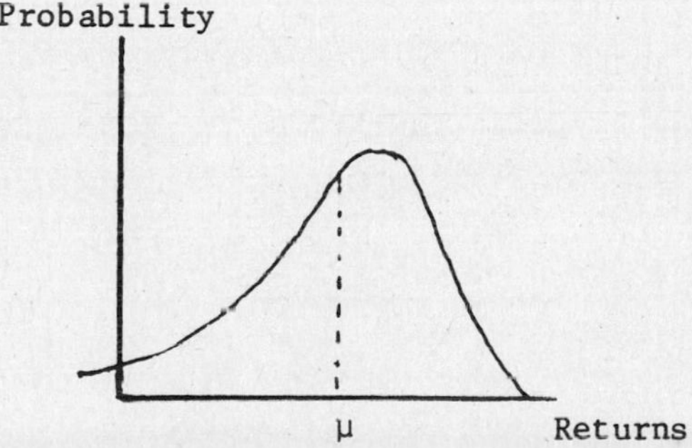

E. Illustrative problem

Davis T.V. and Appliance has the following expectations for sales next year:

State	P_s	Sales (millions)
1	0.1	$2.0
2	0.2	2.4
3	0.4	3.0
4	0.2	3.6
5	0.1	4.0

a. Plot the above points, with sales on the horizontal axis and probability on the vertical. Draw a smooth curve connecting the points.

b. Calculate the mean, standard deviation, and coefficient of variation of the probability distribution.

c. What is the probability that sales will exceed $3.25 million? Fall below $2.25 million? Fall between $2.25 and $3.25 million?

Solution:

a.

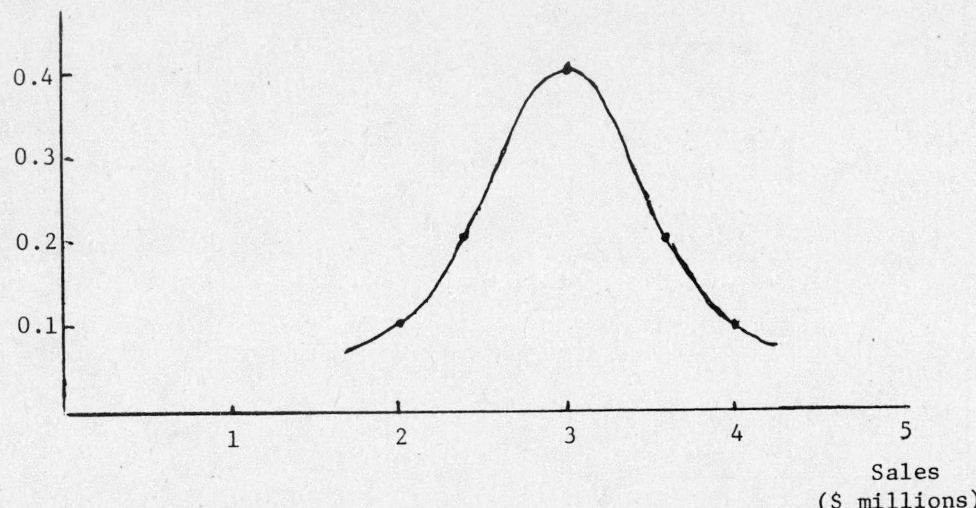

b.

State	$Sales_s \times P_s$	$Sales_s$ - Mean	$(Sales-Mean)^2$	$P_s(Sales-Mean)^2$
1	0.20	-1.0	1.00	0.100
2	0.48	-0.6	0.36	0.072
3	1.20	0.0	0.00	0.000
4	0.72	0.6	0.36	0.072
5	0.40	1.0	1.00	0.100
Mean =	3.00			σ^2 = 0.344
				σ = 0.587 million

$$CV = \frac{\text{Standard deviation}}{\text{Expected sales}} = \frac{0.587}{3} = 0.20$$

Companies with low CV's have less risk per dollar of sales than companies with higher CV's.

c. Exceed \$3.25 million:

$$Z = \frac{X - \mu}{\sigma} = \frac{3.25 - 3}{0.587} = 0.4259$$

From a table of normal values, Z = 0.4259 represents a cumulative probability of 0.1649 + 0.5 = 0.6649. The probability that sales will be above \$3.25 million is equal to 1 - 0.6649 = 0.3351 = 33.5 percent.

Fall below \$2.25 million:

$$Z = \frac{2.25 - 3}{0.587} = -1.2777,$$ which represents a cumulative probability of 0.5 - 0.3993 = .1007 = 10.1 percent.

Fall between \$2.25 and \$3.25 million:

1 - (.335 + .101) = 0.564 = 56.4 percent

Chapter 10 - Illustrative Problems and Solutions

10.1 The Hawks Company's 19X1 sales were $5 million. Its 19X1 Balance Sheet is shown below. The ratio of net profit to sales was 7 percent, with a dividend payout ratio of 45 percent. During 19X2, sales are expected to increase by 25 percent and no long-term debt will be retired. Using the percentage of sales method, determine how much outside financing will be required.

Assets	
Cash	$ 175,000
Accounts receivable	400,000
Inventory	562,500
Total Current Assets	$1,137,500
Net fixed assets	1,700,000
Total Assets	$2,837,500

Claims on Assets	
Accounts payable	$ 162,500
Accruals	87,500
Notes payable	125,000
Total Current Liabilities	$ 375,000
Long-term debt	625,000
Total Debt	$1,000,000
Capital stock	1,115,000
Retained earnings	722,500
Total Liabilities and Net Worth	$2,837,500

Solution:

Cash	3.50%	
Receivables	8.00	
Inventory	11.25	
Current Assets		22.75
Net fixed assets	34.00	
Total Assets		56.75
Accounts payable	3.25	
Accruals	1.75	

Percent of Sales

56.75%	Total Assets
- 5.0%	"Spontaneous" financing
51.75%	Financed by notes payable, long-term debt, and equity

Sales increase by 25% to \$6.25 million; an increase of \$1.25 million.

```
To be financed =     .5175 x $1,250,000 = $646,875
Net profit      =     .07 x $6,250,000   =  437,500
Retained earnings = .55 x Net Profit
                  = .55 x $437,500       =  240,625

Additional financing required = $646,875 - $240,625
                              = $406,250
```

10.2 The 19X2 sales of Zwirlein, Inc. amounted to \$8 million. The dividend payout ratio was 60 percent. Common stock and notes payable were constant. Retained earnings as shown on the December 31, 19X1 balance sheet were \$1,082,000. The percent of sales in each balance sheet item that varies directly with sales is expected to be as follows:

Cash	6%
Receivables	13
Inventories	18
Net fixed assets	26
Accounts payable	12
Accruals	5
Profit rate after taxes on sales	4

a. Complete the balance sheet given:

Zwirlein, Inc.
Balance Sheet
December 31, 19X2

Cash		Accounts payable	
Receivables		Notes payable	\$ 370,000
Inventory		Accruals	
Total current assets		Total current liabilities	
Fixed assets		Common stock	\$2,100,000
Total assets		Retained earnings	
		Total liabilities and net worth	

b. Suppose that 19X3 sales increase 16 percent over the 19X2 sales. How much additional external capital will be needed?

c. Construct the year-end 19X3 balance sheet. Set up an account for "funds available" or "financing needs."

d. What would happen to capital requirements under each of the following conditions?
   1. If the profit margin went:
      (a) from 4 percent to 2 percent.
      (b) from 4 percent to 9 percent.
      Set up an equation to illustrate each answer.
   2. If the dividend payout ratio was:
      (a) raised from 60 percent to 85 percent.
      (b) lowered from 60 percent to 30 percent.
      Set up an equation to illustrate each answer.
   3. If slower collections caused receivables to rise to 55 days of sales (still assuming a 16 percent increase in sales).

Solution:

a.

Zwirlein, Inc.
Balance Sheet
December 31, 19X2

Cash	$ 480,000	Accounts payable	$ 960,000
Receivables	1,040,000	Notes payable	370,000
Inventory	1,440,000	Accruals	400,000
Total current assets	2,960,000	Total current liabilities	$1,730,000
Fixed assets	2,080,000	Common stock	2,100,000
		Retained earnings	1,210,000
Total assets	$5,040,000	Total liabilities and net worth	$5,040,000

(These numbers were arrived at by multiplying percent of sales times sales for each category.)

b.

Cash	6%	Accounts payable	12%
Receivables	13	Accruals	5
Inventory	18		17%
Net fixed assets	26		
	63%		

A sales increase of 16 percent is $1,280,000.

Funds needed: [Total assets as a percent of sales - (Accounts payable + Accruals as a percent of sales)] x (Sales increase) - (Profit rate after taxes as a percent of sales) x (1-Dividend payout) x (New sales volume).

Funds needed = (.63-.17)(1,280,000) - (.04)(.4)(9,280,000)
= 588,800 - 148,480
= 440,320

c.
Zwirlein, Inc.
Balance Sheet
December 31, 19X3

Cash	$ 556,800	Accounts payable	$1,113,600
Receivables	1,206,400	Notes payable	370,000
Inventory	1,670,400	Accruals	464,000
Total current assets	$3,433,600	Total current liabilities	$1,947,600
Fixed assets	2,412,800	Common stock	2,100,000
		Retained earnings	1,358,480
		Financing needed or funds available	440,320
Total assets	$5,846,400	Total liabilities and net worth	$5,846,400

The balance sheet entries were calculated by using the same percent of sales given in the question, but using $9,280,000 ($8,000,000+$1,280,000) as the sales figure.

d. 1. (a) Decrease in profit margin leads to an increase in the requirement of external funds.

$$\text{External funds needed} = \left(\frac{A}{TR} - \frac{L}{TR}\right)\Delta TR - cb(TR_2)$$
= (.63-.17)(1,280,000) -(.02)(.4)(9,280,000)
= 588,800 - 74,240
= $514,560

(b) Increase in profit margin leads to decrease in external funds needed.
EFN = (.63-.17)(1,280,000) - (.09)(.4)(9,280,000)
= 588,800 - 334,080
= $254,720

2. (a) Dividend payout increases from 60 percent to 85 percent; more external funds are needed.
EFN = (.63-.17)(1,280,000) - (.04)(1-.85)(9,280,000)
= 588,800 - 55,680
= $533,120

(b) Dividend payout lowered to 30 percent; decreases the need for external funds.
EFN = (.63-.17)(1,280,000) - (.04)(1-.3)(9,280,000)
= 588,800 - 259,840
= $328,960

3. From the December 31, 19X3 balance sheet:

$$\text{Average collection period} = \frac{\text{Receivables}}{\text{Sales/day}}$$

$$= \frac{1,206,400}{9,280,000/360}$$

$$= 46.8$$

So, if it increases to 55 days:

$$55 = \frac{\text{New receivables}}{9,280,000/360}$$

$$1,417,778 = \text{New receivables}$$

$$1,417,778 - 1,206,400 = \$211,378$$

Increases the need for external funds by $211,378.

10.3 A firm has the following relationships. The ratio of assets to sales is 57 percent. Liabilities that increase spontaneously with sales are 18 percent. The profit margin on sales after taxes is 3 percent. The firm's dividend payout ratio is 60 percent.

a. If the firm's growth rate on sales is 9 percent per annum, what percentage of the sales increase in any year must be financed externally?
b. If the firm's growth rate decreases to 7 percent per annum, what percentage of the sales increase must be financed externally?
c. How will your answer to a. change if the profit margin increases to 7 percent?
d. How will your answer to b. change if the firm's dividend payout is decreased to 40 percent?
e. If the profit margin increases from 3 percent to 5 percent, and the dividend payout ratio is 35 percent, at what growth rate in sales would the external financing needed be exactly $0?

Solution:

Use the formula $PEFR = I - \frac{c}{g}(1+g)b$

$$\text{where } I = \frac{A}{TR} - \frac{L}{TR} = .57 - .18 = .39$$

$$c = .03$$
$$b = .4$$

a. $g = .09$

$$PEFR = .39 - \frac{.03}{.09}(1+.09)(.4)$$

$$= .39 - .145$$
$$= .245$$

24.5 percent of sales increase must be financed externally.

b. $g = .07$

$$PEFR = .39 - \frac{.03}{.07}(1+.07)(.4)$$

$$= .39 - .18$$
$$= .21$$

21 percent of sales increase must be financed externally.

c. $c = .07 \quad g = .09$

$$PEFR = .39 - \frac{.07}{.09}(1+.09)(.4)$$

$$= .39 - .339$$
$$= .05$$

5 percent of sales increase would have to be financed externally.

d. $c = .03 \quad g = .07 \quad b = .6$

$$PEFR = .39 - \frac{.03}{.07}(1+.07)(.6)$$

$$= .39 - .275$$
$$= .115$$

11.5 percent of sales increase must be financed externally.

e. $c = .05 \quad b = .65$

$$0 = .39 - \frac{.05}{g}(1+g)(.65)$$

$$0 = .39 - \frac{.0325}{g} - .0325$$

$$\frac{.0325}{g} = .3575$$

$$.0325 = .3575g$$
$$.091 = g$$

9.1 percent growth rate in sales leads to $0 needed for external financing.

10.4 Daellenbach, Inc. expanded into a new industry in 19X0 and needs a projection of its New Industry Division's financial position for 19X0. One way to get this is to use the industry financial ratio composites. These are given below.

Sales to net worth: 2.5 times
Current debt to net worth: 40%
Total debt to net worth: 80%
Current ratio: 2.5 times
Cash to sales: 13%
Net sales to inventory: 5 times
Net fixed assets to net worth: 80%

a. Complete the pro forma balance sheet for the New Industry Division of Daellenbach, Inc. whose 19X0 sales are $7 million.
b. What other factors will influence the financial structure of the division?

New Industry Division
Daellenbach, Inc.
Pro forma Balance Sheet, 19X0

Cash		Current debt	______
Accounts receivable	______	Long-term debt	______
Inventory	______	Total debt	______
Current assets	______	Net worth	______
Fixed assets	______	Total liabilities	
Total assets	______	and net worth	______

Solution:
a.
New Industry Division
Daellenbach, Inc.
Pro forma Balance Sheet, 19X0

Cash	$ 910,000	Current debt	$1,120,000
*Accounts receivable	490,000	Long-term debt	1,120,000
Inventory	1,400,000	Total debt	$2,240,000
Current assets	2,800,000	Net worth	2,800,000
Fixed assets	2,240,000	Total liabilities	
Total assets	$5,040,000	and net worth	$5,040,000

*Accounts receivable equal current assets less cash and inventory as calculated.

b. Other factors: (1) rate of growth in sales, (2) stage of life cycle, (3) individual policies such as inventory investments, buying versus leasing policies, credit policy, attitudes toward incurring debt.

10.5 The table below gives the relationship between sales and inventory for the United Oil Company for the past 8 years. Next year's forecasted sales are $11 million; management wants to project the level of inventory required to support this level of sales.

Year	Inventory	Sales
19X0	$1.2 million	$4.8 million
19X1	1.4	5.3
19X2	1.5	5.9
19X3	1.8	7.1
19X4	1.5	6.2
19X5	1.8	6.9
19X6	1.9	7.4
19X7	2.0	8.5

a. Find the average value of inventory as a percent of sales. Based on this percentage, what should be the inventory level for the coming year?
b. Calculate the linear regression equation for the data and use it to project next year's inventory based on forecasted sales.
c. What percentage of variation in inventory is explained by sales; that is, what is the coefficient of determination, r^2, of the regression equation?

Solution:

a.

Year	Inventory as a Percent of Sales
19X0	.250
19X1	.264
19X2	.254
19X3	.254
19X4	.242
19X5	.261
19X6	.257
19X7	.235
	2.017

$$\frac{2.017}{8} = .252 = \text{average percentage of sales}$$

Inventory = .252($11 million) = $2.77 million

b. See table on following page.

b.

Year	Inv Y	Sales X	$Y-\overline{Y}$	$(Y-\overline{Y})^2$	$X-\overline{X}$	$(X-\overline{X})^2$	$(Y-\overline{Y})(X-\overline{X})$
19X0	1.2	4.8	-.44	.1936	-1.71	2.9241	.7525
19X1	1.4	5.3	-.24	.0576	-1.21	1.4641	.2904
19X2	1.5	5.9	-.14	.0196	-.61	.3721	.0854
19X3	1.8	7.1	.16	.0256	.59	.3481	.0944
19X4	1.5	6.2	-.14	.0196	-.31	.0961	.0434
19X5	1.8	6.9	.16	.0256	.39	.1521	.0624
19X6	1.9	7.4	.26	.0676	.89	.7921	.2314
19X7	2.0	8.5	.36	.1296	1.99	3.9601	.7164
	13.1	52.1		.5388		10.1088	2.2763

$\overline{Y} = 13.1/8 = 1.64$

$\overline{X} = 52.1/8 = 6.51$

$Var(Y) = .5388/7 = .077$

$\sigma_Y = .277$

$Var(X) = 10.1088/7 = 1.444$

$\sigma_X = 1.202$

$Cov(Y,X) = 2.2763/7 = .325$

$\hat{b} = Cov(Y,X)/\sigma_X^2 = .325/1.444 = .225$

$\hat{a} = \overline{Y} - \hat{b}\overline{X} = 1.64 - (.225)(6.51) = .175$

Inventory = .175 + .225(Sales)

= .175 + .225(\$11) = \$2.65 million

Thus, using the percent-of-sales method would result in overinvestment in inventory by \$1.2 million.

c.

Year	$\hat{Y}$	$\varepsilon = Y-\hat{Y}$	ε^2
19X0	1.2550	-.0550	.00302500
19X1	1.3675	.0325	.00105625
19X2	1.5025	-.0025	.00000625
19X3	1.7725	.0275	.00075625
19X4	1.5700	-.0700	.00490000
19X5	1.7275	.0725	.00525625
19X6	1.8400	.0600	.00360000
19X7	2.0875	-.0875	.00765625
			.02625625

$$\text{Var}(\varepsilon) = \sigma_\varepsilon^2 = .02625625/7 = .00375$$

$$r^2 = (\sigma_Y^2 - \sigma_\varepsilon^2)/\sigma_Y^2 = (.077-.00375)/.077 = .951$$

Thus, 95.1 percent of the variation in inventory is explained by the regression equation.

10.6 The Keene Corporation has the following expectations for next year's economic outlook and its effect on the firm's sales.

Economic State	Probability	Sales
Good	.3	$7 million
Average	.5	5 million
Horrid	.2	3 million

a. Calculate the mean and standard deviation of the probability distribution.

b. If sales fall below $3 million, Keene will have to default on its debt obligations and will be forced into bankruptcy. Assuming that the probability distribution is normal, what is the probability that sales will be below $3 million?

Solution:

a.

State	P_s	Sales	P_sS	$S-\overline{S}$	$(S-\overline{S})^2$	$P_s(S-\overline{S})^2$
G	.3	$7	2.1	1.8	3.24	.972
A	.5	5	2.5	-.2	.04	.020
H	.2	3	0.6	-2.2	4.84	.968
			$\overline{S}$ = 5.2		σ^2 =	1.960
					σ =	1.4

b. $Z = \frac{x-\mu}{\sigma} = \frac{3-5.2}{1.4} = -1.5714$

From a table of normal values, Z = -1.5714 represents a cumulative probability of .5 - .4418 = .0582 = 5.82% that sales will fall below $3 million.

10.7 Farmers' Friend Insurance Company has given you a quote of $600 for fire insurance for 1 year on your new $200,000 home. The probability that your home will be destroyed by fire or incur damages of $200,000 in any 12-month period is 0.0005.

a. What is the insurance company's expected gain on the sale of the policy?

b. If the probability of a $200,000 loss is 0.005, is it likely that Farmers' Friend would still offer you the same policy at the same premium?

Solution:

a.

p_i	Insurance claim
.9995	0
.0005	$200,000

$$E(\text{claim}) = \sum_{i=1}^{N} p_i X_i$$

$$= .9995(0) + .0005(200{,}000)$$

$$= \$100$$

$$E(\text{gain}) = \text{Premium} - E(\text{claim})$$

$$= \$600 - \$100$$

$$= \$500$$

b.

p_i	Insurance claim
.995	0
.005	$200,000

$$E(\text{claim}) = .995(0) + .005(200{,}000)$$

$$= \$1{,}000$$

$$E(\text{gain}) = \text{Premium} - E(\text{claim})$$

$$= \$600 - \$1{,}000$$

$$= -\$400$$

Since the outcome for the insurance company is an expected loss of $400, it is highly unlikely that they would offer you the same policy at the same premium under the higher assumed probability of loss.

PART FOUR. WORKING CAPITAL MANAGEMENT

CHAPTER 11

WORKING CAPITAL POLICY

Theme: Working capital is a firm's investment in short-term assets. Working capital management involves a large portion of the firm's total assets; more than half the typical firm's total investment is in current assets. This chapter focuses on principles and techniques used for effective control of overall working capital management.

I. Working Capital Management is Important for These Reasons:
   A. A large proportion of the financial manager's time is allocated to working capital management.
   B. More than half of the total assets are typically invested in current assets.
   C. The relation between sales growth and the need to invest in current assets is close and direct. For example, if a firm's average collection period is 30 days and its credit sales are $2,000 per day, it has an investment of $60,000 in accounts receivable. If sales rise to $3,000 per day, the investment in accounts receivable will rise to $90,000.
   D. For the small firm, working capital management is particularly important.
      1. Investment in fixed assets can be reduced by renting or leasing, but current asset investment in receivables and inventory is unavoidable.
      2. Because they may have limited access to capital markets, small firms must rely more heavily on short-term credit, increasing current liabilities and reducing net working capital.

II. Two Decision Areas in Working Capital Management Affect Risk and Return.
   A. The level of current assets:
      1. For a given level of production and sales, a higher current asset level reduces risk, but also reduces overall return on assets.
      2. Expected sales influence both fixed and current assets, but only current asset levels can be adjusted to short-run fluctuations in sales.

3. Alternative current asset policies:
   a. Conservative--high current asset level. Sales may be stimulated, but return on assets may be lower.
   b. Average--moderate level of current assets.
   c. Aggressive--low current asset level. Sales may be reduced, but return on assets may be improved.
4. See Figure 11.1.

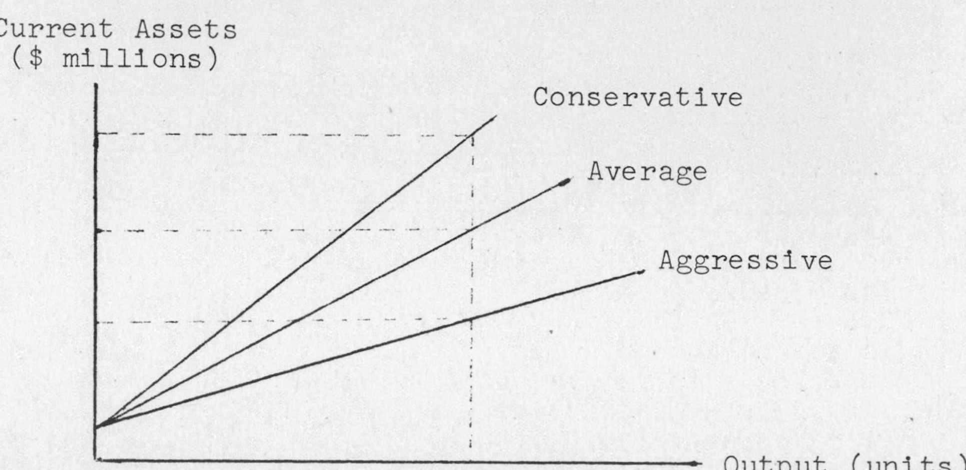

Figure 11.1 Relationship between Current Assets and Output

B. Working capital financing:
   1. As sales increase, funding is needed to acquire new assets.
      a. A steadily rising sales level over a period of years results in a permanent increase in current assets.
      b. Permanent assets--both fixed and current--should be financed from long-term sources.
      c. Fluctuating asset requirements, or temporary increases in assets, may be financed from short-term sources.
   2. Working capital financing policies parallel current asset level policies.
      a. Conservative--greater use of long-term funds for financing current assets. (See Figure 11.2)
      b. Average--use of long-term debt for permanent assets (current and fixed) and short-term debt for fluctuating current assets. (See Figure 11.3)
      c. Aggressive--greater use of short-term funds for financing current assets. (See Figure 11.4)
   3. To analyze decisions in working capital management requires an understanding of the relative costs and risks of short-term and long-term financing.

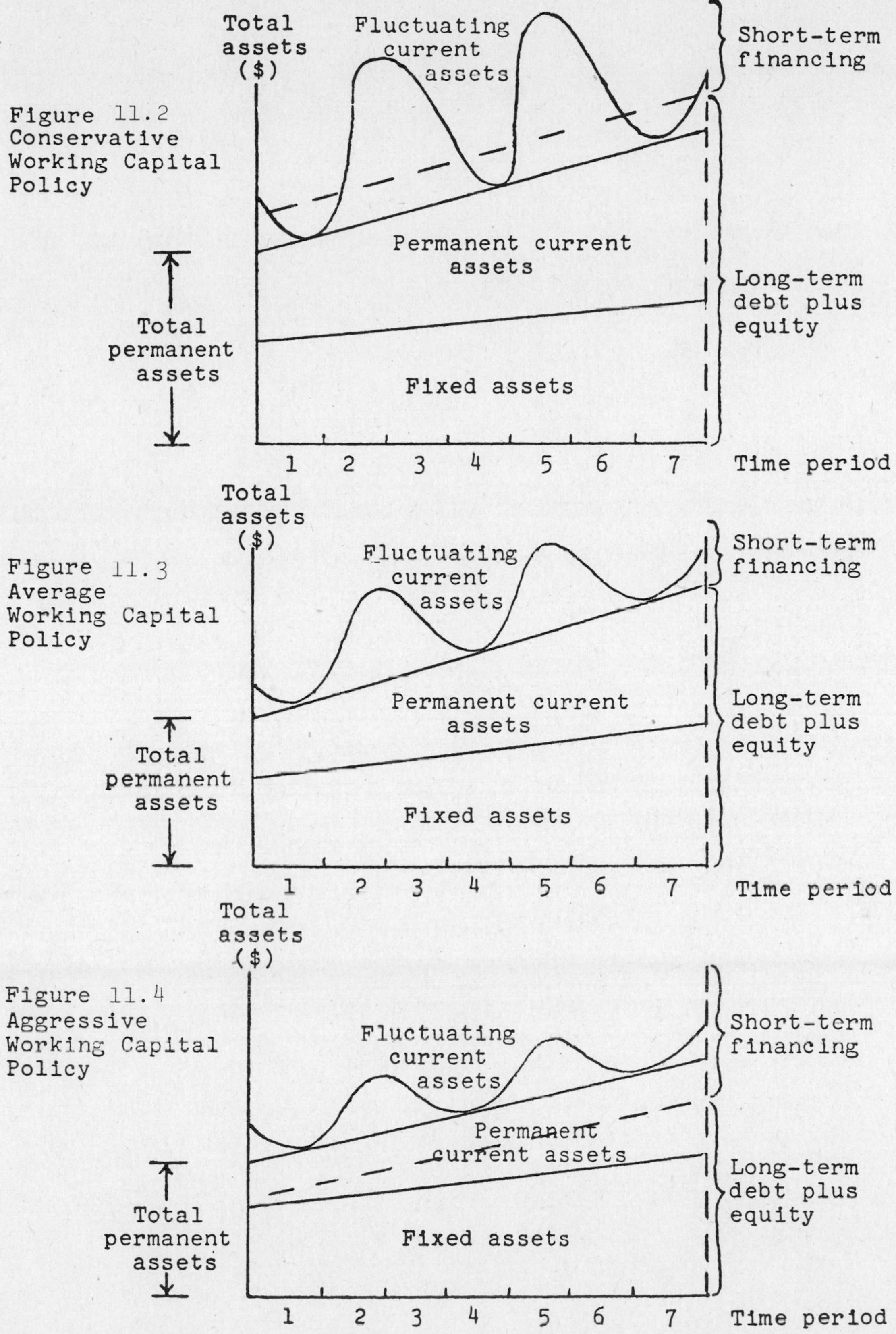

Figure 11.2 Conservative Working Capital Policy

Figure 11.3 Average Working Capital Policy

Figure 11.4 Aggressive Working Capital Policy

III. The Use of Short-term versus Long-term Debt.

   A. During periods of high and uncertain interest rates, firms may be reluctant to issue fixed-rate, long-term debt.
   B. Short-term debt, rolled over as it matures, is the equivalent of using floating-rate, or flexible, debt.
   C. If the health of the economy and of the firm are positively correlated with interest rate levels, the use of floating-rate debt reduces fluctuations in profitability.

Chapter 11 - Illustrative Problems and Solutions

11.1 The Pearson Toy Company wants to determine the optimal level of current assets for the coming year. Management expects sales to increase to $10 million because of a new line of toys based on a popular film. The company plans to maintain a 50 percent debt ratio and fixed assets will remain at $4 million. Pearson's interest cost on both long- and short-term debt is currently 12 percent. Bobby Joe Pearson, the Chief Financial Officer and the president's oldest son, plans to present three alternative current asset policies to the operating committee.

1. A conservative policy under which the current asset level would be 60 percent of sales.
2. The company's traditional policy in which current assets are 50 percent of sales.
3. An aggressive policy requiring current assets to be only 40 percent of sales.

a. What is the expected incremental return on equity under each alternative? Which policy would you recommend? (Assume an EBIT of 10 percent of sales and a 40 percent tax rate.)
b. How will the overall riskiness of the firm vary under each policy? Specifically, discuss questions such as the effect of current asset management on sales, expenses, fixed charge coverage, risk of insolvency, etc.
c. In this problem we have assumed that interest rates and sales levels are independent of the current asset policy. Are these assumptions valid?

Solution:

a. Return on equity may be computed as follows:

	Con-servative	Traditional	Aggressive
Fixed assets	$ 4,000,000	$ 4,000,000	$ 4,000,000
Current assets (sales x percent of sales)	6,000,000	5,000,000	4,000,000
Total assets	$10,000,000	$ 9,000,000	$ 8,000,000
Debt (50% of total assets)	5,000,000	4,500,000	4,000,000
Equity	$ 5,000,000	$ 4,500,000	$ 4,000,000
EBIT (10% x $10,000,000)	1,000,000	1,000,000	1,000,000
Interest expense (12% x debt)	600,000	540,000	480,000
EBT	$ 400,000	$ 460,000	$ 520,000
Taxes (40% x EBT)	160,000	184,000	208,000
Earnings	$ 240,000	$ 276,000	$ 312,000
Return on equity	4.8%	6.13%	7.8%

b. The more aggressive policies lead to higher returns. However, as the current asset level is decreased, some of this is represented by a reduction in the accounts receivable. This is usually accomplished through higher trade discounts, tougher collection policies or higher credit requirements for customers. These policies tend to reduce sales and may reduce total profits. However, a tighter receivables policy may also reduce bad debt expense. Lower current assets also imply a lower liquid assets, impairing the firm's ability to handle unexpected contingencies. Lower liquidity clearly increases the risk of being unable to meet fixed charges. Attempting to accurately quantify these potential risks and cost/benefit tradeoffs is extremely difficult.

c. These assumptions are not likely to be valid in the real world. However, it is difficult to quantify the exact relationship between current asset policy and sales or interest rate levels.

11.2 The Pearson Company (in Problem 11.1) chose to pursue the aggressive current asset policy. On the basis of expected sales of $10,000,000, Pearson's balance sheet appeared as below:

Assets		Liabilities	
Current assets	$4,000,000	Debt (12%)	$4,000,000
Fixed assets	4,000,000	Equity	4,000,000
Total assets	$8,000,000	Total claims	$8,000,000

In fact, actual sales turned out to be only $8,000,000 because of frequent stockouts and delays resulting in cancelled orders. Efforts to placate the customer ill-will caused by these problems had the effect of reducing Pearson's earnings rate (before interest and taxes) to 9 percent of sales.

What is the actual return on equity resulting from the aggressive current asset policy?

Solution:

Sales = $8,000,000	
EBIT = .09($8,000,000) =	$720,000
Interest expense = .12($4,000,000) =	480,000
EBT	$240,000
Taxes (40%)	96,000
Net income	$144,000

Return on equity = $144,000/$4,000,000
= 3.6%

The resulting return on equity is lower than that of the conservative current asset policy (4.8%) because of the adverse effects on sales and earnings.

CHAPTER 12

CASH AND MARKETABLE SECURITIES MANAGEMENT

Theme: Cash management has begun receiving increased emphasis due to inflation and high interest rates that reduce the real value of idle cash and provide incentives for the development of improved cash management techniques.

I. The Cash Management Function.
   A. Two central issues are involved in liquidity management.
      1. The logistics of cash inflows and outflows must be handled efficiently.
      2. A risk-return tradeoff is involved in determining the firm's level of liquid assets (cash and marketable securities).
         a. Liquid assets reduce risk, but generally yield less than the average return to the firm.
         b. The distribution of liquid assets between cash and marketable securities must also be determined.
   B. There are four primary reasons for holding cash.
      1. The transactions motive enables the firm to conduct its ordinary business--making purchases and sales. This provides liquidity to the firm so might also be called the liquidity motive.
      2. The precautionary motive refers to the need to meet fluctuating needs for cash or unexpected cash drains. These needs depend on two factors:
         a. The predictability of cash inflows and outflows
         b. The firm's ability to borrow on short notice
      3. Speculative motive.
         a. Primarily to take advantage of profit-making opportunities that may arise.
         b. Large accumulations of cash for speculative purposes are rarely found.
         c. Both the precautionary and speculative motives are largely satisfied by holdings of marketable securities, which may be regarded as "near money" assets.
      4. Compensating balance requirements of commercial banks represent minimum levels of cash that the firm agrees to maintain in its checking account, for example during the duration of a loan, or to pay for "free" bank services.
   C. Adequate cash provides several kinds of benefits.
      1. Sufficient cash permits taking trade discounts.
         a. When firms offer cash discounts for early payment, an implicit cost is involved if discounts are not (or cannot) be taken.

b. The cost of not taking discounts can be calculated as

$$\text{Cost} = \left(\frac{\text{Discount percent}}{\text{100 minus discount percent}}\right) \times \frac{365}{\text{Final due date minus discount period}}$$

For example, the implicit cost involved in credit terms of "2/15, net 40" is computed:

$$\text{Cost} = \frac{2}{(100-2)} \times \frac{365}{(40-15)} = 29.8 \text{ percent}$$

We may now calculate the APR:

$$\text{APR} = r_e = \left(1+\frac{r}{q}\right)^q - 1 = \left(1+\frac{.298}{14.6}\right)^{14.6} - 1 = 34.3 \text{ percent}$$

where q = 365/ final due date minus discount period

= 365/(40-15) = 14.6

2. Adequate cash is required to strengthen the current and acid test ratios, which are key items in the appraisal of the firm's credit position.
3. Ample cash also is desirable to take advantage of favorable business opportunities.
4. Adequate cash is necessary to provide sufficient liquidity to meet unexpected developments such as natural disasters.

II. Managing Collections.

A. Reduction of float is a key element in expediting cash flows.
   1. Float refers to the time interval between when a buyer of goods writes a check and when the seller has use of the funds.
   2. Sources of float include the following:
      a. Mail-time float--the interval between the mailing of a check and its receipt.
      b. Processing float--the time required to credit the customer's account and deposit the check.
      c. Transit float--clearing time in the banking system.

B. Decentralized collection points can reduce mail-time float and processing float.
   1. Field collections involve field sales offices receiving payments and depositing them in local (field depository) banks.
   2. In a lock-box system, customers mail checks to a post office box in a specified city. A local bank collects the checks, deposits them, and starts the clearing process before notifying the selling firm that payment has been received.

C. A bank gathering system consists of a network of banks to channel funds efficiently.
   1. Local depository banks receive field collections.
   2. Funds are channeled to regional concentration banks to be available for disbursement. Concentration banks usually handle the lock-box arrangement.

a. A concentration bank should be in a Federal Reserve Bank city.
b. It should have access to the bank wire fund transfer system.
c. It should be located so as to receive 80 percent or more customer checks within one day of mailing.
d. It should be competitive with respect to its fees.

3. The central bank is the overall control bank for the firm's pool of cash.
   a. Better control is achieved.
   b. Unused cash is minimized. Cash in excess of local needs is regularly transferred to the central bank.
   c. Marketable securities investment is facilitated.

D. Implementing a cash management system involves an expense to the firm.
   1. Banks impose service charges and/or compensating balance requirements.
   2. The expense is worth incurring as long as marginal returns exceed marginal costs.

E. Monitoring the flows of cash in the gathering system involves a number of elements.
   1. Fund transfers may be initiated by a central or local office or may be put on an automatic basis with transfers made whenever an account balance reaches a predetermined maximum. Cash managers should periodically audit automatic versus actual transfer amounts.
   2. The cash manager must be concerned with actual bank balances so as to avoid possible distortions caused by accounting methods.
   3. A rapid communications system must be developed to monitor available funds.
   4. Bookkeeping processes must not be allowed to interfere with the rapid deployment of cash.

III. A Transfer Mechanism is a Means of Moving Funds Between Banks.

A. Depository transfer checks (DTCs) are checks for deposit only to a firm's account at a particular bank. Electronic depository transfer checks (EDTCs) eliminate mail-time float.

B. Wire transfers make possible immediate availability of funds transferred from one bank to another.
   1. The Federal Reserve Wire System is available to all member banks.
   2. A private bank wire system is used by approximately 300 U.S. banks for transfer of funds, securities and credit information.

C. The cost of a transfer mechanism is related to its speed.
   1. Wire transfers are instantaneous, but cost $6 to $8.
   2. Mail DTC's cost $.40 to $.50, but may take 2 to 7 days.

3. By relating the cost of a faster mechanism to the value of the extra interest which could be earned by the funds after transfer, the breakeven transfer size can be found:

$$S^* = \frac{\Delta \text{ Cost}}{r\Delta T}$$

where

- S^* = The breakeven size of transfer above which the faster, higher cost mechanism should be used.
- Δ Cost = Cost of the faster mechanism minus the cost of the slower mechanism.
- r = The applicable daily interest rate.
- ΔT = The days required for the slower mechanism minus the days required for the faster mechanism.

4. This methodology has been criticized on several counts.
   a. Funds in the depository bank are assumed to have no value when in fact they earn service credits which may reduce bank service charges.
   b. Timing of transfer alternatives may eliminate the advantage of a faster mechanism.
   c. Availability time refers to when checks involving specified distances are presumed by a bank to be available to the payee. If clear time is longer than availability time, a dual balance situation arises with the same funds simultaneously available at two different banks.

IV. Electronic Funds Transfer Systems (EFTS).
   A. Electronic funds transfer system (EFTS) would create a nationwide computer network that would substantially reduce float time to hours or less.
   B. A telecommunications network linking financial institutions with sales outlets would permit rapid credit checking or payment arrangements with a minimum of written documentation.
   C. The goal of EFTS is to reduce the cost of paying bills.
      1. High fixed costs require a high volume of EFTS transactions.
      2. EFTS is in a developmental stage at present.

V. Managing Disbursements.
   A. The goal of managing disbursements is to keep cash on hand longer.
   B. A wide range of methods exists to accomplish this goal.
      1. Delay payments.
      2. Maintain funds in distant banks.
      3. Use of drafts--a draft must be submitted to the issuer for payment. Only then must the issuer deposit funds to cover the draft.

4. Use of float--banks have taken steps to reduce the gain from float, but companies that use float still have an advantage over those that do not.

VI. Marketable Securities.

A. Firms hold portfolios of marketable securities for two primary reasons:
   1. Substitute for cash--as a permanent buffer against cash shortages; most firms, however, prefer to borrow to meet such needs.
   2. Temporary investment--for seasonal surplus cash; to meet predictable financial requirements; to have the funds to respond quickly in volatile industries.

B. Criteria used in selecting security portfolios.
   1. Financial risk refers to fluctuations in price and return, with the extreme fluctuation being default.
   2. Interest rate risk refers to changes in the price of a security caused by changes in the general level of interest rates.
      a. Interest rate fluctuations generally cause substantial price changes in longer term maturities.
      b. As the marketable securities portfolio is used to supply current cash requirements, it is generally advisable to confine security selection to the shorter maturities.
   3. Purchasing power risk is the probability that inflation will reduce the purchasing power of the principal and income received on a marketable security investment.
   4. Liquidity or marketability risk refers to the breadth or thinness of the market for a security which will affect the price realized when sold.
   5. Taxability considerations arise because of differential tax treatment of:
      a. Dividend and interest income
      b. Capital and ordinary gains
      c. Certain types of government and municipal securities
   6. Generally higher relative yields can only be achieved at the cost of higher levels of risk.

C. Alternative marketable securities for investments:
   1. U.S. Treasury bills, notes and bonds
   2. Federal agency issues
   3. Short-term tax exempts
   4. Commercial paper
   5. Bonds of domestic and foreign corporations
   6. Negotiable certificates of deposits (CDs)
   7. Bankers acceptances
   8. Eurodollars
   9. Repurchase agreements
   10. Money market funds

D. Security prices are often quoted on a discount basis. The expressions below are for the calculation of the dollar price for discounted securities.

$$D = \frac{M}{360} \times B \quad \text{and } P = \$100 - D$$

where D = full discount
M = days to maturity
B = discount basis in percent
P = dollar price

For example, for a Treasury bill due in 150 days on a 10 percent discount basis, the dollar price is calculated as follows:

$$D = \frac{150}{360} \times 10\% = 4.167 \text{ percent}$$

$$P = \$100 - 4.167 = \$95.833$$

E. Effects of inflation.
1. During periods of tight money, no firm can be confident of receiving bank loans to meet cash shortages, so it must keep cash reserves for future contingencies.
2. Funds must be invested aggressively in order to protect them against inflation.
3. Certificates of deposit, municipal securities, and commercial paper offer higher rates of return than treasury bills and are thus increasing in popularity.

VII. Cash Management Models.
A. Managing the investment in cash and marketable securities is analogous to managing the investment in inventory.
1. A basic stock is required to balance inflows and outflows.
2. Safety stock should be maintained against unexpected needs.
3. Anticipation stock may be needed to meet future growth needs.

B. The economic ordering quantity (EOQ) is the optimum purchase size to replenish stock periodically.
1. There are costs associated with both too high and too low a level of stock, as well as costs of placing an order.
2. The EOQ balances these costs.

C. Applications to cash management.
1. The cost of too high a level of cash is the opportunity cost of funds tied up in a non-earning asset.
2. The costs of too little cash include the costs of running short (including the inability to take cash discounts), and the transactions costs of borrowing funds or converting marketable securities to cash.

D. The Baumol cash management model calculates the optimal level of cash and the optimal size of transfer from the marketable securities account to cash which minimizes the total cost of cash management.

$$C^* = \sqrt{\frac{2bT}{i}}$$

where C* = the optimal size of cash transfer
T = the total cash usage for the time period
b = the cost of each transaction in the purchase or sale of marketable securities
i = the applicable interest rate on marketable securities = the interest rate foregone by holding cash

1. The average cash balance for the time period will be C*/2.
2. The total cost per time period of maintaining the cash balance can then be calculated:

   $$\text{Total cost} = b(T/C) + i\ (C/2)$$

3. Baumol makes two major assumptions regarding the behavior of cash balances.
   a. Expenditures occur continuously.
   b. Receipts, or cash inflows, come in lump sums at periodic intervals.

E. The Miller-Orr cash management model assumes that changes in a firm's cash balance are random.
1. Cash balances are allowed to drift until they reach some high level, h, or a low level, r.
2. Cash is then restored to the return point, z, by investing excess cash in marketable securities or by selling marketable securities for cash.
3. Formulas to calculate the cost-minimizing z and h are as follows:

   $$z^* = \left(\frac{3b\sigma^2}{4i}\right)^{1/3} \quad \text{and } h^* - 3z^*$$

   where z* = optimal return point
   b = dollar cost per transfer into or out of marketable securities
   σ^2 = variance of daily changes in cash balance
   i = daily interest rate on marketable securities investments

4. The Miller-Orr model appear to be the most flexible and easiest to implement.

F. The Beranek model makes the opposite assumptions from the Baumol model with respect to cash flow patterns.
   1. Receipts are assumed to be continuous and uncontrollable.
   2. Disbursements are lumpy and periodic.
   3. Beranek emphasizes the costs of running out of cash and ignores the alternative of liquidating marketable securities.

G. The models cannot be used mechanically, and their success depends on the extent to which a firm's cash flow patterns fit the assumptions of the particular model.

Chapter 12 - Illustrative Problems and Solutions

12.1 Which of the following credit terms results in the highest cost if the discount is not taken?
a. 2/10, net 45
b. 1/10, net 30
c. 2/15, net 40
d. 3/30, net 60

Solution:

a. $\frac{2}{98} \times \frac{365}{35} = 21.28\%$ $\qquad r_e = \left(1+\frac{.2128}{10.43}\right)^{10.43} - 1 = 23.45\%$

b. $\frac{1}{99} \times \frac{365}{20} = 18.43\%$ $\qquad r_e = \left(1+\frac{.1843}{18.25}\right)^{18.25} - 1 = 20.13\%$

c. $\frac{2}{98} \times \frac{365}{25} = 29.80\%$ $\qquad r_e = \left(1+\frac{.298}{14.6}\right)^{14.6} - 1 = 34.31\%$

d. $\frac{3}{97} \times \frac{365}{30} = 37.63\%$ $\qquad r_e = \left(1+\frac{.3763}{12.17}\right)^{12.17} - 1 = 44.86\%$

Credit terms of 3/30, net 60 result in the highest effective annual percentage rate if the discount is not taken.

12.2 Finance Associates is short on cash and is trying to determine if it would be advantageous to forego the discount on this month's purchases or to borrow funds to take advantage of the discount. The discount terms are 2/10, net 30.

a. What is the maximum annual percentage rate that Finance Associates should pay on borrowed funds? Why?

b. What are some of the intangible disadvantages associated with foregoing the discount?

Solution:

a. The annual cost of credit terms of 2/10, net 30 is $\left(\frac{2}{98} \times \frac{365}{20}\right) = 37.24\%$. The APR is 44.58 percent. Any APR on borrowed funds less than 44.58 percent would make it advantageous to borrow in order to be able to take advantage of the discount.

b. Foregoing of discounts may lead to restricted trade credit and a lowering of a firm's creditworthiness.

12.3 Hope Baking Company has an outstanding account payable of \$400,000, on terms of 2/10, net 60. Because of a cash shortage, Hope would have to borrow \$400,000 to take advantage of the discount. If Hope decides to forego the discount, it will be able to pay off the entire account in 60 days without borrowing. The \$400,000 loan will be a 30-day note on which Hope would have to repay \$406,000. Should Hope borrow the funds or forego the discount?

Solution:

Cost of discount foregone: $\frac{2}{98} \times \frac{365}{50} = 14.90\%$

$$r_c = \left(1+\frac{.149}{7.3}\right)^{7.3} - 1 = 15.89\%$$

Cost of borrowed funds = r:

$$400{,}000\left(1+\frac{r}{12}\right) = 406{,}000$$

$$1+\frac{r}{12} = 1.015$$

$$r = .18 = 18\%$$

$$r_e = \left(1+\frac{.18}{12}\right)^{12} - 1 = 19.56\%$$

Since the cost of borrowed funds exceeds the cost of the discount foregone, Hope should forego the discount and pay the account within 60 days in the absence of significant intangible disadvantages.

12.4 Fonder Mills Company has a centralized billing system with customers scattered throughout the United States. On the average, it takes seven days from the time customers mail payments to the time Fonder Mills receives and deposits the payments. Fonder Mills is considering shortening the time lag through a lock-box collection system. They estimate that the time lag from customer mailing to deposit will be reduced to four days. Fonder Mills has a daily average collection of $725,000.

a. What is the reduction in cash balances that Fonder Mills could achieve by introducing the lock-box system?
b. How much is the lock-box system worth on an annual basis to Fonder Mills, if it has an opportunity cost of 10 percent?
c. What is the maximum monthly charge that Fonder Mills should pay for the lock-box system?

Solution:

a. Reduction in cash balances = Daily average collection x days reduction for collections
   Reduction in cash balances = $725,000 x 3 = $2,175,000
b. Annual worth of lock-box = Reduction in cash balances x opportunity cost = $2,175,000 x .10 = $217,500
c. Maximum monthly charge = Annual worth ÷ 12
   = $217,500/12 = $18,125

12.5 The Los Angeles field office of General Metals Corporation has sold a quantity of aluminum ingots for $25,000. General Metals wants to transfer this amount to its concentration bank in New York as economically as possible. Two means of transfer are being considered.

1. A mail depository transfer check (DTC) costs $0.60 and takes 3 days.
2. A wire transfer costs $8.70 and funds are immediately available in New York.

General Metals earns 16.2 percent annual interest on funds in its concentration bank. Which transfer method should be used?

Solution:

$$S^* = \frac{\Delta \text{ Cost}}{(r)(\Delta T)}$$

$$\Delta \text{ Cost} = \$8.70 - .60 = \$8.10$$

$$r = .162/360 = 0.00045$$

$$\Delta T = 3 \text{ days}$$

$$S^* = \frac{\$8.10}{(.00045)(3)} = \$6,000.$$

General Metals should use the wire transfer since the amount to be transferred is well above the breakeven size.

12.6 Bonwit Farms projects that cash outlays of $5,400,000 will occur uniformly throughout the forthcoming year. Bonwit plans to meet these demands for cash by periodically selling marketable securities from its portfolio. The firm's marketable securities are invested to earn 12 percent, and the cost per transaction of converting funds to cash is $40.

a. Use the Baumol model to determine the optimal transaction size for the transfers from marketable securities to cash.
b. What will be Bonwit's average cash balance?
c. How many transfers per year will be required?

Solution:

a. $C^* = \sqrt{\frac{2bT}{i}}$

$b = \$40$

$T = \$5,400,000$

$i = 12\%$

$$C^* = \sqrt{\frac{2 \times 40 \times 5,400,000}{.12}}$$

$= \$60,000$

b. Average cash balance = $60,000/2 = $30,000

c. Transfers per year = $5,400,000/$60,000 = 90, or every four days.

CHAPTER 13

INVENTORY MANAGEMENT

Theme: Financial managers are concerned with inventory as part of the overall cash flow cycle. In addition, the basic inventory control model (the EOQ, or economic order quantity) has applicability to other areas of asset management as well.

I. Inventories Must be Held by All Firms in Order to Operate. Inventory-to-sales ratios are generally concentrated in the 12-20 percent range, while inventory-to-total-assets ratios range from 16-30 percent. Management strives to minimize investment in inventories.

- A. Types of inventories.
  1. Raw materials
  2. Work-in-process
  3. Finished goods
- B. Determinants of the levels of raw materials inventories.
  1. Anticipated production rate
  2. Seasonality of production
  3. Reliability of supply sources
  4. Efficiency of scheduling purchases
  5. Nature of production operations
- C. Determinants of work-in-process inventories.
  1. Length of the production period
  2. Make versus buy decisions
- D. Determinants of the level of finished good inventories.
  1. Coordination of production and sales
  2. Credit terms and credit policies
- E. General determinants of investment in inventory.
  1. Level of sales
  2. Length and technical nature of the production processes
  3. Durability versus perishability or style factor in the end product
- F. Inventory analysis is generalized.
  1. Managing all types of assets is basically an inventory-type problem.
     - a. A basic stock to balance inflows and outflows is necessary.
     - b. Safety stocks for the unexpected are needed.
     - c. Anticipation stocks for future growth needs should be considered.
     - d. Optimum purchase sizes are economic ordering quantities (EOQs).
  2. Varying the size of investment causes some costs to rise and others to fall.

II. The Nature of Inventory Costs.

A. A larger order size results in fewer orders per year and higher average inventory.

B. Carrying costs generally rise with higher inventory levels.

1. Interest foregone on funds tied up in inventories
2. Storage
3. Insurance
4. Property taxes
5. Depreciation and obsolescence

C. Costs of running short generally decline with higher levels of inventory.

1. Lost sales
2. Loss of customer goodwill
3. Disruption of production schedules

D. Shipping, receiving and ordering costs consist of both fixed and variable components.

1. The personnel costs of a purchasing department are relatively fixed.
2. Other ordering costs will vary according to the number of orders placed.
   a. Costs of placing an order, including production set-up costs
   b. Shipping and handling costs
   c. Quantity discounts lost

E. Rising inventory levels at first cause total inventory costs to decline, until the carrying costs (which rise with inventory levels) offset the declining ordering costs (which decline with the number of orders.)

1. Decision rule: Choose that inventory investment where the curves for the two types of cost intersect; this will minimize the combined inventory investment costs.
2. See Figure 13.1.

III. The EOQ Decision Model Determines the Optimum Order Size to Minimize Total Costs.

A. Formula:

$$EOQ = \sqrt{\frac{2VU}{CP}}$$

where

EOQ = Economic ordering quantity, or the optimum quantity to be ordered each time an order is placed

V = Costs of placing and receiving an order

U = Annual usage in units

C = Carrying cost expressed as a percentage of inventory value.

P = Purchase price per unit of inventory

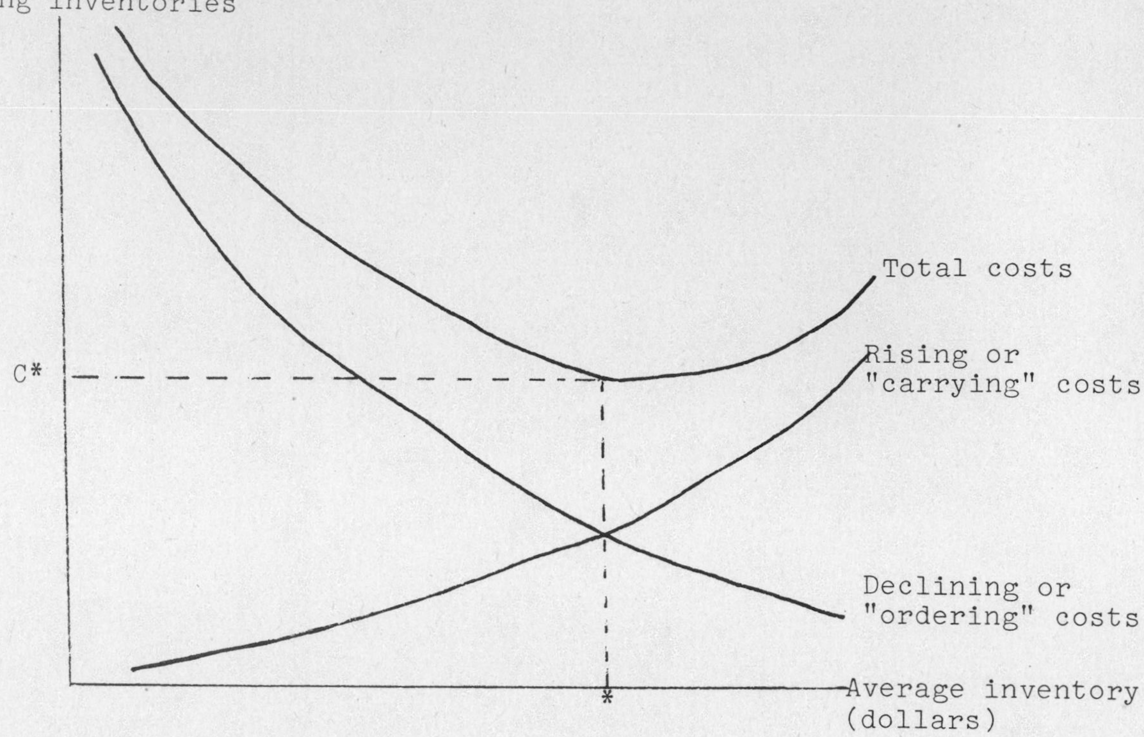

Figure 13.1 Determination of Optimal Investment in Inventory

B. The optimal average inventory, A, is found as

$$A = \frac{EOQ}{2}$$

1. The larger the sales per period or processing costs per order, the larger the EOQ.
2. An increase in sales calls for a less than proportionate increase in the EOQ.
3. The larger the inventory carrying charge, the smaller the EOQ.

C. Total costs of ordering and carrying inventory are

$$T = CPA + VN + F = CP\left(\frac{Q}{2}\right) + V\left(\frac{U}{Q}\right) + F$$

where T = total costs
A = average inventory = Q/2
N = number of orders per year = U/Q
F = fixed ordering costs, regardless of number of orders placed

and all other variables are as defined above.

IV. Use of the EOQ Model.

A. The basic EOQ model makes three assumptions:

1. Predictable sales activity
2. Constant rate of inventory consumption
3. Instantaneous order and delivery of replenishment stock

B. Under conditions of certainty, the instantaneous order and delivery assumption may be relaxed to find the inventory level at which an order should be placed, the reorder point. (With instantaneous order and delivery, the reorder point is zero.)

1. Find the daily rate of usage.
2. The lead time is the number of days required to place an order and receive delivery.
3. Reorder point = (daily usage x lead time).

C. With production of inventory, inventory builds up gradually over the period of the production run, rather than arriving in a lump sum as in a warehouse model.

1. Production run set-up costs are the equivalent of variable ordering costs per order.
2. The number of units produced per production run is the equivalent of the EOQ.

$$EOQ = \sqrt{\frac{2URV}{CP(R-U)}}$$

where R = annual production rate

3. Production results in lower average inventory and lower inventory costs, <u>ceteris paribus</u>, due to continuous rather than intermittent replenishment.

$$A = \frac{Q}{2}\left(1-\frac{U}{R}\right)$$

D. Because neither demand, rate of usage nor order lead time can always be known with certainty, firms add a <u>safety stock</u> to avoid running out of inventory and suffering sales losses.

1. The optimal level of safety stock is where the probable cost of running out of inventory is just offset by the cost of carrying the additional inventory.
2. The costs of a <u>stock-out</u> include:
   a. Customer ill-will
   b. Production delays
   c. Lost sales
3. The probability of a stock-out is influenced by fluctuations in usage rate and delivery time.
4. Inclusion of a safety stock does not affect the EOQ.
   a. The average inventory with safety stock is

$$A = \frac{EOQ}{2} + \text{safety stock}$$

b. The order point is increased by the amount of safety stock.
c. Total inventory costs are increased by the carrying costs of the safety stock, so that minimal total costs will be to the right of the intersection of rising (carrying) and declining (ordering) costs.

E. An increase in sales results in a less than proportional increase in inventories.

V. Effects of Inflation on EOQ.

A. Values used in the EOQ equation may not remain constant for an appreciable length of time.
B. A firm needs more flexible inventory management so it can take advantage of bargains and provide for future contingencies.
C. The basic logic for inventory models is still valid, only finding the optimum becomes more difficult.

Chapter 13 - Illustrative Problems and Solutions

13.1 Given the following information:

Annual demand: 100,000 units
Cost per order placed: $35
Carrying cost for inventory: 25% annually
Price per unit: $1.00

a. Complete the following table.

Order size (units)	1,000	3,000	5,000	7,000	10,000
Number of orders					
Average inventory (units)					
Carrying cost ($)					
Ordering cost ($)					
Total cost ($)					

b. What is the EOQ?

Solution:

a.

Order size (units)	1,000	3,000	5,000	7,000	10,000
Number of orders	100	34	20	15	10
Average inventory (units)	500	1,500	2,500	3,500	5,000
Carrying cost ($)	125	375	625	875	1,250
Ordering cost ($)	3,500	1,190	700	525	350
Total cost ($)	3,625	1,565	1,325	1,400	1,600

b.

$$EOQ = \sqrt{\frac{2VU}{CP}}$$

U = 100,000
V = $35 per order
C = 25%
P = $1.00

$$EOQ = \sqrt{\frac{2(\$35)(100,000)}{(.25)(1.00)}} = 5,291.5$$

$$\cong 5,292 \text{ units}$$

13.2 Advanced Microcircuits Inc. operates in the very competitive market for semiconductor chips. The president of the company, Mr. Chips, is very sensitive to the loss of customer goodwill caused by stock-outs. He has ordered his warehouse manager to maintain a safety stock of 100,000 units. Annual sales are expected to be 5 million units. The price of manufacturing a semiconductor is $1.50. The cost of holding inventory is 40% because of the high rate of obsolescense. The costs of scheduling a production run are $1,500.

a. What is the economic size of a production run? (Hint: solve for the EOQ.)
b. What are total annual inventory costs?
c. If the safety stock were reduced to 50,000 units, what effect would this have on total inventory costs?
d. If the cost of a production run increases to $4,500, what is the optimal production quantity?
e. If the fixed cost of a production run is $1,500, but the manufacturing cost of a semiconductor drops to 25¢, what is the optimal production quantity?

Solution:

a. When goods are to be manufactured rather than purchased, the EOQ formula can be used to approximate the optimal size of a production run. The manufacturing cost is equivalent to the purchase price of a good. The fixed costs of starting a production run can be viewed as the cost of ordering product. In this example:

U = 5,000,000 units
P = $1.50/unit
V = Cost of production run = $1,500
C = 40 percent

Economic size of a production run = EOQ

$$EOQ = \sqrt{\frac{2VU}{CP}} = \sqrt{\frac{2(\$1,500)(5 \text{ million})}{(.40)(\$1.50)}} = 158,114 \text{ units}$$

b. Annual inventory costs:

Number of production runs: $\frac{5,000,000}{158,114} = 31.6$

x cost per production runs	= $1,500
"Ordering" costs	$47,400

Average inventory (units) = $\frac{158,114}{2} + 100,000 = \$179,057$

x price per unit	$1.50
Average inventory ($)	$268,586
x carrying cost percentage	.40
Carrying costs	$107,434

Total costs = $47,400 + $107,434
= $154,834

c. Average inventory (units) = $\frac{158,114}{2}$ + 50,000 = \$129,057

x price per unit	=	\$1.50
Average inventory (\$)		\$193,586
x carrying cost percentage		.40
Carrying costs		\$ 77,434

Total costs = \$47,400 + \$77,434
= \$124,834

d. Substituting V = \$4,500,

$$EOQ = \sqrt{\frac{2(\$4,500)(5 \text{ million})}{(.40)(\$1.50)}} = 273,861 \text{ units}$$

e. V = \$1,500, P = \$.25

$$EOQ = \sqrt{\frac{2(\$1,500)(5 \text{ million})}{(.40)(.25)}} = 387,298 \text{ units}$$

This problem illustrates the sensitivity of the EOQ model to changes in ordering costs or product costs. In the real world, these are the parameters which are likely to exhibit the greatest variance.

13.3 The Petrox Company uses 12,000 electronic memories annually in its products. These memories are needed at a constant rate throughout the year. The purchasing manager for Petrox, Joe Stove, recently called to place his regular order with their supplier of these memories, Hasty Electronics. The sales manager at Hasty said that his company was facing a cash crunch because of poor current asset management. He then offered Mr. Stove a one-time 5 percent discount if Petrox would order 6,000 units. Petrox usually pays \$10 each for these memories. The costs of ordering are \$104 per shipment and the inventory holding costs are 25 percent annually.

a. What is the normal EOQ for Petrox at the \$10 price?
b. What would be the incremental carrying costs of inventory for 6 months if Mr. Stove buys 6,000 units?
c. What are ordering cost savings of a 6,000 unit purchase?
d. Should Mr. Stove accept the offer?
e. At what price discount would Mr. Stove be indifferent to the offer?

Solution:

a. U = 12,000 units
C = 25%
P = \$10
V = \$104

$$EOQ = \sqrt{\frac{2(\$104)(12,000)}{(.25)(\$10)}}$$

$$= \sqrt{998,400} \approx 1,000 \text{ units}$$

b.

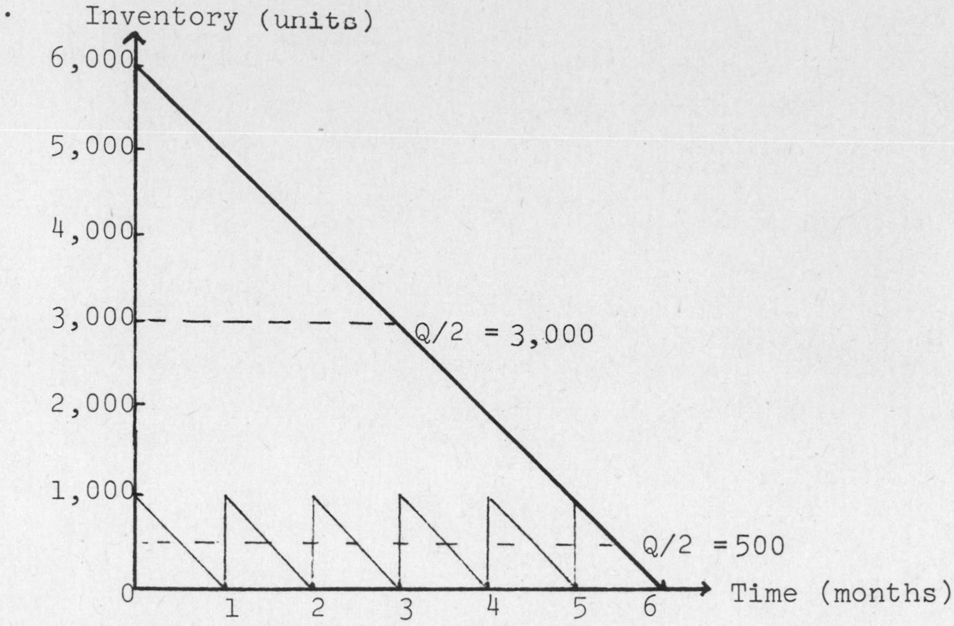

The graph above illustrates the pattern of inventory for the next 6 months under each alternative. If 6,000 units are purchased, then the average inventory level will be Q/2 = 3,000 units. If the normal pattern of purchase is maintained, then the average inventory level will be Q/2 = 500 units.

Since total inventory holding costs
= (Av. inventory)(Price of unit)(Holding cost percentage)

Incremental inventory holding costs for half of year $= 3{,}000(\$9.50)\left(\frac{.25}{2}\right) - 500(\$10)\left(\frac{.25}{2}\right)$

$= \$3{,}562.50 - \$625$

ΔInventory costs = \$2,937.50

c. Mr. Stove would place only one order rather than the usual 6 during this period. The ordering cost savings are therefore:

5(\$104) = \$520

d. The additional costs incurred by Petrox would be:

Δ Inventory holding costs =	\$2,937.50
- Ordering cost savings	520.00
Net cost	\$2,417.50

The savings realized by Petrox are:

$$6{,}000 \text{ units} \times \$10 \times 5\% \text{ discount}$$
$$= \$60{,}000(.05)$$
$$= \$3{,}000$$

Based on this information alone, the net benefit to Petrox is \$3,000 - \$2,417.50 = \$582.50. Mr. Stove should make the bulk purchase.

e. To find the point at which Petrox will be indifferent, set the incremental savings equal to the incremental costs and solve for x, the critical discount rate.

$$3{,}000\left(\frac{.25}{2}\right)(10-10x) - 500\left(\frac{.25}{2}\right)(10) - 520 = 6{,}000(10)(x)$$

$$3{,}750 - 3{,}750x - 1{,}145 = 60{,}000x$$

$$2{,}605 = 63{,}750x$$

$$x = .0409 = 4.09\%$$

13.4 The Dai-Wo Company of Taiwan assembles television sets from components manufactured elsewhere. Dai-Wo purchases 112,500 tuners annually from an Australian firm. The tuners cost \$25 each, and 5 weeks are required for delivery from the time an order is placed. Fixed costs are \$50 per order and carrying costs are 20 percent.

a. What is the EOQ for the tuners?
b. How often must Dai-Wo place an order?
c. If Dai-wo wants to maintain a safety stock of 5,000 units, at what inventory level should an order be placed?

Solution:

a. $$\text{EOQ} = \sqrt{\frac{2VU}{CP}}$$

$$= \sqrt{\frac{2(\$50)(112{,}500)}{(.20)(\$25)}}$$

$$= \sqrt{2{,}250{,}000}$$

$$= 1{,}500 \text{ units}$$

b. Orders per year = 112,500/1,500 = 75

365/75 = 4.9 or one order approximately every 5 days.

c. Reorder point = Safety stock + (daily usage x lead time) - goods in transit

Safety stock = 5,000 units
Daily usage = 112,500/365 = 308
Lead time = 35 days

Goods in transit = 6 x 1,500 = 9,000
See below:

O#1 = Order number 1, etc.

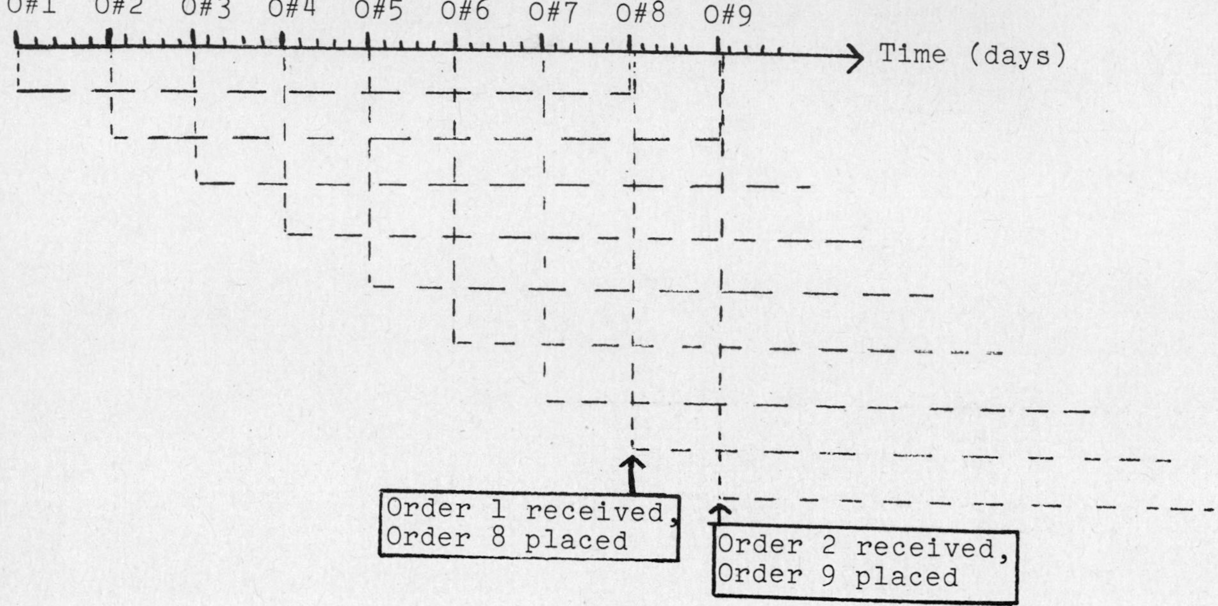

At O#8, steady-state is reached; from this point forward, every 5 days on the same day an order is placed, the order placed 5 weeks earlier is received, and 6 orders are in transit.

Reorder point = 5,000 + (308x35) - 9,000
= 5,000 + 10,780 - 9,000
= 6,780 units

Dai-Wo should reorder when inventory is down to 6,780 units.

CHAPTER 14

CREDIT MANAGEMENT AND POLICY

Theme: Credit and collection policies become increasingly important during a period of persistent inflation. New approaches to the analysis of credit policy decisions have led to a greater understanding of this vital area.

I. Management of Accounts Receivable.
   A. Determinants of the level of receivables.
      1. Volume of credit sales
      2. Average period between sales and collections which is dependent upon:
         a. Economic conditions
         b. Credit policy variables (controllable factors)
            (1) Credit standards
            (2) Credit period
            (3) Discounts for early payment
            (4) Collection policy
   B. Credit standards.
      1. The optimal credit policy involves relating the marginal costs of credit to the marginal profits on increased sales.
         a. Marginal costs include production and selling expense.
         b. Marginal costs relating to credit quality consist of:
            (1) Cost of bad debt losses or defaults
            (2) Credit investigation and collection expense
            (3) Cost of capital tied up in accounts receivable
      2. The evaluation of credit-risk--the five C's of credit.
         a. Character--the probability that the customer will try to honor his obligation.
         b. Capacity--subjective judgment or evaluation of the ability of the customer to pay.
         c. Capital--measured by the general financial position of the firm as indicated by financial ratio analysis.
         d. Collateral--represented by assets the customer may offer as a pledge for security.
         e. Conditions--the impact of general trends on the firm or special developments in certain areas of the economy.

II. Sources of Credit Information.
   A. Financial statements submitted by credit applicants are analyzed with special emphasis on liquidity, leverage and profitability ratios.

B. Credit information exchanges involve periodic meetings of credit managers of firms selling to firms in a particular industry for the purpose of exchanging credit experiences.

C. Credit interchange bureaus are formal networks that compile data from local credit bureaus and member firms; they provide credit reports to clients for a fee. Examples include:
   1. The National Credit Interchange System.
   2. TRW, a private firm which compiles credit bureau information.

D. Credit reporting agencies.
   1. Dun and Bradstreet, Inc.
      a. Publishes reference books giving credit ratings and measures of overall strength for 3 million firms.
      b. Clients can also purchase more detailed business information reports including discussion of business operations and payment experience.
   2. Some agencies specialize in coverage of a limited number of industries:
      a. National Credit Office
      b. Lyon Furniture Mercantile Agency

E. Banks can provide general background information useful to credit managers.

III. Analysis and Use of Credit Information.

A. Financial ratios are compared to industry norms.
   1. Trend analysis of liquidity, leverage and profitability ratios is emphasized.
   2. Multiple discriminant analysis may be used to develop a formal system for credit scoring.

B. Information on a firm's payment pattern is compared to two standards.
   1. The credit terms of the selling firm
   2. The average payment pattern for the customer's industry

C. Qualitative and quantitative analysis go into the development of the firm's credit policy.
   1. Credit limits set a maximum on the total amount of credit without a detailed review of the customer.
      a. It may be related to experience with the customer.
      b. If there has been no experience, it may be related to probable loss ratio.
      c. It may be a fraction of the firm's net worth.
   2. Risk class groupings can be developed on the basis of credit information indicating probable loss ratio as a percentage of total sales to firms in that risk group.
   3. The probable loss ratio may be related to the firm's margin of profit and overhead in relation to revenues.
   4. Credit terms to each risk class will vary according to the probability of default.
   5. Statistical techniques, such as regression or

multiple discriminant analysis,are more useful for firms that have a large number of customers with relatively small accounts.

D. A credit manager can play an active role in increasing sales by counseling customer firms.
   1. Credit analysis may reveal problems or deterioration of a firm's financial condition which reduce its creditworthiness.
   2. The credit manager alerts the customer firm to the problems and may assist in correcting them.
   3. Sales increase as the customer firm expands profitably.

IV. Terms of Credit.

A. Specify the period for which credit is extended, and the discount, if any, for early payment. The credit term "2/10, net 30" means that a two percent discount is allowed if the purchase is paid within 10 days; otherwise the entire amount is due in 30 days.
   1. The credit term "net 30" indicates that no discount is offered, and the full amount is due in 30 days.
   2. A credit term "2/10, net 30, May 1 dating," means that the effective invoice date is May 1. The discount may be taken until May 10, and the net is due May 30. Seasonal dating on invoices is used when sales are seasonal.

B. The credit period.
   1. Lengthening the credit period stimulates sales.
   2. The higher level of receivables caused by both the higher sales and longer credit terms increases the cost of carrying receivables.

C. Cash discounts.
   1. Increasing the size of the discount will attract customers desiring to take discounts.
   2. Average collection period will decrease.
   3. Cost of the discount will increase.
   4. Optimal discount point should be established at the point where costs and benefits are exactly offsetting.

D. Collection policy.
   1. The firm can attempt to collect past due accounts in several ways.
      a. Letter
      b. Telephone call
      c. Collection agency
   2. The collection process may be expensive.
      a. Firmness is required to prevent increased collection periods.
      b. Losses must be minimized.
   3. Optimal policy again is where costs and benefits are offsetting.

E. When goods are sold on credit:
   1. Accounts receivable is an asset item that appears on the books of the selling firm.
   2. Accounts payable is a liability item that appears on the books of the purchaser.

V. Evaluating Changes in Credit Policy.
   A. The Sartoris-Hill decision model uses an NPV framework to integrate all the elements of current asset management affected by credit policy.
      1. Evaluation of a credit policy change extends beyond its effect on the level of accounts receivable.
      2. Interrelationships between credit policy, production and sales impact the timing and amount of cash flows.
   B. The model finds the NPV of one day's operations under the current and the proposed policies; the policy with the higher positive NPV is chosen.
      1. The basic model:

$$NPV_0 = \frac{P_0Q_0(1-b_0)}{(1 + k_0)^{t_0}} - C_0Q_0$$

where P = price per unit
C = cost per unit
Q = daily sales
b = bad debt loss rate
t = collection period
k = daily interest rate

         a. The subscript "0" refers to the current policy; the subscript "1" is used to refer to the proposed policy.
         b. Inventory is assumed to be purchased, or produced, and paid for on the date of sale.
      2. The model can be expanded to include changes in working capital requirements, trade discounts, inventory effects and the growth rate of sales, as well as any of the above variables, all simultaneously or in any combination.
   C. The value of the model depends on the validity of the data inputs.
      1. Estimates may be based on market research or on the basis of existing product line and credit policy combinations.
      2. The model can also be used in a sensitivity analysis framework to determine what level of reduction in bad debt losses, for example, would be necessary to justify a particular change in credit policy.

VI. Computers in Credit Management.
   A. The collection, analysis, compilation, storage and retrieval of data involved in credit management make it well-suited to computerization.
   B. Computer capabilities can enhance the effectiveness of the credit department staff.
      1. Analytical reports may be drawn on individual companies, groups of companies, or on the status of accounts receivable as a whole.

2. Computers can monitor delinquency.
3. Accounts approaching credit limits can be flagged.
4. Accounts exhibiting abnormal payment behavior may be detected early enough to avoid serious credit problems.
5. Selected credit decisions can be made on the basis of quantitative guidelines.

VII. Two Widely-Used Methods of Accounts Receivable Control--Days' Sales Outstanding (DSO) and the Aging Schedule (AS)--May Give a Credit Manager Misleading Signals.

A. The DSO indicates how many days' sales are represented by the accounts receivable balance.

1. $\text{DSO} = \frac{\text{Total Accounts Receivable}}{\text{Daily Sales}}$
2. An increase in DSO could indicate a problem with receivables collection.
3. DSO may be distorted by the level and pattern of sales, and by the averaging period used to determine daily sales.

B. The Aging Schedule shows the percentage of end-of-quarter receivables in different age groups relative to the time of sale.

1. A high percentage of receivables based on old sales could indicate a collection problem.
2. The AS can also give misleading signals if sales patterns are not level, or if the payment pattern varies.

C. The Payments Pattern Approach relates accounts receivable to sales in the month of origin.

1. A payments pattern indicates the proportions of a particular period's sales which are paid in that period and in each subsequent period.
   a. The balance fractions are the corresponding proportions remaining in accounts receivable for a particular period's sales.
   b. The payments horizon is the number of periods required for the initial period's credit sales to be completely collected.
2. The payments pattern approach is not dependent on sales level or pattern.
3. Once a consistent payments pattern is established, changes in payment behavior are obvious to the credit manager.

D. Carpenter and Miller build on the payments pattern approach.

1. The C-M model enables the credit manager to distinguish between efficiency variances (collection experience) and sales volume variances.
2. Variances may be calculated relative to the previous period or to some standard period.

Chapter 14 - Illustrative Problems and Solutions

14.1 The Putney Company is considering a change in its credit policy. Currently the firm sells 100 units per day at a price of $100. Each unit costs Putney $85. The firm offers a 2 percent discount for early payment; 35 percent of Putney's customers take the discount and pay at the end of 10 days. The remainder have an average collection period of 40 days, with a bad debt loss rate of 2 percent.

Putney's supplier has announced that it is raising its price to $90; Putney, in turn, plans to raise its price to $115 while simultaneously relaxing credit standards. Sales are expected to rise to 125 units per day; however, the percentage of customers paying within 10 days is expected to drop to 25 percent, with the remaining customers having an average collection period of 60 days and a bad debt loss rate of 4 percent. Putney's cost of capital is 9 percent.

Should Putney make the change, assuming its estimates are correct?

Solution:

P_0 = \$100 $\qquad$ P_1 = \$115

Q_0 = 100 units $\qquad$ Q_1 = 125 units

C_0 = \$85 $\qquad$ C_1 = \$90

d_0 = 2% $\qquad$ d_1 = 2%

D_0 = 35% $\qquad$ D_1 = 25%

t_{d0} = 10 days $\qquad$ t_{d1} = 10 days

b_0 = 2% $\qquad$ b_1 = 4%

t_0 = 40 days $\qquad$ t_1 = 60 days

$k_0 = .09/360 = .00025$ $\qquad$ $k_1 = .09/360 = .00025$

where P = price per unit
Q = number of units sold
C = cost per unit
d = discount for early payment
D = percentage of customers taking discount
t_d = collection period for discounted payments
b = bad debt loss rate
t = average collection period (non-discount)
k = interest rate

$$NPV = D\frac{PQ(1-d)}{(1+k)^{t_d}} + (1-D)\frac{PQ(1-b)}{(1+k)^{t}} - CQ$$

$$NPV_0 = .35\frac{(\$100)(100)(1-.02)}{1.00025^{10}} + .65\frac{(\$100)(100)(1-.02)}{1.00025^{40}} - \$85(100)$$

$$= .35\frac{9,800}{1.002503} + .65\frac{9,800}{1.010049} - 8,500$$

$$= 3,421 + 6,307 - 8,500$$

$$= \$1,228$$

$$NPV_1 = .25\frac{(\$115)(125)(1-.02)}{1.00025^{10}} + .75\frac{(\$115)(125)(1-.04)}{1.00025^{60}} - \$90(125)$$

$$= .25\frac{14,088}{1.002503} + .75\frac{13,800}{1.015111} - 11,250$$

$$= 3,513 + 10,196 - 11,250$$

$$= \$2,459$$

Since NPV_1 is greater than NPV_0 the change in credit policy should be made.

14.2 The Crane Manufacturing Company is considering a change in credit policy. Under the current policy, Crane sells 200 units per day at a price of $45 each. The average collection period is 60 days and the bad debt loss rate is 4 percent. Crane's gross profit margin is 30 percent.

It is estimated that the proposed new policy will reduce the average collection period to 45 days and will reduce bad debt losses to 3 percent; however, sales will drop to 175 units per day because of the higher credit standards. Crane's cost of capital is 18 percent.

a. Should the change in credit policy be made?
b. If not, what reduction in bad debt losses would be required to make the change beneficial?

Solution:

a.

$P_0 = \$45$ | $P_1 = \$45$

$Q_0 = 200$ units | $Q_1 = 175$ units

$C_0 = .7(45) = \$31.50$ | $C_1 = \$31.50$

$b_0 = 4\%$ | $b_1 = 3\%$

$t_0 = 60$ days | $t_1 = 45$ days

$k_0 = .18/360 = .0005$ | $k_1 = .18/360 = .0005$

$$NPV_0 = \frac{\$45(200)(1-.04)}{1.0005^{60}} - \$31.50(200)$$

$$= \frac{8,640}{1.03045} - 6,300$$

$$= \$2,085$$

$$NPV_1 = \frac{\$45(175)(1-.03)}{1.0005^{45}} - \$31.50(175)$$

$$= \frac{7,639}{1.02275} - 5,512.50$$

$$= \$1,957$$

Since NPV_0 is greater than NPV_1, the change should not be made.

b. Solve the equation for the value of b which will make NPV_1 at least equal to $NPV_0 = \$2,085$.

$$NPV_1 = \$2,085 = \frac{45(175)(1-b)}{1.0005^{45}} - 5,512.50$$

$$7,597.50 = \frac{7,875(1-b)}{1.02275}$$

$$7,597.50 = 7,699.8(1-b)$$

$$.9867 = 1-b$$

$$b = .0133$$

The new policy would have to reduce bad debt losses to below 1.3 percent in order for the change to be beneficial.

CHAPTER 15

SHORT-TERM FINANCING

Theme: Short-term credit is defined as debt originally scheduled for repayment within one year. The three major sources of short-term financing are trade credit among firms, loans from commercial banks, and commercial paper.

I. Trade Credit is the Largest Category of Short-term Financing.
  A. Purchase of materials or supplies on credit from other firms is recorded as accounts payable.
  B. Trade credit is a "spontaneous" source of financing in that it arises from ordinary business transactions.
  C. Credit terms are determined by the following:
    1. Economic nature of the product--shorter terms for:
      a. Higher turnover
      b. Higher perishability
    2. Seller circumstances--longer terms for:
      a. Greater financial strength of seller
      b. Larger size of seller
      c. Greater use of credit terms in sales promotion
      d. Higher degree of excess capacity of seller
    3. Buyer circumstances--longer terms for:
      a. Higher degree of financial strength
      b. Lower risks associated with the product.
  D. Cash discounts may be given.
    1. Savings from the discount frequently exceed the rate of interest on borrowed funds; therefore, trade credit can be expensive.
    2. The length of the credit period is influenced by the size of the discounts offered.
  E. Concept of "net credit."
    1. Trade credit is a source of credit for financing purchases.
    2. It is a use of funds to the extent that the firm finances credit sales to customers.
    3. Net credit extended is the difference between accounts receivable and accounts payable.
  F. Advantages of trade credit as a source of financing.
    1. It is convenient and informal.
    2. Its wise use promotes sound customer relations.
    3. A firm that does not qualify for credit from a financial institution may receive credit from the seller because of his greater experience and knowledge of the firm.
    4. The cost of trade credit may be higher or lower than bank borrowing.

a. Cost is commensurate with risks to the seller.
b. The buyer may not have better alternatives.
c. Sometimes the buyer has not calculated the cost of trade credit.

G. The importance of good supplier relations during inflation.
1. Suppliers become more selective when extending trade credit.
2. A firm must earn the confidence of its suppliers by:
a. Having good financial ratios
b. Paying promptly
c. Offering realistic plans for improving its situation when necessary

II. Commercial Bank Loans.
A. Importance.
1. Banks occupy a pivotal position in the short-term money market.
2. Banks often provide the marginal credit that allows firms to expand.
B. Characteristics.
1. Forms of loans.
a. Single loan
b. Line of credit--a maximum loan balance is agreed upon in advance, with the firm borrowing up to the limit as needed. May involve a commitment fee on the unused portion of the loan.
2. Size of customers--small firms account for 40 percent of the number (not dollar amount) of bank loans.
3. Maturity--concentration on the short-term lending market.
4. Security--high risk borrowers must provide collateral.
5. Minimum average balance--up to 15 percent of the loan may be required as a "compensating balance."
6. Repayment of bank loans--a periodic "clean up" of the borrowings is required for firms to demonstrate their ability to repay their loans.
C. Measuring the effective costs of bank loans.
1. The <u>prime rate</u> is the interest rate charged to a bank's most creditworthy customers, generally one-half to three-quarters of a percent above the Federal Reserve rediscount rate.
2. Smaller, financially weaker firms must pay higher rates and may be required to provide collateral.
3. Interest rates are quoted in three ways.
a. Regular compound interest--interest is paid at maturity.

$$\text{Effective rate} = \frac{\text{Interest}}{\text{Borrowed amount}}$$

b. Discount interest--interest is deducted in advance.

$$\text{Effective rate} = \frac{\text{Interest}}{\text{Borrowed amount less interest}}$$

c. Installment loans--the load is repaid in 12 monthly installments, each consisting of both interest and principal components.

Computed interest rate = r_c

Amount received = Periodic payment x PVIFA(r_c, n)

(i) Add-on installment loan:

$$\text{Monthly payment} = \frac{(1+\text{nominal rate})(\text{Borrowed amount})}{12}$$

Amount borrowed = amount received

(ii) Discounted installment loan:

$$\text{Monthly payment} = \frac{\text{Borrowed amount}}{12}$$

Amount received = Amount borrowed - [nominal interest rate x amount borrowed]

4. Compensating balances may increase the effective cost of a loan.
5. Fees may also be charged.

D. In choosing a bank, the financial manager should consider:
1. The bank's policy toward risk.
2. The availability of management counseling services.
3. The loyalty of the bank when the firm encounters difficulties.
4. The stability of the bank's deposits as a measure of possible repayment pressure.
5. A matching of the loan areas in which the bank specializes with the borrower's area of operations.
6. The maximum size loan a bank can make.
7. The range of financial and business services offered by the bank.

III. Commercial paper consists of promissory notes of large firms that are sold primarily to other business firms, insurance companies, investment funds, pension funds, and small banks.

A. Maturities vary from up to one to two years with an average of about six months.

B. Costs are generally one-half of 1 percent below the prime rate.

C. The open market for commercial paper is limited to firms which are good credit risks.

1. Advantages.
   a. The commercial paper market provides more funds at relatively low rates.

b. The borrower avoids the inconvenience and expense of financing arrangements.
c. Publicity and prestige are enhanced.

2. Disadvantages.
a. The amount of funds available is limited to the excess liquidity of the main suppliers of funds at a particular time.
b. A commercial paper borrower who is in temporary financial difficulty receives little consideration because of the impersonal nature of the commercial paper market.

D. Commercial paper issuers may be forced to use higher cost bank financing during inflationary periods since the size of the commercial paper market is limited to the excess liquidity of those firms which purchase commercial paper.

E. Bankers acceptances are another form of short-term financing.
1. A bankers acceptance is a check drawn by a firm and accepted by a bank to pay a specific sum to a third party at a particular time; that is, it is a bank guarantee of a draft drawn by a firm.
2. They are traded in an active secondary market.
3. They are usually backed by collateral.
4. The return to investors is comparable to the return on a good certificate of deposit.
5. Bankers acceptances are widely used on import-export activity.

IV. Use of Security in Short-term Financing.

A. Conditions for offering collateral or security.
1. The borrower's credit strength is not sufficient to justify a loan without providing collateral.
2. Lenders may quote lower interest rates for a secured loan.

B. Types of collateral offered:
1. Marketable stocks or bonds.
2. Real property and equipment are usually used to secure long-term loans.
3. Short-term assets may also be used as collateral.
a. Accounts receivable
b. Inventories

V. Accounts Receivables Financing.

A. Two major forms.
1. In <u>pledging</u> accounts receivable as security for financing no notification is made to the buyer of the goods, and the lender has recourse to the holder of the account receivable in case of default. The receivable is <u>not</u> sold to the lender; it is merely used as a security for a loan.

2. In factoring, the buyer of the goods makes payment directly to the factor who has no recourse to the seller of the goods in case of default. The receivable is sold outright to the factoring firm.

B. Procedure for pledging accounts receivable.
   1. A contract setting forth legal rights and procedures is agreed upon.
   2. The firm takes its invoices to the financial institution, where they are reviewed and either accepted or rejected.
   3. Upon acceptance, payment is made to the firm.
   4. When the buyer of the goods makes payment to the firm, the proceeds are turned over to the financial institution.
   5. Normally, the firms which use this service are relatively small.

C. Procedure for factoring accounts receivable.
   1. A legal contract is drawn up.
   2. The firm receives an order for goods.
   3. The purchase order is drawn up and sent to the factor for a credit check.
   4. If the factor disapproves the purchase order, the selling firm can make the sale, but the seller bears the credit risk.
   5. If the factor approves the purchase order, it is processed and the invoice is usually stamped with instructions to remit payment to the factor.
   6. For a small firm, the credit checking service of the factor can be utilized as a cost-saving device.
   7. Once a factoring agreement is in force, financing from this source takes place on a regular basis as described.

D. The cost of receivable financing.
   1. Interest rates on borrowed funds under receivables financing are usually above the prevailing prime rate.
      a. The credit rating of the borrower is usually below that of firms qualifying for prime rate loans.
      b. The processing of the invoices (receivables) involves additional expenses.
   2. The computed interest rate, r*, in pledging accounts receivables is found:

$$r^* = \frac{1}{(1/r) - (1/n)}$$

where r = nominal interest rate
n = annual accounts receivable turnover

   3. Factoring charges consist of two elements:
      a. A fee for credit checking of 1 to 3 percent.
      b. An interest charge (somewhat above the prevailing prime rate) on the funds provided by the factor.
      c. Also, where the risk is high, the factor may purchase the invoices at a discount from face value.

E. Advantages of receivable financing.
   1. It is a flexible method.
   2. The security provided may make financing possible.
   3. Factoring may provide the services of a credit department.

F. Disadvantages of accounts receivable financing.
   1. When invoices are numerous, administrative costs may be high.
   2. The firm is using a highly liquid asset as security.

G. In the future, accounts receivable financing will increase in relative importance as automation reduces the costs and increases the convenience of employing receivables financing. Credit card use is a prime example of a type of automated accounts receivable financing.

VI. Inventory Financing.

A. Major forms.
   1. Blanket inventory lien
   2. Trust receipts
   3. Field warehousing
   4. Collateral certificates

B. The blanket inventory lien gives the lending institution a lien against all inventories of the borrowing firm.
   1. The firm is considered a relatively poor risk.
   2. The firm is free to sell the inventories. This reduces the value of the collateral.

C. A trust receipt is an instrument acknowledging that the borrower holds goods in trust for the lender.
   1. The borrower may keep the goods in his possession, but he must remit the proceeds of the sale of the specific goods to the lender.
   2. Disadvantages:
      a. Must be issued for specific goods
      b. Other complex legal requirements

D. Field warehousing.
   1. Establishment requires two elements:
      a. Public notification of the arrangement
      b. Supervision of the warehouse by the lender or his agent
   2. Financing procedure.
      a. Goods are segregated in a "field warehouse" on the borrower's premises.
      b. Custodian describes the goods and notifies the lender of the delivery.
      c. The lender deposits funds for the use of the borrower.
      d. The borrower receives purchase orders and transmits them to the lender.
      e. The lender notifies the custodian to release the goods.

3. Nonperishable goods that are sold in organized markets are good candidates for field warehousing.
4. The costs for a field warehousing operation are relatively high.
5. Field warehousing is a good source of funds.
   a. Amount is flexible.
   b. It increases the acceptability of inventories as loan collateral.
   c. May result in improved warehouse practices.

E. A collateral certificate guarantees the existence of the amount of inventory pledged as loan collateral.
   1. No need for physical segregation of inventories.
   2. It allows financing to continue smoothly as inventories are converted into receivables.
   3. The certificate issuer provides a number of services to simplify loan administration.

Chapter 15 - Illustrative Problems and Solutions

15.1 Newton Corporation is negotiating a $100,000, one-year loan from Goodwill National Bank and Goodwill National has offered the following three alternatives:

a. An 18 percent interest rate with a 10 percent compensating balance and interest due at the end of the year.
b. A 21 percent interest rate with no compensating balance and the loan is discounted.
c. A 15 percent interest rate with a 20 percent compensating balance and the loan is discounted.

Which alternative will result in the lowest effective rate for Newton?

Solution:

a. $$\text{Effective rate} = \frac{\text{Interest}}{\text{Usable funds}}$$

$$= \frac{.18(100{,}000)}{100{,}000-(.10)100{,}000} = \frac{18{,}000}{90{,}000} = 20.0\%$$

b. $$\text{Effective rate} = \frac{\text{Interest}}{\text{Borrowed amount-Interest}}$$

$$= \frac{.21(100{,}000)}{100{,}000-(.21)(100{,}000)} = \frac{21{,}000}{79{,}000} = 26.6\%$$

c. $\text{Effective rate} = \frac{\text{Interest}}{\text{Usable funds-Interest}}$

$$= \frac{.15(100,000)}{100,000-.20(100,000)-.15(100,000)}$$

$$= \frac{15,000}{65,000} = 23.1\%$$

Alternative (a) has the lowest effective cost to Newton.

15.2 In Problem 15.1, suppose Newton Corporation needs the entire \$100,000. Compute the amount which must be borrowed for Newton to receive a net amount of \$100,000 under each alternative. Are the effective interest rates affected?

Solution:

a. Amount, X, which must be borrowed to net \$100,000 after compensating balance:

$$\$100,000 = X - .1X$$

$$X = \$100,000/.9 = \$111,111$$

$$\text{Effective rate} = \frac{\text{Interest}}{\text{Usable funds}} = \frac{.18(111,111)}{100,000}$$

$$= \frac{20,000}{100,000} = 20.0\%$$

b. Amount which must be borrowed to net \$100,000 after interest:

$$\$100,000 = X - .21X$$

$$X = \$100,000/.79 = \$126,582$$

$$\text{Effective rate} = \frac{\text{Interest}}{\text{Usable funds}} = \frac{.21(126,582)}{100,000}$$

$$= \frac{26,582}{100,000} = 26.6\%$$

c. Amount which must be borrowed to net \$100,000 after interest and compensating balance:

$$\$100,000 = X - .15X - .2X$$

$$X = \$100,000/.65 = \$153,846$$

$$\text{Effective rate} = \frac{\text{Interest}}{\text{Usable funds}} = \frac{.15(153,846)}{100,000}$$

$$= \frac{23,077}{100,000} = 23.1\%$$

Note that the effective interest rates are not affected and alternative (a) still remains the one with the lowest cost to Newton Corporation.

15.3 George Jacobs wants to borrow \$50,000 to expand his small business. The Friendly Finance Company has offered a one-year installment loan at a nominal interest rate of 14 percent.

a. What will the monthly payments be if the transaction is treated as an add-on installment loan? What will be the effective rate of interest?

b. Calculate the monthly payments and effective rate of interest if the loan is discounted.

Solution:

a. Add-on installment loan:

Amount borrowed	\$50,000
Nominal interest rate	14%
Add-on interest	\$7,000
Total	\$57,000
Monthly payment 57,000/12	\$4,750

Amount received = Periodic payment x PVIFA(r_c , n periods)

$$\$50,000 = \$4,750\left[\frac{1 - \frac{1}{[1+(r/q)]^q}}{r/q}\right]$$

$$10.5623 = \left[\frac{1 - \frac{1}{[1+(r/12)]^{12}}}{r/12}\right]$$

$$r/12 = .02076$$

$$r_c = 24.9\%$$

$$APR = (1.02076)^{12} - 1 = 27.96\%$$

Thus the effective annual percentage rate on the installment loan is 27.96 percent.

b. Discounted installment loan:

Amount borrowed	\$50,000
Nominal interest rate	14%
Subtract interest	\$7,000
Amount received	\$43,000
Monthly payment 50,000/12	\$4,166.67

Amount received = Periodic payment x PVIFA(r_c, n periods)

$$\$43{,}000 = \$4{,}166.67\left[\frac{1 - \dfrac{1}{[1+(r/q)]^q}}{r/q}\right]$$

$$10.32 = \left[\frac{1-\dfrac{1}{[1+(r/12)]^{12}}}{r/12}\right]$$

$$r/12 = .024$$

$$r_c = 28.8\%$$

$$APR = (1.024)^{12} - 1 = 32.92\%$$

Discounting the installment loan results in a lower monthly payment (\$4,166.67 versus \$4,750), but also results in a higher annual percentage rate. In both cases, the effective rate is about double the stated rate.

15.4 Clout Industries is having difficulty paying its bills and is considering foregoing discounts on \$200,000 of accounts payable. As an alternative, Clout can obtain a sixty-day note with a 15 percent annual interest rate. The note will be discounted. The trade credit terms are 2/15, net 60.

a. Which alternative has the lower effective cost?

b. If Clout does not take the discount, what conclusions may its creditors draw?

Solution:

<u>Trade discount</u>: Computed annual interest rate = $\frac{2}{98} \times \frac{365}{45} = 16.55\%$

$$APR = \left[1+\frac{.1655}{8.11}\right]^{8.11} - 1 = 17.8\%$$

<u>Loan</u>: Computed annual interest rate = $\dfrac{.165}{1-\left[\dfrac{.165}{6.083}\right]} = 16.96\%$

$$APR = \left[1+\frac{.1696}{6.083}\right]^{6.083} - 1 = 18.21\%$$

On an effective cost basis, Clout will be better if it foregoes the discount than if it borrows to be able to take advantage of it.

b. Foregoing of discounts may cause creditors to question a firm's creditworthiness and lead to restricted trade credit in the future.

15.5 Pioneer Mines Corporation is considering the following two alternatives for financing next year's tin mining operation:

1. Establishing a $1,500,000 line of credit with a 12 percent annual interest rate on the used portion and a 3 percent commitment fee on the unused portion. A $300,000 compensating balance is required at all times on the entire $1,500,000 credit line.
2. Using field warehousing to finance $1,200,000 of inventory. Financing charges are a flat fee of $5,000, plus 4 percent of the maximum amount of credit extended, plus a 9 percent annual interest rate on all outstanding credit.

Pioneer Mines has $300,000 available funds for inventory financing. All financing is done on the first of the month and is sufficient to cover the value of the inventory at the end of the month. Expected month-end inventory levels are as follows:

Month	Amount	Month	Amount
January	$ 190,000	July	$900,000
February	450,000	August	500,000
March	700,000	September	400,000
April	800,000	October	360,000
May	1,500,000	November	150,000
June	1,200,000	December	0

Which financing plan should Pioneer Mines Corporation select and why?

Solution:

Required Financing

Month	Line of Credit	Interest Charge	Commitment Fee	Field Warehousing	Interest Charge
January	$ 190,000	1,900	3,275	0	0
February	450,000	4,500	2,625	150,000	1,125
March	700,000	7,000	2,000	400,000	3,000
April	800,000	8,000	1,750	500,000	3,750
May	1,500,000	15,000	0	1,200,000	9,000
June	1,200,000	12,000	750	900,000	6,750
July	900,000	9,000	1,500	600,000	4,500
August	500,000	5,000	2,500	200,000	1,500
September	400,000	4,000	2,750	100,000	750
October	360,000	3,600	2,850	60,000	450
November	150,000	1,500	3,375	0	0
December	0	0	3,750	0	0
Total		71,500	27,125		30,825

Line of credit

Interest charge	$71,500
Commitment fee	27,125
	$98,625

Field Warehousing

Interest charge	$30,825
Flat fee	5,000
4% on $1,200,000	48,000
	$83,825

Pioneer Mines should select field warehousing because it offers the lowest cost.

15.6 Clay Ceramics needs $300,000 which can be obtained either through a bank loan or a factoring arrangement. The bank will charge 15 percent per year, discount basis, with a 10 percent compensating balance. The factor will purchase Clay's accounts receivable, advancing the invoice amount less a 5 percent commission on the invoices purchased each month. All sales are on 30-day terms. In addition the factor will charge an 18 percent annual interest rate on the total invoice price, deducted in advance. Under the factoring arrangement Clay will reduce its bad debt losses by 5 percent on the receivables factored, and will be able to cut the staff in its credit department for a savings of $4,200 per month.

a. What amount of accounts receivable must be factored to net $300,000?
b. How large must the bank loan be to net $300,000?
c. What are the effective interest rate and total dollar costs associated with each alternative? (Include the costs of bad debt losses and credit department expenses.)

Solution:

a. Accounts receivable to be factored = $\frac{\$300,000}{1-[.05+(.18/12)]}$

= \$320,856

b. Size of bank loan = $\frac{\$3-0,000}{1-(.15+.10)}$ = \$400,000

c. Bank loan:

Computed interest rate = r_c = $\frac{\text{Interest}}{\text{Amount received}}$

$$= \frac{.15(400,000)}{400,000-.15(400,000)-.10(400,000)}$$

$$= \frac{60,000}{300,000} = 20\%$$

Alternatively, $r_c = \frac{.15}{1-(.15+.10)} = 20\%$

Factoring worksheet:

Receivables factored	\$320,856
Less commission @ 5%	16,043
Less interest @ 18%/12	4,813
Net amount received	\$300,000
Costs per advance	\$20,856
Advances per year	12
Annual costs	\$250,272

Computed interest rate = $\frac{250,272}{300,000}$ = 83.42%

Dollar costs

Bank loan: \$400,000(.20) = \$80,000

Factoring:	Monthly costs:	Commission	\$16,043
		Interest	4,813
	Monthly savings:	Credit dept.	(4,200)
		Bad debt exp.	(16,043)
	Net monthly cost		\$613
	Annual cost		\$7,356

In spite of the vast difference in computed interest rates for the factoring arrangement versus the bank loan, the factoring arrangement should be chosen on the basis of dollar costs. The computed interest rate is inflated by the factoring commission. However, the dollar cost calculation takes into consideration that with factoring, Clay can avoid the expense of a credit department as well as its rather high bad debt losses of 10 percent.

Thus the factoring commission might be considered as a fee for the credit-checking and risk-bearing functions performed by the factor rather than as an interest expense. Note also that if the need for additional funds is permanent, Clay should perhaps contemplate long-term debt or equity rather than short-term remedies.

15.7 The Markell Company has annual sales of $4,000,000 and an average accounts receivable balance of $800,000. Markell is considering pledging its accounts receivable to provide needed funds. The terms of the agreement specify a 20 percent reserve to be deducted from funds advanced to protect against returns on disputed items. The nominal interest rate is 14 percent, to be deducted in advance.

a. What is the effective rate of interest implicit in the pledging agreement?
b. Calculate the annual cost of the pledging arrangement.

Solution:

a. Accounts receivable turnover = n = 4,000,000/800,000 = 5

$$r_c = \frac{1}{(1/r)-(1/n)}$$

$$r_c = \frac{1}{(1/.14)-(1/5)} = \frac{1}{7.14-0.2} = 14.4\%$$

$$APR = r_e = \left[1+\frac{.144}{5}\right]^5 - 1 = 15.25\%$$

b.

Average duration of advance	360/5	= 72 days
Periodic interest rate	14%/5	= 2.8%
Reserve	(.20)$800,000	= $16,000
Periodic interest charge	.028($800,000-$16,000)	= $21,952
Annual interest charge	5($21,952)	= $109,760

We can use the annual interest charge to verify the computed interest rate found in part a:

Net amount received	$800,000-$16,000-$21,952	= $762,048
Interest rate	$109,760/$762,048	= 14.4%

The APR is higher than the computed interest rate due to the fact that interest is collected 5 times per year, in advance of the issuance of funds.

15.8 Evaluate the following three options available to Sunny Fashions for meeting a temporary financing need of $400,000 for the month of July.

a. Establish a one-year line of credit for $400,000 with a commercial bank. The commitment fee will be 0.6 percent and the interest charge on the used funds will be 18 percent per annum. The minimum time the funds can be used is thirty days.

b. Forego the July discount of 2/10, net 40 on $400,000 of accounts payable.

c. Issue $400,000 of sixty-day commercial paper at 15 percent per annum. Since the funds are required for only thirty days, the excess funds can be invested in 12 percent per annum marketable securities for the month of August. The transaction fee on the purchasing and selling of the marketable securities is 0.6 percent of the fair value.

Solution:

a. <u>Line of credit</u>

Commitment fee	= (.006)(400,000)(11/12)	=	$2,200
Interest	= (400,000)(.18)/12	=	6,000
			$8,200

b. <u>Trade discount</u>

Discount foregone = (.02)(400,000) = $8,000

c. <u>Commercial paper</u>

Interest charge	= (.15)(400,000) $\frac{60}{360}$	=	$10,000
Transaction fee	= (.006)(400,000)	=	2,400
			$12,400
<u>Less</u> interest on marketable securities	= (.12)(400,000)/12	=	4,000
			$ 8,400

Foregoing the discount has the lowest cost.

PART FIVE. DECISION MAKING UNDER UNCERTAINTY

CHAPTER 16

PORTFOLIO THEORY: DECISION MAKING UNDER UNCERTAINTY

Theme: Portfolio theory is necessary to understand corporate finance because the firm is, in essence, a portfolio of risky assets and liabilities. The manager must select the combination of risk and return that maximizes shareholder wealth.

I. Portfolio Theory Deals with the Selection of Optimal Portfolios.
   A. The objects of choice are the set of attainable portfolios, or combinations of risky assets.
   B. The theory of choice concerns the way in which investors decide upon a portfolio within the investment opportunity set.

II. The Theory of Choice--Indifference Curves.
   A. Three possible attitudes toward risk are identified:
      1. Risk-seeker--given the same level of expected return, selects the investment with the higher risk.
      2. Risk-neutral--selects solely on the basis of expected return regardless of risk.
      3. Risk-averter--given the same level of expected return, selects the investment with the lower risk.
   B. Business managers and stockholders are generally risk-averters who prefer a higher mean and lower variance of return.
   C. Utility theory explains why risk aversion generally holds.
      1. Utility theory is based on the diminishing marginal return for money--that is, the second increment of money received brings less satisfaction (utility) than the first (equal) amount.
      2. The risk-averse investor gets more pain from a dollar lost than pleasure from a dollar gained.
      3. The expected utility of an investment, not its expected monetary value, motivates the investment decision.
   D. Indifference curves are a graphic representation of an individual's subjective attitude toward risk and return.
      1. Risk, measured by the standard deviation of return, is plotted on the horizontal axis.
      2. Expected return is plotted on the vertical axis.
      3. A single indifference curve is a map of all the combinations of risk and return which provide the investor the same total utility.
         a. Each individual has a family of parallel indifference curves representing the risk-return tradeoffs for different levels of total utility.
         b. If the individual can receive a higher return for the same level of risk, he will move to a higher indifference curve.

4. Figure 16.1 illustrates the indifference curves of two risk-averse individuals.
   a. Individual A is more risk-averse than individual B.
   b. Both individuals will have higher total utility on indifference curves farther to the left (for example, I_{A3} and I_{B3}); these curves offer higher expected return for a given amount of risk.

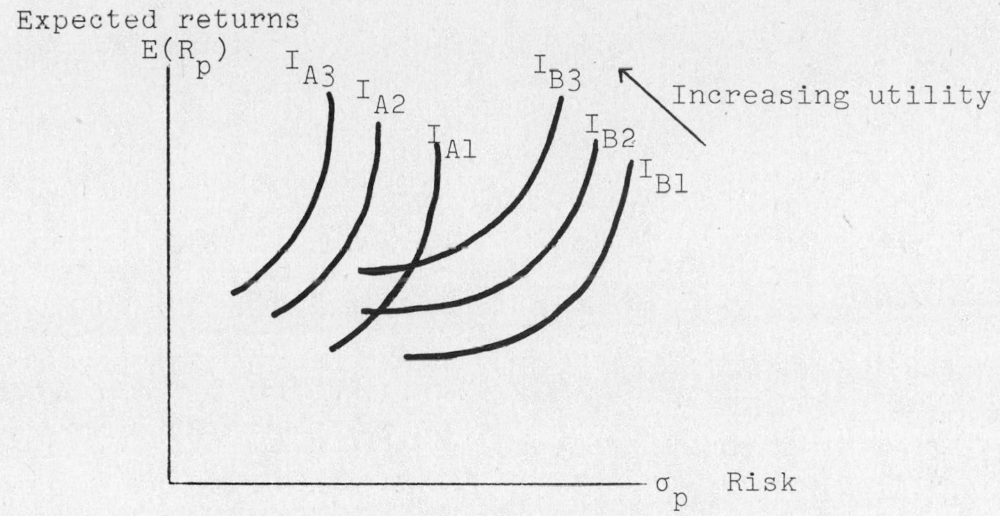

Figure 16.1 Indifference Curves

III. The Objects of Choice--The Portfolio Opportunity Set.
   A. Mean and variance (or standard deviation, the square root of the variance) are measures of return and risk for risky assets in isolation. (See Chapter 10 for formulas.)
   B. When assets are combined into portfolios, the mean portfolio return is simply the weighted average of the individual asset returns.

$$R_p = wR_A + (1-w)R_B$$

where R_p = return on the portfolio
w = percent of the portfolio invested in asset A
$1-w$ = percent of the portfolio invested in asset B
R_A = return on asset A
R_B = return on asset B

C. A fundamental aspect of portfolio theory is that the risk of an asset in a portfolio is different from the risk of that same asset held in isolation.

1. The risk of a portfolio depends not only on the variances of its assets, but also on the covariances between them.

$$Var(R_p) = w^2 Var(R_A) + 2w(1-w)Cov(R_A,R_B) + (1-w)^2 Var(R_B)$$

where Var = variance of returns
Cov = covariance between returns

2. The correlation coefficient, ρ, indicates how assets covary.

a. $\rho_{AB} = \dfrac{Cov(A,B)}{\sigma_A \sigma_B}$

b. $-1 < \rho < +1$

$\rho = -1$: Asset returns are perfectly inversely correlated; covariance is negative.
$\rho = 0$: Asset returns are unrelated; zero covariance.
$\rho = +1$: Asset returns are perfectly correlated; covariance is positive.

c. Whenever asset returns are less than perfectly positively correlated, the portfolio variance will be reduced by the diversification effect of offsetting returns.

$$Var(R_p) = w^2 Var(R_A) + 2w(1-w)\rho_{AB}\sigma_A\sigma_B + (1-w)^2 Var(R_B)$$

d. For all correlation coefficients other than +1, there can be found some value of w which will minimize the risk of the portfolio, σ_p. This value is calculated as:

$$w_A = \frac{\sigma_B(\sigma_B - \rho_{AB}\sigma_A)}{\sigma_A^2 + \sigma_B^2 - 2\rho_{AB}\sigma_A\sigma_B} = \frac{\sigma_B^2 - Cov(A,B)}{\sigma_A^2 + \sigma_B^2 - 2Cov(A,B)}$$

D. The set of attainable portfolios can be found graphically.

1. Given the correlation between assets, calculate the resulting portfolio mean and standard deviation for a range of asset weights.
2. Plot these attainable risk-return combinations on a graph to form the portfolio opportunity set. (See Figure 16.2.)

3. Portfolios exist to the right of curve VWXYZ in Figure 16.2, however, the curve VWXYZ defines the minimum variance portfolio opportunity set which provides minimum standard deviation (risk) for a given rate of return.

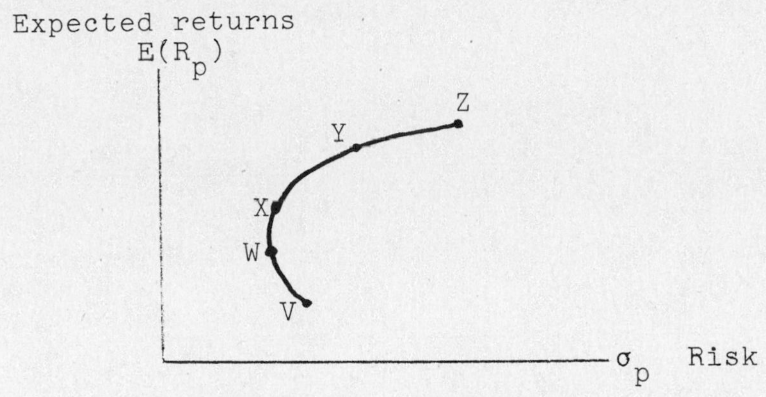

Figure 16.2 Minimum Variance Portfolio Opportunity Set

IV. Optimal Portfolio Choice--Individual.

A. An individual is endowed with a particular level of risk and return at point A on one of his indifference curves in Figure 16.3a.

1. The slope of a line tangent to the indifference curve at that point is the individual's marginal rate of substitution (MRS) between risk and return.
2. This subjective price of risk is the amount of additional return required by the individual to accept an additional unit of risk.

B. The slope of a line tangent to the portfolio opportunity set (see Figure 16.3b) is the marginal rate of transformation (MRT) between return and risk offered by nature.

C. Plot the individual's indifference curve on the same graph as the portfolio opportunity set. (See Figure 16.3c.)

D. If the individual's marginal rate of substitution is greater than the marginal rate of transformation, the individual is willing to give up more return to avoid risk than the market requires.

1. The individual can increase his utility (move to a higher indifference curve) by changing the mix of assets in his portfolio and moving along the portfolio opportunity set to point B in Figure 16.3c.
2. At this optimal portfolio, the individual's indifference curve will be tangent to the portfolio opportunity set, and MRS = MRT.

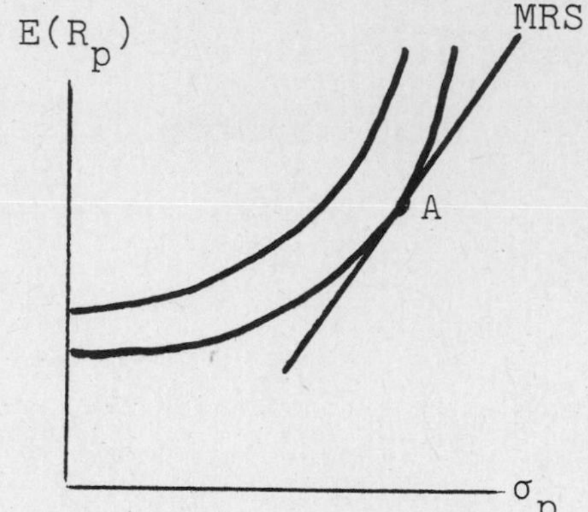

Figure 16.3a
Indifference Curves and the Marginal Rate of Substitution

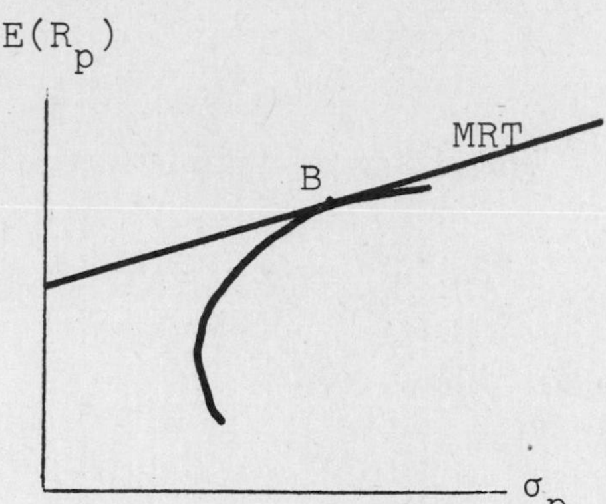

Figure 16.3b
Portfolio Opportunity Set and the Marginal Rate of Transformation

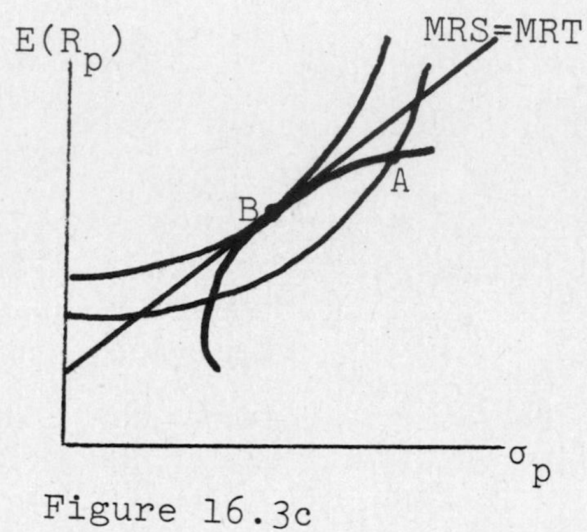

Figure 16.3c

E. Different investors will choose optimal portfolios of different risk depending on their degrees of risk aversion.
   1. All risk-averse investors will choose portfolios along the upper half of the portfolio opportunity set.
   2. This portion of the portfolio opportunity set offers the highest return for a given level of risk; it is called the <u>efficient set</u>. (See curve WXYZ in Figure 16.2.)

V. Optimal Portfolio Choice--Market Equilibrium.

A. We introduce borrowing and lending at the risk-free rate.

B. The opportunity set now includes all feasible portfolios made up of one riskless asset and one (or many) risky assets.

C. The Captial Market Line (CML) is tangent to the investment opportunity set along line $R_F M$.

D. In equilibrium, all risk-averse investors will choose their optimal portfolios from combinations of the riskless asset and the risky portfolio, M.

   1. The risky portfolio, M, is the market portfolio of all assets in the economy held according to their market value weights.

E. Opportunities to borrow or lend at the riskless rate combined with investment in the risky portfolio allow all investors to reach their highest possible indifference curves; that is, for each investor, the indifference curve that is tangent to the CML, and not necessarily tangent to the investment opportunity set. (See Figure 16.4.)

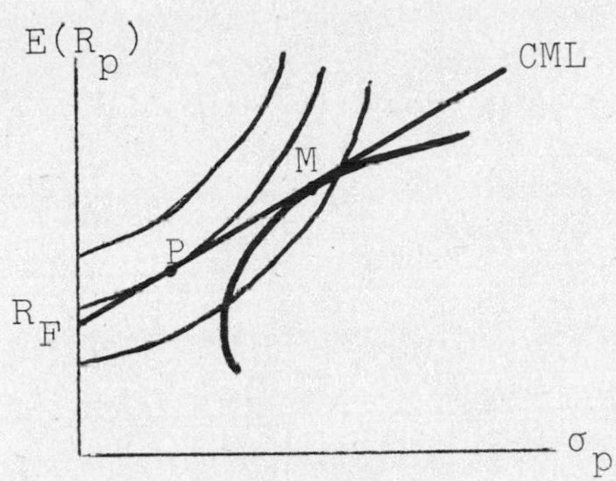

Figure 16.4
The Capital Market Line
(Point P is the optimal portfolio for the investor whose indifference curves are shown.)

F. The slope of the CML is the market equilibrium tradeoff between risk and return.
   1. The equation of the CML is:

$$E(R_p) = R_F + \frac{E(R_M) - R_F}{\sigma_M}(\sigma_p)$$

   2. The slope of the CML is: $\frac{E(R_M) - R_F}{\sigma_M}$

   3. In equilibrium, all investors will use the market price of risk as the appropriate marginal rate of substitution = marginal rate of transformation.

VI. Diversification Effects.
   A. The total risk of an inefficient asset (or portfolio) can be partitioned into two parts.
      1. Diversifiable or unsystematic risk.
         a. This type of risk can be virtually costlessly eliminated through diversification, that is, by combining the asset or portfolio with other assets with which it is imperfectly correlated.
         b. The market does not offer a premium to avoid this type of risk.
      2. Undiversifiable or systematic risk.
   B. As the number of securities in a portfolio increases, the standard deviation of the portfolio decreases.
      1. Portfolio risk decreases at a decreasing rate.
      2. Further risk reductions are small after about ten securities have been added to the portfolio.
   C. The systematic risk of a portfolio cannot be diversified away.
      1. A broadly diversified portfolio is highly correlated with the market portfolio.
      2. Risk arises due to general market movements.

VII. Summary of Portfolio Risk Analysis.
   A. Portfolio risk is measured by the standard deviation of its rate of return.
   B. The relevant risk of an individual security is its contribution to portfolio risk.
   C. A stock's standard deviation reflects both diversifiable (unsystematic) and undiversifiable (systematic) risk; only systematic risk is relevant and is priced in the marketplace.
   D. A stock's systematic risk is measured by the covariance of its returns with the general market's returns.

Chapter 16 - Illustrative Problems and Solutions

16.1 Graph the indifference curves of a risk neutral investor.

Solution:

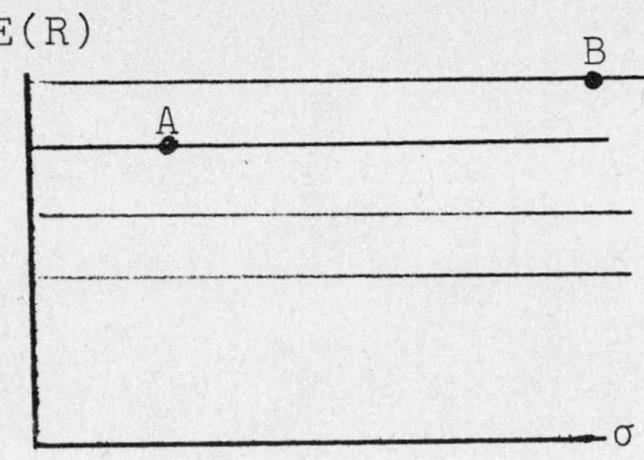

Since the risk-neutral investor is indifferent to risk, his total utility depends solely on the level of return. Thus, for example, point B above would be preferred to point A because it is on a higher indifference curve; its utility is higher even though its risk is far greater for only a small increment of return.

16.2 The figure below shows the family of indifference curves for risk-averse Investor I.

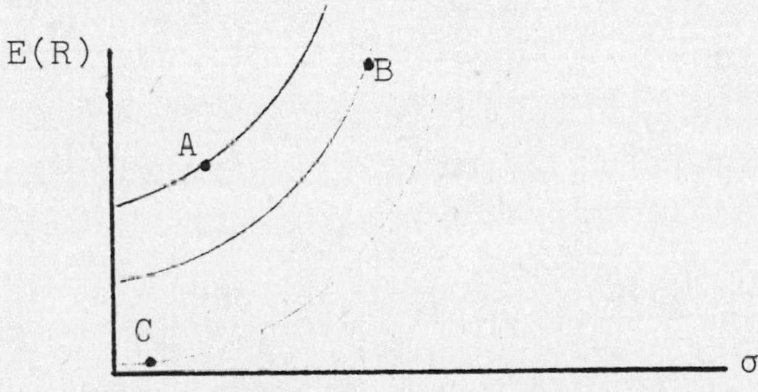

a. Which point on the graph would Investor I prefer?
b. Draw an indifference curve for Investor II who is indifferent between points C and B.
c. Which investor, I or II, is the more risk-averse?

Solution:

a. Point A will be preferred because it is on the highest indifference curve. Although point B has higher expected return, its risk is also greater, and its utility is less.

b.

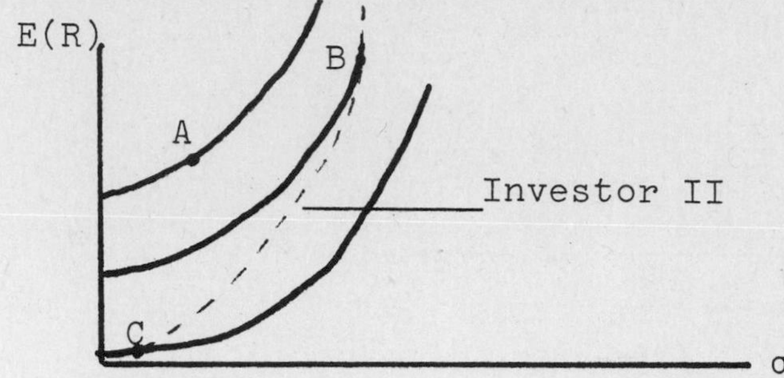

c. Investor II is more risk-averse than Investor I because his indifference curve slopes more steeply upward; that is, Investor II requires more return to compensate him for taking on additional risk than does Investor I.

16.3 Based on the following historical market data, calculate the expected return on the market, the variance of returns on the market, the standard deviation of the returns on the market, and the expected risk-free return.

Year	S&P 500 Price Index	Dividend Yield	Risk-free return (R_F)
1	79.58		.039
2	85.26	.0306	.041
3	92.48	.0320	.045
4	87.24	.0284	.049
5	91.93	.0307	.056
6	98.70	.0314	.068
7	88.45	.0324	.076
8	98.29	.0396	.084
9	109.20	.0340	.086
10	119.63	.0317	.119

Solution:

Year	(P) S&P Index	Capital Gain (Loss) $\frac{P_t - P_{t-1}}{P_{t-1}}$	Dividend Yield	R_M	$R_M - \bar{R}_M$	$(R_M - \bar{R}_M)^2$	R_F
1	79.58						.039
2	85.26	.0714	.0306	.1020	.0207	.00043	.041
3	92.48	.0847	.0320	.1167	.0354	.00125	.045
4	87.24	(.0567)	.0284	(.0283)	(.1096)	.01201	.049
5	91.93	.0538	.0307	.0845	.0032	.00001	.056
6	98.70	.0736	.0314	.1050	.0237	.00056	.068
7	88.45	(.1039)	.0324	(.0715)	(.1528)	.02335	.076
8	98.29	.1112	.0396	.1508	.0695	.00483	.084
9	109.20	.1110	.0340	.1450	.0637	.00406	.086
10	119.63	.0955	.0317	.1272	.0459	.00211	.119
				.7314		.04861	.663

$$\bar{R}_M = \sum_{t=1}^{9} R_M/9 = .7314/9 = .0813$$

$$Var(R_M) = \sum_{t=1}^{9} (R_M - \bar{R}_M)^2/8 = .04861/8 = .00608$$

$$\sigma_M = \sqrt{.00608} = .0780$$

$$\bar{R}_F = \sum_{t=1}^{10} R_F/10 = .663/10 = .0663$$

Note that in the calculation of the variance we divide by 8, not 9 because one degree of freedom has been lost since the variance calculation is dependent on the mean.

16.4 The Goodman Plastics Company has developed the following data regarding a proposed new product line:

State	P_s	Market Return (R_M)	Project Return (R_j)
1	.1	.04	.02
2	.3	.10	.12
3	.4	.15	.18
4	.2	.18	.20

Calculate:

a. The expected return on the project
b. The variance of project returns
c. The standard deviation of project returns
d. The coefficient of variation of project returns
e. The covariance of the project returns with the market returns
f. The correlation coefficient between the project returns and the market returns

Solution:

S	P_s	R_M	R_j	P_sR_M	P_sR_j	$R_M-\bar{R}_M$	$(R_M-\bar{R}_M)^2$	$P_s(R_M-\bar{R}_M)^2$
1	.1	.04	.02	.004	.002	-.09	.0081	.00081
2	.3	.10	.12	.030	.036	-.03	.0009	.00027
3	.4	.15	.18	.060	.072	.02	.0004	.00016
4	.2	.18	.20	.036	.040	.05	.0025	.00050
				$\bar{R}_M$ = .130	$\bar{R}_j$ = .150			σ_M^2 = .00174
								σ_M = .04171

$R_j-\bar{R}_j$	$(R_j-\bar{R}_j)^2$	$P_s(R_j-\bar{R}_j)^2$	$(R_M-\bar{R}_M)(R_j-\bar{R}_j)$	$P_s(R_M-\bar{R}_M)(R_j-\bar{R}_j)$
-.13	.0169	.00169	.0117	.00117
-.03	.0009	.00027	.0009	.00027
.03	.0009	.00036	.0006	.00024
.05	.0025	.00050	.0025	.00050
		σ_j^2 = .00282		$Cov(R_j,R_M)$ = .00218
		σ_j = .05310		

a. $\bar{R}_j = .15$

b. $Var(R_j) = \sigma_j^2 = .00282$

c. $\sigma_j = \sqrt{.00282} = .05310$

d. $CV_j = \sigma_j/\bar{R}_j = .05310/.15 = .354$

e. $Cov(R_j,R_M) = .00218$

f. $\rho_{jM} = Cov(R_j,R_M)/\sigma_j\sigma_M = .00218/(.0531)(.04171) = .9843$

16.5 The expected returns of the Ascar and Belker Companies are estimated as follows:

State	P_s	R_a	R_b
1	.20	(.11)	.20
2	.25	.10	.18
3	.35	.14	.16
4	.15	.18	.10
5	.05	.22	.08

a. Calculate the expected return and standard deviation for the two companies.

b. Calculate the covariance (Cov_{ab}) and correlation coefficient (ρ_{ab}) of the firms' returns.

c. Assume that Belker Company is 3 times larger than Ascar, and that the two companies merge to form a new company, Portco.

(1) What is the expected return for Portco ($\overline{R}_p$)?

(2) What is the standard deviation of returns for Portco (σ_p)?

Solution:

a.

S	P_s	R_a	R_b	P_sR_a	P_sR_b	$R_a-\overline{R}_a$	$(R_a-\overline{R}_a)^2$	$P_s(R_a-\overline{R}_a)^2$
1	.20	-.11	.20	-.022	.040	-.20	.0400	.008000
2	.25	.10	.18	.025	.045	.01	.0001	.000025
3	.35	.14	.16	.049	.056	.05	.0025	.000875
4	.15	.18	.10	.027	.015	.09	.0081	.001215
5	.05	.22	.08	.011	.004	.13	.0169	.000845
				$\overline{R}_a$ = .090	$\overline{R}_b$ = .160			σ_a^2 = .010960
								σ_a = .104690

$R_b-\overline{R}_b$	$(R_b-\overline{R}_b)^2$	$P_s(R_b-\overline{R}_b)^2$
.04	.0016	.00032
.02	.0004	.00010
0	0	0
-.06	.0036	.00054
-.08	.0064	.00032
		σ_b^2 = .00128
		σ_b = .03578

b.

$(R_a-\bar{R}_a)(R_b-\bar{R}_b)$	$P_s(R_a-\bar{R}_a)(R_b-\bar{R}_b)$
-.0080	-.00160
.0002	.00005
0	0
-.0054	-.00081
-.0104	-.00052

$$Cov_{ab} = -.00288$$

$$\rho_{ab} = Cov_{ab}/\sigma_a\sigma_b = (-.00288)/(.10469)(.03578) = -.7689$$

c. If Belker is 3 times as large as Ascar, then the weights for Portco will be 75% Belker, 25% Ascar.

(1) $\bar{R}_p = w_a\bar{R}_a + w_b\bar{R}_b$

$= .25(.09) + .75(.16)$

$= .1425$

(2) $\sigma_p = \sqrt{w_a^2\sigma_a^2 + w_b^2\sigma_b^2 + 2w_aw_b\rho_{ab}\sigma_a\sigma_b}$

$= \sqrt{.25^2(.01096)+.75^2(.00128)+2(.25)(.75)(-.7689)(.10469)(.03578)}$

$= \sqrt{.000685 + .00072 + (-.001080057)}$

$= \sqrt{.000324943}$

$= .018026$

Notice that the standard deviation of the merged firm is below the standard deviations of the two individual companies. This is because the two companies' returns are negatively correlated. At the extreme of $\rho = -1$, the merged firm's standard deviation could be zero.

16.6 You have $1,000,000 to invest. Two securities, A and B, are available to you. You may invest in either one alone, or in a portfolio containing both. A broker has provided the following probability distribution of returns:

State	Probability	Security A	Security B
1	.2	-10%	15%
2	.3	0%	4%
3	.4	4%	0
4	.1	8%	-15%

a. Calculate the expected return and standard deviation for Securities A and B.
b. Calculate the correlation coefficient between the securities.
c. Construct a table of expected portfolio returns and standard deviations based on 100%, 75%, 50%, 25%, and 0% of wealth in Security A, with the remainder in Security B.
d. Graph the portfolio opportunity set from the data in part c. Identify the efficient section of the feasible set.
e. Assuming that you are risk-averse, draw hypothetical indifference curves and indicate your optimal portfolio.

Solution:

a.

State	P_s	R_A	R_B	P_sR_A	P_sR_B
1	.2	-.10	.15	-.020	.030
2	.3	0	.04	0	.012
3	.4	.04	0	.016	0
4	.1	.08	-.15	.008	-.015
				$\bar{R}_A$ = .004	.027 = $\bar{R}_B$

$(R_A-\bar{R}_A)$	$(R_A-\bar{R}_A)^2$	$P_s(R_A-R_A)^2$	$(R_B-\bar{R}_B)$	$(R_B-\bar{R}_B)^2$	$P_s(R_B-\bar{R}_B)^2$
-.104	.010816	.0021632	.123	.015129	.0030258
-.004	.000016	.0000048	.013	.000169	.0000507
.036	.001296	.0005184	-.027	.000729	.0002916
.076	.005776	.0005776	-.177	.031329	.0031329
	Var_A =	.003264		Var_B =	.006501
	σ_A =	.05713		σ_B =	.08063

b. To find ρ, the correlation coefficient between Securities A and B, we must first find the covariance between A and B.

State	$P_s(R_A-\bar{R}_A)(R_B-\bar{R}_B)$	
1	.2(-.104)(.123) =	-.0025584
2	.3(-.004)(.013) =	-.0000156
3	.4 (.036)(-.027) =	-.0003888
4	.1 (.076)(-.177) =	-.0013452
	Cov_{AB}	-.0043080

$$\rho_{AB} = \frac{Cov_{AB}}{\sigma_A\sigma_B} = \frac{-.004308}{(.05713)(.08063)} = -.935$$

c. $\underline{w_A = 100\%:}$

$R_p = w_A(\overline{R}_A) + w_B(\overline{R}_B)$

$= 1(.004) + 0(.027)$

$= .004$

$\sigma_p = (w_A^2\sigma_A^2 + 2w_Aw_B\rho_{AB}\sigma_A\sigma_B + w_B^2\sigma_B^2)^{1/2}$

$= [1^2(.003264)+2(1)(0)(-.935)(.05713)(.08063)+0^2(.006501)]^{1/2}$

$= (.003264 + 0 + 0)^{1/2}$

$= .05713$

$\underline{w_A = 75\%:}$

$R_p = .75(.004) + .25(.027)$

$= .003 + .00675$

$= .00975$

$\sigma_p = [.75^2(.003264) + 2(.75)(.25)(-.935)(.05713)(.08063) + .25^2(.006501)]^{1/2}$

$= [.001836 + (-.001615116) + .000406313]^{1/2}$

$= (.000627197)^{1/2}$

$= .02504$

$\underline{w_A = 50\%:}$

$R_p = .5(.004) + .5(.027)$

$= .002 + .0135$

$= .0155$

$$\sigma_p = [.5^2(.003264) + 2(.5)(.5)(-.935)(.05713)(.08063) + .5^2(.006501)]^{1/2}$$

$$= [.000816 + (-.002153488) + .00162525]^{1/2}$$

$$= (.000287762)^{1/2}$$

$$= .01696$$

$\underline{w_A = 25\%:}$

$$R_p = .25(.004) + .75(.027)$$

$$= .001 + .02025$$

$$= .02125$$

$$\sigma_p = [.25^2(.003264) + 2(.25)(.75)(-.935)(.05713)(.08063) + .75^2(.006501)]^{1/2}$$

$$= [.000204 + (-.001615116) + .003656813]^{1/2}$$

$$= (.002245697)^{1/2}$$

$$= .04739$$

$\underline{w_A = 0\%:}$

$$R_p = 0(.004) + 1(.027)$$

$$= .027$$

$$\sigma_p = [0^2(.003264) + 2(0)(1)(-.935)(.05713)(.08063) + 1^2(.006501)]^{1/2}$$

$$= (0 + 0 + .006501)^{1/2}$$

$$= .08063$$

w_A	R_p	σ_p	Points
1.00	.00400	.05713	C
.75	.00975	.02504	D
.50	.01550	.01696	A
.25	.02125	.04739	B
0	.02700	.08063	C

d. and e.

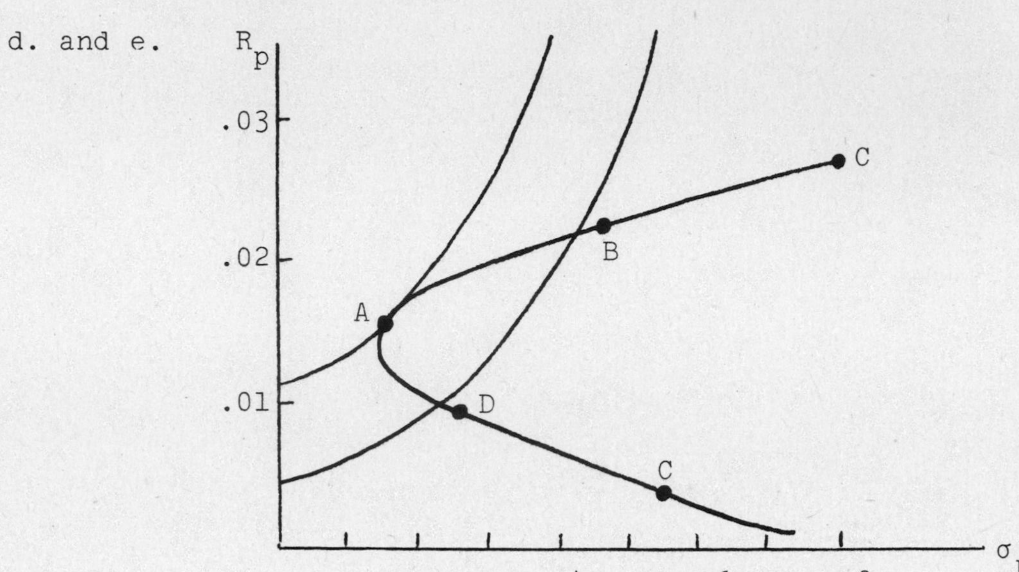

The line ABC represents the efficient set.

For the indifference curves drawn, the optimal portfolio is at point A which represents a portfolio equally divided between the two securities.

16.7 The risk-free rate is 9.5 percent. The expected return on the market portfolio is 14 percent, and the standard deviation of returns on the market portfolio is .18.

a. What is the marginal rate of transformation?
b. What percentage of your wealth should you invest in the market portfolio and in the riskless asset to earn an expected return of 20 percent?
c. What is the standard deviation of the portfolio in part b?

Solution:

a. The marginal rate of transformation is the equilibrium market price of risk; it is the slope of the Capital Market Line.

Equation of the CML: $R_p = R_F + \dfrac{E(R_M)-R_F}{\sigma_M}\sigma_p$

Slope of the CML: $\dfrac{E(R_M)-R_F}{\sigma_M} = \dfrac{.14 - .095}{.18} = .25$

b. The return to a 2-asset portfolio is the weighted average of the expected returns of the assets:

$R_p = w(R_1) + (1-w)(R_2)$

$.20 = w(.095) + (1-w)(.14)$

$.20 = .095w + .14 - .14w$

$.06 = -.045w$

$w = -1.33$

$1-w = 2.33$

To earn an expected return of 20 percent, you would have to invest 233 percent of your wealth in the market portfolio, borrowing at the risk-free rate in order to do so.

c. $\sigma_p = [w^2\sigma^2_{R_F} + 2w(1-w)Cov(R_F,R_M) + (1-w)^2\sigma^2_M]^{1/2}$

$= [(-1.33)^2(0) + 2(-1.33)(2.33)(0) + (2.33)^2(.18)^2]^{1/2}$

$= (0 + 0 + .175896)^{1/2}$

$= .4194$

Borrowing to invest 233% of your wealth in the market portfolio is obviously a very risk position. The risk is 2.33 times greater than the risk of investing only 100 percent of your wealth in the market portfolio.

16.8 Probable returns for the market portfolio and for Security Z are given below:

Probability	Security Z Return	Market Return
1/8	-8%	12%
1/8	12	14
1/8	10	8
1/8	2	-6
1/8	0	-2
1/8	-4	8
1/8	20	18
1/8	16	20

a. Estimate the undiversifiable risk of Security Z using linear regression.
b. What is the correlation between Security Z and the market portfolio?
c. What percentage of the total risk of Security Z is undiversifiable?

Solution:
Preliminary calculations

p_s	R_Z	p_sR_Z	R_M	p_sR_M	$R_M-\overline{R}_M$	$(R_M-\overline{R}_M)^2$
.125	-.08	-.0100	.12	.0150	.03	.0009
.125	.12	.0150	.14	.0175	.05	.0025
.125	.10	.0125	.08	.0100	-.01	.0001
.125	.02	.0025	-.06	-.0075	-.15	.0225
.125	0	0	-.02	-.0025	-.11	.0121
.125	-.04	-.0050	.08	.0100	-.01	.0001
.125	.20	.0250	.18	.0225	.09	.0081
.125	.16	.0200	.20	.0250	.11	.0121
		$\overline{R}_Z = .06$		$\overline{R}_M = .09$		

$p_s(R_M-\bar{R}_M)^2$	$R_Z-\bar{R}_Z$	$(R_Z-\bar{R}_Z)^2$	$p_s(R_Z-\bar{R}_Z)^2$
.0001125	-.14	.0196	.00245
.0003125	.06	.0036	.00045
.0000125	.04	.0016	.00020
.0028125	-.04	.0016	.00020
.0015125	-.06	.0036	.00045
.0000125	-.10	.0100	.00125
.0010125	.14	.0196	.00245
.0015125	.10	.0100	.00125

$Var(R_M) = .0073$ $\qquad$ $Var(R_Z) = .0087$

$\sigma_M = .0854$ $\qquad$ $\sigma_M = .0933$

$p_s(R_Z-\bar{R}_Z)(R_M-\bar{R}_M)$
-.000525
.000375
-.000050
.000750
.000825
.000125
.001575
.001375

$Cov(R_Z,R_M) = .00445$

a. $\text{Undiversifiable risk} = b = \frac{Cov(R_Z,R_M)}{Var(R_M)} = \frac{.00445}{.0073}$

$= .6096$

b. $\rho_{MZ} = \frac{Cov(R_M,R_Z)}{\sigma_M\sigma_Z} = \frac{.00445}{(.0854)(.0933)}$

$= \frac{.00445}{.007968}$

$= .5585$

c. Total risk = undiversifiable risk + diversifiable risk

$Var(R_Z) = b^2Var(R_M) + Var(\varepsilon)$

$.0087 = (.6096)^2(.0073) + Var(\varepsilon)$

Undiversifiable risk = $(.6096)^2(.0073) = .00271$

Diversifiable risk = $Var(\varepsilon) = .00599$

Thus, 31.1 percent (= .00271/.0087) of Security Z's risk is undiversifiable risk and 68.9 percent of total risk can be costlessly diversified away.

CHAPTER 17

RISK AND RETURN: THEORY, EVIDENCE, AND APPLICATIONS

Theme: The Capital Asset Pricing Model (CAPM) and the Arbitrage Pricing Model (APM) are theories about the pricing of risky assets. They have applications to capital budgeting, the cost of capital and security valuation.

I. The Capital Market Line (CML) and the Capital Asset Pricing Model (CAPM).

A. The equation of the CML is:

$$E(R_p) = R_F + \left[\frac{E(R_M)-R_F}{\sigma_M}\right]\sigma(R_p)$$

where $E(R_p)$ = expected return on a portfolio

R_F = risk-free rate

$E(R_M)$ = expected return on the market portfolio

σ_M = standard deviation of the market portfolio

$\sigma(R_p)$ = standard deviation of a portfolio

1. The equation uses the standard deviation as the measure of risk to predict the expected return of all portfolios along the CML.
   a. All points on the CML represent combinations of the riskless asset and the market portfolio.
   b. The CML cannot predict the expected return for inefficient securities or portfolios which do not lie on the CML.
2. For inefficient securities, there is no unique relationship between standard deviation and expected (and required) return.

B. The total risk of an asset (its standard deviation or variance) consists of diversifiable risk plus undiversifiable risk.

1. Diversifiable risk:
   a. Uncorrelated with the market portfolio.
   b. Can be completely eliminated through costless diversification, therefore not associated risk premium.
   c. Irrelevant in determining risk-adjusted rate of return.

2. Undiversifiable risk:
    a. Correlated with the market portfolio.
    b. Measured by $\beta = \frac{Cov(R_j, R_M)}{Var(R_M)}$ = beta.

C. The equation of the CAPM is:

$$E(R_j) = R_F + [E(R_M) - R_F]\beta_j$$

1. The CAPM uses β as the measure of risk to predict security returns.
2. The CAPM is also called the Security Market Line (SML).
3. In equilibrium, all securities (whether efficient or not) must be priced so they fall on the SML.

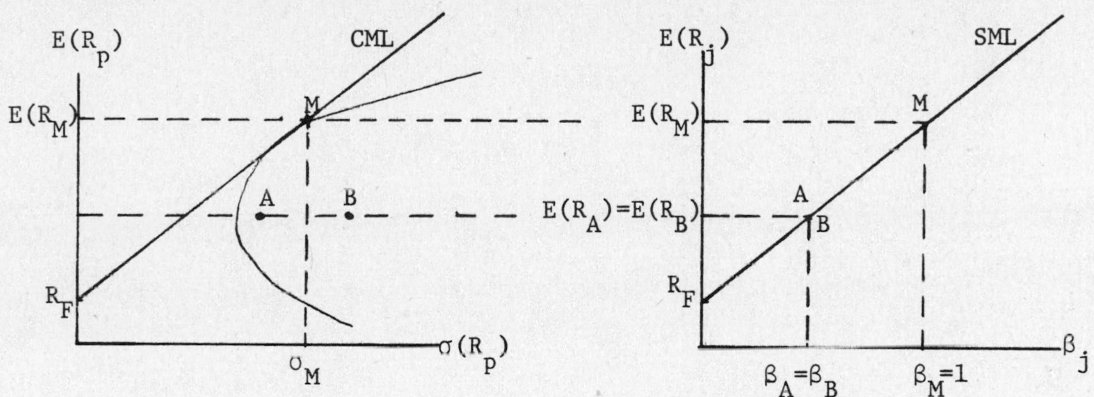

D. The price of risk per unit of risk is the same for both the CML and the SML.

$$\text{Price of risk} = \frac{E(R_M) - R_F}{\sigma_M}$$

II. Characteristics of Beta and the CAPM.
  A. According to the SML, the required return on any asset is equal to the risk-free rate plus a risk-adjustment factor.
    1. The market risk premium $[E(R_M)-R_F]$ is weighted by the index of systematic, or undiversifiable, risk, β.
    2. $\beta = 1$.
        a. Security returns fluctuate by exactly the same degree as the market return.
        b. Required return = market return.
    3. $\beta < 1$.
        a. Security returns are less volatile than market returns.
        b. Required return < market return.
    4. $\beta > 1$.
        a. Security returns are more volatile than market returns.
        b. Required return > market return.

B. The beta of a portfolio (β_p) of assets is the weighted average of the β's of the individual assets, weighted by the value of the asset relative to the value of the portfolio.
   1. A firm can be thought of as a portfolio of risky assets or projects.
   2. The beta of the firm (its undiversifiable risk) is thus the weighted average of its project betas.

C. The beta of a security reflects the stability or instability of its firm's industry characteristics and management policies.

D. Except for beta, all the parameters of the CAPM are market-wide measures which are not subject to a great range of subjective interpretation.

E. The CAPM includes all four elements of the nominal rate of return.
   1. R_F includes: expected real rate, expected inflation, and liquidity.
   2. $[E(R_M)-R_F]\beta_j$ includes the risk factor.
   3. Changes in expected inflation do not change the slope of the SML [that is, $E(R_M)-R_F$)], merely the y-axis intercept which moves from R_F^* to $R_F^* + i$, where R_F^* is the real risk-free rate.

III. The CAPM and the Cost of Capital.

A. The cost of risky debt.
   1. The interest rate at which discounted expected payments equal the present value (price) of a bond is the market-determined, risk-adjusted required rate of return on the bond.
   2. The market prices only undiversifiable risk.
   3. Two possible risk scenarios:
      a. Default risk is independent of economy, i.e. uncorrelated with the market portfolio.
         (i) It can be completely and costlessly diversified away.
         (ii) The return on a well-diversified portfolio of risky bonds equals the risk-free rate equals the market-determined, risk-adjusted rate.
      b. Default risk is somewhat correlated with the economy.
         (i) The market-determined, risk-adjusted rate will exceed the risk-free rate.
         (ii) The beta will be positive; use the CAPM to solve for beta using the known required return, market return and risk-free rate.
         (iii) Beta will usually be quite small; most default risk can be diversified away.

B. The cost of equity.
   1. The equity beta is easier to estimate because of the ready availability of stock price data.
   2. Estimates of beta for firms on the NYSE and AMEX are prepared by various investor services.
   3. The equity beta is used in the CAPM to determine the required return, or cost, of equity.

C. The weighted average cost of capital (WACC).
   1. $WACC = k_b(1-T)\frac{B}{B+S} + k_s\left(\frac{S}{B+S}\right)$.
   2. k_b and k_s are estimated using the debt and equity betas respectively in the CAPM.
   3. $\frac{B}{B+S}$ and $\frac{S}{B+S}$ represent the target market values of debt and equity divided by the market value of the firm.
   4. Expected cash flows discounted at the WACC will result in the total market value of the firm, V, = B+S.

IV. The CAPM in Capital Budgeting.
   A. All projects must earn at least the rate of return required by the CAPM for projects of equivalent risk.
   B. Each project has its own WACC.
   C. The project WACC, not the firm WACC, is the appropriate discount rate to use in capital budgeting.
      1. The firm WACC is the weighted average of the WACC's of all the projects which comprise the firm.
      2. If a project earns more than its own required WACC, according to the CAPM, it will have a positive NPV.

V. Risk and Time.
   A. In a one-period framework, the CAPM can be used to find NPV using either of two techniques.
      1. The risk-adjusted discount rate technique:
         a. Present value (PV) is determined by discounting the expected cash flow at the risk-adjusted rate as determined by the CAPM.

$$PV = \frac{E(CF)}{1+E(R_j)}$$

         b. $E(R_j)$ can be written as $R_F+[E(R_M)-R_F]\beta_j$.

         c. Thus, $PV = \frac{E(CF)}{1+R_F+[E(R_M)-R_F]\beta_j}$

         d. As in any capital budgeting framework, NPV = PV - I; if NPV is positive, project should be accepted.

2. The <u>certainty equivalent method</u> reduces the expected cash flows by a risk premium, and then discounts this amount by the risk-free rate of return.
   a. The certainty equivalent risk premium is expressed as

$$\lambda COV(CF,R_M)$$

where $\lambda = \frac{E(R_M)-R_F}{\sigma_M^2}$

   b. The present value (PV) of cash flows can then be expressed as

$$PV = \frac{E(CF)-\lambda COV(CF,R_M)}{1+R_F}$$

   c. As before, NPV = PV - I.

B. For multiple-period projects, the certainty equivalent method must be adjusted.
   1. The risk-adjusted discount rate method accounts for both time and risk simultaneously; no adjustment is required for evaluating multiple-period projects.

$$PV = \sum_{t=0}^{N} \frac{E(CF_t)}{[1+E(R_j)]^t}$$

   2. To use the certainty equivalent method in a multi-period framework, two stages are necessary.
      a. Calculate the certainty equivalent factor, cef.

$$cef = \frac{E(CF)-\lambda COV(CF,R_M)}{E(CF)}$$

      b. Each year's cash flows are then adjusted by the cef and discounted at the risk-free rate.

$$PV = \sum_{t=0}^{N} \frac{(cef)^t E(CF_t)}{(1+R_F)^t}$$

C. Both projects assume implicitly that a project's systematic risk (beta) does not change over its life.
   1. If project risk changes, the risk-adjusted discount rate must change.
   2. The certainty equivalent risk premium must also be adjusted to reflect changes in project risk.

VI. Discounting Cost Streams.
   A. Equipment replacement decisions often involve data on costs alone.
      1. Outputs and revenues remain unchanged.

2. Costs are reduced through the use of more efficient new equipment.

B. A higher variance cost stream should be discounted at a <u>lower</u> risk-adjusted rate of return.
   1. A greater variance in costs implies that the absolute value of the cost stream is positively correlated with the market.
   2. Systematic risk (beta) will be lower for projects with greater cost variance.
      a. Favorable economy--higher costs reduce profits below what they otherwise would be in a favorable economy.
      b. Slack economy--lower costs will result in profits above what they otherwise would be in a slack economy.
      c. Overall effect is to reduce variability of project returns.
   3. Lower beta results in lower risk-adjusted discount rate.

VII. Factors Affecting the Beta of Firms.
   A. Line of business, business risk.
      1. Cyclical nature of revenues.
      2. Operating leverage.
   B. Financial leverage.
      1. Beta increases in a linear fashion with financial leverage.
      2. $\beta(\text{equity}) = \beta(\text{assets}) + [\beta(\text{assets})-\beta(\text{debt})]\frac{B}{S}$
   C. Other factors include:
      1. Dividend payout policies.
      2. Liquidity.
      3. Firm size.
      4. Rate of growth.
   D. To estimate a project beta, compare your subjective estimate of project beta with the published betas of firms similar in nature to the project.

VIII. Empirical Evidence on the CAPM.
   A. The empirical CAPM $R_{jt} = R_{Ft}+(R_{Mt}-R_{Ft})\beta_j + \varepsilon_{jt}$ differs from the theoretical CAPM $E(R_j) = R_F +[E(R_M)-R_F]\beta_j$ in three ways:
      1. Time subscripts.
      2. No expectations operators since the CAPM is tested using ex post data.
      3. The error term, ε_{jt}
   B. The testing form of the CAPM is written as

$$R_{jt}-R_{Ft} = a + b\,\beta_j + \varepsilon_{jt}$$

1. If the CAPM is true, then the following conditions should hold:
   a. a should not be significantly different from zero.
   b. β_j should be the only factor which explains the rate of return; adding other terms to the regression should not improve its explanatory power.
   c. The relationship should be linear in β; the slope should be b and the y-axis intercept should be a.
   d. The coefficient of β (that is, b_j) should be equal to $(R_{Mt}-R_{Ft})$.
   e. Over the long term, R_{Mt} should be greater than R_{Ft}; that is, the linear relationship should have a positive slope.
2. Evidence from empirical tests of the CAPM cause us to reject the CAPM.
   a. a is significantly different from zero and b is less than $R_{Mt}-R_{Ft}$.
      (i) This implies that low-beta securities earn more than predicted by the CAPM and
      (ii) High-beta securities earn less than the CAPM predicts.
   d. Other factors in addition to beta help to explain security returns (although beta does dominate).
      (i) P/E ratio--low P/E ratio portfolios outperform CAPM predictions.
      (ii) Firm size--smaller firms outperform CAPM predictions.
      (iii) Dividend policy--required return rises with higher dividend yields.
      (iv) Seasonality of stock returns.
3. Notwithstanding, the Empirical Market Line (EML) can still be useful in estimating required returns given beta.
   a. The EML differs from the SML in that it has a higher intercept and a lower slope.

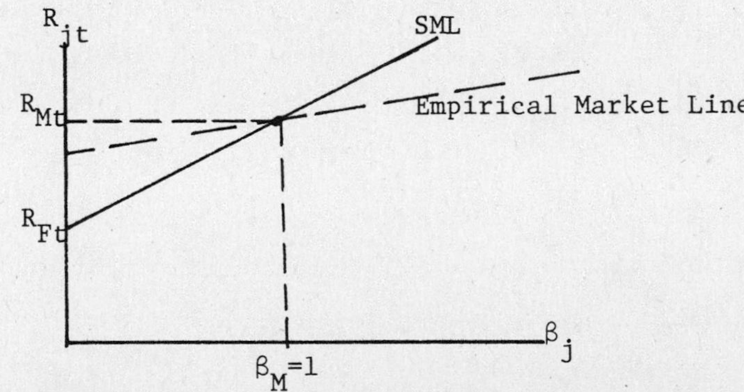

IX. The Arbitrage Pricing Model (APM) Uses Many Factors to Explain Security Returns.

A. Like the CAPM, the APM prices only systematic risk.
   1. In the CAPM, systematic risk is based solely on the market return and each asset's sensitivity (beta) to the market return.
   2. In the APM, systematic risk (and thus asset return) is based on any number of underlying macroeconomic variables. Four have been identified as significant:
      a. Industrial production (the market portfolio).
      b. Changes in the default risk premium, measured as the difference between the AAA and Baa corporate bond yields.
      c. Twists in the yield curve, measured as the difference between long- and short-term government bond yields.
      d. Unanticipated inflation.

B. The APM is based on the concept of the arbitrage portfolio (which cannot exist, or persist, in market equilibrium). Characteristics of the arbitrage portfolio are:
   1. No risk.
   2. No capital investment required.
   3. Positive return.

C. Construction of an arbitrage portfolio.
   1. Eliminate diversifiable risk by limiting extent of investment in any single asset. Asset weights in the portfolio should approach 1/N where N is the number of assets in the economy.
   2. Eliminate systematic risk by choosing asset weights such that the weighted average of systematic risk components for each underlying factor is set equal to zero.
   3. Eliminate investment requirement by choosing asset weights such that some assets are sold short and proceeds are used for long positions in other assets.
   4. Given conditions above, portfolio return must be zero in market equilibrium, not positive.

D. Formulation of the APM:

$$E(R_j) = R_F + [\overline{\delta}_1 - R_F]b_{j1} + \dots + [\overline{\delta}_k - R_F]b_{jk}$$

where $E(R_j)$ = expected return on asset j

R_F = risk-free rate

$\overline{\delta}_k$ = expected return on a mimicking portfolio which has unitary sensitivity to the kth factor and zero sensitivity to all other factors

b_{jk} = sensitivity of jth asset to the kth factor

1. According to the APM, the expected return is equal to the risk-free rate plus a set of risk premia.
   a. Risk premium = $(\bar{\delta}_k - R_F)b_{jk}$

      = (market price of risk for the kth factor) times (sensitivity of the jth asset to the kth factor)
   b. $b_{jk} = \dfrac{COV(R_j, \delta_k)}{Var(\delta_k)}$
   c. The CAPM is equivalent to a single-factor APM; that single factor being the return on the market, R_M, which is used in a way that parallels the use of δ_k in the APM.
      (i) Beta in the CAPM is equivalent to b_{jk} in the APM.
      (ii) The beta of the market portfolio is 1; that is, the market portfolio has unitary sensitivity to itself, and zero sensitivity to all other factors (no other factors enter into the CAPM).
2. Arbitrage profits (i.e., positive returns requiring no change in risk and no net investment) can result from asset mispricing.
   a. If an individual's subjective estimate of a security's return differs from that predicted by the APM, the individual can reap arbitrage profits if his estimate turns out to have been the more accurate ex post.
   b. Portfolio weights are rearranged to take advantage of the mispricing.
   c. As long as there are more securities than underlying factors, an infinite number of portfolio weights exists satisfying the conditions that no net investment will be required and that there will be no risk change for any factor.

X. Applications and Empirical Evidence on the APM.
   A. The APM may be used in exactly the same situations as the CAPM, for example, cost of capital, valuation, capital budgeting.
   B. The APM results in an improvement over the CAPM in many applications.
      1. Improves estimates of cost of capital in electric utilities industry.
      2. Eliminates effect of firm size.
      3. The APM can explain CAPM residuals, but not vice versa.

C. Advantages of the APM over the CAPM.

1. No assumptions are made about the empirical distribution of asset returns.
2. No strong assumptions are made about individuals' utility functions, beyond greed and risk aversion.
3. Equilibrium returns are dependent on many factors, not only beta.
4. The APM enables relative pricing of any subset of assets without the need to measure the entire universe of assets to test theory.
5. No special role is required for the market portfolio; the CAPM requires that the market portfolio be efficient.
6. Easily extended to a multi-period framework.

XI. Sensitivity Analysis of Risky Projects.

A. Sensitivity analysis involves calculating a project's NPV under various alternative assumptions to see how sensitive the NPV is to changing conditions.

B. Decision trees are useful when decisions are made in stages rather than once and for all at one point in time.

1. Subsequent decisions are based on the outcomes of previous decisions, represented as branches from a decision point.
2. The decision tree may be used in a variety of ways to arrive at a decision.
    a. Expected NPV of alternative decision paths.
    b. Risk of alternative decision paths as measured by the coefficient of variation.

C. Computer simulation methods can also be used in conjunction with the above methods.

1. Assign probability distributions to each of the major cost and revenue components.
2. The computer will simulate what is likely to happen.
    a. This will be repeated for several hundred trials to get many possible rates of return.
    b. The frequency distribution of the rates of return can be computed, plotted, and further analyzed to aid in judgments about the most probable results on the investments.
3. The costs of full-scale simulation may be such that it is not worthwhile except for large and expensive projects.

Chapter 17 - Illustrative Problems and Solutions

17.1 The Lone Star Oil Company is evaluating two mutually exclusive drilling projects. Each costs $5,000,000 and has an expected life of 8 years. Annual cash flows are projected as follows:

Project A		Project B	
Probability	Cash Flow	Probability	Cash Flow
0.3	$ 750,000	0.5	$ 0
0.4	1,000,000	0.1	1,000,000
0.3	1,250,000	0.4	2,500,000

Lone Star has decided to evaluate the riskier project at 12 percent and the less risky project at 10 percent.

a. What is the expected value of the annual net cash flows from each project?
b. Which project is riskier?
c. What is the risk-adjusted NPV of each project?
d. If Lone Star expects Project B to be negatively correlated with the firm's other cash flows, while Project A would be positively correlated, which project should be chosen?

Solution:

a. Project A expected cash flow = 0.3($750,000) + 0.4($1,000,000) + 0.3($1,250,000) = $1,000,000.
Project B expected cash flow = 0.5(0) + 0.1($1,000,000) + 0.4($2,500,000) = $1,100,000
b. Project B is riskier because it has greater variability in its expected cash flows. (You can calculate the variance for each project to verify this.)
c. NPV_A = -$5,000,000 + $1,000,000 $PVIFA_{10\%, 8\ yrs.}$
= -$5,000,000 + $1,000,000(5.3349)
= $334,900
NPV_B = -$5,000,000 + $1,100,000 $PVIFA_{12\%, 8\ yrs.}$
= -$5,000,000 + $1,100,000(4.9676)
= $464,360
Lone Star should select Project B, even though it is riskier.
d. The portfolio effects from Project B would tend to make it less risky than otherwise, which reinforces the decision to accept Project B.

17.2 The data below has been provided for three investment projects under consideration:

Project	Estimated Beta
J	0.9
K	1.3
L	2.1

$E(R_M) = 12\%$

$R_F = 6\%$

What are the rates of return required for the projects by the CAPM?

Solution:

$$CAPM = SML = R_j = R_F + [E(R_M)-R_F]\beta_j$$

Project J: $R_j = .06 + (.12-.06)(0.9)$
$= .06 + (.06)(0.9)$
$= .114$

Project K: $R_k = .06 + (.06)(1.3)$
$= .138$

Project L: $R_l = .06 + (.06)(2.1)$
$= .186$

17.3 The Kayson Company is evaluating a project with an initial investment outlay of $4,000. The expected net cash flows from the project are $1,500 per year for 5 years, and the project beta is 1.5. The risk-free rate of return is 5 percent and the market risk premium is 6 percent.

a. What is the required rate of return on the project according to the SML?

b. Should the project be accepted?

Solution:

a. $R_j = R_F + [E(R_M)-R_F]\beta_j$

$= .05 + (.06)(1.5)$

$= .14$

b. $NPV = \sum_{t=1}^{N} \frac{CF_t}{(1+k)^t} - I_0$

$= \$1,500[PVIFA(14\%, 5 \text{ yrs})] - \$5,000$

$= \$1,500(3.4331) - \$5,000$

$= \$5,149.65 - \$5,000$

$= \$149.65$

Since the NPV is positive, when discounted at the risk-adjusted required rate of return, the project should be accepted.

17.4 Multiglomerates, Inc. discounts cash flows for each potential project at a rate determined by the following formula:

Required return = Risk-free rate + 15 CV

The risk-free rate is 6 percent. The company is considering two investments A and B, with the following projected cash flows:

A		B	
Probability	Cash Flow	Probability	Cash Flow
0.3	$ 50,000	0.2	$ 25,000
0.4	100,000	0.6	150,000
0.3	150,000	0.2	350,000

a. Calculate the coefficient of variation for cash flows from each project and find the required rates of return.
b. The beta is 1.1 for returns on Project A and 1.9 for Project B. The market risk premium is 5 percent. What is the required rate of return for each project using the SML?
c. Project A has a cost of $400,000, and Project B costs $600,000. Each has a life of 10 years and no residual value. Using the required rates of return you have calculated (rounded to whole percents) find the NPV for each project.
d. What should Multiconglomerates do if the two projects are independent? Mutually exclusive?

Solution:
a. See next page.

b. $R_A = 6 + 5(1.1) = 11.5\%$
$R_B = 6 + 5(1.9) = 15.5\%$
The SML gives the same required return for Project B and a slightly lower R_A for Project A.

17.4

a.

A		B	
0.3($50,000)	= $ 15,000	0.2($25,000)	= $ 5,000
0.4($100,000)	= 40,000	0.6($150,000)	= 90,000
0.3($150,000)	= 45,000	0.2($350,000)	= 70,000
Expected cash flow	= $100,000	Expected cash flow	= $165,000

Ignoring the zeros:

$F_A - \bar{F}_A$	$(F_A-\bar{F}_A)^2 \times P_s$		$F_B - \bar{F}_B$	$(F_B-\bar{F}_B)^2 \times P_s$	
50 - 100 = -50;	2,500 x 0.3 =	750	25 - 165 = -140;	19,600 x 0.2 =	3,920
100 - 100 = 0;	0 x 0.4 =	0	150 - 165 = -15;	225 x 0.6 =	135
150 - 100 = 50;	2,500 x 0.3 =	750	350 - 165 = 185;	34,225 x 0.2 =	6,845
	σ_A^2 =	1,500		σ_B^2 =	10,900

$\sigma_A = \sqrt{1,500} = 38.730$ or \$38,730 $\qquad \sigma_B = \sqrt{10,900} = 104.403$ or \$104,403

$CV_A = \frac{\sigma_A}{\bar{F}_A} = \frac{\$38,730}{\$100,000} = 0.387 \qquad CV_B = \frac{\sigma_B}{\bar{F}_B} = \frac{\$104,403}{165,000} = 0.633$

With a larger coefficient of variation, Project B is riskier than Project A.

The required rates of return are:

$R_A = 6 + 15(0.387) = 6 + 5.8 = 11.8\%$

$R_3 = 6 + 15(0.633) = 6 + 9.5 = 15.5\%$

c. $NPV_A = \$100,000 \times PVIFA_{12\%,\ 10\ yrs} - \$400,000$
$= \$100,000 \times 5.6502 - \$400,000$
$= \$165,020$

$NPV_B = \$165,000 \times PVIFA_{16\%,\ 10\ yrs} - \$600,000$
$= \$165,000 \times 4.8332 - \$600,000$
$= \$197,478$

d. If the projects are independent, both should be accepted. If they are mutually exclusive, Project B should be chosen. Even though its returns are riskier, Project B still has the higher NPV when discounted at the appropriate risk-adjusted rate.

17.5 An investment project is presented to your company as follows:

P = \$12 per unit R_F = 6 percent
VC = \$8 per unit $Var(R_M) = 0.01$
FC = \$1,200

State	Probability (p_s)	R_M	Q
1	0.2	-0.03	0
2	0.6	0.10	500
3	0.2	0.15	900

a. What is the price of risk, i.e. $[E(R_M)-R_F]/\sigma_M^2$? (The price of risk is also called lambda, λ.)

b. What is the value of the project?

c. What is the required return on the project?

Solution:

a.

State	$P_s R_M$	$(R_M-\bar{R}_M)$	$(R_M-\bar{R}_M)^2$	$P_s(R_M-\bar{R}_M)^2$
1	-0.006	-0.114	0.0130	0.0026
2	0.060	0.016	0.0003	0.0002
3	0.030	0.066	0.0044	0.0009
	$\bar{R}_M = 0.084$			$\sigma_M^2 = 0.0037$

$$\lambda = \frac{\bar{R}_M - R_F}{\sigma_M^2} = \frac{0.084 - 0.06}{0.0037} = 6.5$$

b.

(1) State	(2) $X=(cQ-FC)$	(3) P_sX	(4) $(X-\bar{X})(R_M-\bar{R}_M)$	(5) $\times P_s =$
1	-1,200	-240	(-1,920)(-0.114) = 219	44
2	800	480	(80)(0.016) = 1	0
3	2,400	480	(1,680)(0.066) = 111	22
		$\bar{X}$ = 720		$Cov(X,R_M)$ = 66

$$V_j = \frac{\bar{X} - \lambda Cov(X,R_M)}{R_F} = \frac{720 - 6.5(66)}{0.06} = \$4,850$$

c. Since $\bar{R}_J = \frac{\bar{X}_j}{V_j}$, $\bar{R}_j = \frac{\$720}{\$4,850} = 15\%$

This problem illustrates a method for calculating required returns when the expected returns on a project are calculated in dollar figures (in this case, from quantity projections and price data) rather than in percentages. Because market risk and project risk are accounted for in calculating the value of the project, the usual required return equation, $\bar{R}_j = R_F + \lambda Cov(R_j,R_M)$, need not be used to find $\bar{R}_j$.

17.6 The following facts relate to market returns and returns on two investment projects with equal costs.

State	P_s	R_{Ms}	Return to Project 1	Return to Project 2
1	0.3	-0.1	-0.1	0
2	0.5	0.1	0.1	0.2
3	0.2	0.2	0.4	0.1

a. Calculate the three means, variances, and standard deviations, the covariance of each project with the market; the covariance of Project 1 with Project 2; and the correlation coefficients ρ_{1M}, ρ_{2M}, and ρ_{12}.

b. What is the expected return and standard deviation of a portfolio which has 6% in Project 1 and 94% in in Project 2?

c. Calculate the Security Market Line $R_F = 0.04$. On a graph, plot the Security Market Line and points for Projects 1 and 2.

d. If the projects are mutually exclusive, which would you select?

Solution:

a. Market mean, variance and standard deviation.

State	$P_s R_{Ms}$	$R_{Ms} - \bar{R}_M$	$(R_{Ms} - \bar{R}_M)^2$	$P_s(R_{Ms} - \bar{R}_M)^2$
1	-0.03	-.16	0.0256	0.00768
2	0.05	0.04	0.0016	0.00080
3	0.04	0.14	0.0196	0.00392
	$\bar{R}_M = 0.06$			$\sigma_M^2 = 0.0124$
				$\sigma_M = 0.111$

Project 1 mean, variance, and standard deviation.

State	$P_s R_{1s}$	$R_{1s} - \bar{R}_1$	$(R_{1s} - \bar{R}_1)^2$	$P_s(R_{1s} - \bar{R}_1)^2$
1	-0.03	-0.2	0.04	0.012
2	0.05	0.0	0.00	0.000
3	0.08	0.3	0.09	0.018
	$\bar{R}_1 = 0.10$			$\sigma_1^2 = 0.030$
				$\sigma_1 = 0.173$

Project 2 mean, variance and standard deviation.

State	P_sR_{2s}	$R_{2s}-\bar{R}_2$	$(R_{2s}-\bar{R}_2)^2$	$P_s(R_{2s}-\bar{R}_2)^2$
1	0.0	-0.12	0.0144	0.00432
2	0.1	0.08	0.0064	0.00320
3	0.02	-0.02	0.0004	0.00008
	$\bar{R}_2$ = 0.12			σ_2^2 = 0.0076
				σ_2 = 0.0872

Covariances and correlation coefficients.

State	$P(R_{1s}-\bar{R}_1)(R_{Ms}-\bar{R}_M)$
1	(0.3)(-0.2)(-0.16) = 0.0096
2	(0.5)(0.0)(0.04) = 0.0000
3	(0.2)(0.3)(0.14) = 0.0084
	$Cov(R_1,R_M)$ = 0.0180

State	$P(R_{2s}-\bar{R}_2)(R_{Ms}-\bar{R}_M)$
1	(0.3(-0.12)(-0.16) = 0.00576
2	(0.5)(0.08)(0.04) = 0.00160
3	(0.2)(-0.02)(0.14) = -0.00056
	$Cov(R_2,R_M)$ = 0.00680

$$\rho_{1M} = \frac{Cov(R_1,R_M)}{(\sigma_1)(\sigma_M)} = \frac{0.0180}{(0.173)(0.111)} = 0.940$$

$$\rho_{2M} = \frac{0.00680}{(0.0872)(0.111)} = 0.703$$

State	$P(R_{1s}-R_1)(R_{2s}-R_2)$
1	(0.3)(-0.2)(-0.12) = 0.0072
2	(0.5)(0.0)(0.08) = 0.0000
3	(0.2)(0.3)(-0.02) = -0.0012
	$Cov(R_1,R_2)$ = 0.006

$$\rho_{12} = \frac{Cov(R_1,R_2)}{(\sigma_1)(\sigma_2)} = \frac{0.006}{(0.173)(0.0872)} = 0.398$$

b. Portfolio weights are 6% in Project 1 and 94% in Project 2. Portfolio expected return and standard deviation.

State	w_1R_{1s}	+	w_2R_{2s}	=	R_{Ps}	P_sR_{Ps}	$R_{Ps}-\bar{R}_P$	$P_s(R_{Ps}-\bar{R}_P)^2$
1	-0.006		0.000		-0.006	-0.0018	-0.125	0.00469
2	0.006		0.188		0.194	0.0970	0.075	0.00282
3	0.024		0.094		0.118	0.0236	0.001	0.00000
					$\bar{R}_p$ =	0.1188	σ_p^2 =	0.00751
							σ_p =	0.087

c. Security Market Line

$$E(R_j) = R_F + \lambda \text{Cov}(R_j, R_M),$$

$$\text{where } \lambda = \frac{R_M - R_F}{\sigma_M^2} = \frac{0.06 - 0.04}{0.0124} = 1.61$$

$$E(R_j) = 0.04 + 1.61 \text{ Cov}(R_j, R_M)$$

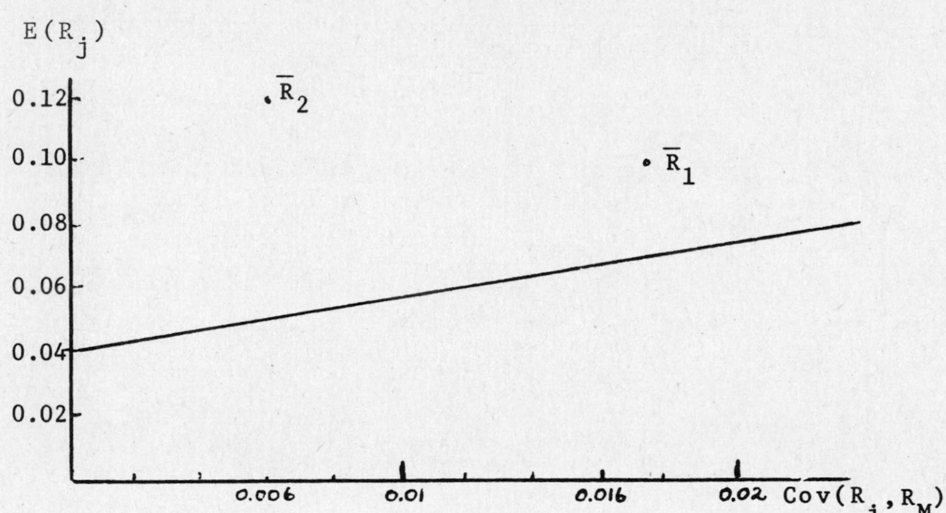

d. $E(R_1) = 0.04 + 1.61(0.0180) = 0.07$

$E(R_2) = 0.04 + 1.61(0.008) = 0.05$

	Project 1	Project 2
Expected return	0.10	0.12
Required return	0.07	0.05
Excess return	0.03	0.07

Since the cost is the same for both projects, the higher excess return for Project 2 makes it the clean choice. If project costs were different, the choice would be based on excess return weighted by cost.

17.7 Your firm is considering two investment projects of different risk. Project A has a required rate of return of 14 percent; Project B is risk-free and has a required return of 7 percent.

Calculate the certainty equivalent factor, $(cef)^t$ for each project for the risky project for years 0, 1, 5, 10, 20, and 30.

Solution:

Since both riskless and risky projects lie on the SML,

$$PV = \sum_{t=0}^{N} \frac{E(CF_t)}{(1+R_j)^t} = \sum_{t=0}^{N} \frac{(cef)^t E(CF_t)}{(1+R_F)^t}$$

For one period, $\frac{E(CF)}{(1+R_j)} = \frac{cef[E(CF)]}{(1+R_F)}$

Multiply both sides of the equation by 1/E(CF):

$$\frac{1}{1+R_j} = \frac{cef}{1+R_F}$$

Thus, $cef = \frac{1+R_F}{1+R_j}$

and by extension, $(cef)^t = \left(\frac{1+R_F}{1+R_j}\right)^t$

$cef = \frac{1.07}{1.14} = .9386$

$cef^0 = 1$
$cef^1 = .9386$
$cef^5 = .7284$
$cef^{10} = .2886$
$cef^{20} = .2816$
$cef^{30} = .1494$

The problem assumes that Project A's systematic risk, or beta does not change over time; thus the cef does not change either. This assumption may not be valid. If the beta of Project A changes, then so will its risk-adjusted required rate of return change, as will the cef.

17.8 The risk-free rate of return is 5 percent, the expected return on the market is 12 percent, and the variance of market returns is 1 percent. The expected net operating income (X) of Armor Corporation is $1,200,000, and the covariance of Armor's net operating income with the market return is $150,000.

a. Calculate the value of the firm using the certainty equivalent method.
b. Calculate the value of the firm using the risk-adjusted return method (CAPM).
c. Comment on your results.

Solution:

a. Certainty equivalent risk premium = $\lambda \text{Cov}(CF, R_M)$

$$\text{where } \lambda = [E(R_M)-R_F]/\sigma_M^2$$

$$= (.12-.05)/.01$$
$$= 7$$

Thus, the certainty equivalent risk premium

$$= 7(150,000) = 1,050,000$$

$$\text{Value of the firm} = PV = \frac{E(CF)-\lambda \text{Cov}(CF, R_M)}{R_F}$$

$$= \frac{1,200,000-1,050,000}{.05}$$

$$= \$3,000,000$$

b. Value of the firm = PV = $\frac{X}{R_j}$

$$\text{where } R_j = R_F + [E(R_M)-R_F]\beta_j$$

$$\text{and } \beta_j = \frac{Cov(R_j, R_M)}{\sigma_M^2} = \frac{Cov[(X/V), R_M]}{\sigma_M^2}$$

$$= \frac{Cov[(1{,}200{,}000/V),\ .12]}{.01}$$

$$\text{Value of the firm} = \frac{1{,}200{,}000}{.05 + (.07)\dfrac{Cov[(1{,}200{,}000/V),\ .12]}{.01}}$$

$$V\left\{.05 + (.07)\frac{Cov[(1{,}200{,}000/V),\ .12]}{.01}\right\} = 1{,}200{,}000$$

$$.05V + 7(150{,}000) = 1{,}200{,}000$$

$$.05V + 1{,}050{,}000 = 1{,}200{,}000$$

$$.05V = 150{,}000$$

$$V = \$3{,}000{,}000$$

c. The results are equivalent using the risk-adjusted return method and the certainty equivalent method.

17.9 The Teletronics Corporation has risky debt with a beta (β_d) of 0.3 and its stock has a beta (β_s) of 1.8.

a. Teletronics has a debt-to-total-assets ratio of 40 percent. What is the beta of the firm, β_{assets}?

b. If Teletronics is able to increase leverage (B/(B+S)) to 60 percent without changing the risk of its debt, or of the firm as a whole, what will its equity beta (β_s) become?

Solution:

a. B/(B+S) = .40, thus S/(B+S) = .60

$$\beta_{assets} = \beta_d\left(\frac{B}{B+S}\right) + \beta_s\left(\frac{S}{B+S}\right)$$

$$= .3(.4) + .6(1.8)$$

$$= .12 + 1.08$$

$$= 1.2$$

The beta of the firm is the weighted average of the debt and equity betas.

b. $\frac{B}{B+S} = .6$ $\frac{S}{B+S} = .4$

$$\beta_{equity} = \beta_{assets} + [\beta_{assets} - \beta_{debt}]\frac{B}{S}$$

$$= 1.2 + [1.2 - .3]\frac{.6}{.4}$$

$$= 1.2 + (.9)(1.5)$$

$$= 2.55$$

The equity beta increases with increased leverage since shareholders are residual claimants to the firm's cash flows. Using more debt shifts more of the asset risk to the firm's shareholders.

17.10 A risky bond is selling for $1,087. The expected return on the market is 15 percent and the risk-free rate is 8 percent. The coupon rate on the bond is 12 percent (coupons are paid annually) and its face value is $1,000. The bond has 4 years to maturity. All coupons on the bond are expected to be paid with certainty, but there is a 10 percent chance that the bond will default on its face value and pay only $850.

What is the beta of the bond?

Solution:

$$B_0 = \sum_{t=1}^{N} \frac{\text{coupon}_t}{(1+r)^t} + \frac{\text{face value}}{(1+r)^N}$$

$$E(\text{face value}) = .9(\$1{,}000) + .1(\$850)$$

$$= \$985$$

$$\$1{,}087 = \sum_{t=1}^{4} \frac{\$120}{(1+k_b)^t} + \frac{\$985}{(1+k_b)^4}$$

By trial and error we find that k_b = 9 percent.

$$k_b = E(R_j) = R_F + [E(R_M)-R_F]\beta_j$$

$$.09 = .08 + (.15-.08)\beta_j$$

$$.09 = .08 + .07\beta_j$$

$$.01 = .07\beta_j$$

$$\beta_j = .14$$

17.11 The following data is provided for the Filex Company:

Year	Filex Return	Market Return
19X1	4%	-2%
19X2	8	8
19X3	7	10
19X4	8	11
19X5	-2	12
19X6	-3	13
19X7	6	12
19X8	10	15
19X9	11	18

a. Calculate the historical beta for the equity of the Filex Company.

b. If R_F = 8 percent, and the currently expected market return is 16 percent, what is Filex's cost of equity?

Solution: Preliminary calculations:

Year	R_j	$R_j-\overline{R}_j$	R_M	$R_M-\overline{R}_M$	$(R_M-\overline{R}_M)^2$	$(R_j-\overline{R}_j)(R_M-\overline{R}_M)$
19X1	.04	-.014	-.02	-.128	.016384	.001792
19X2	.08	.026	.08	-.028	.000784	-.000728
19X3	.07	.016	.10	-.008	.000064	-.000128
19X4	.08	.026	.11	.002	.000004	.000052
19X5	-.02	-.074	.12	.012	.000144	-.000888
19X6	-.03	-.084	.13	.022	.000484	-.001848
19X7	.06	.006	.12	.012	.000144	.000072
19X8	.10	.046	.15	.042	.001764	.001932
19X9	.11	.056	.18	.072	.005184	.004032
	.49		.97		.024956	.004288

$\overline{R}_j = .49/9 = .054$ $\overline{R}_M = .97/9 = .108$

$\sigma_M^2 = .024956/8 = .0031195$ $COV(R_j,R_M) = .004288/8 = .000536$

a. $\beta_j = \dfrac{COV(R_j,R_M)}{\sigma_M^2} = \dfrac{.0005360}{.0031195} = .172$

b. $R_j = R_F + [E(R_M)-R_F]\beta_j$

$= .08 + (.16-.08)(.172)$

$= .08576$

Filex's cost of equity is approximately 8.6 percent. In order to use the CAPM in this way, it is necessary to assume that a firm's current systematic risk is unchanged from that of the historical period used to estimate beta.

17.12 The Parish Company has two divisions of approximately the same size. The treasurer's staff has estimated each division's expected return for possible future states of nature as indicated below:

State of Nature	p_s	R_M	Divisional Rate of Return: Division 1	Divisional Rate of Return: Division 2
Great	.25	.25	.30	.20
Good	.25	.15	.18	.10
Average	.25	.08	.12	.06
Horrid	.25	-.04	-.02	-.05

a. If R_F = 8 percent, what is the required return for each division?
b. What is the beta of the firm?
c. If the firm has 40 percent of its funds in the form of riskless debt and the remainder in equity, what is Parish's equity beta?
d. Would it be advisable for Parish to spin-off either division? Why?
e. What will Parish's firm beta be if a division is spun-off as in part d?

Solution:
Preliminary calculations:

State	p_sR_M	p_sR_1	p_sR_2	$R_M-\bar{R}_M$	$(R_M-\bar{R}_M)^2$	$p_s(R_M-\bar{R}_M)^2$
1	.0625	.075	.0500	.14	.0196	.0049
2	.0375	.045	.0250	.04	.0016	.0004
3	.0200	.030	.0150	-.03	.0009	.0002
4	-.0100	-.005	-.0125	-.15	.0225	.0056

$\bar{R}_M = .11$ $\sigma_M^2 = .0111$

$\bar{R}_1 = .145$

$\bar{R}_2 = .0775$

$R_1-\bar{R}_1$	$(R_1-\bar{R}_1)(R_M-\bar{R}_M)$	$p_s(R_1-\bar{R}_1)(R_M-\bar{R}_M)$
.155	.02170	.0054250
.035	.00140	.0003500
-.025	.00075	.0001875
-.165	.02475	.0061875
	$COV(R_1,R_M) =$	.0121500

$R_2-\bar{R}_2$	$(R_2-\bar{R}_2)(R_M-\bar{R}_M)$	$p_s(R_2-\bar{R}_2)(R_M-\bar{R}_M)$
.1225	.017150	.00428750
.0225	.000900	.00022500
-.0175	.000525	.00013125
-.1275	.019125	.00478125
	$COV(R_2,R_M) =$	.00942500

$$\beta_1 = \frac{COV(R_1,R_M)}{\sigma_M^2} = \frac{.01215}{.0111} = 1.09$$

$$\beta_2 = \frac{COV(R_2,R_M)}{\sigma_M^2} = \frac{.009425}{.0111} = .85$$

a. $R_j = R_F + [E(R_M)-R_F]\beta_j$

$R_1 = .08 + (.11-.08)(1.09) = .1127$ = required return

$R_2 = .08 + (.11-.08)(.85) = .1055$ = required return

b. $\beta_{firm} = .5\beta_1 + .5\beta_2$

$= .5(1.09) + .5(.85)$

$= .545 + .425$

$= .97$

The beta of the firm is the weighted average of the betas of the divisions which make up the firm.

c. For riskless debt, the beta (β_d) = 0.

$$\beta_{assets} = \beta_d\left(\frac{B}{B+S}\right) + \beta_s\left(\frac{S}{B+S}\right)$$

$$.97 = (0)(.4) + \beta_s(.6)$$

$$.97 = \beta_s(.6)$$

$$\beta_s = 1.62$$

d. The expected return for Division 2 is .0775. This is below its required return of .1127. Division 1 has an expected return of .145 versus a required return of only .1055. Since Division 2 earns less than its required return Parish should consider eliminating this division.

e. If Division 2 is spun-off, the firm beta will be the same as the beta of Division 1, or 1.09.

17.13 Projects X and Y are mutually exclusive equipment replacement projects. Both require the same cash outlay of $1,500, both last one year, and both have the same end-of-year revenues $3,500. End-of-year cash outflows however may vary. Estimates of end-of-year outflows for the two projects plus the market return are given for various states of nature below:

State of Nature	p_s	End-of-Year Outflows Project X	Project Y	R_M
Great	.25	$500	$400	.20
Good	.25	700	500	.15
Average	.25	800	600	.08
Horrid	.25	1,000	1,500	0

Which project will have the higher NPV?

Solution:

State	p_s	R_X	R_Y
1	.25	(3500-500)/1500 = 2.00	(3500-400)/1500 = 2.07
2	.25	(3500-700)/1500 = 1.87	(3500-500)/1500 = 2.00
3	.25	(3500-800)/1500 = 1.80	(3500-600)/1500 = 1.93
4	.25	(3500-1000)/1500 = 1.67	(3500-1500)/1500 = 1.33

p_sR_M	$R_M-\overline{R}_M$	$(R_M-\overline{R}_M)^2$	$p_s(R_M-\overline{R}_M)^2$
.0500	.0925	.00856	.00214
.0375	.0425	.00181	.00045
.0200	−.0275	.00076	.00019
.0000	−.1075	.01156	.00289
$\overline{R}_M$ = .1075			σ_M^2 = .00567

p_sR_X	$R_X-\overline{R}_X$	$(R_X-\overline{R}_X)(R_M-\overline{R}_M)$	$p_s(R_X-\overline{R}_X)(R_M-\overline{R}_M)$
.5000	.165	.01526	.003815
.4675	.035	.00149	.000373
.4500	−.035	.00096	.000240
.4175	−.165	.01774	.004430
$\overline{R}_X$ = 1.8350			$COV(R_X,R_M)$ = .008858

p_sR_Y	$R_Y-\overline{R}_Y$	$(R_Y-\overline{R}_Y)(R_M-\overline{R}_M)$	$p_s(R_Y-\overline{R}_Y)(R_M-\overline{R}_M)$
.5175	.2375	.02197	.00549
.5000	.1675	.00712	.00178
.4825	.0975	−.00268	−.00067
.3325	−.5025	.05402	.01350
$\overline{R}_Y$ = 1.8325			$COV(R_Y,R_M)$ = .02010

$$\beta_X = \frac{COV(R_X,R_M)}{\sigma_M^2} = \frac{.008858}{.00567} = 1.56$$

$$\beta_Y = \frac{COV(R_Y,R_M)}{\sigma_M^2} = \frac{.02010}{.00567} = 3.55$$

All else being equal, Project Y will be discounted at a higher discount rate since its beta is higher than the beta of Project X. Thus the NPV of project Y will be lower than the NPV of Project X.

Both projects have the same expected value of cash outflows at the end of the period (Expected value = $750). However, Project Y's cash outflows have a higher variance, and thus more risk, than those of Project X.

17.14 The Donat Corporation is considering the purchase of a welding machine. The welder will cost $4,000 and will produce revenues of $1,000 per year; it will be depreciated via the straight line method over its expected 8-year life. There is some debate over the useful life of the welder, which may be as long as 10 years or as short as 5 years. Prepare a sensitivity analysis of the effect of asset life on the NPV of the investment. Assume a 40 percent tax rate, zero salvage value, and a cost of capital of 12 percent.

Solution:

If actual life is 5 years:

Outflows	Amount Before Tax	Amount After Tax	Year Event Occurs	PV Factor @ 12%	PV
Investment in welder	$4,000	$4,000	0	1.0	$4,000
Inflows or Benefits					
Revenues [Use (1-T)]	$1,000	$600	1-5	3.6048	$2,162.88
Depreciation [Use T]	500	200	1-5	3.6048	720.96
Tax savings on loss at end of year 5 [Use T]	1,500	600	5	.5674	340.44
Total					$3,224.28

NPV = PV of benefits - PV of costs = $3,224.28 - $4,000

= -$775.72

If actual life is 10 years:

Outflows remain unchanged at $4,000

Inflows or Benefits

Revenues [Use (1-T)]	$1,000	$600	1-10	5.6502	$3,390.12
Depreciation [Use T]	500	200	1-8	4.9676	993.52
Total					$4,383.64

NPV = $4,383.64 - $4,000 = $383.64

If actual life = depreciable life = 8 years:

Outflows remain unchanged at $4,000

	Amount Before Tax	Amount After Tax	Year Event Occurs	PV Factor @ 12%	PV
Inflows or Benefits					
Revenues [Use (1-T)]	$1,000	$600	1-8	4.9676	$2,980.56
Depreciation [Use T]	500	200	1-8	4.9676	993.52
Total					$3,974.09

NPV = $3,974.09 - $4,000 = -$25.91

This investment decision is very sensitive to asset life; its margin for error is small. Only if it has a 10-year life will it have a positive NPV. Donat might want to do more research on the actual useful life it may expect from the welding machine.

(NOTE that annual depreciation is independent of the actual life of the machine. Depreciation must be based on ex ante expected life; actual life is not known when the machine is purchased and depreciation is begun.)

17.15 Mellonson Corporation is planning an investment project in South America. Because of political and other considerations, both investment outlays and cash inflows are uncertain. Mellonson's financial staff has prepared the following cost and revenue estimates and their probabilities.

Investment outlay		Annual cash inflows	
Probability	Cash outlay	Probability	Cash inflow
.20	$200,000	.20	$25,000
.40	300,000	.30	40,000
.35	400,000	.40	50,000
.05	800,000	.10	80,000

The applicable risk-adjusted cost of capital is 16 percent, project life is 20 years, and salvage value is zero.

a. Prepare a decision-tree analysis showing probabilities, payoffs, and expected NPV.
b. Calculate expected NPV using expected cash outlay and expected cash inflows.
c. What is the probability and NPV of the worst possible outcome?
d. What is the probability and NPV of the best possible outcome?
e. What is the probability that the investment will have a positive NPV?

Solution:

a. Present value of cash inflows:
$25,000[PVIFA(16%, 20 yrs)] = $25,000(5.9288) = $148,220

$40,000(5.9288) = $237,152

$50,000(5.9288) = $296,440

$80,000(5.9288) = $474,304

Prob	PV of Cash Flow	Prob	Outlay	NPV	Joint Prob	Joint Prob times NPV
.2	148,220	.20	200,000	-51,780	.04	-2,071
		.40	300,000	-151,780	.08	-12,142
		.35	400,000	-251,780	.07	-17,625
		.05	800,000	-651,780	.01	-6,518
.3	237,152	.20	200,000	37,152	.06	2,229
		.40	300,000	-62,848	.12	-7,542
		.35	400,000	-162,848	.105	-17,099
		.05	800,000	-562,848	.015	-8,443
.4	296,440	.20	200,000	96,440	.08	7,715
		.40	300,000	-3,560	.16	-570
		.35	400,000	-103,560	.14	-14,498
		.05	800,000	-503,560	.02	-10,071
.1	474,304	.20	200,000	274,304	.02	5,486
		.40	300,000	174,304	.04	6,972
		.35	400,000	74,304	.035	2,601
		.05	800,000	-325,696	.005	-1,628
					Expected NPV =	-73,204

b. Expected cash flows = .2(25,000) + .3(40,000) + .4(50,000) + .1(80,000)
= 5,000 + 12,000 + 20,000 + 8,000
= $45,000

Expected outlay = .2(200,000) + .4(300,000) + .35(400,000) + .05(800,000)
= 40,000 + 120,000 + 140,000 + 40,000
= $340,000

Expected NPV = -340,000 + 45,000(5.9288)
= -340,000 + 266,796
= -73,204

This result agrees with the result obtained using the decision tree methodology.

c. The worst possible outcome is a loss of $651,780; its probability is .01, or one chance in 100.

d. The best possible outcome is a gain of $274,304; its probability is .02.

e. Summing the joint probabilities associated with positive NPV's we have .06 + .08 + .02 + .04 + .035 = .235.

The outlook is not particularly promising for this investment project, and Mellonson would be wise to abandon it.

CHAPTER 18

OPTIONS ON RISKY ASSETS

Theme: Trading in options has increased in recent years. Theoretical developments include Option Pricing Models (OPM) and the extension of option pricing principles to the valuation of equity and risky debt and to the effects of mergers.

I. Introduction to Options.
   A. An option is a contract that gives its holder the right to buy (or sell) an asset at a predetermined price for a given period.
      1. The right to buy is a call option.
      2. The right to sell is a put option.
      3. The predetermined price is called the exercise, or striking price.
         a. Out-of-the-money call option--Exercise price exceeds current asset price.
         b. In-the-money call option--Exercise price is below current asset price.
         c. The converse is true for put options.
      4. European options may be exercised only at maturity.
      5. American options may be exercised at any time up to and including maturity.
   B. Many other types of financial assets can be thought of as options:
      1. Stocks of levered firms.
      2. Risky bonds.
      3. Warrants.
      4. Convertible bonds.

II. Put-Call Parity.
   A. Any pattern of financial payoffs can be constructed using combinations of four basic building blocks.
      1. The four basic building blocks are:
         a. Stocks--S
         b. Risk-free discount bonds--B
         c. Call options--C
         d. Put options--P
      2. Their relationship is such that $S + P = B + C$.
         a. $S + P$ represents the payoff resulting from a long position in 1 share of stock and a put option on that stock, with exercise price X.
         b. $B + C$ represents the payoff on a bond with face value X and a call option on the same stock as above, also with exercise price X.

B. Put-call parity means that for European options there is a fixed relationship between the market values of put and call options written on the same asset, with the same maturity (T) and exercise price (X).

C. Consider the risk-free position: B = S + P - C (which is derived from S + P = B + C).

1. A risk-free position, B, can be constructed by buying 1 share of stock and 1 put option on the stock and selling 1 call option on the stock.
2. The net payoff from this position is constant (i.e. riskless) at X regardless of stock price changes.
3. Thus the present value of the position is equal to the present value of the payoff discounted at the risk-free rate. Using continuous discounting:

$$S_o + P_o - C_o = Xe^{-r_f T}$$

D. Put-call parity is expressed as:

$$C_o - P_o = S_o - Xe^{-r_f T}$$

1. The relationship between the values of the put and call options is fixed.
2. Once a formula is derived for the pricing of call options, we can also price put options.

III. The Value of a Call Option is Affected by Five Factors.

A. Stock price, S.

1. Call value or price, C, increases with stock price.
2. $C \geq 0$, since there is always some chance that it will mature in-the-money.
3. $C \leq S$, since the call price cannot exceed the value of the underlying stock.
4. $C \geq S-X$, since the call price must at least equal its value if exercised, that is the difference between the stock price and the exercise price.

B. Exercise price, X.

1. The lower the exercise price, the greater the value of the call.
2. If X = 0, call price is equal to share price.

C. Time to maturity, T.

1. The longer the maturity, the greater the call value, since the greater chance that the stock price will rise above exercise price.
2. If maturity were infinite, call price would be equal to stock price.

D. Price variance of underlying stock, σ_s^2.

1. The greater the variance, the higher the value of the call, since there is a greater likelihood that stock price will exceed exercise price.
2. Increased variance causes no change in downside effect which has a minimum of C = 0.

E. Risk-free rate of interest, r_f.

1. The higher the risk-free rate, the higher the call price.

2. $C_o \geq MAX[0, S_o - Xe^{-r_f T}]$

   a. $Xe^{-r_f T}$ declines as $r_f T$ increases.

   b. Thus, $S_o - Xe^{-r_f T}$ increases as $r_f T$ increases.

F. Summary of factors affecting the price of a call option:

$$C_o = f(S_o, X, T, \sigma_s^2, r_f)$$

1. S_o--positive effect.
2. X--negative effect.
3. T--positive effect.
4. σ_s^2--positive effect.
5. r_f--positive effect.

IV. Binomial Option Pricing Model.

A. Assume a 1-period framework.

1. At end of period, stock price can be higher or lower than at beginning of period.
   a. S_o = current stock price.
   b. q = probability that stock price will rise.
   c. 1-q = probability that stock price will fall.
   d. $1+r_f$ = 1 plus the risk-free rate.
   e. u = multiplicative upward movement in price.
      (i) $u > 1+r_f > 1$.
      (ii) If stock price rises, end-of-period stock price will be uS.
      (iii) No upside limit.
   f. d = multiplicative downward movement in price.
      (i) $d < 1 < 1+r_f$.
      (ii) If stock price falls, end-of-period stock price will be dS.
      (iii) Stock price cannot decline below 0.
2. Call option on the stock has the same probabilities [q and (1-q)] of upside or downside impact.
   a. Payoff to call if stock price rises = MAX[0, uS-X].
   b. Payoff to call if stock price falls = MAX[0, dS-X].

B. The binomial OPM depends on the existence of a risk-free hedge portfolio which earns the risk-free rate regardless of stock price movement.

1. The hedge portfolio consists of buying 1 share and writing m units of call option against the share $= S-mC$.
2. m = hedge ratio.
   a. Set upside and downside payoffs equal:
   $$uS-mC_u = dS-mC_d$$
   b. Solve for m:
   $$m = \frac{S(u-d)}{C_u-C_d}$$
3. Since the hedge portfolio earns the risk-free rate, its end-of-period value can be found by multiplying its present value by $1+r_f$:
   $$(1+r_f)(S-mC) = uS-mC_u \qquad (= dS-mC_d)$$
   a. Solving for C and substituting for m we have:
   $$C = \frac{C_u\left[\frac{1+r_f-d}{u-d}\right] + C_d\left[\frac{u-1-r_f}{u-d}\right]}{1+r_f}$$
   b. Let $p = \frac{1+r_f-d}{u-d}$ and $(1-p) = \frac{u-1-r_f}{u-d}$
   c. Then $C = \frac{pC_u + (1-p)C_d}{1+r_f}$
   d. p = hedging probability = q for risk-neutral investor.

C. Insights provided by the binomial OPM:

1. Investor expectations as to the probability of stock price changes do not affect option price.
2. Individual attitude toward risk is irrelevant; only requirement is that people prefer more wealth to less.
3. The only random variable on which option price depends is stock price.

D. The binomial OPM can be extended to a multi-period framework; at the limit, the binomial model approaches the Black-Scholes OPM discussed next.

V. The Black-Scholes Option Pricing Model.

A. The Black-Scholes formula is:

$$C = SN(d_1) - Xe^{-r_f T} N(d_2)$$

$$\text{where } d_1 = \frac{\ln(S/X)+r_f T}{\sigma\sqrt{T}} + \tfrac{1}{2}\sigma\sqrt{T}$$

$$d_2 = d_1 - \sigma\sqrt{T}$$

1. $N(d_1)$ and $N(d_2)$ are cumulative normal probabilities as found in Appendix Table D.
2. The value of the call is a function of:
   a. S = stock price.
   b. X = exercise price.
   c. T = time to maturity.
   d. σ^2 = instantaneous variance of stock returns.
   e. r_f = risk-free rate.

B. Like the binomial OPM, the Black-Scholes OPM depends on the existence of a hedge portfolio which earns the risk-free rate.

1. The value of the hedge portfolio = V_H = S-mC.
2. m = $1/N(d_1)$; or alternatively, $N(d_1)$ is the inverse of the hedge ratio.
3. The hedge portfolio is riskless only for very small stock price changes.
4. Thus, the hedge ratio must be adjusted whenever the stock price changes.
5. $N(d_2)$ = probability that the option will finish in-the-money.

VI. Applications of the OPM to Corporate Finance.

A. The equity of a levered firm may be viewed as a call option on the value of the firm.

1. The face value of the debt is the exercise price and the maturity of the debt is the maturity of the option.
   a. If the value of the firm exceeds the face value of the debt at maturity:
      (i) The option (the equity) has a positive value.
      (ii) The option will be exercised. (The debt will be repaid.)
   b. If the value of the firm is less than the face value of the debt at maturity:
      (i) The option (the equity) has a zero value.
      (ii) The option will not be exercised. (The debt will not be repaid.)

(iii) The firm will be in default; however the shareholders' loss will be limited to the the amount of their equity (the value of the option).

2. Shareholders' wealth (S) at maturity of debt is:

$$S = MAX[0, V-D]$$

where V = value of the firm
D = face value of risky debt

3. Recall that S + P = B + C. (18.4)
   a. When using the OPM for equity pricing we have:
      V = value of the levered firm = underlying asset
      S = equity in the firm = call option.
      So substitute V for S and S for C in 18.4. So V+P = B+S.
   b. Thus V = (B-P) + S.
4. Firm value is partitioned into two parts:
   a. S = equity = call option.
   b. B-P = present value of risk-free debt plus short position in a European put option on the value of the firm.
5. The application of the OPM to the pricing of corporate securities can be extended to the analysis of various corporate finance decisions:
   a. Risky investments.
   b. Dividend policy.
   c. Spinoffs.
   d. Equity repurchases.
   e. Subordinated debt.
   f. Mergers.

B. The OPM framework emphasizes the inherent divergence between the interests of shareholders and creditors.
   1. Increasing the riskiness (σ^2) of a firm's operations increases the value of equity and reduces the value of debt.
   2. Bondholders will require a higher rate of return on risky debt; a higher interest rate will be required to equate their future payoff with the reduced current market value of the risky debt:

$$B_o = De^{-k_b T}$$

C. The OPM can be used in financial leverage decisions by illustrating the relationship between leverage and the cost of risky debt.
   1. Use the OPM to calculate the market values of debt and equity corresponding to various levels of the face value of debt.
   2. The implied k_b can be computed from the face and market values of debt.
   3. The required yield rises with increased leverage.

D. Mergers result in portfolio diversification (risk-reduction) effects whenever the cash flows of the two firms are less than perfectly correlated.
   1. According to the OPM, this lower risk will cause a wealth transfer from shareholders to bondholders.
   2. Utilization of greater debt capacity after the merger may restore shareholder value loss.
   3. Mergers may also have divergent effects on different groups of bondholders.
      a. Holders of longer-maturity bonds become, in effect, holders of subordinate debt.
      b. Bond covenants may restrict merger activity.

VII. Empirical Evidence on Option Pricing Models.
   A. Variations on the models discussed above have been developed for specific situations.
      1. Since equity is an option, an option on stock is like an option on an option; including firm leverage and debt maturity in the option pricing model improve its accuracy.
      2. The model has been extended to dividend-paying stock.
   B. Some studies have found OPM predictions to have no economically exploitable biases, net of transaction costs.
   C. Other studies have found biases in the Black-Scholes model.
      1. The model underprices options on low-variance assets and vice versa.
      2. The model may misprice depending on the in-the-money/out-of-the-money status of the option and its time to maturity.

VIII. The OPM is Consistent with the CAPM.
   A. Increase in option price when variance is higher does not imply that investors prefer more risk to less.
      1. The undiversifiable risk of a call option is related to the undiversifiable risk of the underlying asset. (The beta of a call option is generally greater than that of the underlying asset.)
      2. Call option risk decreases (and value increases) with:
         a. Increase in stock price.
         b. Increase in risk-free rate.
         c. Increase in stock variance.
         d. Increase in option maturity.
      3. Call option risk increases (and value decreases) with increase in exercise price.

4. $E(r_c) = r_f + [E(r_m)-r_f]\beta_c$
   a. where $E(r_c)$ = expected return on the call option
      β_c = beta of the call option = $N(d_1)(S/C)\beta_S$
   b. Option risk changes daily with approaching maturity.

B. Unlike the CAPM, the OPM is not an equilibrium model.
   1. The OPM requires fewer assumptions.
   2. An option is merely a contingent claim based on the equilibrium pricing of the underlying asset.

Chapter 18 - Illustrative Problems and Solutions

18.1 Use the one-period binomial OPM to price a call option which has an exercise price of $15. The current price of the underlying stock is $20, u = 1.2 and d = 0.9. The risk-free rate is 10 percent.

Solution:

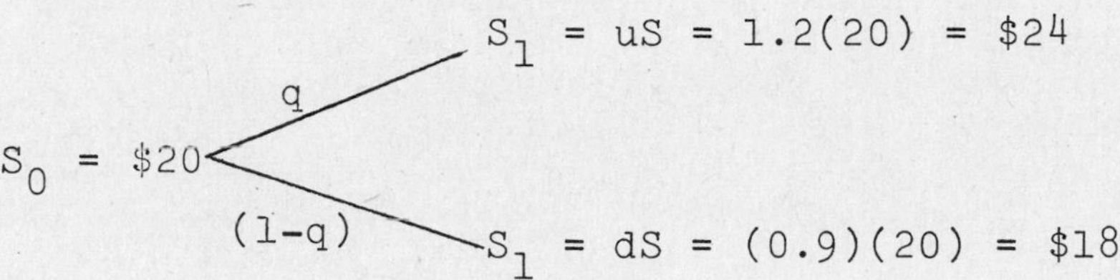

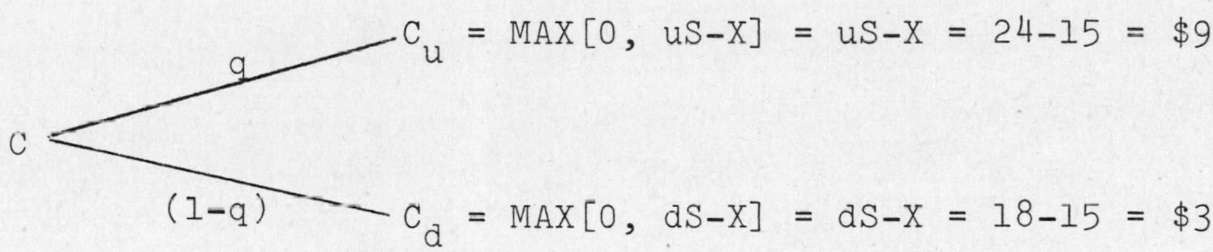

$$m = \frac{S(u-d)}{C_u-C_d} = \frac{20(1.2-0.9)}{9-3} = \frac{20(0.3)}{6} = \frac{6}{6} = 1$$

The riskless hedge portfolio consists of buying 1 share of the stock and selling 1 call option against it.

$$C = \frac{[pC_u+(1-p)C_d]}{1+r_f}$$

$$p = \frac{1+r_f-d}{u-d} = \frac{1.10-0.9}{0.3} = .67$$

$$1-p = \frac{u-1-r_f}{u-d} = \frac{1.2-1-.10}{0.3} = .33$$

$$C = \frac{.67(9) + .33(3)}{1.10} = \frac{6.03 + 1}{1.10} = \frac{7.03}{1.10} = \$6.39$$

18.2 A call option has an exercise price of $18. The current price of the underlying stock is $24. The instantaneous variance of the underlying stock returns is 16 percent, the risk-free rate is 10 percent, and the option has 6 months to maturity.

a. Use the Black-Scholes OPM to find the value of the call option.

b. How many call options must you write to create a riskless hedge if you own 50 shares of the stock?

Solution:

a. $C = SN(d_1) - Xe^{-r_f T} N(d_2)$

$S = \$24$
$X = \$18$

$$d_1 = \frac{\ln(S/X) + r_f T}{\sigma\sqrt{T}} + \tfrac{1}{2}\sigma\sqrt{T}$$

$$= \frac{\ln(24/18) + (.10)(180/365)}{.4(\sqrt{180/365})} + (.5)(.4)(\sqrt{180/365})$$

$$= \frac{.28768 + .04932}{.2809} + .14045$$

$$= 1.19972 + .14045$$

$$= 1.34017$$

$$d_2 = d_1 - \sigma\sqrt{T}$$

$$= 1.34017 - (.4)(\sqrt{180/365})$$

$$= 1.34017 - .2809$$

$$= 1.05927$$

From Appendix Table D:

$$N(d_1) = .5 + .4099 = .9099$$

$$N(d_2) = .5 + .3554 = .8554$$

$$C = 24(.9099) - 18[e^{-(.10)(180/365)}](.8554)$$

$$= 21.84 - 18(.95188)(.8554)$$

$$= 21.84 - 14.66$$

$$= \$7.18$$

b. The hedge ratio is the inverse of $N(d_1)$.

$$m = \frac{1}{N(d_1)} = \frac{1}{.9099}$$

$$= 1.099$$

To hedge against 50 shares, you must write 50(1.099) or 54.95 call options.

18.3 You are given the following facts:

Stock price = S = \$20
Call price = C = \$0.94
Exercise price = X = \$22
Call maturity = T = 90 days
Risk-free rate = r_f = 0.10

Estimate the instantaneous variance of the stock.

Solution:
We know from the Black-Scholes OPM that

$$C = SN(d_1) - Xe^{-r_f T} N(D_2)$$

$$\text{where } d_1 = \frac{\ln(S/X)+r_f T}{\sigma\sqrt{T}} + (1/2)\sigma\sqrt{T}$$

$$\text{and } d_2 = d_1 - \sigma\sqrt{T}$$

We can substitute the equation for d_1 into the equation for d_2.

$$d_2 = \frac{\ln(S/X)+r_fT}{\sigma\sqrt{T}} + (1/2)\sigma\sqrt{T} - \sigma\sqrt{T} = \frac{\ln(S/X)+r_fT}{\sigma\sqrt{T}} - (1/2)\sigma\sqrt{T}$$

Thus, $C = SN\left[\frac{\ln(S/X)+r_fT}{\sigma\sqrt{T}} + (1/2)\sigma\sqrt{T}\right]$

$$- Xe^{-r_fT}N\left[\frac{\ln(S/X)+r_fT}{\sigma\sqrt{T}} - (1/2)\sigma\sqrt{T}\right]$$

Substituting in the values we are given we have:

$$0.94 = 20N\left[\frac{\ln(20/22)+(.10)(90/365)}{\sigma\sqrt{90/365}} + (1/2)\sigma\sqrt{90/365}\right]$$

$$- 22e^{-(.10)(90/365)}N\left[\frac{\ln(20/22)+(.10)(90/365)}{\sigma\sqrt{90/365}} - (1/2)\sigma\sqrt{90/365}\right]$$

$$0.94 = 20N\left[\frac{-.142267}{\sigma} + .24828\sigma\right] - 21.4642N\left[\frac{-.142267}{\sigma} - .24828\sigma\right]$$

We must solve for σ using trial and error.

We find $\sigma \cong .387$

$\sigma^2 \cong 15$ percent

18.4 The common stock of Wrangler Corporation sells for \$42 per share. Warrants are also available for purchasing the stock at a price of \$36. The warrants have 4 years to maturity. The instantaneous variance of returns on the common stock is 16 percent and the risk-free rate is 12 percent.

a. Using the option pricing model, determine the value of a warrant.

b. What would be the value of a warrant if the maturity were 9 years?

Solution:

a. $C_o = S_oN(d_1) - X_oe^{-R_fT}N(d_2)$

$S_o = \$42$

$X_o = \$36$

$T = 4$ years

$R_f = .12$

$\sigma^2 = .16$

$C_o = \$42N(d_1) - \$36e^{-(.12)(4)}N(d_2)$

$$d_1 = \frac{\ln(42/36) + [.12 + (.16/2)]4}{.4(2)} = 1.1927$$

$d_2 = 1.1927 - [.4(2)] = .3927$

$N(d_1) = .5 + .3830 = .8830$

$N(d_2) = .5 + .1517 = .6517$

$C_o = \$42(.8830) - \$36e^{-.48}(.6517)$

$= \$37.09 - \$14.52$

$= \$22.57$

b. $T = 9$ years

$$C_o = \$42N(d_1) - \$36e^{-(.12)(9)}N(d_2)$$

$$d_1 = \frac{\ln(42/36) + [.12 + (.16/2)]9}{.4(3)} = 1.6285$$

$$d_2 = 1.6285 - [.4(3)] = .4285$$

$$N(d_1) = .5 + .4484 = .9484$$

$$N(d_2) = .5 + .1664 = .6664$$

$$C_o = \$42(.9484) - \$36e^{-1.08}(.6664)$$

$$= \$39.83 - \$8.15$$

$$= \$31.68$$

The higher warrant value for the longer maturity reflects the probability that over the longer period, the price of the stock may increase more.

18.5 Clareville Corporation has outstanding debt of \$4,000,000 on its balance sheet with 25 years to maturity. On the market, Clareville is currently valued at \$18,000,000. The total risk of the company's percentage returns is $\sigma = 0.71$. The riskless rate of return is 12 percent. Using the OPM,

a. Determine the value of equity.
b. Determine the value of debt.
c. Assume that Clareville revises its long-term strategy such that the risk of its percentage returns rises to 0.83. What is the effect on the value of debt and equity?
d. Instead of revising its long-term strategy, Clareville decides to merge with Scorpio Corporation, a firm with the same market value as Clareville., and identical to it in several respects:

$D_c = D_s = \$4,000,000$	Face Value of Debt
$T_c = T_s = 25$ years	Maturity of Debt
$\sigma_c = \sigma_s = 0.71$	Instantaneous Std. Deviation
$R_f = .12$	
$\rho_{cs} = -.5$	

The combined value of the merged firm will be \$36,000,000. What will be the value of debt and equity?

Solution:

a. The total value of the firm, \$18,000,000, is

$$V = S + B$$

We can use the OPM to determine the market value of the stock (expressed as a call option on the value of the firm) and subtract this from \$18,000,000 to find B, the market value of the debt.

For valuing corporate securities, the OPM can be expressed as:

$$S = VN(d_1) - De^{-R_f T} N(d_2)$$

where

S = market value of stock
V = market value of the firm = \$18,000,000
D = face value of debt = \$4,000,000

$$S = \$18N(d_1) - 4e^{-(.12)(25)}N(d_2)$$

$$d_1 = \frac{\ln(18/4) + [.12 + (.5041/2)]\ 25}{(.71)(5)} = 3.04$$

$$d_2 = 3.04 - [(.71)(5)] = -.51$$

$$N(d_1) = .5 + .4988 = .9988$$

$$N(d_2) = .5 - .1950 = .305$$

$$S = 18(.9988) - 4(e^{-3})\ (.305)$$

$$= 17.9784 - .0607$$

$$= \$17,917,700$$

b. $V = S + B$

$\$18,000,000 = \$17,917,700 + B$

$B = \$82,300$

The high value of equity relative to debt reflects the long maturity of the debt. Over 25 years, the probability is high that the value of the firm will be greater than the face value of the debt, and thus the option will be exercised.

c. $S = 18N(d_1) - 4e^{-(.12)(25)}N(d_2)$

$$d_1 = \frac{\ln(18/4) + [.12 + (.6889/2)]\ 25}{(.83)(5)} = 3.16$$

$$d_2 = 3.16 - [(.83)(5)] = -.99$$

$$N(d_1) \approx 1$$

$$N(d_2) = .5 - .3389 = .1611$$

$S = 18(1) - 4e^{-3}(.1611)$

$= 18 - .03208$

$= \$17,967,920$

$B = \$32,080$

The greater risk has increased the value of equity and reduced the value of debt.

d. To obtain the market value of debt and equity for the new firm, we must calculate the instantaneous standard deviation of the merged entity.

$$\sigma_{cs}^2 = w_c^2\sigma_c^2 + w_s^2\sigma_s^2 + 2w_c w_s \rho_{cs}\sigma_c\sigma_s$$

$$= (.5)^2(.5041) + (.5)^2(.5041) + 2(.5)(.5)(-.5)(.71)(.71)$$

$$= .126025 + .126025 - .126025$$

$$= .126025 = .126$$

$$\sigma_{cs} = .35$$

$$S = 36N(d_1) - 8e^{-(.12)(25)}N(d_2)$$

$$d_1 = \frac{\ln(36/8) + [.12 + .126/2]\ 25}{(.35)(5)} = 3.47$$

$$d_2 = 3.47 - [.35(5)] = 1.72$$

$$N(d_1) \cong 1$$

$$N(d_2) = .5 + .4573 = .9573$$

$S = 36(1) - 8(e^{-3})(.9573)$

$= 36 - .38129$

$= \$35,618,710$

$B = \$36,000,000 - \$35,618,710 = \$381,290$

The value of equity is still very high relative to debt. However, the value of equity is less than double the original value of equity (\$17,917,700 x 2 = \$35,835,400) by over \$200,000. This is because the negative correlation between Clareville and Scorpio has reduced the risk of the merged firm. If no other merger effects were involved, the shareholders of both firms should oppose the merger.

18.6 The Corral Corporation has a current market value of \$2,000,000. Forty percent of the current value is the face amount of pure discount debt which matures in 3 years. The risk-free rate is 10 percent, and the variance of percentage returns is 36 percent.

a. What is the market value of equity?
b. What is the market value of debt?
c. What is the yield to maturity on the debt?

Solution:

a. $r_f = 10\%$
$T = 3$
$\sigma^2 = .36$
$\sigma = .6$
V = value of the firm = \$2,000,000
D = face value of debt = .4(2,000,000) = \$800,000

The Black-Scholes OPM is written as follows for the valuation of corporate securities.

$$S = VN(d_1) - De^{-r_f T} N(d_2)$$

$$\text{where } d_1 = \frac{\ln(V/D)+r_f T}{\sigma\sqrt{T}} + (1/2)\sigma\sqrt{T}$$

$$\text{and } d_2 = d_1 - \sigma\sqrt{T}$$

For the facts of this problem

$$d_1 = \frac{\ln(2/.8)+.10(3)}{.6\sqrt{3}} + (1/2)(.6)(\sqrt{3})$$

$$= \frac{1.21629}{1.03923} + .519615$$

$$= 1.68999$$

$$d_2 = 1.68999 - 1.03923$$

$$= .65076$$

From Appendix Table D we find

$$N(d_1) = .5 + .4545 = .9545$$

$$N(d_2) = .5 + .2422 = .7422$$

$$S = 2(.9545) - .8e^{-(.10)(3)}(.7422)$$

$$= 1.909 - .8(.74082)(.7422)$$

$$= 1.909 - .439868$$

$$= \$1,469,132 = \text{market value of equity}$$

b. The market value of debt is equal to the market value of the firm less the market value of equity.

$$B = 2,000,000 - 1,469,132$$

$$= \$530,868$$

c. The yield to maturity on the debt is found as follows:

$$\$530,868 = \frac{\$800,000}{(1+r)^3}$$

$$(1+r)^3 = 1.50696595$$

$$1+r = 1.14648$$

$$r \cong 14.65 \text{ percent}$$

18.7 The King Company has outstanding debt with a face value of \$3 million. The current market value of the firm is \$8 million. The debt consists of pure discount bonds which mature in 4 years. The firm pays no cash dividends and has a variance of percentage returns of 0.25. Inflation is expected to fall by 5 percentage points, lowering the nominal risk-free rate of interest from 12 to 7 percent.

a. Use the OPM to determine the current market values of debt and equity.
b. Which class of security holders will benefit more from the expected change in the risk-free rate?

Solution:

a. V = market value of the firm = \$8 million
D = face value of debt = \$3 million
$r_f = 0.12$
$\sigma^2 = .25$
$T = 4$

$$S = VN(d_1) - De^{-r_f T} N(d_2)$$

$$d_1 = \frac{\ln(V/D)+r_f T}{\sigma\sqrt{T}} + (1/2)\sigma\sqrt{T}$$

$$= \frac{\ln(8/3)+(.12)(4)}{.5(2)} + (1/2)(.5)(2)$$

$$= \frac{.9808+.48}{1} + .5$$

$$= 1.96$$

$$d_2 = d_1 - \sigma\sqrt{T}$$

$$= 1.96 - 1$$

$$= .96$$

From Appendix Table D we find

$$N(d_1) = .5 + .475 = .975$$

$$N(d_2) = .5 + .3315 = .8315$$

$$S = (.975) - 3e^{-.12(4)}(.8315)$$

$$= 7.8 - 3(.618783392)(.8315)$$

$$= 7.8 - 1.543555$$

= \$6,256,445 = market value of equity

Market value of debt = V - S = \$1,743,555

b. All facts are the same except that r_f now equals 7 percent.

$$d_1 = \frac{\ln(8/3)+(.07)(4)}{1} + .5$$

$$= .9808 + .28 + .5$$

$$= 1.76$$

$$d_2 = 1.76 - 1$$

$$= .76$$

$$N(d_1) = .5 + .4608 = .9608$$

$$N(d_2) = .5 + .2764 = .7764$$

$$S = (.9608) - 3e^{-.07(4)}(.7764)$$

$$= 7.6864 - 3(.755783741)(.7764)$$

$$= 7.6864 - 1.760371$$

$$= \$5,926,029$$

The market value of debt = B = V-S = \$2,073,971

Debtholders benefit from the decline in the risk-free rate at the expense of shareholders. The market value of debt has increased by \$330,416, and the market value of equity has declined by the same amount.

18.8 The Squires Corporation has a current market value of \$250 million; its capital structure consists of equity and \$100 million in pure discount bonds which will mature in 4 years. The total risk of Squires' assets is $\sigma = 0.9$. The expected return on the market is 14 percent. The firm's equity beta is 1.3 and the beta of its debt is 0.2. Assume that Squires pays no cash dividends and that $r_f = 10$ percent.

a. What are the market values of Squires' debt and equity?
b. What is the cost of debt and the cost of equity? (Disregard taxes.)
c. If everything else remains the same, what will Squires' equity beta be two years from now?

Solution:

a. $V = \$250$
$D = \$100$
$r_f = 0.10$
$\sigma = 0.9$
$T = 4$

$$S = VN(d_1) - De^{-r_f T}N(d_2)$$

$$d_1 = \frac{\ln(V/D)+r_f T}{\sigma\sqrt{T}} + (1/2)\sigma\sqrt{T}$$

$$= \frac{\ln(250/100)+(.10)(4)}{(.9)(2)} + (1/2)(.9)(2)$$

$$= \frac{.91629 + .4}{1.8} + 0.9$$

$$= 1.6313$$

$$d_2 = d_1 - \sigma\sqrt{T}$$

$$= 1.6313 - 1.8$$

$$= -.16873$$

$$N(d_1) = .5 + .4484 = .9484$$

$$N(d_2) = .5 - .0675 = .4325$$

$$S = 250(.9484) - 100e^{-(.10)(4)}(.4325)$$

$$= 237.1 - 100(.67032)(.4325)$$

$$= 237.1 - 28.991342$$

$= \$208,108,658$ = market value of equity

$B = V - S$

$= \$250,000,000 - \$208,108,658$

$= \$41,891,342$ = market value of debt

b. Since we know the betas of debt and equity, as well as the market return and the risk-free rate, we can use the CAPM to find the costs of debt and equity.

Equity: $k_e = r_f + [E(R_M) - r_f]\beta_e$

$= .10 + (.14-.10)1.3$

$= 15.2$ percent

Debt: $k_b = r_f + [E(R_M) - r_f]\beta_b$

$= .10 + (.04)(.2)$

$= 10.8$ percent

c. If nothing else changes (i.e. the variance of the market portfolio and Squires' covariance with the market portfolio), then the equity beta should also remain unchanged.

The relative values of debt and equity will change, however, since the time to maturity on the debt is now only two years instead of four.

$$d_1 = \frac{\ln(250/100)+(.10)(2)}{(.9)(\sqrt{2})} + (1/2)(.9)(\sqrt{2})$$

$$= \frac{.91629 + .2}{1.2728} + .6364$$

$$= 1.513$$

$$d_2 = 1.513 - 1.2728$$

$$= .2406$$

$N(d_1) = .5 + .4345 = .9345$

$N(d_2) = .5 + .0948 = .5948$

$$S = 250(.9345) - 100e^{-.10(2)}(.5948)$$

$$= 233.625 - 100(.81873)(.5948)$$

$$= 233.625 - 48.698105$$

$$= \$184,926,895$$

$$B = V\text{-}S = \$250,000,000 - \$184,926,895 = \$65,073,105$$

The market value of the debt has increased and the market value of equity has declined with the approaching maturity of the debt, all else being equal.

18.9 Suppose the government has imposed an interest rate ceiling of 10 percent. Demand for borrowing exceeds the funds available at that rate. The Foursquare Insurance Company has a customer, the Schwartz Drug Company, who is willing to pay 20 percent interest to borrow $200,000 for 5 years. Schwartz is willing to put up his business (with a current market value of $250,000) as collateral to secure the loan.

To get around the interest rate ceiling, Foursquare proposes the following contract:

--Foursquare will hold title to the business assets for the next five years.
--Foursquare receives a right to sell the business back to Schwartz for $X at the end of five years. That is, Foursquare has a put option. If Foursquare decides to sell, Schwartz must buy.
--Foursquare will advance the $200,000 immediately.
--Schwartz receives the right to buy his company back from Foursquare for $X at the end of five years. That is, Schwartz has a call option.

What value must X have in order to provide Foursquare with a riskless 20 percent annual rate of return?

Solution:

This problem illustrates put-call parity. There are 2 possible outcomes at maturity:

1. The business is worth more than $X. Schwartz will willingly buy back the company for $X.

Schwartz will exercise his call option.

2. The business is worth less than $X. Foursquare will exercise its put option and require Schwartz to buy back the business for $X.

In either outcome, Foursquare receives $X, and the only issue is to find the value of X which results in a 20 percent annual return.

Put-call parity is expressed as:

$$S_0 + P_0 - C = B_0$$

The amount lent is $200,000; thus

$$S_0 + P_0 - C = \$200,000$$

B_0 is the present value of X; thus

$$B_0 = \frac{X}{(1+r)^t} = \frac{X}{(1.20)^5} = \$200,000$$

Solving for X we find

$$X = \$200,000(1.20)^5$$

$$= \$497,664$$

Foursquare is lending $200,000 today and wants to receive an annual return of 20 percent for five years. This is merely a present value problem where $200,000 is the present value of the loan and X is the future value which, when discounted at 20 percent for 5 years equals the present value.

CHAPTER 19

MARKET EFFICIENCY AND FINANCIAL DECISIONS

Theme: Capital market efficiency is an assumption of many financial decision models. Capital market efficiency deals with the issue of whether or not security prices accurately reflect relevant information.

I. Information and Market Efficiency.
   A. Information is defined as a set of messages which may be used to alter the actions of the recipient to change his or her welfare.
      1. The ability of the recipient to act is critical.
      2. A message which never changes has no value.
      3. Inversely correlated messages can be as valuable as positively correlated messages.
   B. The fair game model says that, on average, the actual change in security prices over an interval of time will be the same as the change predicted given the information available at the beginning of the period.
      1. The expected return is based on the information available at the beginning of the period.
      2. Any return above the expected return is defined as an excess or abnormal return.
   C. The fair game model partitions market efficiency into three information subsets:
      1. Weak-form efficiency--The information set consists of historical price and return data.
      2. Semi-strong-form efficiency--The information subset consists of all publicly available information, including, but not limited to:
         a. Historical price data.
         b. Ticker tape information.
         c. Corporate reports.
         d. Investment advisory reports.
      3. Strong-form efficiency--The information subset consists of all information, whether publicly available or not.

II. Weak-Form Market Efficiency.
   A. Weak-form efficiency holds that security prices fully reflect past price data.
   B. Excess returns cannot be earned on the basis of past price patterns, according to the weak-form hypothesis.
   C. Empirical tests strongly support weak-form market efficiency.
      1. Technical trading rules called filter rules attempt to exploit historical price patterns to earn excess returns.

a. The logic of a filter rule is: Buy a stock if its current price has risen X percent from a previous low. Hold the stock until its price falls X percent from its high, then sell and go short. Maintain the short position until the price rises X percent, then cover the short position and establish a long position (buy the stock).
b. Filter rules are tested by comparing the returns from using the filter rule over an interval of time to the returns from a buy-and-hold strategy on the same stock for the same interval.

2. Results of tests on filter rules:
   a. Filters above 1.5 percent cannot beat the buy-and-hold strategy even before transactions costs.
   b. Filters below 1.5 percent do earn small excess returns before transactions costs; these profits are eliminated by the transactions costs involved in the frequent trading required by the rule.
3. The market appears to be a fair game with positive expected returns.

III. Semi-Strong-Form Market Efficiency.

A. Semi-strong-form market efficiency holds that security prices fully and immediately reflect all publicly available information.

B. The hypothesis holds that no investor can earn excess returns based on publicly available information.

C. Empirical tests generally support semi-strong-form market efficiency, although some anomalous results have been reported.
   1. Two elements are involved in empirical tests of semi-strong-form efficiency.
      a. Security prices should respond quickly and fully to new public information.
      b. If security prices do not change when "news" is published, then the "news" contained no information.
   2. Empirical tests have looked at the information content of annual and quarterly accounting earnings reports, and block trading.

D. Tests of annual accounting earnings reports support semi-strong-form market efficiency.
   1. The annual report appears to contain no new information.
      a. Stock prices fully react to any unexpected change in earnings well before the publication of the annual report.
      b. The annual report appears to contain no new information which has not been anticipated by the market.
   2. No profitable trading rule can be formed based on the information in published annual reports.

E. Quarterly accounting earnings reports and announcements of dividend changes do appear to contain new information.
   1. Stock prices change significantly when the change in earnings or dividends is unexpected.
   2. There is some evidence of market inefficiency in that excess returns persist well beyond the announcement date of the unexpected change--that is, stock prices do not appear to react fully and immediately to the new information.

F. Block trades involve the sale of blocks of 10,000 or more shares of stock.
   1. Evidence on block trades supports semi-strong-form efficiency.
   2. Block trades do contain information which affects stock prices.
   3. Stock prices following block trades exhibit both temporary price pressure and permanent information effects.
      a. Price-pressure--To sell a large block requires that the price per share be below the opening price of the stock before the block sale.
      b. Information effects--The closing price after a block sale is above the block price, but the stock price does not make a full recovery to its previous opening price.
   4. Information on block trades becomes publicly available when the trade appears on the ticker tape.
      a. Buying at the block price and selling at the day's closing price could result in excess returns.
      b. Stock prices react so quickly to an unbiased estimate of the new closing price that generally only stock exchange insiders would be able to participate at the block price.
   5. Evidence on block trades tends to support semi-strong-form efficiency, buy may refute strong-form efficiency.

IV. Strong-Form Market Efficiency.

A. Strong-form efficiency holds that security prices reflect all information, whether publicly available or not.

B. According to strong-form efficiency, even insiders with access to privileged information cannot earn excess returns.

C. Empirical tests do not support strong-form efficiency; SEC data on insider trading indicates that insiders can and do earn excess returns.

D. Stock prices can reflect the impact of all information (public and private) in two ways:
   1. <u>Fully-aggregating</u> market--Stock prices reflect the full impact of all information, even though individual market participants have incomplete information. A fully-aggregated market would occur in the following way:

a. Informed (insider) traders would take market positions based on their superior private information.
b. Uninformed traders would be able to infer the private information by observing stock prices.
2. An <u>information-averaging</u> market would reflect only some average of each bit of information held by various market participants.
3. Even insiders could not make excess returns in a fully-aggregating market because the act of trading would make the private information public.
4. Evidence that insiders do earn excess returns indicates that markets are not fully-aggregating.

V. Implications of Market Efficiency for Managerial Decision-Making.
A. If markets are efficient, stock prices let managers know what the market thinks of their decisions.
B. The rapid adjustment of security prices to new information has many implications.
1. All securities are perfect substitutes. In the absence of insider information, the NPV of any securities investment is zero when discounted at the appropriate risk-adjusted rate of return.
2. Securities investors can duplicate management decisions, using homemade leverage, diversification, merger, etc. to undo management errors or to create results left undone by management.
3. The market cannot be fooled by changes which do not impact discounted cash flows.
4. Current security prices are the best estimate of future security prices.

VI. Efficient Markets with Transactions Costs and Costly Information.
A. The securities analysis industry thrives in spite of evidence that security prices reflect all publicly available information, thus precluding abnormal returns.
1. Securities analysts attempt to discover valuable private information which they sell to investors.
2. Investors who pay for costly, good information must earn abnormal gross rates of return; net of costs their return is equal to the return of uninformed investors who randomly select their portfolio.
3. In equilibrium there will be both informed and uninformed investors, the proportions of each determined by the point at which the net returns to each type of trader are equal (and zero).
a. In a world comprised mostly of informed traders, uninformed traders will begin to proliferate.
b. In a world of uninformed traders, informed traders will begin to proliferate.

B. Empirical evidence on mutual funds suggests that they are able to earn positive abnormal returns sufficient to cover expenses of research costs, management fees, brokerage commissions, etc.
   1. Net mutual fund performance is no better than a naive investment strategy.

C. The Value Line Investor Survey is one of the best known investment advisory services.
   1. An empirical study of the Value Line Investor Survey showed positive abnormal risk-adjusted rates of return for one portfolio, based on the CAPM methodology.
   2. The CAPM methodology has been criticized as a methodology for finding abnormal returns.
      a. Results will show no abnormal returns if the market index portfolio is _ex post_ efficient.
      b. Results will show meaningless abnormal returns if the market index portfolio is _ex post_ inefficient.
   3. Another empirical study using the APM model showed no significant abnormal performance for Value Line net of transactions costs.

D. It is often possible to find market inefficiencies gross of transactions costs.
   1. Most of these inefficiencies are economically insignificant net of transactions costs.
   2. _Allocational efficiency_ refers to the degree to which security prices reflect information.
   3. _Operational efficiency_ refers to competitively determined transactions costs at the lowest possible level.

PART SIX: COST OF CAPITAL AND VALUATION

CHAPTER 20

FINANCIAL STRUCTURE AND THE USE OF LEVERAGE

Theme: Since both the returns and risks to stockholders are affected by financial structure, the use of leverage potentially affects the firm's cost of capital.

I. Basic Definitions for Financial Leverage.
   A. Asset structure is the left-hand side of the balance sheet (the firm's assets which must be financed).
   B. Financial structure is the right-hand side of the balance sheet (the sources of financing).
   C. Capital structure is the permanent financing of the firm, represented by long-term debt plus preferred stock and common equity but excluding all short-term credit.
   D. Shareholders' equity includes common stock, paid-in (or capital) surplus and retained earnings. When preferred stock is included, the term net worth is used.
   E. Financial leverage, or the leverage factor, is the ratio of total debt (B) to total assets (TA) or the total market value of the firm (V). The ratio of debt (B) to common stock (S) may be calculated using the B/V ratio:

   $B/S = B/V \div (1-B/V)$

   Examples:
   If B/V = .50, B/S = .5/.5 = 1.00
   B/V = .25, B/S = .25/.75 = 0.33
   B/V = .60, B/S = .60/.40 = 1.50

   F. Business risk is the inherent variability of expected pre-tax returns on the firm's portfolio of assets.
      1. One source is the riskiness of the product markets in which the firm operates.
      2. Another source is the degree of fixed costs in the firm's cost structure--its degree of operating leverage.
   G. Financial risk is additional risk to common stock resulting from the use of financial leverage.

II. The Nature and Impact of Financial Leverage.
   A. The effects of financial leverage on the returns to shareholders. (See also Problem 20.1.)
      1. Illustration of the effects of financial leverage: Here leverage is measured by the debt-to-total-asset ratio at book values. Assume that total assets equal $200,000:

Leverage ratio (D/TA)	0	20%	40%	50%	60%
Amount of debt	0	$40,000	$80,000	$100,000	$120,000
Amount of equity	$200,000	$160,000	$120,000	$100,000	$ 80,000

2. No taxes: Assume that the cost of debt is 10 percent and that the return on total assets (ROA) is alternatively 5 percent, 10 percent, or 15 percent. What is the return on equity? (See also Figure 20.1.)

		ROA = 5% NOI = $10,000		ROA = 10% NOI = $20,000		ROA = 15% NOI = $30,000	
Debt	Interest	Net Income	Return on Equity	Net Income	Return on Equity	Net Income	Return on Equity
$ 0	$ 0	$10,000	5.00%	$20,000	10%	$30,000	15.00%
40,000	4,000	6,000	3.75%	16,000	10%	26,000	16.25%
80,000	8,000	2,000	1.67%	12,000	10%	22,000	18.33%
100,000	10,000	0	0%	10,000	10%	20,000	20.00%
120,000	12,000	(2,000)	(2.50%)	8,000	10%	18,000	22.50%

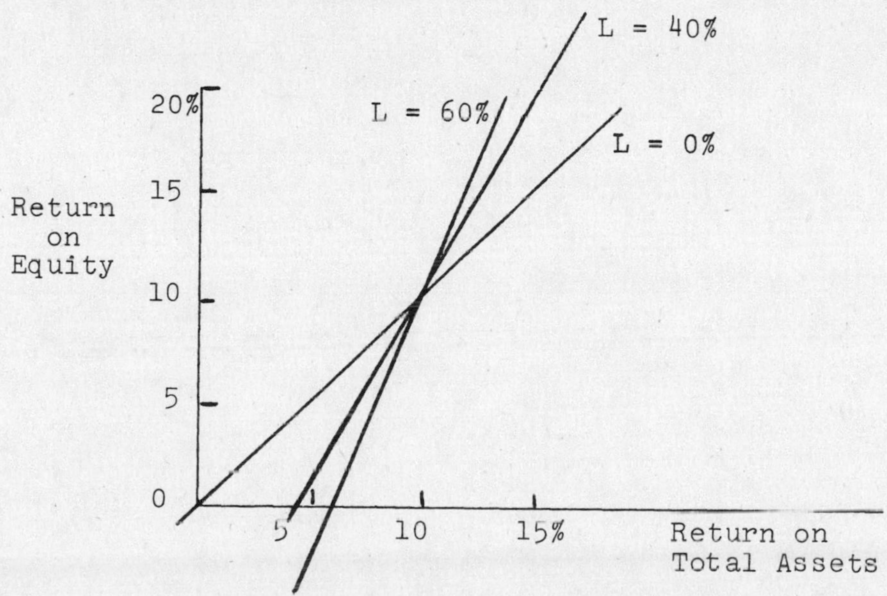

Figure 20.1 Impact of Leverage on Return on Equity (No Taxes)

3. With taxes at 40%: (See also Figure 20.2.)

ROA = 5%
EBIT = $10,000

Debt	Income Before Tax	Tax @ .4	Net Income	Return on Equity
$	$10,000	$4,000	$6,000	3.00%
40,000	6,000	2,400	3,600	2.25%
80,000	2,000	800	1,200	1.00%
100,000	0	0	0	0%
120,000	(2,000)	(800)	(1,200)	(1.50%)

ROA = 10%
EBIT = $20,000

Debt	Income Before Tax	Tax @.4	Net Income	Return on Equity
$ 0	$20,000	$8,000	$12,000	6.00%
40,000	16,000	6,400	9,600	6.00%
80,000	12,000	4,800	7,200	6.00%
100,000	10,000	4,000	6,000	6.00%
120,000	8,000	3,200	4,800	6.00%

ROA = 15%
EBIT = $30,000

Debt	Income Before Tax	Tax @.4	Net Income	Return on Equity
$ 0	$30,000	$12,000	$18,000	9.00%
40,000	26,000	10,400	15,600	9.75%
80,000	22,000	8,800	13,200	11.00%
100,000	20,000	8,000	12,000	12.00%
120,000	18,000	7,200	10,800	13.50%

4. The above illustrates that greater financial leverage leads to greater volatility in return on equity.
   a. A small change in EBIT/TA leads to a large change in NI/SHE.
   b. In the next section, we shall begin to quantify the increased risk.

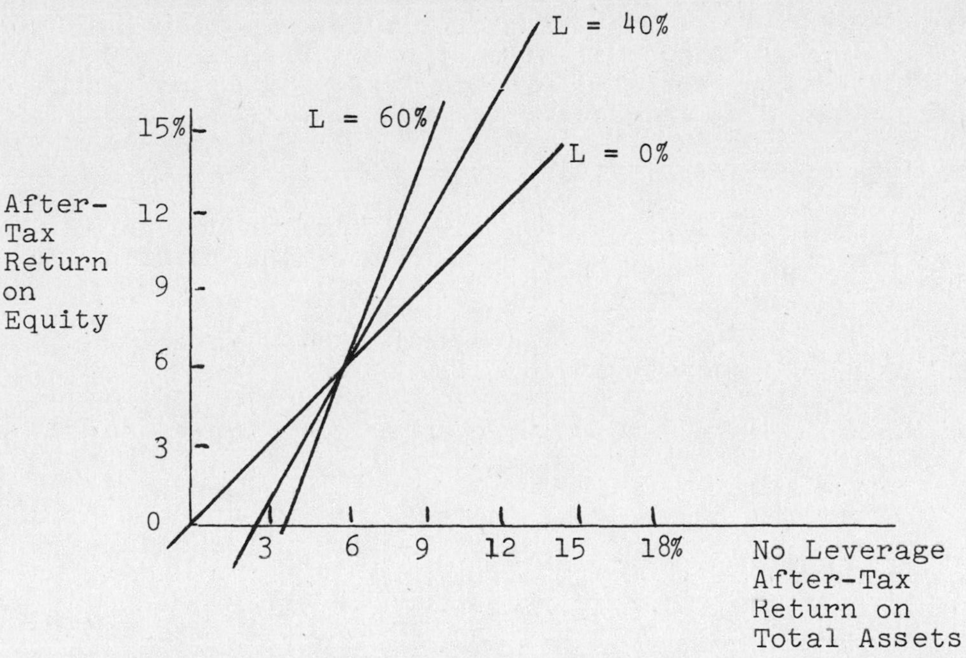

Figure 20.2 Impact of Leverage on Return on Equity (With Taxes)

B. The impact of financial leverage on risk can be demonstrated by its effects on two risk measures--the coefficient of variation (CV) and the beta coefficient (β).
   1. First construct a probability distribution for possible sales levels.
   2. For each sales level calculate EBIT and EBIT/TA (= return on assets = ROA).
   3. Use the probabilities to find the expected return on assets ($\overline{ROA}$), the standard deviation of return on assets (σ_{ROA}), and the coefficient of variation ($CV = \sigma_{ROA} \div \overline{ROA}$).
   4. Introduce financial leverage into the analysis by calculating return on equity (ROE) for each sales level at alternative leverage factors.
      a. Subtract interest expense from EBIT and apply the appropriate tax rate to get net income after taxes.
      b. Divide net income after taxes by shareholders' equity to get return on equity (ROE).
   5. As in step 3, find the expected ROE ($\overline{ROE}$), the standard deviation of ROE (σ_{ROE}) and the coefficient of variation $\left(CV = \frac{\sigma_{ROE}}{\overline{ROE}}\right)$ for each financial structure.

6. The coefficient of variation of return on equity will be larger than the coefficient of variation of return on total assets for all leverage factors greater than zero, indicating increased risk with increased leverage. (See Problem 20.2.)
7. The beta of a security also rises with increased leverage.
   a. The relationship between the beta of an unlevered firm (β_u) and the beta for an otherwise identical but levered firm (β_j) can be calculated as:

   $$\beta_j = \beta_u[1+B/S(1-T)]$$

   b. When leverage (as measured by B/S) is increased, the firm's beta increases linearly. (See Problem 20.4.)
   c. Therefore, higher debt increases risks to the holders of common stock, causing required returns on commom stock to rise.
   d. By relating the required return on equity (calculated using $\underline{\beta}$ and the SML) to the expected return on equity ($\overline{ROE}$) for each financial structure (calculated in step 5), one guide to capital structure decisions is provided. (See Problems 20.5 and 20.7.)

C. If the return on assets (net operating income/total assets) is greater than the cost of debt, leverage is favorable.
   1. If the return on assets is above the cost of debt, higher leverage factors (B/TA) will lead to a higher rate of return on net worth.
   2. If the return on assets is below the cost of debt, higher leverage factors will lead to a lower rate of return on net worth.

D. For any given change in sales, increased leverage increases the fluctuations in EPS and returns on stockholders' equity.
   1. If leverage is used successfully, it increases the returns to owners.
   2. If leverage is used unsuccessfully, it can ultimately lead to bankruptcy.
   3. At some degree of leverage, the cost of debt rises because of increased risk with the higher fixed charges in relation to expected future EBIT.

III. Financial Leverage is Related to Operating Leverage.
   A. Both operating and financial leverage have similar effects on profits, and a greater use of either has these effects:
      1. The breakeven point is raised.
      2. The impact of a change in the level of sales on profitability is magnified.
   B. Operating and financial leverage have reinforcing effects.
      1. Operating, or first stage, leverage affects earnings before interest and taxes (EBIT).
      2. Financial, or second stage, leverage affects return on net income, equity, and EPS.
   C. The data in Table 20.1 for the Gamble Grinder Company are used to illustrate these relationships.

Table 20.1

Gamble Grinder Company

Probability of indicated sales	.30	.50	.20
Sales in units	10,000	30,000	50,000
Sales in dollars	$1,000,000	$3,000,000	$5,000,000
Fixed costs	1,000,000	1,000,000	1,000,000
Variable costs (40% of sales)	400,000	1,200,000	2,000,000
Earnings before interest and taxes (EBIT)	$ (400,000)	$ 800,000	$2,000,000

Debt Financing

Interest expense (.10x$1,000,000)	100,000	100,000	100,000
Earnings before tax	$(500,000)	700,000	$1,900,000
Taxes @ 40%*	(200,000)	280,000	760,000
Net profit after tax	$(300,000)	$420,000	$1,140,000
EPS (100,000 shares)	$(3.00)	$4.20	$11.40
Market price of common (12X)**	--	$50.40	$136.80

Stock Financing

Earnings before tax	$(400,000)	$800,000	$2,000,000
Taxes @ 40%*	(160,000)	320,000	800,000
Net profit after tax	$(240,000)	$480,000	$1,200,000
EPS (120,000 shares)	$(2.00)	$4.00	$10.00
Market price of common (14X)**	--	$56.00	$140.00

*Assumes tax credit on losses.
**Use of negative values is not meaningful.

D. The degree of operating leverage (DOL) is:

$$DOL = \frac{\%\text{ change in EBIT}}{\%\text{ change in Sales}} = \frac{C}{X}$$

For the data in Table 20.1, as sales increase from \$3,000,000 to \$5,000,000,

$$DOL = \frac{1,200,000/800,000}{2,000,000/3,000,000} = \frac{150\%}{67\%} = 2.25 = \frac{1,800,000}{800,000}$$

A 10 percent increase in volume will lead to a 22.5 percent increase in operating income; in this example, a 67 percent increase in sales, from \$3 million to \$5 million, leads to a 150 percent (= 67 x 2.25) increase in EBIT.

E. The degree of financial leverage (DFL) is:

$$DFL = \frac{\%\text{ change in Net Income or in Return on Equity or in EPS}}{\%\text{ change in EBIT}} = \frac{X}{X-rD} \quad (20.1)$$

Using data from the Debt Financing section of Table 20.1, corresponding to the sales increase from \$3,000,000 to \$5,000,000,

$$DFL = \frac{720,000/420,000}{1,200,000/800,000} = \frac{171.43\%}{150.0\%} = 1.14 = \frac{800,000}{800,000-100,000}$$

F. Combining Operating and Financing Leverage to obtain the Degree of Combined Leverage (DCL).

1. The magnification effect is a product:

$$DCL = \left(\frac{\%\text{ change in EBIT}}{\%\text{ change in Sales}}\right)\left(\frac{\%\text{ change in Net Income}}{\%\text{ change in EBIT}}\right)$$

$$= \frac{\%\text{ change in Net Income}}{\%\text{ change in Sales}} = \frac{C}{X-rD} \quad (20.2)$$

2. For the data in Table 20.1

$$DCL = \frac{720,000/420,000}{2,000,000/3,000,000} = \frac{171.43\%}{66.67\%} = 2.57 = \frac{1,800,000}{700,000}$$

3. Alternatively, DCL = DOL x DFL
   = 2.25 x 1.14
   = 2.57

4. Firms can make tradeoffs between financial and operating leverage to provide the same combined leverage factor.

G. See Problems 20.6 and 20.7.

H. Use of degree of leverage concepts.
   1. Analysis of magnification effects on EBIT and net income.
   2. Analysis of interaction between operating and financial leverage.
   3. Analysis of relation between expected returns and required returns.

IV. Frequently a firm will combine a decision to expand with an analysis considering alternative leverage structures. The procedure for calculating the comparative costs of alternative forms of financing is shown in Table 20.1 for the Gamble Grinder Company.

A. Basic assumptions of the example:
   1. Gamble is considering an increase in capacity involving a $1,000,000 investment. Demand is strong, and sales could be as high as $5,000,000. However, the industry is subject to fluctuations in demand, so the level of sales could also be as low as $1,000,000. The estimated probabilities for each level of sales are given in Table 20.1.
   2. The firm has no interest-bearing debt at present.
   3. If the $1,000,000 is obtained through debt, the cost of debt will be 10 percent.
   4. Alternatively, the additional funds could be raised by the sale of common stock, netting the company $50 per share. Gamble currently has 100,000 shares of common stock outstanding.
   5. Fixed costs are $1,000,000, variable costs are 40 percent of sales, and the tax rate is 40 percent.
   6. The current P/E ratio is 13. If debt financing is used, the P/E ratio will fall to 12; with equity financing it will rise to 14.

B. Analysis of the two alternative methods of financing:

	Debt Financing	Stock Financing
Expected EPS	$3.48	$3.40
Coefficient of variation of EPS	1.44	1.24

   1. The expected EPS is lower for stock financing than for debt financing.
   2. Stock financing has a lower coefficient of variation of EPS so is less risky than debt financing.
   3. A risk-return tradeoff is required.

C. Breakeven analysis is one method of evaluating the risk-return tradeoff.
   1. Breakeven sales is when net income is zero;
      let breakeven sales = net income
      = (sales-fixed costs-variable costs-interest)(1-T)

For debt financing:

$$\text{Net income} = (S^*-\$1,000,000-.4S^*-\$100,000).6 = 0$$
$$S^* = \$1,833,333$$

For equity financing:

$$\text{Net income} = (S^*-\$1,000,000-.4S^*).6 = 0$$
$$S^* = \$1,666,667$$

2. Equity financing has a lower breakeven level of sales so is less risky than debt financing.

D. Crossover analysis.
   1. Figure 20.3 portrays the pattern of EPS in relation to alternative levels of sales for debt vs equity financing.
   2. Crossover point for debt vs equity financing occurs when the EPS is the same. EPS is the net income relation above divided by the number of shares of common stock.

$$EPS_s = \frac{(S-\$1,000,000-.4S).6}{120,000}$$

$$= \frac{(S-\$1,000,000-.4S-\$100,000).6}{100,000} = EPS_b$$

The crossover sales level = \$2,666,667
At this level of sales, EBIT for both is \$600,000 and EPS is \$3.00.

   3. Below the crossover level of sales, EPS is higher when stock financing is used. Above the crossover level of sales, EPS is higher for debt financing.
   4. The final decision will depend upon management's assessment of whether the future sales levels are more likely to be above the crossover point or below it.

V. Effects of Fluctuating Interest Rates.
   A. Changes in interest rates affect the market value of fixed rate debt and may affect the value of firm assets.
      1. Rising interest rates cause a decline in the market value of fixed rate debt.
      2. Asset values may be positively or negatively correlated with interest rates.
         a. If asset values decline with rising interest rates, the decline in the value of fixed rate debt is offset, or immunized.
         b. If asset values rise with higher interest rates, the firm may be destabilized.
      3. And conversely in periods of falling interest rates.

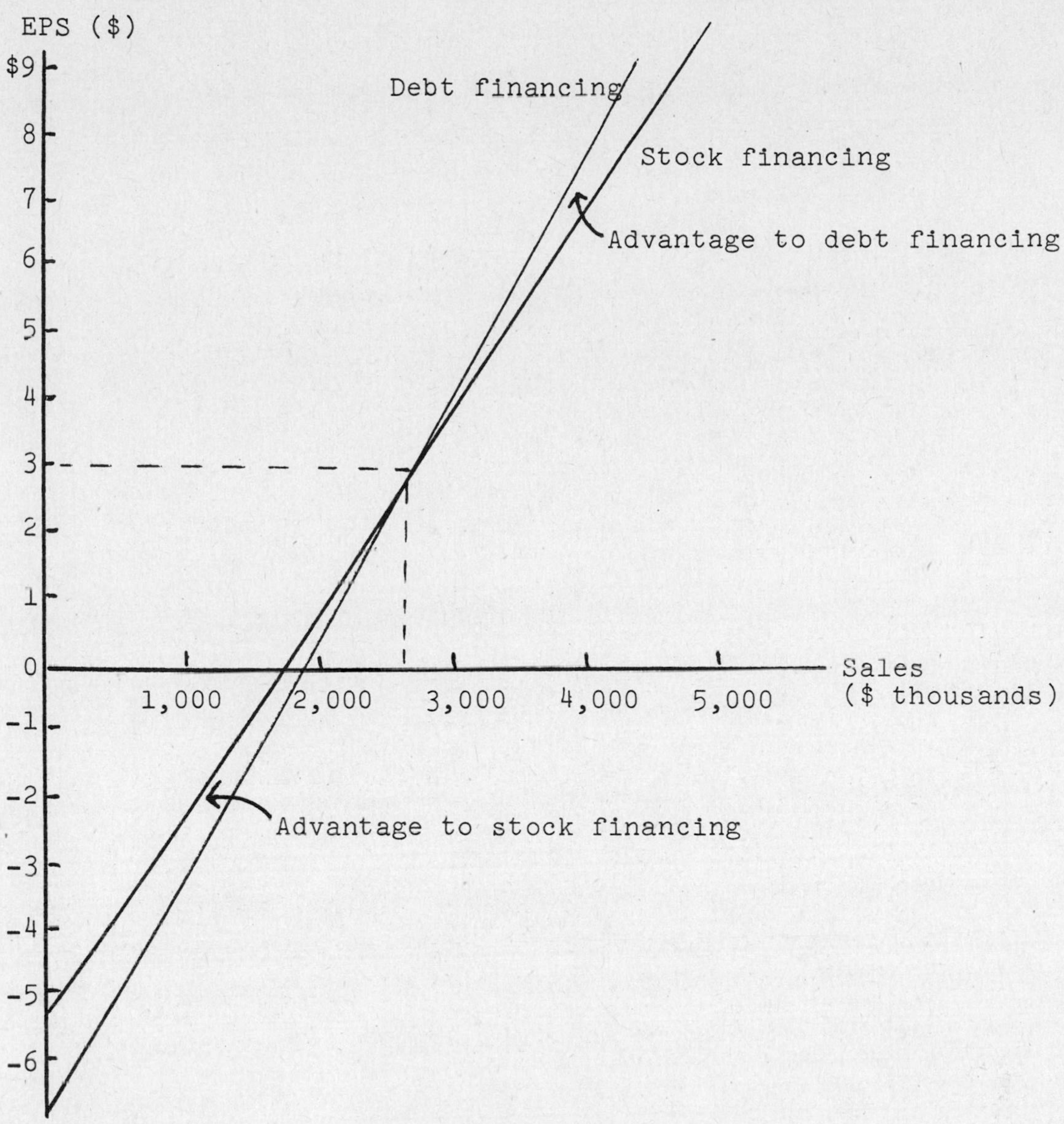

Figure 20.3 EPS Crossover Chart for Debt and Stock Financing

B. The effect of using floating rate debt during a period of fluctuating interest rates depends upon the correlation between interest rates and the borrower's NOI.
   1. If interest rates are positively correlated with NOI, floating rate coupons reduce borrower risk.
   2. If interest rates are negatively correlated with NOI, floating rate coupons increase risk.

VI. Among the Factors Influencing Financial Structure:
   A. Growth rate of future sales--higher growth, more leverage.
   B. Stability of future sales--greater stability, more leverage.
   C. Asset structure of the industry--good collateral may encourage use of secured debt.
   D. Competitive structure of the industry--ease of entry may erode profit margins.
   E. Control position and attitudes toward risk of owners and management--greater risk aversion of owners, less debt.
   F. Lender attitudes toward the firm and the industry--greater risk aversion of lenders, less debt.

VII. Detailed study of financial ratios among different industries and among firms in the same industry reveals a considerable range of variation.
   A. Service industries use the most leverage because:
      1. Services include financial institutions which use high leverage because they can draw on a central bank for additional financing if their assets are sound.
      2. There are many small firms which are heavy users of debt.
   B. Utilities use debt:
      1. Due to a heavy investment in fixed assets.
      2. Because they historically have had relatively stable sales.
   C. Manufacturing companies use less debt because their sales fluctuate more. However, among manufacturing firms there is a wide variation in the amount of leverage used.
      1. The highest amounts of leverage are found in consumer goods industries, because demand is relatively inelastic with respect to price and low in sensitivity to fluctuations in the economy.
      2. Lower debt ratios are found among durable goods industries due to their greater instability.

Chapter 20 - Illustrative Problems and Solutions

20.1 The Frankel Corporation has total assets of $5 million. Earnings before interest and taxes were $1 million in 19X0 and the tax rate was 40 percent. Using the leverage ratios and corresponding interest rates given below, calculate Frankel's return on equity (net income/equity) for each level of debt.

Leverage (Debt/Total Assets)	Interest Rate on Debt
0%	--
20	9%
40	11%
50	11%
60	15%

Solution:

TA = $5,000,000
T = Tax rate = 0.40
EBIT = Earnings before interest and taxes = $1,000,000
B = Amount of debt
R_b = Interest rate on debt
S = Amount of equity
R_s = Return on equity = $(EBIT - R_bB)(1-T)/S$

B/TA	B	R_b	$EBIT-R_bB$	$(EBIT-R_bB)(1-T)$	S	R_s
0%	$ --	--	$1,000,000	$600,000	$5,000,000	.120
20%	1,000,000	.09	910,000	546,000	4,000,000	.137
40%	2,000,000	.11	780,000	468,000	3,000,000	.156
50%	2,500,000	.11	725,000	435,000	2,500,000	.174
60%	3,000,000	.15	550,000	330,000	2,000,000	.165

At first, the return on equity increases as leverage increases. But because lenders charge higher interest rates as leverage increases, the return on equity begins to decline when leverage rises beyond a certain optimum ratio.

20.2 The Frankel Corporation estimates next year's earnings before interest and taxes as follows:

Probability	EBIT
0.3	\$1,500,000
0.5	1,000,000
0.2	750,000

Using the data in Problem 20.1, calculate Frankel's expected return on equity, the standard derivation, and the coefficient of variation at each debt ratio given.

Solution:

$\bar{R}_s$ = Expected return on equity

σ^2 = Variance

σ = Standard deviation

C.V. = Coefficient of variation

0% Leverage: B = 0, S = \$5,000,000

State	P_s	EBIT	$(EBIT-R_bB)(1-T)$	R_s	P_sR_s	$P_s(R_s-\bar{R}_s)^2$
1	.3	\$1,500,000	\$900,000	.18	.054	.00069
2	.5	1,000,000	600,000	.12	.060	.00007
3	.2	750,000	450,000	.09	.018	.00035
				$\bar{R}_s$ =	.132	σ^2=.00111
						σ =.033

$$C.V. = \sigma/\bar{R}_s = .033/.132 = .25$$

20% Leverage: B = \$1,000,000, S = \$4,000,000, R_b = 9%

State	P_s	EBIT	$(EBIT-R_bB)(1-T)$	R_s	P_sR_s	$P_s(R_s-\bar{R}_s)^2$
1	.3	\$1,500,000	\$846,000	.212	.064	.00104
2	.5	1,000,000	546,000	.137	.069	.00013
3	.2	750,000	396,000	.099	.020	.00058
				$\bar{R}_s$ =	.153	σ^2=.00175
						σ =.042

$$C.V. = .042/.153 = .275$$

40% Leverage: B = \$2,000,000, S = \$3,000,000, R_b = 11%

State	P_s	EBIT	$(EBIT-R_bB)(1-T)$	R_s	P_sR_s	$P_s(R_s-\bar{R}_s)^2$
1	.3	\$1,500,000	\$768,000	.256	.077	.00192
2	.5	1,000,000	468,000	.156	.078	.00020
3	.2	750,000	318,000	.106	.021	.00098
				$\bar{R}_s$ =	.176	σ^2=.00310
						σ =.056

C.V. = .056/.176 = .318

50% Leverage: B = \$2,500,000, S = \$2,500,000, R_b = 11%

State	P_s	EBIT	$(EBIT-R_bB)(1-T)$	R_s	P_sR_s	$P_s(R_s-\bar{R}_s)^2$
1	.3	\$1,500,000	\$735,000	.294	.088	.00276
2	.5	1,000,000	435,000	.174	.087	.00029
3	.2	750,000	285,000	.114	.023	.00141
				$\bar{R}_s$ =	.198	σ^2=.00446
						σ =.067

C.V. = .067/.198 = .338

60% Leverage: B = \$3,000,000, S = \$2,000,000, R_b = 15%

State	P_s	EBIT	$(EBIT-R_bB)(1-T)$	R_s	P_sR_s	$P_s(R_s-\bar{R}_s)^2$
1	.3	\$1,500,000	\$630,000	.315	.095	.00425
2	.5	1,000,000	330,000	.165	.083	.00048
3	.2	750,000	180,000	.090	.018	.00225
				$\bar{R}_s$ =	.196	σ^2=.00698
						σ =.084

C.V. = .084/.196 = .429

As in Problem 20.1, return on equity increases with increasing leverage up to a point, then begins to fall. The two measures of risk, the standard deviation and coefficient of variation of the returns, rise with each increase in leverage.

20.3 In 1978, Catron Printers, Inc., had 100,000 shares outstanding, with a $5 par value, and no debt. Each year thereafter until 1982, Catron increased its debt and used the borrowed money to retire shares of stock. Total assets did not change, and earnings before interest and taxes were stable at $100,000. The tax rate was 40 percent. The amount of debt, applicable interest rate, and required return on equity for each year are shown below. For each year, calculate earnings per share, price per share, and the leverage ratio at both book and market values of equity.

Year	Debt (B)	Interest Rate (R_b)	Required Return (R_s)
1978	$ 0	-	12%
1979	125,000	8%	12%
1980	225,000	10%	13%
1981	300,000	11%	15%
1982	350,000	14%	18%

Solution:
(See table on next page.)
In column 3, the number of shares outstanding each year is given. The number of shares retired is found by dividing the increase in debt by the price per share for the previous year (column 5). Calculation of the other columns is straightforward.

According to the EPS criterion, Catron should have stopped issuing debt in 1981, when EPS reached a maximum of $0.87. But management's goal should be to maximize shareholder wealth, not EPS. Therefore, Catron should have stopped issuing debt in 1980, when share price was highest at $6.15.

Solution:

20.3

(1) Year	(2) Earnings: $(EBIT-R_bB)(1-T)$	(3) N	(4) EPS (2)÷(3)	(5) p $(4)÷R_s$	(6) S_A (3)x$5	(7) S (3)x(5)	(8) $\frac{B}{B+S_A}$	(9) $\frac{B}{B+S}$
1978	$60,000	100,000	$0.60	$5.00	$500,000	$500,000	0.0%	0.0%
1979	54,000	75,000	0.72	6.00	375,000	450,000	25.0	21.7
1980	46,500	58,333	0.80	6.15	291,665	358,748	43.5	38.5
1981	40,200	46,138	0.87	5.80	230,690	267,600	56.5	52.9
1982	30,600	37,517	0.82	4.56	187,585	171,078	65.1	67.2

N = shares outstanding

EPS = earnings per share

p = market price per share

S_A = equity at book value

S = equity at market value

$\frac{B}{B + S_A}$ = leverage ratio at book value

$\frac{B}{B + S}$ = leverage ratio at market value

20.4 Catron Printers had a beta of 0.75 in 1978, when the firm had no debt. From the data in Problem 20.3, calculate Catron's beta as leverage increased in each of the following years, using market values for equity.

Solution:

20.4

The equation is $\beta_L = \beta_u + \beta_u(B/S)(1-T)$

Year	B	S	B/S	β_L
1978	$	$500,000	0.00	0.75
1979	125,000	450,000	0.28	0.88
1980	225,000	358,748	0.63	1.03
1981	300,000	267,600	1.12	1.25
1982	350,000	171,078	2.05	1.67

This illustrates how the beta measure of risk rises with leverage.

20.5 The estimated risk-free return is 7 percent, and the market risk premium is 6 percent. For each year in Problem 20.4, calculate the required return on Catron Printers' equity by means of the SML.

Solution:

$$R_s^* = R_F + (\bar{R}_M - R_F)\beta_j$$

$$= .07 + (.06)\beta_j$$

Year	R_s^*
1978	11.50%
1979	12.28
1980	13.18
1981	14.50
1982	17.02

The required return on equity that is used in cost of capital calculations rises with leverage.

20.6 The Dallas Devices Corporation produces a successful line of hand-held electronic calculators. In 1980, DD sold 100,000 calculators at $50 each. DD's income statement for 1980 is as follows:

Sales			$5,000,000
Less:	Variable Costs	$2,500,000	
	Fixed Costs	1,500,000	4,000,000
EBIT			1,000,000
Less:	Interest		125,000
EBT			875,000
Less:	Income tax (40%)		350,000
Net Income			525,000
EPS (100,000 shares)			$5.25

Calculate DD's degree of operating leverage, degree of financial leverage, and combined leverage.

Solution:

First, create a pro forma income statement for a 10 percent sales increase, that is, 110,000 units sold:

Sales (110,000 x $50)		$5,500,000
Less: Variable costs*(110,000 x $25)	$2,750,000	
Fixed costs	1,500,000	4,250,000
EBIT		$1,250,000
Less: Interest		125,000
EBT		$1,125,000
Less: Income tax (40%)		450,000
Net income		$ 675,000
EPS (100,000 shares)		$ 6.75

*Variable costs per unit = $2,500,000/100,000 - $25

Degree of operating leverage:

$$DOL = \frac{\%\text{ change in EBIT}}{\%\text{ change in sales}} - \frac{C}{X}$$

$$= \frac{\dfrac{\$1,250,000 - \$1,000,000}{\$1,000,000}}{.10} - \frac{\$2,500,000}{\$1,000,000}$$

$$= 2.5$$

Degree of financial leverage:

$$DFL = \frac{\%\text{ change in net income}}{\%\text{ change in EBIT}} = \frac{X}{X-rD}$$

$$= \frac{\frac{\$675,000 - \$525,000}{\$525,000}}{.25} = \frac{\$1,000,000}{\$1,000,000-\$125,000}$$

$$= 1.14$$

Degree of combined leverage:

$$DCL = \frac{\%\text{ change in net income}}{\%\text{ change in sales}} = \frac{C}{X-rD}$$

$$= \frac{.2857}{.10} = \frac{\$2,500,000}{\$875,000}$$

$$= 2.857$$

Alternatively, DCL = DOL x DFL = (2.5)(1.14) = 2.85

20.7 The 1980 balance sheet for Dallas Devices (Problem 20.6) is shown below:

Current assets	$1,000,000	Current liabilities	$ 500,000
Net fixed assets	1,500,000	Long-term liabilities	1,250,000
		Common stock	100,000
		Retained earnings	650,000
Total assets	$2,500,000		$2,500,000

DD expects sales for 1981 as follows:

Sales	Probability
$3,000,000	0.2
5,000,000	0.3
7,000,000	0.5

DD plans to install $1,500,000 of efficient new production machinery at the beginning of 1981. To finance the equipment, common stock can be sold to net $50 per share, or bonds paying 10 percent can be issued. With the new equipment, fixed costs will rise to $2,000,000 and variable costs will fall to $20 per unit.

a. Calculate earnings per share at each possible level of sales under both financing alternatives. What are the expected earnings per share under each financing plan?
b. For 1981, calculate operating leverage, financial leverage, and combined leverage effects for each financing method at sales of $5,000,000.

c. In 1980, DD had a beta of 1.8. The risk-free rate is 6% and the market risk premium 5%. Calculate beta and the required return on equity for 1981 under both financing alternatives.

d. DD pays half its earnings as dividends. Its stock sold at $17.50 in 1980. If DD wants its stock price to grow, which financing plan should it use?

Solution:

a. Earnings per share under equity financing, 1981:

Sales	$3,000,000	$5,000,000	$7,000,000
Less: Variable costs*	1,200,000	2,000,000	2,800,000
Fixed costs	2,000,000	2,000,000	2,000,000
EBIT	(200,000)	1,000,000	2,200,000
Less: Interest	125,000	125,000	125,000
EBT	(325,000)	875,000	2,075,000
Less: Tax (40%)	(130,000)	350,000	830,000
Net Income	$ (195,000)	$ 525,000	$1,245,000
EPS (130,000 shares)**	($1.50)	$4.04	$9.58

*Q = Sales/$50, Variable costs = Q x $20

**N =[$1,500,000/$50] + 100,000 = 130,000

Earnings per share under bond financing, 1981:

Sales	$3,000,000	$5,000,000	$7,000,000
EBIT	(200,000)	1,000,000	2,200,000
Less: Interest*	275,000	275,000	275,000
EBT	475,000	725,000	1,925,000
Less: Tax (40%)	(190,000)	290,000	770,000
Net Income	$ (285,000)	$ 435,000	$1,155,000
EPS (100,000 shares)	($2.85)	$4.35	$11.55

*Interest = (0.10)($1,500,000) + $125,000 = $275,000

Expected EPS(equity financing) = .2(-$1.50) + .3($4.04) + .5($9.58) = $5.70

Expected EPS(bond financing) = .2(-$2.85) + .3($4.35) + .5($11.55) = $6.51

Notice that at $5,000,000 sales, EPS is lower under either financing plan than it was for 1980. The new equipment is being installed in expectation of higher sales in 1981. Debt financing produces higher expected EPS, but results in much greater losses if 1981 is a slow year for sales.

b. First, create pro forma income statements for each financing alternative for a 10 percent increase in sales:

Equity financing

Sales		$5,500,000
Less: Variable costs (110,000 x $20)	$2,200,000	
Fixed costs	2,000,000	4,200,000
EBIT		$1,300,000
Less: Interest		125,000
EBT		$1,175,000
Less: Income tax (40%)		470,000
Net income		$ 705,000

Bond financing (same as above through EBIT)

EBIT	$1,300,000
Less: Interest	275,000
EBT	$1,025,000
Less: Income tax (40%)	410,000
Net income	$ 615,000

Degree of operating leverage: (Same under both alternatives)

$$DOL = \frac{\%\text{ change in EBIT}}{\%\text{ change in sales}} = \frac{C}{X}$$

$$= \frac{\frac{\$1{,}300{,}000 - \$1{,}000{,}000}{\$1{,}000{,}000}}{.10} = \frac{\$3{,}000{,}000}{\$1{,}000{,}000}$$

$$= 3$$

Degree of financial leverage:

Equity financing

$$DFL = \frac{\%\text{ change in net income}}{\%\text{ change in EBIT}} = \frac{X}{X-rD}$$

$$= \frac{\frac{\$705{,}000 - \$525{,}000}{\$525{,}000}}{.30} = \frac{\$1{,}000{,}000}{\$1{,}000{,}000-\$125{,}000}$$

$$= 1.14$$

Bond financing

$$DFL = \frac{\frac{\$615{,}000 - \$435{,}000}{\$435{,}000}}{.30} = \frac{\$1{,}000{,}000}{\$1{,}000{,}000-\$275{,}000}$$

$$= 1.38$$

Degree of combined leverage:

Equity financing

$$DCL = \frac{\%\text{ change in net income}}{\%\text{ change in sales}} = \frac{C}{X-rD}$$

$$= \frac{.3429}{.10} = \frac{\$3,000,000}{\$1,000,000-\$125,000}$$

$$= 3.43$$

$$DCL = DOL \times DFL = (3)(1.14) = 3.42$$

Bond financing

$$DCL = \frac{.4138}{.10} = \frac{\$3,000,000}{\$1,000,000-\$275,000}$$

$$= 4.14$$

$$DCL = DOL \times DFL = (3)(1.38) = 4.14$$

Operating leverage in 1981 is higher than in 1980 due to the installation of more efficient capital equipment. Financial leverage under equity financing is the same for both years only because total costs happen to be the same at the $5 million sales level. You can verify that the results would differ at other sales levels. Financial leverage under debt financing is, of course, higher.

The combined leverage effect in 1981 is much higher under both financing methods. The combined effect is higher under equity financing due to a change in one component, operating leverage. The combined effect under debt financing is higher because both components have changed. The combined leverage effect of 4.14 under debt financing means that a one percent change in 100,000 units sold will produce a 4.14% change in net income.

CHAPTER 21

CAPITAL STRUCTURE AND THE COST OF CAPITAL

Theme: The cost of debt, equity and hybrid securities such as preferred stock are based on the fundamental theories of risk and return. The influence of leverage results in an optimal financing mix which minimizes the firm's overall cost of capital, thus maximizing firm value. Combining the marginal efficiency of investment schedule with the marginal cost of capital schedule determines the firm's capital budget.

I. The Modigliani-Miller Propositions on the Effects of Leverage.
   A. Two key assumptions are made.
      1. No bankruptcy costs.
      2. Homemade leverage--personal and corporate leverage are perfect substitutes.
   B. With no taxes, firm value is independent of financial structure.
      1. Value of firm = $V = \frac{NOI}{k} = \frac{X}{k}$
      2. Cost of capital = $k = \frac{X}{V}$
   C. With taxes, the value of a levered firm is greater than the value of an unlevered firm because of the interest tax shelter on debt.
      1. Value of an unlevered firm = $V_u = \frac{X(1-T)}{k_u}$
      2. Unlevered cost of capital = $k_u = \frac{X(1-T)}{V_u}$
      3. Using a homemade leverage arbitrage process, it can be demonstrated that

$$V_L = V_u + TB$$

   D. The M-M equation for the cost of equity of a levered firm, with taxes, is:

$$k_s = k_u + (k_u - k_b)(1-T)(B/S)$$

      1. This is the equation for a straight line with intercept, k_u and slope, $(k_u - k_b)(1-T)$.
      2. Thus, k_s rises linearly with increased leverage measured as B/S.

3. The cost of equity rises with increased leverage because shareholders are exposed to greater risk.

E. The weighted average cost of capital is the return on assets that the firm must earn, given its leverage level, to increase shareholder wealth.

1. The weighted average cost of capital (WACC) changes with increasing leverage.
   a. Shareholder wealth increases when firms undertake projects which earn more than the WACC.
   b. All the increase in firm value accrues to shareholders.
   c. Cash flows discounted at the WACC are defined as the after-tax operating cash flows the firm would have if it had no debt.
2. The M-M propositions result in three formulations of the firm's WACC.
   a. $\text{WACC} = k = k_b(1-T)(B/V) + k_s(S/V)$
   b. $\text{WACC} = k = \dfrac{X(1-T)}{V}$
   c. $\text{WACC} = k = k_u(1-TL)$, where $L = B/V$

F. In the M-M model, with corporate taxes only, the tax subsidy on debt reduces the WACC and increases firm value.

1. At the extreme, this implies that firms should use debt financing exclusively.
2. Possible reasons for an optimal capital structure including both debt and equity are discussed in the following sections.

II. Possible Explanations for an Optimal Capital Structure.

A. Impact of personal as well as corporate taxes.

1. The gain from leverage is the tax benefit of corporate debt:

$$G = \left[1 - \frac{(1-T_c)(1-T_{ps})}{(1-T_{pb})}\right]B$$

where T_c = corporate tax rate

T_{ps} = personal capital gains tax rate (applicable to stock)

T_{pb} = ordinary personal income tax rate (applicable to interest income on debt)

   a. $V_L = V_u + G$
   b. If $T_{ps} = T_{pb}$, then $V_L = V_u + T_cB$, the M-M result.

2. Personal taxes result in a corporate leverage clientele effect.
   a. For lower ordinary personal income tax rates, the gain from corporate debt is higher, and vice versa.
   b. High-tax bracket investors should invest in low leverage firms and vice versa.
3. Personal tax rates also have implications for the supply and demand for corporate debt.
   a. Assume personal taxes on capital gains can be avoided, $T_{ps} = 0$.

   b. $G = 1 - \frac{(1-T_c)}{(1-T_{pb})}$

   c. The supply curve of corporate debt is a horizontal line:

      $r_b = r_0/(1-T_c)$

      where r_b = rate of return on corporate bonds

      r_0 = rate paid on the debt of tax-free institutions
   d. The demand curve for corporate debt rises due to the progressive personal tax structure.
      (i) If all corporate debt paid only r_0, only other tax-free institutions would hold it.
      (ii) Individuals require a return of

      $r_0/(1-T_{pb})$
   e. The dollar amount of bonds supplied and demanded is where the curves intersect at

      $r_0/(1-T_{pb}) = r_0/(1-T_c)$

B. Impact of multiple tax shields.
1. Other tax shields include:
   a. Investment tax credits (if they exist)
   b. Depreciation and oil depletion allowances
2. The expected value of the interest tax shield declines with higher levels of debt.
   a. Increased debt levels increase the probability that earnings will not be sufficient to utilize all available substitute tax shields.
   b. This results in a downward sloping supply curve for corporate debt.
3. The marginal expected benefit of the interest tax shield is related to the marginal expected cost of bankruptcy.

C. Exchange offers are pure financial restructurings in which one form of security (e.g. debt) is exchanges for another (e.g. stock).

1. An empirical study of exchange offers found significant positive stock returns as a result of leverage-increasing exchange offers and vice versa.
2. Possible explanations include:
   a. Bondholders may suffer a wealth loss due to the greater risk of a smaller equity base; shareholders may benefit from a wealth redistribution effect.
   b. Stock value increases due to the increased interest tax shelter.
   c. Leverage increase may signal favorable future prospects.
3. The sale of new debt to retire equity also has option pricing model implications.
   a. Sale of debt is equivalent to writing (selling) a covered call option.
   b. Original bondholders suffer loss of wealth due to:
      (i) Smaller proportionate claim on same asset pool.
      (ii) Increase in risk with no compensation.
   c. No expropriation would occur if original bondholders precluded the possibility in the bond indenture, or if they demanded higher return to compensate them for this eventuality.

D. Agency costs may be minimized by some optimal combination of debt and equity, even in the absence of taxes or bankruptcy costs.
   1. Agency costs rise with increased debt--the costs of writing and monitoring the bond indenture agreement.
   2. Agency costs also rise with increased outside equity since original owner-manager may indulge in perquisites for which he bears only part of the expense.
   3. Other agency cost considerations for leverage:
      a. Durable goods market--consumers monitor firm to assess probability of bankruptcy which would prevent the firm from providing follow-up service. Lower debt ratios in the durable goods industry.
      b. Labor contracts--workers assess the probability of bankruptcy. Results in lower debt ratios in industries requiring job-specific human capital which would be less transferrable in the event of bankruptcy.
      c. Collateral value of goods--lenders assess the probability of bankruptcy; higher leverage will be permitted for firms with more tangible, non-specialized assets.

E. Information asymmetry and signalling may result in an optimal capital structure.
   1. Managers know more about their firms' prospects than investors.
   2. An optimal capital structure may exist if:
      a. The nature of a firm's investment policy is signalled to the market by the firm's capital structure decision.

   b. Managers' compensation is tied to the signal in a way that rewards truthful signalling.
3. Information asymmetry may also explain the financial intermediation industry.
   a. It is difficult for investors to assess the value of financial intermediary assets such as mortgages, loans, etc.
   b. Financial intermediaries accumulate the information necessary to evaluate such assets, and buy and hold these assets accordingly.
   c. Investors can judge the quality of the information by the financial intermediary's returns and by the willingness of its organizers to invest in their own equity.
   d. The higher the proportion of equity held by organizers, the greater the debt capacity.

III. The Effects of Bankruptcy Costs on Optimal Capital Structure.

A. Interest on debt is tax deductible, therefore the tax shelter effect causes the value of the firm to rise with increased leverage--to a point.

B. At some point, the risks of rising bankruptcy costs will outweigh the tax shelter effect, and the value of the firm will decrease with increased leverage. Bankruptcy costs include:

1. Legal, accounting, and administrative costs associated with the actual bankruptcy proceedings.
2. Before the actual legal bankruptcy proceedings take place, the following costs may result from the firm's deteriorating position:
   a. Financing under increasingly undesirable terms.
   b. Loss of key employees.
   c. Loss of important suppliers.
   d. Loss of sales.
   e. Complete loss of financing.
   f. Liquidation of fixed assets to meet working capital requirements.

C. Increased probability of bankruptcy increases costs of both debt and equity with increased debt levels.
Payoffs to shareholders and debtholders:

1. Return to debtholders = Min[V,D], without bankruptcy.
   Return to debtholders = Min[V-θV, D], with bankruptcy, where θ = bankruptcy costs as a percentage of firm value.
   Thus, return required by debtholders increases with increased probability of bankruptcy.
2. Return to equity = MAX[0,V-D], with or without bankruptcy.
3. As debtholders require higher returns, the probability of bankruptcy increases, increasing the likelihood that shareholders will receive 0 instead of V-D; thus shareholders will also increase their required return.

IV. The Capital Structure Decision: Two Criteria.

A. Minimize the weighted average cost of capital.

1. For a given level of financing (or capital budget), find the weighted average cost of capital at alternative leverage ratios.

   a. The WACC is relatively flat over a fairly broad range, giving the financial manager some flexibility.

   b. For a different level of financing, the cost relationships among the weighted average cost of capital components might not be the same.

2. Choose the capital structure that minimizes the weighted average cost of capital.

B. Maximize firm value.

1. Increased leverage causes firm value to rise due to the tax shelter effect of interest expense.

2. With further increases in leverage, firm value begins to fall due to bankruptcy cost effects.

3. Choose the capital structure that maximizes firm value.

V. The Cost of External Equity if Higher than the Cost of Internal Equity, or Retained Earnings.

A. The dividend growth model is an all internal equity financing model used to find the cost of retained earnings.

$$k_r = \frac{d_1}{p_o} + g$$

where k_r = cost of internal equity, or retained earnings

d_1 = expected dividend per share

p_o = current stock price

g = growth rate in dividends per share

B. The traditional approach to the cost of external equity has been to adapt the dividend growth model to include the flotation costs involved in issuing new financing.

$$k_e = \frac{d_1}{p_o(1-f)} + g$$

where k_e = the cost of external equity financing

f = percentage flotation costs on the new stock issue

1. This approach also provides a basis for determining the availability of dividends.

a. If the marginal efficiency of investment (MEI) schedule crosses the MCC curve before internal funds are exhausted, dividends could be paid.
b. If the MEI schedule crosses the MCC curve at a point beyond funds available from internal sources, dividends would not generally be paid.

2. This approach has been criticized for violating the logic of the dividend growth model which hypothesizes all internal equity financing.
   a. The growth rate assumption of the dividend growth model is violated.
   b. Since old shareholders will have to share future earnings and dividends with new shareholders, all terms of the formula will not grow at the same rate for all shareholders.
3. A newer approach posits that flotation costs increase the investment outlay, not the cost of capital.
   a. According to this view,

$$NPV = \sum_{t=1}^{N} \frac{NCF_t}{(1+k)^t} - \frac{\Delta I}{(1-f)}$$

   b. A problem with this approach is that it may be difficult to associate individual projects with their sources of financing.
4. The application of flotation costs to the cost of external financing, rather than to the investment outlay, is a more practical, if less theoretically sound, approach.

B. An argument has been made that the cost differential between internal and external equity is caused by personal tax rates.
   1. This is based on personal tax rates for dividend income versus capital gains, and the need for shareholders to reinvest dividends received.
   2. This argument is discussed in Chapter 22 on dividend policy.

VI. The Cost of Depreciation-Generated Funds.
   A. A cost of capital schedule that includes replacement of depreciable assets should include depreciation.
   B. The cost of depreciation-generated funds is the weighted average cost of capital before outside equity.
   C. A cost of capital schedule concerned solely with net increases in assets should not include depreciation.
      1. Depreciation-generated funds should be distributed to creditors and shareholders if the funds cannot be invested to yield the cost of capital.
      2. Retention of these funds will occur if the internal rate of return exceeds the cost of capital.

VII. The Cost of Capital is Calculated as a Weighted Average of the Opportunity Costs of the Various Types of Funds Used.

A. The cost of each capital component is its current opportunity cost, not its historical cost.

B. If debt is used to finance a project, the cost of the project is not the cost of debt, but is equal to the weighted average cost of capital because the firm has used up some of its debt capacity and will have to use equity financing in the future to restore the capital structure.

C. In order to calculate the cost of capital as a weighted average, it is necessary to estimate the cost of each type of funds used.

1. Capital or financial components are items on the right-hand side of the balance sheet which finance the firm's assets--such as debt, preferred stock and common equity.
2. The cost of each component is called its component cost.
3. Component costs are placed on an after-tax basis because shareholders are concerned with after-tax returns.

D. The capital structure components and their component costs are identified by the following symbols:

k_b = Interest on firm's new debt = component cost of debt, before tax

$k_b(1-T)$ = Component cost of debt, after tax, where T = marginal tax rate; $k_b(1-T)$ is the debt cost used to calculate the marginal weighted average cost of capital

k_{ps} = Component cost of preferred stock

k_r = Component cost retained earnings (or internal equity

k_e = Component cost of new issues of common stock (or external equity)

k = Weighted average, or composite, cost of capital. If a firm raises $1 of new capital to finance asset expansion, and if it is to keep its capital structure in balance (that is, if it is to keep the same percentages of debt, preferred stock and common equity), then it will raise part of the dollar as debt, part as preferred stock, and part as common equity (with equity coming either as retained earnings or from the sale of new common stock). k is also a marginal cost; there is a value of k for each dollar of new capital the firm raises.

E. Management's target weights for each capital component are the appropriate weights to use.

1. If management's target weights are unknown, market value weights are closer approximations than book value weights.

2. When the market/book value ratio is greater than 1, the firm's prospects are viewed as relatively favorable, justifying a higher target leverage ratio, and vice versa when the market/book value ratio is less than 1.

VIII. The Component Cost of Debt Depends on the Cost of New Debt and Ignores the Cost of Any Previously Outstanding Debt.

A. The before-tax component cost of debt is equal to the rate of return earned by investors, or the interest rate:

$$\text{Before-tax component cost of debt} = k_b = \frac{\text{Interest}}{\text{Principal}}$$

B. The after-tax component cost of debt is equal to the before-tax component cost of debt adjusted for the tax shelter resulting from the deductibility of interest payments:

$$\text{After-tax component cost of debt} = k_b(1-T)$$

C. There are two methods of estimating k_b:

1. Use the published yield to maturity for the published bond rating of the firm.
2. Calculate the effective yield to maturity based on expected returns and the current price of the bonds.

IX. The Component Cost of Preferred Stock.

A. The cost of preferred stock is the effective yield as measured by the annual preferred dividend, divided by the price of the preferred stock.

B. The cost of preferred stock is already on an "after-tax" basis because preferred stock dividends are not tax-deductible to the issuing firm.

$$k_{ps} = \frac{d_{ps}}{P_{ps}}$$

C. The nature of preferred stock depends on point of view:

1. For the issuer, preferred is riskier than common but less risky than debt.
2. For the shareholder, preferred is riskier than debt but less risky than common stock.
3. Preferred stock is an attractive investment for other corporations, because 85 percent of all dividends (whether common or preferred) are excluded from corporate income taxation.

X. The Cost of Common Equity.

A. There are four approaches to calculating the cost of equity.

1. Three approaches are based on financial market data and give an estimate of the cost of external equity:
   a. CAPM approach.
   b. Debt-equity yield relation.
   c. Realized investor yield approach.
2. The fourth method, the dividend growth model, is a

theoretical approach which gives the cost of internal equity, or retained earnings.

B. In the CAPM approach, the cost of equity is expressed as a premium over the risk-free rate:

$$k_s = R_F + (\bar{R}_M - R_F)\beta_j$$

1. The market risk premium, $(\bar{R}_M - R_F)$, has historically been 6 to 8 percent.
2. U.S. Treasury rates (short or longer term) are used to estimate R_F.
3. Estimates of beta are published by investment services.

C. Using the debt-equity yield relation, a firm's equity must pay more than the firm's long-term debt because of the higher risk.

D. The realized investor yield approach says that the required return on equity is approximately equal to its long-run average return on equity over some past period--that is, its average dividend yield plus its average capital gain.

E. The dividend growth model expresses the cost of internal equity in relation to dividends and the growth rate:

$$k_r = \frac{d_1}{P_o} + g$$

Alternatively,

$$k_r = \frac{E_o(1+g)(1-b)}{P_o} + br$$

where E_o = earnings
b = fraction of earnings retained
r = internal profitability rate
br = growth rate

1. This model assumes all internal equity financing.
2. The model requires a constant growth rate through infinity; all factors of the model grow at the same rate.
3. To estimate the growth rate, use the actual growth rate over some past period, or an estimate of g provided by an investment service.
4. This method is also used to estimate the cost of external equity by including flotation costs as discussed above.

XI. Cost of Capital for a Division.

A. If project or division risk differs from firm risk, it is not appropriate to use the firm's overall WACC for capital budgeting.

B. The CAPM enables us to calculate a divisional cost of capital related to the division's risk.

1. Difficulties arise because market price and return data are not available on a divisional basis.
2. The methodology that follows can also be used to find the cost of capital for a firm whose stock is not publicly traded.

C. Calculation of the cost of capital for a division or a non-public firm.

1. Express the value of the division's after-tax unlevered cash flows with the market return based on historical data or subjective estimates of future values.

$$V_j = \frac{E(X_j) - \lambda Cov(X_j, R_M)}{R_F}$$

$$\text{where } \lambda = \frac{\bar{R}_M - R_F}{\sigma_M^2}$$

2. The covariance of the rate of return of the division with the market can then be expressed as:

$$Cov(R_j, R_M) = \frac{Cov(X_j, R_M)}{V_j}$$

3. Use these relationships to find the unlevered beta of the division.

$$\beta_u = \frac{Cov(R_j, R_M)}{Var(R_M)}$$

4. Choose a target leverage ratio and calculate β_j.

$$\beta_j = \beta_u[1+(B/S)(1-T)]$$

   a. Check the calculated beta against the published betas of publicly traded firms whose activities are similar to the division's activities.
   b. Adjust the comparable firm's leverage if necessary to make the betas equivalent.
      (i) Convert the firm's beta to an unlevered beta.
      (ii) Compare unlevered betas.
      (iii) Calculate the firm's levered beta using the same target leverage as the division.
      (iv) Compare levered betas.

5. Use the SML to find the cost of equity capital.

$$E(R_j) = R_F + (\bar{R}_M - R_F)\beta_j$$

6. Use the cost of equity with the cost of debt and any other capital components in their target proportions to find the appropriate investment hurdle rate for a division to use in evaluating new projects.

D. Divisional betas can also be used to check the accuracy of published firm betas since the firm beta should simply be a value-weighted average of its divisions' betas.

E. Estimates of divisional investment hurdle rates improve capital budgeting decisions. Using a firm-wide rate would result in poor decisions if divisional risk varies.
   1. Highly risky projects could be adopted when they should be rejected.
   2. Low-risk projects could be rejected when they should be accepted.

XII. Developing the Firm's Overall Capital Budget.

A. The marginal efficiency of investment (MEI) and MCC curves are plotted on the same graph.
   1. Total investment (financing) is plotted on the x-axis.
   2. The return on investment (cost of capital) is plotted on the y-axis.

B. The MEI declines with additional investment because the investment opportunities available to the firm are limited.

C. The MCC curve rises with additional financing for a number of reasons.
   1. Flotation costs and tax effects cause a higher cost for external equity than for retained earnings.
   2. The market might require a premium for a firm growing substantially faster than its industry.
      a. The price-pressure argument suggests that the market is unwilling to accept too large a supply of securities from a single firm; there is little empirical support for this argument.
      b. The organizational development argument says that rapid growth will result in organizational problems.
      c. The competitive reaction hypothesis says that rapid growth will attract imitators to the industry, reducing the growth rate of the original firm.
      d. One view is that the organizational development and competitive reaction arguments should be reflected not in a higher MCC curve, but in a lower MEI curve. The result, however, would be the same--a lower capital budget.

D. The point at which the MEI and MCC curves intersect determines the size of the optimal capital budget.

XIII. Extensions and Criticisms of the M-M Model.

A. The M-M proposition which shows most clearly the tax benefits of debt is:

$$k = k_u(1-TL)$$

1. The M-M model is based on unchanging cash flows in perpetuity.
2. Alternatively, the M-M model can be thought of as a one-period model.

B. Miles and Ezzell (M-E) have extended the M-M model so that the time pattern and duration of the unlevered cash flows are immaterial.

$$k = k_u - rTL\left(\frac{1+k_u}{1+r}\right)$$

where $r = k_b$ = cost of debt of an unlevered firm

1. The M-E model assumes that a constant leverage ratio is maintained.
2. The model results in a different cost of capital from that of the M-M model.
   a. Where k_u is greater than r (the typical case), the M-E k is greater than the M-M k.
   b. If k_u is less than r, the M-E k is lower than the M-M k.

C. Some critics have argued that the M-M model must be adjusted to account for the change in value caused by depreciation of assets.
1. Assume that a firm makes an annual investment outlay, K, sufficient to maintain operating cash flows at a constant level.
2. The annual investment outlay is equal to the annual depreciation charge.
3. Under these assumptions, the M-M valuation model works equally well for firms with depreciable assets.

D. The M-M WACC has been criticized as being incorrectly specified for use as an investment hurdle rate in NPV analysis.
1. The target leverage ratio must be maintained with respect to the increase in market value of the firm caused by a new investment, rather than with respect to the book value of the new investment.
2. When used correctly, as above, the M-M relationships are appropriate for use in investment analysis.

XIV. The State Preference Model (SPM) is Based on a Consideration of Alternative Future States of the World that May Occur.

A. If securities are available such that some payoff will be received regardless of which future state occurs, then by a combination of investment strategies, a <u>pure</u>, or <u>primitive</u> security is possible.

1. A pure or primitive security is one which pays $1 if a specified state occurs, and nothing if any other state occurs.
2. An example with two securities and two alternative states-of-the-world will illustrate the concept.

	Payoff in State 1	Payoff in State 2	Price
Security j	$\$20 = F_{j1}$	$\$30 = F_{j2}$	$\$19 = P_j$
Security k	$40 = F_{k1}$	$24 = F_{k2}$	$20 = P_k$

Two pure securities (p_1 and p_2) can be found (p_1 which will pay $1 if State 1 occurs and nothing if State 2 occurs and p_2 which will pay $1 if State 2 occurs and nothing if State 1 occurs) by simultaneously solving these two equations:

$$p_1F_{j1} + p_2F_{j2} = P_j$$

$$p_2F_{k1} + p_2F_{k2} = P_k$$

$$p_1 20 + p_2 30 = 19$$

$$p_1 40 + p_2 24 = 20$$

$$p_1 = \$.20$$

$$p_2 = .50$$

B. The SPM has been used to calculate optimal financial leverage.

1. Estimates are made of the EBIT which a firm may expect under alternative future states.
2. Primitive security prices are calculated which represent a claim on $1 under one state only.
3. The after-tax amounts to be received by stockholders and debtholders are calculated for the various states, taking into consideration the bankruptcy or failure costs if the firm's EBIT in a state is insufficient to make the fixed debt payments required.
4. The amounts received by debt and equity holders under each state are multiplied by the price of the primitive security for that state.

5. By repeating the above process for varying levels of debt, we can find the leverage factor which will maximize the value of the firm.
6. The SPM leverage analysis illustrates that where taxes and bankruptcy costs are present, there exists an optimal leverage level.

C. Under complete capital markets a security exists for every possible state of the world such that a full set of primitive securities is possible.
1. Under such conditions, and in the absence of imperfections (e.g. taxes, bankruptcy costs), capital structure would not matter, as in the Modigliani-Miller propositions.
2. A firm's leverage policy consists of repackaging the claims on its assets in various ways to increase the value of the firm, because of some types of market imperfections.

Chapter 21 - Illustrative Problems and Solutions

21.1 The Baylor Corporation is expected to grow at 10 percent per year. Baylor common stock pays a dividend of $2.00 and sells for $25 per share. What is Baylor's cost of retained earnings?

Solution:

$$k_e = \frac{d_1}{p_0} + g = \frac{\$2.00}{\$25.00} + 0.10 = 0.18 = 18\%$$

21.2 Lilly LaMonte Cosmetics, Incorporated carries no debt in its capital structure. Its beta is 1.8.

a. The risk-free rate is 9 percent and the expected return on the market is 15 percent. What is Lilly LaMonte's cost of capital?

b. Should the company invest in a project that earns 13 percent with a beta of 0.8?

Solution:

a. $k_s = R_F + \rho_1 + \rho_2$

There is no debt, so $\rho_2 = 0$

$\rho_1 = \beta_u(\bar{R}_M - R_F) = 1.8(0.15-0.09) = 0.108$

$k_s = 0.09 + 0.108 = 0.198 = 19.8\%$

b. $k_j^* = R_F + (\bar{R}_M - R_F)\beta_j$
$= 0.09 + (0.15 - 0.09)(0.8) = 0.09 + 0.048 = 13.8\%$

The required rate of return k_j^*, calculated by means of the Security Market Line, is 13.8%. The project is expected to return only 13 percent and should be rejected.

21.3 The Klaus Company recently issued 25-year bonds with a par value of $1,000 and a 9 percent coupon. Interest is paid semiannually. The bonds sold for $950. Klaus's tax rate is 35 percent. What is Klaus's after-tax cost of debt?

Solution:
First, find the yield to maturity:

$950 = $45 x PVIFA(r, 50) + $1,000 x PVIF(r, 50)
at r = 4.75%:
$950 = $45 x PVIFA(4.75%, 50) + $1,000 x PVIF(4.75%, 50)
= $45(18.9844) + $1,000(0.0982)
= $854.30 + $98.20
$950 ≈ $952.50
YTM = 4.75% x 2 = 9.5%

The after-tax cost of debt is $k_b(1-T) = 9.5\%(1-0.35) = 6.18\%$

21.4 The Grimes Corporation is planning to issue $4,000,000 of 12 percent, non-convertible preferred stock with a par value of $50 per share. After flotation costs, the company will net $3,600,000. What is Grimes's cost of preferred stock?

Solution:

$$k_{ps} = \frac{D_{ps}}{P_{ps}}$$

$$= \frac{.12(4,000,000)}{3,600,000}$$

$$= \frac{480,000}{3,600,000}$$

$$= .133 = 13.3 \text{ percent}$$

Alternatively, on a per share basis:

$$k_{ps} = \frac{d_{ps}}{p_{ps}(1-f)}$$

where f = percentage flotation costs

$$f = \frac{4,000,000 - 3,600,000}{4,000,000}$$

$$= \frac{400,000}{4,000,000}$$

$$= .10$$

$$k_{ps} = \frac{.12(50)}{50(1-.1)}$$

$$= \frac{6}{45}$$

$$= .133 = 13.3 \text{ percent}$$

21.5 Coarsegold Mining earns \$3.50 per share. Last year's dividend was \$1.65 per share. The current share price is \$36. Coarsegold's earnings, dividends, and stock price have been growing at 6 percent per year for the last six years, and this growth rate is expected to continue indefinitely. What is the cost of retained earnings?

Solution:

$$k_r = \frac{d_1}{p_0} + g$$

$$= \frac{d_0(1+g)}{p_0} + g$$

$$= \frac{\$1.65(1.06)}{36} + .06$$

$$= 10.86\%$$

21.6 Sanford Corporation is expected to pay a year-end dividend of \$2.00. Sanford earns \$5 per share and its stock sells at \$40 per share. Stock price, earnings and dividends are expected to grow at 10 percent per year indefinitely.

a. Calculate the cost of retained earnings for Sanford.
b. Assume that Sanford reinvests retained earnings at 10 percent rather than its cost of capital. Assume that the resulting new growth rate is permanent, that dividends remain constant, and that Sanford continues to earn the same rate of return on its original capital

as it has in previous years. What will be the price of one share at the end of one year?

c. If Sanford has a zero growth rate and a 100 percent pay-out ratio, what is the stockholders rate of return? (Use the original stock price.)

Solution:

a. $k_s = \frac{d_1}{p_0} + g$

$= \frac{\$2.00}{\$40} + .10$

$= 15.0\%$

b. Calculate new EPS:

\$5.00	EPS
-2.00	Dividend
\$3.00	Retained earnings per share

\$3.00 x .10 = \$.30 Incremental EPS

\$5.00	Past year's EPS
.30	Incremental EPS
\$5.30	New EPS

New growth rate:

$\frac{\$5.30}{\$5.00} = 1.06 = 6\%$ growth

New price per share:

$p_0 = \frac{d_1}{k_s - g}$

$= \frac{\$2.00}{.15-.06}$

$= \frac{\$2.00}{.09}$

$= \$22.22$

The stock price has fallen because the reinvestment rate is below the stockholders required rate of return of 15.0 percent.

c. $k_s = \frac{d_1}{p_0} + g$

$= \frac{\$5}{\$40} + 0$

$= 12.5\%$

21.7 RCN, Incorporated has $587.5 million in total net assets at the end of 1984. It plans to increase fixed assets during 1985 by $100 million. Bond financing can be arranged to sell at par value with a 13 percent coupon. Preferred stock financing is available at 12 percent interest and will sell at a par value of $100. Common stock is currently selling at $86 per share. Over the past several years, RCN's dividend yield has been 8 percent. The firm's growth rate is 7 percent per year which is expected to continue indefinitely. RCN is expected to have $25 million of retained earnings available for financing. The current risk-free rate is 8 percent; the return on the market portfolio is 14 percent; and RCN's equity beta is 1.26. The tax rate is 40 percent. The current capital structure (considered by management to be optimal) is shown below.

Debt (9 percent bonds)		$180,000,000	
(10 percent bonds)		150,000,000	$330,000,000
Preferred stock			22,500,000
Common stock	$100,000,000		
Retained earnings	135,000,000		235,000,000
			$587,500,000

a. How much of the $100 million increase in fixed assets must be financed with equity to maintain the current capital structure?
b. How much of the equity must come from the sale of new common stock?
c. What is RCN's cost of equity?
d. What is RCN's cost of capital on the $100 million incremental financing?

Solution:

a. Current equity proportion $= \frac{\$235,000,000}{\$587,500,000}$

$= 40\%$

New financing	$100,000,000
	x.40
Equity financing	$ 40,000,000

b.

Equity financing	$40,000,000
Less retained earnings	25,000,000
External equity	$15,000,000

c. Cost of external equity (using the CAPM approach)

$$k_s = R_F + (\bar{R}_M - R_F)\beta_j$$
$$= .08 + (.14-.08)1.26$$
$$= 15.6 \text{ percent}$$

Cost of retained earnings = dividend yield + growth
= .08 + .07
= 15%

Average cost of equity:

	Amount	Percent	x Cost	= Product
New external equity	$15,000,000	37.5%	15.6%	5.85 %
Retained earnings	25,000,000	62.5	15	9.375
	$40,000,000		Equity cost =	15.225%

d. Weights:

Debt $\frac{\$330,000}{\$587,500} = 56.2\%$

Preferred $\frac{\$22,500}{\$587,500} = 3.8\%$

Equity $\frac{\$235,000}{\$587,500} = 40\%$

	Cost		x Weight =	Product
Debt	.13(1-.4)	7.8%	56.2%	4.38%
Preferred		12	3.8	0.46
Equity		= 15.225	40	6.09
		Incremental cost of capital =		10.93%

21.8 At the beginning of 1985, the total assets of Chriswell Corporation were $150 million. By year-end, total assets are expected to be $250 million. Chriswell's capital structure (below) is considered to be optimal.

Debt (11.5% coupon bonds)	$ 64.5 million
Preferred stock (12%)	18.0
Common equity	67.5
	$150.0 million

New bonds can be sold at par with a 12 percent coupon. Preferred stock can also be sold at par with a 13 percent dividend rate. Common stock is currently selling at $45. The expected year-end dividend is $3.83. The past and expected future growth rate is 6 percent. External equity can be sold at a 3 percent risk premium over the cost of Chriswell's long-term debt. Chriswell expects to retain $15 in earnings during 1985. The applicable corporate tax rate is 40 percent.

a. Assuming that all asset expansion is included in the capital budget, what is the dollar amount of the 1985 capital budget?
b. To maintain the optimal capital structure, how much of the capital budget should be financed with equity?
c. How much of the new equity funds must be raised externally?
d. What is the cost of retained earnings?
e. What is the cost of external equity?
f. At what level of the capital budget will there be a break in the marginal cost of capital schedule?
g. Calculate the MCC below and above the break.
h. Plot the MCC schedule. Draw in a hypothetical MEI schedule that is consistent with the MCC schedule and the projected capital budget.

Solution:

a.

Total assets, beginning of year	$150 million
Expected assets, end of year	250 million
Capital budget	100 million

b. Current weight of equity $= \frac{\$67.5}{\$150}$

$= 45\%$

.45 x \$100 = \$45 million of capital budget to be financed with equity

c. \$45 million
-15 million retained earnings
\$30 million to be raised externally

d. Cost of retained earnings

$$k_r = \frac{d_1}{P_o} + g$$

$$= \frac{3.83}{45} + .06$$

$$= 14.5 \text{ percent}$$

e. Cost of external equity = bond yield plus risk premium

= .12 + .03

= 15 percent

f. Break in MCC = $\frac{\text{Retained earnings}}{\text{Equity/total capital}}$

$= \frac{\$15 \text{ million}}{.45}$

$= \$33,333,333$

g. (i) Cost below break:

	Percent	x	After-Tax Cost	=	Product
Debt (12%)	43%		7.2%	=	3.096%
Preferred stock (13%)	12		13		1.560
Equity (retained earnings)	45		14.5		6.525
			MCC below break		11.181%

(ii) Cost above break:

Debt (12%)	43%	7.2%	3.096%
Preferred (13%)	12	13	1.560
New equity	45	15	6.750
		MCC above break	11.406%

h.

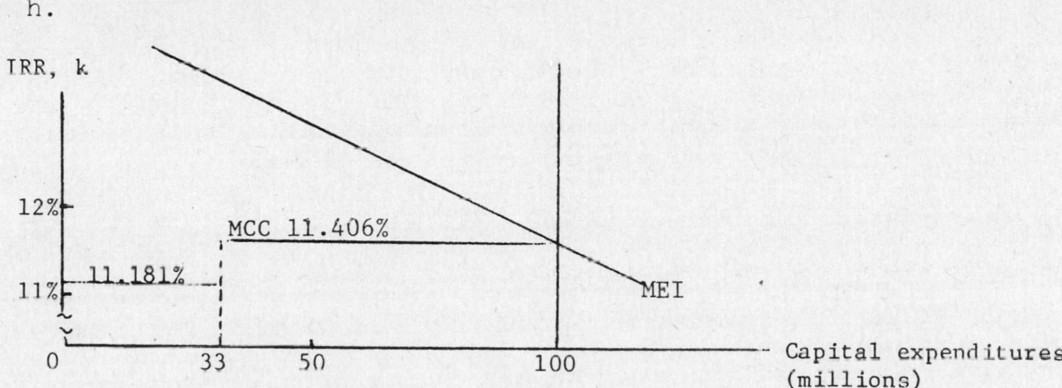

The slope of the MEI curve is not relevant to this problem. It must, however, cut the MCC at $100 million.

21.9 Andiman Corporation is unlevered. A partial balance sheet is shown below:

Andiman Corporation Balance Sheet
for year ending 12/31/X0 ($ millions)

		Common stock par value $2	$10
		Paid-in capital	10
		Retained earnings	20
Total assets	$40	Total claims	$40

Net operating earnings for the year ending 12/31/X0 were $10 million and the effective tax rate is 40 percent. The common stock has a market value of $9 per share. To finance additional projects Andiman can issue $18 million in long-term debt to sell at par with a 12 percent coupon rate. Alternatively, the expansion can be financed by the sale of 2 million additional shares of common stock. Net operating earnings are expected to rise to $15 million per year as a result of the additional investment.

a. Before the new financing:
   1. What are earnings per share of common stock?
   2. What is the P/E ratio?
   3. What is the relationship between book value and market value?
   4. What is the cost of capital?

b. After new financing by debt:
   5. What is the new value of the firm?
   6. What is the new level of earnings per share?
   7. What is the new market price per share?
   8. What is the new P/E ratio?
   9. What is the new cost of equity, k_s?
   10. What is the new weighted average cost of capital (WACC)?
   11. What is the new market to book relationship?

c. After new financing with equity?
   12-18. Answer the same questions as part b, 5-11.

Solution:

a. 1.

NOI	$10,000,000
Tax @ 40%	4,000,000
Net income	$6,000,000

$$\text{Number of shares} = \frac{\$10,000,000}{\$2 \text{ par}} = 5,000,000$$

EPS = $6,000,000/5,000,000 = $1.20

2. P/E ratio = $9/$1.20 = 7.5X

3. Book value per share = $\frac{\$40,000,000}{5,000,000}$ = $8

Market/Book = $9/$8 = 1.125

On a firm-wide basis, the market value of the firm equals V_u, which equals market value per share times number of shares outstanding.

$$V_u = \$9(5,000,000) = \$45,000,000$$

Market/Book = $45,000,000/$40,000,000 = 1.125

4. $k = k_u = \frac{X(1-T)}{V_u}$

$$= \frac{\$10,000,000(.6)}{\$45,000,000}$$

$$= \frac{\$6,000,000}{\$45,000,000}$$

$$= .133 = 13.3\%$$

b. After financing by debt:

5. $V_L = \frac{X(1-T)}{k_u} + TB$

$$= \frac{\$15,000,000(.6)}{.133} + .4(\$18,000,000)$$

$$= \$67,669,173 + \$7,200,000$$

$$= \$74,869,173$$

6.

NOI		$15,000,000
Interest expense	(.12)(18,000,000)	2,160,000
EBT		12,840,000
Tax @ 40%		5,136,000
Net income		$7,704,000

EPS = $7,704,000/5,000,000 = $1.54

7. $S = V_L - B$

$= \$74,869,173 - \$18,000,000$

$= \$56,869,173$

Market price per share $= \dfrac{\$56,869,173}{5,000,000} = \$11.37$

8. P/E ratio = \$11.37/\$1.54 = 7.38X

9. $k_s = \dfrac{NI}{S} = \dfrac{\$7,704,000}{\$56,869,173} = .13547 = 13.547\%$

Alternatively, $k_s = k_u + (k_u - k_b)(1-T)(B/S)$

$= .133 + (.133-.12)(.6)\dfrac{\$18,000,000}{\$56,869,173}$

$= .133 + .00247$

$= .13547 = 13.547\%$

10. $WACC = k = k_b(1-T)\dfrac{B}{V_L} + k_s \dfrac{S}{V_L}$

$= .12(.6)\left(\dfrac{18,000,000}{74,869,173}\right) + .13547\left(\dfrac{56,869,173}{74,869,173}\right)$

$= .0173 + .1029$

$= .1202 = 12.02\%$

Alternatively,
$k = k_u(1-TL)$ where $L = \dfrac{B}{V_L} = \dfrac{18,000,000}{74,869,173} = .2404$

$= .133[1-(.4)(.2404)]$

$= .133(.9038)$

$= .1202 = 12.02\%$

Also,
$k = \dfrac{X(1-T)}{V_L} = \dfrac{\$15,000,000(.6)}{\$74,869,173} = .1202 = 12.02\%$

11. Market/Book value = 74,869,173/58,000,000

= 1.29

c. After financing with equity:

12. $V_u = \frac{X(1-T)}{k_u} = \frac{\$15,000,000(.6)}{.133}$

= \$67,669,173

13.

NOI	\$15,000,000
Tax @ 40%	6,000,000
Net income	\$9,000,000

Number of shares = 5,000,000 + 2,000,000 = 7,000,000

EPS = \$9,000,000/7,000,000 = \$1.29

14. $S = V_u$ = \$67,669,173

Market price per share = S/N

= \$67,669,173/7,000,000

= \$9.66

15. P/E ratio = \$9.66/\$1.29 = 7.5X

16. $k_s = k_u$ = NI/S = \$9,000,000/\$67,669,173

= .133 = 13.3%

17. WACC = k_u = .133 = 13.3%

18. Market/Book = \$67,669,173/\$58,000,000

= 1.17

On a per share basis, \$9.66/\$8.29 = 1.17.

Summarizing some of the key factors involved we have:

	No expansion	With Equity	With Debt
WACC	13.3%	13.3%	12.02%
Firm Value	\$45,000,000	\$67,669,173	\$74,869,173
Share Price	\$9.00	\$9.66	\$11.37

The analysis suggests that Andiman should go ahead with the expansion using debt financing to maximize firm value and share price. Note that P/E = $\frac{1}{k_s}$. When financed with debt, MM II states that k_s rises. Hence P/E falls. But share price can increase as this example illustrates.

21.10 The Upson Company, Inc. and Luxon Corporation are identical in every respect except that Upson has no debt in its capital structure, while Luxon has $18 million in 10 percent bonds outstanding. Assume:

1. All the Modigliani-Miller assumptions are met.
2. The tax rate for both firms is 40 percent.
3. EBIT is $3.5 million.
4. Upson's cost of equity is 12 percent.

a. What is the value of each firm according to the M-M model?
b. What is the cost of equity for Luxon Corporation?
c. What is the cost of capital for Luxon Corporation?

Solution:

a.

$$V_u = \frac{X(1-T)}{k_u}$$

$$= \frac{3.5(.6)}{.12}$$

$$= \$17.5 \text{ million} = \text{value of Upson Company}$$

$$V_L = V_u + TB$$

$$= \$17.5 + .4(18)$$

$$= \$24.7 \text{ million} = \text{value of Luxon Corporation}$$

b. $k_s = k_u + (k_u - k_b)(1-T)(B/S)$

$$= .12 + (.12-.10)(.6)(18/6.7)$$

$$= 15.2 \text{ percent}$$

c.

$$k = \frac{X(1-T)}{V_L} = \frac{3.5(.6)}{24.7} = .085 = 8.5 \text{ percent}$$

Check on value of Luxon.

$$V_L = \frac{X(1-T)}{k} = \frac{3.5(.6)}{.085} = \$24.71 \text{ million}$$

Alternatively,

$$k = k_u(1\text{-}TL) \quad \text{where } L = B/V$$

$$= .12[1-(.4)(18/24.7)]$$

$$= .12(1-.2915)$$

$$= .085 = 8.5 \text{ percent}$$

As a final check:

$$k = WACC = k_b(1\text{-}T)(B/V) + k_s(S/V)$$

$$= .10(.6)(18/24.7) + .152(6.7/24.7)$$

$$= .044 + .041$$

$$= 8.5 \text{ percent}$$

21.11 The following projections of after-tax NOI and market returns have been made by the consumer products division of the Macrosonics Corporation for the coming year:

State of the Economy	p_s	X_j (\$000)	R_M
Terrible	.2	\$-10	.02
Average	.4	25	.10
Good	.3	40	.14
Great	.1	80	.18

The risk-free rate is 8 percent and the corporate tax rate is 40 percent.

a. What is the value of the consumer products division?
b. What is the unlevered beta of the consumer products division?

Solution:
Preliminary calculations:

State	p_s	X_j	p_sX_j	$X_j-\overline{X}_j$
Terrible	.2	\$-10	-2	-38
Average	.4	25	10	-3
Good	.3	40	12	12
Great	.1	80	8	52
			$\overline{X}_j$ = 28	

R_M	$p_s R_M$	$R_M-\bar{R}_M$	$(R_M-\bar{R}_M)^2$	$p_s(R_M-\bar{R}_M)^2$
.02	.004	-.084	.007056	.0014112
.10	.040	-.004	.000016	.0000064
.14	.042	.036	.001296	.0003888
.18	.018	.076	.005776	.0005776
$\bar{R}_M$ =	.104		$Var(R_M)$ =	0023840

$p_s(X_j-\bar{X}_j)(R_M-\bar{R}_M)$
.6384
.0048
.1296
.3952
$Cov(X_j,R_M)$ = 1.1680

a. $$V_j = \frac{E(X_j)-\lambda Cov(X_j,R_M)}{R_F}$$

$$\text{where } \lambda = \frac{\bar{R}_M-R_F}{\sigma_M^2} = \frac{.104-.08}{.002384} = 10$$

$$V_j = \frac{28-(10)(1.168)}{.08}$$

$$= \frac{28-11.68}{.08}$$

= \$204 = Value of the consumer products division

b. $$Cov(R_j,R_M) = \frac{Cov(X_j,R_M)}{V_j}$$

$$= \frac{1.168}{204}$$

$$= .0057255$$

$$\beta_u = \frac{Cov(R_j,R_M)}{\sigma_M^2} = \frac{.0057255}{.002384} = 2.4$$

21.12 Security X pays \$5 if State 1 occurs and \$15 if State 2 occurs. Security Y pays \$25 if State 1 occurs and \$10 if State 2 occurs.

The price of Security X is \$25; the price of Security Y is \$60.

a. Set up a payoff table for Securities X and Y.
b. What are the prices of pure securities 1 and 2?

Solution:

a.

	State 1	State 2	Price
Security X	\$5	\$15	\$25
Security Y	\$25	\$10	\$60

b.

$$p_1 5 + p_2 15 = 25 \qquad (1)$$

$$p_1 25 + p_2 10 = 60 \qquad (2)$$

Multiply equation (1) by 5; subtract equation (2) from it and solve for p_2. Use the value of p_2 to find p_1.

$$p_1 25 + p_2 75 = 125$$

$$-\ [p_1 25 + p_2 10 = 60\ ]$$

$$p_2 65 = 65$$

$$p_2 = \$1$$

$$p_1 5 + (1)(15) = 25$$

$$p_1 5 = 10$$

$$p_1 = \$2$$

21.13 The Kalish Company is evaluating three alternative production plans (A, B, and C) as follows:

State	p_s	Cost of Failure	EBIT (\$000) A	B	C
1	.2	\$ 2	\$ 5	\$10	\$ 8
2	.3	10	20	25	15
3	.4	25	50	45	52
4	.1	40	65	50	60

The prices of the pure securities (p_s) and the cost of failure (f_s) are also given.

Production will be financed with \$50,000 in debt. Which plan will maximize the value of the firm? (The corporate tax rate is 40 percent.)

Solution:

Plan A

$X_s < B$ for states 1, 2 $\quad V = (X_s - f_s)p_s$

$X_s \geq B$ for states 2, 3

$$V = Bp_s + (X_s - B)(1-T)p_s$$

State	Value of firm's state payoff
1	(5-2)(.2) = 0.6
2	(20-10)(.3) = 3.0
3	(50)(.4)+(50-50)(.6)(.4) = 20.0
4	(50)(.1)+(65-50)(.6)(.1) = 5.9
	Value of firm under Plan A = 29.5

Plan B

$X_s < B$ for states 1,2,3 $\quad V = (X_s - f_s)p_s$

$X_s \geq B$ for state 4 $\quad V = Bp_s + (X_s - B)(1-T)p_s$

State	Value of firm's state payoff
1	(10-2)(.2) = 1.6
2	(25-10)(.3) = 4.5
3	(45-25)(.4) = 8.0
4	(50)(.1)+(50-50)(.6)(.1) = 5.0
	Value of firm under Plan B = 19.1

Plan C

$X_s < B$ for states 1, 2 $\quad V = (X_s - f_s)p_s$

$X_s \geq B$ for states 3, 4 $\quad V = Bp_s + (X_s - B)(1-T)p_s$

State	Value of the firm's state payoff
1	(8-2)(.2) = 1.20
2	(15-10)(.3) = 1.50
3	(50)(.4)+(52-50)(.6)(.4) = 20.48
4	(50)(.1)+(60-50)(.6)(.1) = 5.60
	Value of firm under Plan C = 28.78

Firm value is maximized under Plan A.

CHAPTER 22

DIVIDEND POLICY

Theme: Dividend policy affects the financial structure, the flow of funds, corporate liquidity, and investor attitudes. Thus, it is one of the central decision areas related to policies seeking to maximize the value of the firm's common stock.

I. Dividend Payments.
   A. Management generally tries to convey to investors certain ideas:
      1. The regular dividend will be maintained.
      2. Earnings will be sufficient to maintain dividends.
   B. In order to attain these goals, what may firms with volatile cash flows and investment needs do?
      1. They will set a lower regular dividend rate than firms with the same average earnings but less volatility.
      2. They may also declare extra dividends in years when earnings are high and funds are available.

II. The Payment Procedure.
   A. On the declaration date directors declare the dividends and the payment date.
   B. On the holder of record date the stock transfer books are closed. If the company is notified of the sale and transfer of stock on or before the holder of record date, the new owner receives the dividend.
   C. To avoid conflicts concerning whether a company will be notified of a sale in time to meet the holder of record date, the brokerage business has set up the convention that the right to the dividend expires on the ex-dividend date, four days prior to the holder of record date. The value of the stock is normally expected to drop by the amount of the dividend on the ex-dividend date.
   D. The company mails checks to the holders of record on the payment date.

III. These are Legal Rules Influencing Dividend Policy.
   A. The net profits rule states that dividends must be paid from present and/or past retained earnings.
   B. The capital impairment rule states that dividends cannot be paid out of invested capital.
   C. The insolvency rule states that no dividends can be paid during insolvency (when liabilities exceed assets).

IV. Within the Framework Set by Legal Rules, Business Factors Affect Dividend Policy.

A. The cash or liquidity position of a firm influences its ability to pay dividends. A firm may have sufficient retained earnings, but if they are invested in physical assets, cash may not be available to make dividend payments.

B. The need to repay debt also influences the availability of cash flow to pay dividends.

C. Restrictions in debt contracts may specify that dividends may be paid only out of earnings generated after signing the loan agreement and only when net working capital is above a specified amount. Also, preferred stock agreements often specify that preferred dividends take precedence over common stock dividends.

D. A high rate of asset expansion creates a need to retain funds rather than to pay dividends.

E. A high rate of profit on net worth makes it desirable to retain earnings rather than to pay them out if the investor will earn less on them.

F. Stability of earnings will allow a high payout ratio, which can be maintained even during difficult economic times.

G. A firm's access to capital markets will be influenced by the age and size of the firm, therefore a well-established firm is likely to have a higher payout ratio than a smaller, newer firm.

H. Control considerations may influence dividend policy, since additional external financing is influenced by the dividend payout. If the owners rely on internal financing in order to maintain control, the dividend payout will be reduced.

I. The tax position of stockholders also affects dividend policy.

1. Corporations owned largely by taxpayers in high income tax brackets tend toward lower dividend payouts because the tax rate on capital gains is lower than the personal tax rate applied to dividends.

2. Corporations owned by small investors tend toward higher dividend payouts.

3. Sometimes there may be a conflict between stockholders in high income tax brackets and stockholders in lower tax brackets.

a. The dividend policy may be a compromise--an intermediate payout ratio.

b. If one group dominates, the members of the other group are likely to sell their shares, over time. Therefore, a firm's dividend policy dictates the type of stockholders it has, and vice versa. This is called the clientele effect.

J. In addition, the <u>tax position of the corporation</u> affects its dividend policies. Possible penalties for excess accumulation of retained earnings may induce higher payout ratios.

V. General Dividend Patterns in the Economy.
   A. For the period 1947-55, the dividend payout ratio was relatively stable, with an average payout of 49 percent.
   B. During the period of price stability from 1956-66, the average dividend payout ratio declined to 42 percent.
   C. With continuing inflation and the rise in oil prices after 1972, the average payout rose to 58 percent for the 1980-83 period.
   D. Deflating both after-tax profits and dividends by the consumer price index (CPI) for the 1966 to 1983 period shows a pattern of relatively stable real dollar value dividends in spite of declining real after-tax profits.

VI. Alternative Dividend Policies.
   A. <u>Stable-dollar amount per share</u>. This is the policy followed by most firms.
      1. Maintenance of a stable-dollar amount per share or a <u>target dividend</u> will lead to low payout ratios when profits are temporarily high and to high payout ratios when profits are temporarily depressed. This will cause dividend growth to lag profit growth, and dividends will be more stable than earnings.
      2. The rationale for keeping stable dividends but allowing the payout ratio to fluctuate is that this practice leads to higher stock prices, because:
         a. Fluctuating dividends are riskier than stable ones, therefore a lower discount factor will be applied to the stable dividends, and they will be valued more highly.
         b. Stockholders who live on income received in the form of dividends seek a relatively assured minimum dollar dividend and will be willing to pay a premium for the stock.
         c. Qualification for legal lists (that is, listings of securities in which institutions of a fiduciary nature are allowed to invest) requires a stable and uninterrupted dividend history. Placement on legal lists increases the breadth of the market and the potential demand for the firm's securities.

B. Constant payout ratio. A few firms pay out a constant percentage of earnings.
   1. Earnings fluctuate, therefore, the dollar amount of dividends fluctuates.
   2. This policy is not likely to maximize the value of the firm's stock.

C. Low regular dividend plus extras. A compromise policy between the first two, giving a little more flexibility to the firm.

VII. The Theory of Dividend Policy.

A. There is nothing in dividend theory to suggest that dividends are desirable or that changes in dividend policy can affect shareholder wealth.

B. We first consider dividend policy in a world without taxes.
   1. Assumptions:
      a. Two firms are identical in all respects except for dividends paid out in the current period; all future dividends will be the same for both firms.
      b. No debt in capital structure.
      c. Investment decisions are unaffected by the level of dividends paid out.
      d. There are no transactions costs associated with raising external funds.
   2. The sources and uses of funds statements of the two firms illustrate that dividend payout does not affect firm value.
      a. External sources of funds (sale of equity) and uses of funds (equity repurchase) enable firms to pursue the same investment program regardless of the level of dividend payout.
      b. Dividends do not appear in the valuation equation; firm value depends on the discounted value of expected future cash flows resulting from planned investment which is assumed to be the same for both firms.
   3. Without taxes, shareholders are indifferent to receiving cash flows in the form of dividends or capital gains if earnings are retained.

C. Next consider dividend policy in a world with taxes.
   1. We make the same assumptions as above except that there are now three different tax rates to consider:
      a. T_c = corporate tax rate
      b. T_p = personal tax rate on income from bonds, dividends and wages
      c. T_g = tax rate on capital gains

2. If T_p is greater than T_g, which is generally the case, then shareholders will prefer a policy of no dividends.
   a. Dividend income can be neutralized such that only capital gains rates will be paid through a combination of borrowing and risk-free investing, making shareholders indifferent to cash received as dividends or capital gains.
   b. In practice, the usefulness of this strategy is limited by law and by the transactions costs involved.

D. In spite of the foregoing analysis, firms continue to pay dividends.

VIII. Toward a Theory of Optimal Dividend Policy.

A. An optimal dividend policy requires that dividend payments entail benefits as well as costs.

B. Dividends can reduce the agency costs of outside shareholders.
   1. Outside shareholders must monitor the performance of owner-managers.
   2. Higher dividend payouts increase the probability that a firm will have to seek external capital.
   3. The firm's management comes under the scrutiny of the capital market when it raises external capital.
   4. Thus, some of the costs of monitoring performance are shifted to the capital market.

C. The higher costs of external financing result in different dividend payout policies depending on firm characteristics.
   1. Firms with more variable cash flows (higher beta) will have lower payout ratios to avoid external financing in the bad years.
   2. Growth firms will have lower payout ratios to be able to finance more investment opportunities with less expensive internal financing.
   3. The higher the percentage of insider shareholders, the less need to monitor management, and the lower the payout ratio.

D. Dividends are also useful as signals to transmit information.
   1. Managers have monopolistic access to information about the firm's prospects.
   2. An increase in dividends signals management's belief that future cash flows will be sufficient to sustain the higher dividend level.

3. A useful signal must satisfy four conditions:
   a. Managers must have incentive to send a truthful signal even if the information is bad.
   b. The signal of a successful firm should be difficult for an unsuccessful firm to copy.
   c. The signal must be correlated with observable events.
   d. There should be no more cost-effective way to convey the same message.

E. The tax status of shareholders helps to determine an optimal dividend/investment policy.
   1. The firm can make two types of investments:
      a. Real asset investments have diminishing returns to scale because the profitable investment opportunities available to the firm are limited.
      b. Investments in the securities of other firms have a constant return to scale; 85 percent of the dividends received are not taxable.
   2. The after-tax return to individual shareholders depends on their tax brackets.
      a. The after-tax return to shareholders on earnings paid out as dividends is

$$r_b(1-T_c)(1-T_d)$$

where r_b = pre-tax return on the firm's investments in real assets
T_c = corporate tax rate
T_d = individual tax rate on dividend income

      b. If earnings are retained, shareholders will be satisfied with a lower pre-tax return on real assets.
      c. EXAMPLE:
      Individual 1 is a high-tax-bracket shareholder.

$$r_b = .18 \quad T_c = .40 \quad T_{d1} = .50$$

After-tax return on dividend income

$$= r_b(1-T_c)(1-T_{d1})$$

$$= .18(.6)(.5) = .054$$

The pre-tax return on real assets at which Individual 1 would be indifferent between retained earnings and dividends:

$$r_b(1-T_c) = .054$$

$$r_b(.6) = .054$$

$$r_b = .09$$

Individual 2 is a low-tax bracket shareholder.

$$r_b = .18 \quad T_c = .40 \quad T_{d2} = .20$$

After-tax return on dividend income

$$= r_b(1-T_c)(1-T_{d2})$$

$$= .18(.6)(.8) = .0864$$

The pre-tax return on real assets at which Individual 2 would be indifferent between retained earnings and dividends:

$$r_b(1-T_c) = .0864$$

$$r_b(.6) = .0864$$

$$r_b = .144$$

d. The low-bracket shareholder receives a higher after-tax return on dividends than the high-bracket shareholder, and thus has a greater preference for dividends.

e. The high-bracket shareholder would let the firm retain earnings to invest until the pre-tax return fell to below 9 percent; the low-bracket shareholder would require a pre-tax earnings rate of 14.4 percent or more.

3. Shareholders in different tax brackets self-select into clienteles, reducing shareholder conflicts; high-bracket investors buy low-dividend stocks and vice versa.

4. The tax model has implications for dividend/investment policy.
   a. Firms will not use more expensive external financing to invest in the securities of other firms; these investments will be financed with any excess internal funding after more profitable real asset investments are exhausted, depending on the tax bracket of shareholders.
   b. Growth firms with many investment opportunities use up all their internal financing, plus external financing, and do not pay dividends. Older, mature firms have leftover internal funds after exhausting investment opportunities, which they use to pay dividends.
   c. Mergers are predicted between firms with excess internal financing and firms which require all their internal financing plus external financing.
   d. Earnings decreases have more impact on the investment policies of firms which had intended to finance internally.

e. The greater the amount of internal funding relative to investment opportunities, the greater the potential for shareholder conflict.

F. Empirical evidence suggests that shareholders do not like dividends and require higher rates of return (i.e. place a lower value) on high-dividend stocks.

IX. More on Dividend Clientele Effects.

A. The clientele effect posits that each firm attracts to itself a clientele of shareholders who prefer the firm's particular payout policy, without implications for the value of stock.

1. Shareholder clientele preferences are based on tax categories.
2. According to the theory, changes in dividend payout policies would require shareholders to incur transactions costs to relocate to another firm with their preferred payout.

B. While empirical evidence on the clientele effect is mixed, there is some support for the theory that high-dividend payouts are associated with lower implied tax-bracket shareholders and vice versa.

C. One study found several non-tax characteristics for the clientele of low-dividend stocks:

1. High income investors.
2. Younger investors.
3. Investors with a big difference between capital gain and ordinary tax rates.
4. Investors with high systematic risk portfolios.

X. Stock Dividends and Stock Splits.

A. There are some distinctions between them.

1. A stock dividend simply involves a bookkeeping transfer from the retained earnings to the capital stock account. It is paid in shares of stock instead of cash.
2. A stock split simply increases the number of shares outstanding.

B. There are also some similarities.

1. No cash is distributed in either case.
2. Both result in a larger number of shares outstanding.
3. Total net worth remains unchanged.
4. In a practical sense, there is no difference between the two. The NYSE recognizes this by defining a stock dividend as a stock distribution up to 25 percent of the outstanding stock of the firm, and a stock split as any distribution of 25 percent or more.

C. Identifying Characteristics.

1. A split does not affect the capital accounts, whereas a stock dividend increases the capital stock account and reduces retained earnings.
2. A split may result in change in the par or stated value, but a stock dividend does not.

D. Empirical evidence supports the common rationale that stock splits and dividends increase shareholder wealth.
   1. A 1969 study found that shareholder wealth is increased by stock splits associated with dividend increases.
   2. A 1983 study found significant positive returns even for pure stock splits unassociated with dividend increases.
   3. Positive results were even greater for stock dividends.
      a. Stock dividends require a reduction in retained earnings.
      b. Thus, the firm must be confident that the reduced retained earnings will not violate debt restrictions.
   4. Stock splits appear to be interpreted as favorable signals.

E. Stock splits reduce trading liquidity contrary to the rationale that splits reduce stock price to an optimal price range which increases liquidity.
   1. Trading volume is proportionately lower than the pre-split level.
   2. Brokerage commissions are proportionately higher.
   3. Bid-ask spreads are higher as a percentage of the bid price.

F. Stock dividends and splits are effective in increasing the number of shareholders by reducing the unit price of stock to a more popular trading range.

XI. Stock Repurchases as an Alternative to Dividends.

A. Stock repurchased by the issuing firm is called treasury stock.

B. Acquisition of treasury stock is an alternative to dividend payments.
   1. Fewer shares remain outstanding, increasing EPS.
   2. Increased EPS increases market price of remaining shares.

C. Corporations can repurchase either on the open market or via tender offers.
   1. Open-market repurchases are generally gradual programs over a period of time.
   2. In a tender offer repurchase, the tender price, the number of shares to be repurchased and the tender offer period are specified in advance.

D. Tender offer repurchases are significant corporate events with an average cash distribution of almost 20 percent of the market value of the firm.

E. Five hypotheses have been tested to explain the significant increase in the market value of equity associated with tender offer repurchases.

1. Signalling.
   a. The tender offer could be interpreted as good news or as an indication that the firm had no profitable investment opportunities.
   b. Empirical evidence indicates that tender offers are interpreted as a favorable reassessment of the firm's earnings prospects.
   c. The signalling hypothesis appears to be the most important explanation of the positive returns.
2. Leverage effects.
   a. If the repurchase is financed by debt, there may be a gain from the increased leverage.
   b. While leverage effects do exist, they are not the predominant explanation for the positive returns.
3. Dividend tax avoidance.
   a. The cash distributions in repurchases are almost always taxed as capital gains and not as dividends.
   b. Empirically, the personal tax savings are too small to explain the magnitude of positive returns.
4. Bondholder expropriation.
   a. Repurchase may reduce the asset base, undermining bondholders' collateral.
   b. This hypothesis is refuted by empirical evidence.
5. Wealth transfers between shareholders.
   a. Not all shareholders tender their shares, resulting in a wealth transfer from non-tendering to tendering shareholders.
   b. While tendering shareholders benefit more, non-tendering shareholders also benefit from tender offer repurchases.

Chapter 22 - Illustrative Problems and Solutions

22.1 The Kirkman Company plans to expand its manufacturing facilities in the coming year by $13 million. Kirkman's current debt/total assets ratio is 40 percent (considered to be optimal) and current earnings after taxes are $6 million. If Kirkman wishes to maintain a 60 percent dividend payout ratio, how much external equity will be required to finance the expansion?

Solution:

$6,000,000 Earnings
.60 Dividend payout rate
$3,600,000 Dividends

$6,000,000
-3,600,000
$2,400,000 Retained earnings

$13,000,000 Capital budget
.60 (1 - Debt/Total Assets) = percent to be financed with equity
$ 7,800,000 New equity needed
-2,400,000 Retained earnings
$ 5,400,000 External equity required

22.2 Richmond Electronics declared a dividend of $2.50 per share following a 4-for-1 stock split. This new dividend represents a 10 percent increase over last year's pre-split dividend. Richmond's stock sold for $160 prior to the stock split. What was last year's dividend per share?

Solution:

Post-split dividend $ 2.50
x4
Equivalent pre-split dividend $10.00

1.10 x Last year's dividend = $10.00
Last year's dividend = $ 9.09

22.3 Green Mountain Forest Products had earnings of $11 million last year and paid out $3.96 million in dividends. Earnings have grown at a rate of 6 percent per year over the 10 years, and this growth rate is expected to continue in the future in spite of the fact that this year's earnings were unusually high at $14 million. Green Mountain has investment opportunities totalling $10 million. Calculate Green Mountain's dividends for this year under each of the following policies:

a. Constant payout ratio.
b. Stable, growing dollar dividend.
c. Residual policy dividend (assuming that the company wishes to maintain a 40 percent debt-to-total-assets ratio).

Solution:

a. Payout ratio = $\frac{\$3,960,000}{11,000,000}$ = 36%

.36($14,000,000) = $5,040,000

b. 1.06($3,960,000) = $4,197,600

c.

Investment	$10,000,000
% financed with equity	.60
Amount financed with equity	$ 6,000,000
Earnings	$14,000,000
Amount of equity financing	6,000,000
Dividends	$ 8,000,000

22.4 The Gaylin Corporation's common stock is selling for $45.00 per share following a 2-for-1 stock split. This stock price represents a P/E ratio of 15. Prior to the stock split the P/E ratio was 10, and dividends per share were $1.00. The post-split dividend is $.75 per share.

a. What was the pre-split stock price?
b. By what percentage has the stock price increased?
c. By what percentage has the dividend increased?

Solution:

a. Price/EPS = 15

$45/EPS = 15

EPS = $3 per new share

Post-split EPS	$ 3.00
2-for-1 stock split	x 2
Pre-split EPS	$ 6.00
Pre-split P/E ratio	10
Pre-split stock price	$60.00

b.

Post-split stock price	$45.00
2-for-1 stock split	x 2
Equivalent pre-split stock price	$90.00

$\frac{\$90 - \$60}{\$60}$ = .5 = 50% increase in stock price

c. Post-split dividend $ .75
2-for-1 stock split x 2
Equivalent pre-split dividend $1.50

$$\frac{\$1.50 - \$1.00}{\$1.00} = .5 = 50\% \text{ increase in dividend}$$

22.5 The owners' equity accounts of the Lundberg Company are shown below.

Common stock ($4 par)	$ 4,000,000
Paid-in capital	10,000,000
Retained earnings	29,000,000
Shareholders' equity	$43,000,000

Lundberg's stock is currently selling at $50 per share.
a. Show the equity accounts after a 4-for-1 stock split.
b. Show the equity accounts after a 20 percent stock dividend.

Solution:

a.

Common stock ($1 par, 4,000,000 shares)	$ 4,000,000
Paid-in capital	10,000,000
Retained earnings	29,000,000
Shareholders' equity	$43,000,000

b.

Number of shares	1,000,000
% stock dividend	.20
New shares to be distributed	200,000
Price per share	$50
Amount to be transferred from retained earnings	$10,000,000

Number of new shares	200,000
Par value	$4
To be transferred to common stock	$800,000

To be transferred to paid-in capital:
$10,000,000 - 800,000 = $9,200,000

Equity accounts

Common stock ($4 par, 1,200,000 shares)	$ 4,800,000
Paid-in capital	19,200,000
Retained earnings	19,000,000
Shareholders' equity	$43,000,000

Neither the stock split nor the stock dividend changes the total amount of shareholders' equity. The stock split merely increases the number of shares and reduces par value accordingly. With the stock dividend there are accounting changes within the shareholders' equity account, but the total remains the same.

CHAPTER 23

VALUATION

Theme: The goal of financial management is to maximize the value of the firm. The elements of valuation are the future revenue stream and the discount factor applied to it. Varying patterns of expected future revenues in the form of interest, dividends or capital gains affect current valuation.

I. These are Some Basic Definitions.
   A. Liquidating value vs. going-concern value.
      1. Liquidating value is the amount that could be realized by selling an asset or group of assets separately from the organization that has been using them.
      2. Going-concern value is the amount realized if the firm is sold as an operating business.
      3. Any excess of going-concern value over liquidating value may be called organization value.
   B. Book value vs. market value.
      1. Book value is the accounting value at which an asset is carried, usually historical cost.
      2. Market value is the price at which an asset can be sold, generally the higher of going-concern or liquidating value.
      3. In the case of stock:
         a. Book value is the firm's total common equity divided by shares outstanding.
         b. Market value is what people will pay for a share of stock.
   C. "Fair" or "reasonable" or intrinsic value.
      1. This value is arrived at by estimating future net cash flows and discounting at an appropriate capitalization rate to arrive at a present value.
      2. This capitalization-of-income method of valuation is the same as the present value of assets method used in capital budgeting.

II. Bond Values and Their Fluctuations.
   A. The expected cash flows consist of the periodic interest payments plus the principal due when the bond matures.
   B. A perpetual bond is a bond which never matures.
      1. the value of a perpetuity is found as

$$v_b = \frac{c}{k_b}$$

where
v_b = Value of the bond
c = Annual interest payment
k_b = The appropriate interest rate for securities of similar risk

2. If the price and coupon are known, the cost of debt, or yield on the perpetuity, can be found by solving for k_b:

$$k_b = \frac{c}{v_b}$$

3. If the going rate of interest rises, the value of the perpetual bond will fall, and vice versa.

C. The value of any finite maturity bond can be found as

$$v_b = \frac{c_1}{(1+k_b)^1} + \frac{c_2}{(1+k_b)^2} + \ldots + \frac{c_n + M}{(1+k_b)^n}$$

where
M = Maturity value of the bond.

1. Alternatively,
$v_b = c[PVIFA(k_b, t\ yrs)] + M[PVIF(k_b, n\ yrs)]$
2. The yield on a finite-maturity bond, or cost of debt, is found by solving the above equations for k_b.
3. As with perpetual bonds, finite-maturity bonds fluctuate in value depending on the required yield level.

D. The degree of responsiveness to changes in interest rates varies with the level of rates and with the maturity of the bond.
1. At lower required yields, longer maturity bonds have greater price changes in response to a given change in interest rates, and thus the risk in holding them is greater.
2. For deep-discount bonds, at higher required yields, the further decline in value associated with an increase in required yield is at a lesser rate for longer-term bonds than for shorter-term bonds.

III. Preferred Stock Valuation.
A. The cash flows consist of the regular, fixed dividend payments.
B. The valuation and cost of preferred stock are based on the perpetuity formulation:

$$k_{ps} = \frac{d_{ps}}{p_{ps}}$$

$$p_{ps} = \frac{d_{ps}}{k_{ps}}$$

where

d_{ps} = Preferred stock dividend

k_{ps} = Required return on preferred stock

p_{ps} = Price of preferred stock

IV. Common Stock Valuation and Rates of Return.
  A. Two factors complicate common stock valuation.
    1. Forecasting future dividends, earnings and stock prices is difficult.
    2. Earnings and dividends are expected to grow, not remain constant.
  B. The single-period valuation model consists of:
    1. Expected dividends
    2. Expected capital gain (or loss) when the stock is sold
    3. The risk-adjusted required rate of return
  C. The fair or intrinsic value of a share of stock can be found as

$$p_o = \frac{d_1}{k_s - g}$$

where

p_o = Current stock price

d_1 = Expected dividend in the coming year = $d_o(1+g)$

k_s = Risk-adjusted required rate of return

g = Expected growth rate in earnings and dividends.

  D. The model can also be used to calculate the rate of return an investor can expect in purchasing the stock at the current market price.
    1. If the expected return is above the required return, the investor should buy the stock.
    2. If the expected return is below the required return, the investor should not buy, or should sell.
    3. The buying or selling pressure caused by a disparity between expected and required returns results in market equilibrium where expected and required returns are equal.
  E. Securities prices respond rapidly to disequilibrium conditions:

1. A change in the general level of interest rates
2. Altered expectations as to the growth prospects of the firm

V. Multi-period Stock Valuation Models.

A. Stock prices are determined as the present value of the stream of cash the stocks provide according to the capitalization of income procedure.

B. The stream of dividends approach results in several models corresponding to different growth patterns in firms.

C. The general form of the dividend formulation is

Value of stock = P_o = PV of expected future dividends

$$= \sum_{t=1}^{\infty} \frac{d_t}{(1+k)^t}$$

D. Variations of this general model can accomodate any pattern of growth or decline in dividends.

1. No growth: $P_o = \frac{d_1}{k_s}$

2. Constant (normal) growth:

$$P_o = \frac{d_1}{k_s - g}$$

a. A necessary condition for this formula is that k_s be greater than g.

b. This formula also applies to a declining firm with constant negative growth.

3. Supernormal growth:
Present price = PV of dividends during supernormal growth period + value of stock price at end of supernormal growth period discounted back to present.

$$P_o = \sum_{t=1}^{n} \frac{d_o(1+g_s)^t}{(1+k_s)^t} + \left(\frac{d_{n+1}}{k_s - g}\right)\left(\frac{1}{(1+k_s)^n}\right)$$

E. The stream of dividends models implicitly incorporate both the dividends and capital gain expectations of investors. Under conditions of equal initial dividends and required returns, the following will result:

1. For the no growth firm, there is neither a capital gain nor loss expectation. The entire return will be from the dividend yield.
2. The constant growth model implies a lower relative current dividend yield, but also the expectation of a capital gain. (For the constantly declining firm, the current dividend yield will be relatively high, with a capital loss expectation.)
3. The supernormal growth firm has the lowest current dividend yield, but the highest capital gain expectation.

VI. The Free Cash Flow Model is More General.

A. For an unlevered firm, the value of the firm is equal to the value of its equity under various growth patterns.

1. No growth:

$$V_u = \frac{X(1-T)}{k_u}$$

where V_u = Value of an unlevered firm
X = Net operating income
k_u = Cost of capital of an unlevered firm
T = Corporate tax rate

2. Constant (normal) growth:

$$V_u = \frac{X(1-T)(1-b)(1+g)}{k_u-g}$$

where b = Ratio of net investment, I, in period t to after-tax NOI in period t
$= I_t/X_t(1-T)$

g = Growth rate of $X(1-T)$
$= br$ where r = internal profitability rate of investment in the firm; that is, $r = \Delta X(1-T)/I$

3. Temporary supernormal growth:
   a. Supernormal growth is temporary due to competitive factors.
   b. A forecast of conditions beyond the supernormal growth period is essential. Two models have been developed.
   c. Temporary supernormal growth followed by no growth:

$$V_u = X_o(1-T)(1-b) \sum_{t=1}^{n} \frac{(1+g_s)^t}{(1+k_u)^t} + \frac{X_o(1-T)(1+g_s)^t}{k_u(1+k_u)^n}$$

where g_s = Supernormal growth rate
n = Years of supernormal growth

   d. Temporary supernormal growth followed by constant normal growth:

$$V_u = X_o(1-T)(1-b) \sum_{t=1}^{n} \frac{(1+g_s)^t}{(1+k_u)^t}$$

$$+ \frac{X_o(1-T)(1-b)(1+g)}{k_u-g}\left[\frac{(1+g_s)^n}{(1+k_u)^n}\right]$$

B. Price/earnings and market-to-book-value-of-stock ratios are positively affected by the growth rate of earnings.

C. The free cash flow model is easily extended to the valuation of a levered firm.
   1. The value of a levered firm is greater than the value of the firm's equity.
   2. Simply substitute the firm's weighted average cost of capital, k, for k_u in the valuation equations above.
   3. k may be determined by the methods described in Chapter 21 on the cost of capital.

Chapter 23 - Illustrative Problems and Solutions

23.1 The Rockland Mining Company owns several silver mines which are near depletion. The increased costs of extracting the remaining ore have resulted in declining profits, dividends and share price. The rate of decline has been 3 percent per year. Rockland paid \$6 in dividends during the most recent year. The appropriate capitalization rate is 16 percent. What is the market price per share?

Solution:

$$p_o = \frac{d_1}{k_s - g} \qquad d_1 = d_o(1+g)$$

$$= \$6(1-.03)$$

$$= \$5.82$$

$$p_o = \frac{\$5.82}{.16-(-.03)}$$

$$= \frac{\$5.82}{.19}$$

$$= \$30.63$$

23.2 North Haven Resorts, Inc. was in an excellent position to take advantage of liberalized casino gambling laws and as a result is experiencing growth of 40 percent per year. After four years this growth rate is expected to decline to 12 percent per year as other companies are able to complete construction. Stockholders require an 18 percent return on stock of the risk of North Haven's. The current dividend is \$1.50 per share. What is the most that a shareholder could pay for North Haven stock and still earn 18 percent?

Solution:

$$p_o = \sum_{t=1}^{n} \frac{d_o(1+g_s)^t}{(1+k_s)^t} + \frac{d_{n+1}}{(k_s-g)}\left[\frac{1}{(1+k_s)^n}\right]$$

d_o = \$1.50

g_s = .40

k_s = .18

g = .12

n = 5

$$p_o = \sum_{t=1}^{5} \frac{\$1.50(1.40)^t}{(1.18)^t} + \frac{\$1.50(1.40)^5(1.12)}{(.18-.12)} \left[\frac{1}{(1.18)^5}\right]$$

PV value of dividends during supernormal growth period:

Year	Dividend $\$1.50(1.40)^t$	PVIF at 18%	Present Value
1	\$2.10	.8475	\$ 1.78
2	2.94	.7182	2.11
3	4.12	.6086	2.51
4	5.76	.5158	2.97
5	8.07	.4371	3.53

$$\sum_{t=1}^{5} d_o\left(\frac{1+g_s}{1+k_s}\right)^t = \$12.90$$

Alternatively,

$$\frac{1 + g_s}{1 + k_s} = 1 + h = \frac{1.40}{1.18} = 1.18644$$

$$h = .18644$$

Present value of dividends during supernormal growth period

$$= d_o(1+h)[\text{FVIFA}(h\%, \text{ n yrs})]$$

$$= 1.50(1.18644)\left[\frac{1.18644^5-1}{.18644}\right]$$

$$= 1.77966(7.2456)$$

$$= \$12.895 \approx \$12.90$$

Stock price at the end of supernormal growth period:

$$p_5 = \frac{d_6}{k_s - g}$$

$$= \frac{d_5(1+g)}{k_s - g}$$

$$= \frac{8.07(1.12)}{.18 - .12}$$

$$= \$150.64$$

Discount p_5 back to present:

$$\$150.64\left(\frac{1}{1.18}\right)^5 = \$150.54[\text{PVIF}(18\%,\ 5\text{ yrs})]$$

$$= \$150.64(.4371)$$

$$= \$65.84$$

Current stock price = \$12.90 + \$65.84

= \$78.74

23.3 The Delta Company's current dividend is \$2 per share. The capitalization rate appropriate for common stock of the same risk as Delta is 16 percent. Compute the value of a share of Delta stock under each of the following assumptions:

a. The future growth rate is expected to be zero.
b. The growth rate is expected to be 10 percent per year for the foreseeable future.
c. The company is declining at a rate of 4 percent per year.
d. The growth rate is expected to be 22 percent per year for the next 4 years, and 8 percent per year indefinitely thereafter.

Solution:

a. $k_s = .16$

$d_1 = d_o = \$2.00$

$$p_o = \frac{d_1}{k_s} = \frac{\$2.00}{.16} = \$12.50$$

b. $g = .10$

$d_1 = d_o(1+g) = \$2.00(1.10) = \$2.20$

$$p_o = \frac{d_1}{k_s - g} = \frac{\$2.20}{.16 - .10} = \frac{\$2.20}{.06} = \$36.67$$

c. $g = -.04$

$d_1 = d_o(1+g) = \$2.00(.96) = \$1.92$

$$p_o = \frac{\$1.92}{.16 - (-.04)} = \frac{\$1.92}{.20} = \$9.60$$

d. $g_s = .22$
$g = .08$
$n = 4$ years

$$p_o = \sum_{t=1}^{n} \frac{d_o(1+g_s)^t}{(1+k_s)^t} + \left(\frac{d_{n+1}}{k_s - g}\right)\left[\frac{1}{(1+k_s)^n}\right]$$

$$p_o = \sum_{t=1}^{4} \frac{\$2(1.22)^t}{(1.16)^t} + \frac{2(1.22)^4(1.08)}{(.16-.08)}\left[\frac{1}{(1.16)^4}\right]$$

$$p_o = 2(1+h)[\text{FVIFA}(h\%, 4 \text{ yrs.})] + \frac{2(1.08)}{(.16-.08)}\left(\frac{1.22}{1.16}\right)^4$$

$$\text{where } (1+h) = \left(\frac{1+g_s}{1+k_s}\right) = \frac{1.22}{1.16} = 1.052 \cong 1.05$$

$$h = .05$$

$$p_o = 2(1.05)(4.3101) + \frac{2.16}{.08}(1.05)^4$$

$$= 9.05 + 32.82$$
$$= \$41.87$$

23.4 You require a 16 percent rate of return on stock of the risk of Telco Corporation. Telco's earnings and dividends have been growing at a 6 percent annual rate, and this growth is expected to continue. During the most recent year Telco had \$4.18 in EPS. The company has maintained a 50 percent dividend payout rate for the past 15 years, the corporate tax rate is 40 percent, and the stock is selling for \$32. Should you invest in Telco stock?

Solution:

$$p_o = \frac{d_1}{k_s - g}$$

$$d_o = .50(\$4.18) = \$2.09$$

$$d_1 = \$2.09(1.06) = \$2.22$$

$$\$32 = \frac{\$2.22}{k_s - .06}$$

$$k_s = \frac{\$2.22}{\$32} + .06$$

$$= 12.94\%$$

The expected return on Telco stock is only 12.94 percent. Since you require 16 percent on investments of this risk, you should not purchase the stock.

23.5 A perpetual bond pays $70 annual interest. Its par value is $100. What is the yield to maturity if the current market price is
a. $300?
b. $400?
c. $700?

Solution:

a. $k_b = \frac{c}{v_b} = \frac{\$70}{\$300} = 23.3\%$

b. $k_b = \frac{c}{v_b} = \frac{\$70}{\$400} = 17.5\%$

c. $k_b = \frac{c}{b_b} = \frac{\$70}{\$700} = 10.0\%$

Note that with perpetual bonds the par value is meaningless since the bond has no maturity. Based on the par value the bond pays a 70 percent coupon, however based on the range of market values here, the yield is a more realistic 10 to 23 percent.

23.6 Calculate the yield to maturity for the bond in Problem 23.5 for the $300 and $400 market prices under the assumption that the bond has 5 years to maturity.

Solution:

$$v_b = \sum_{t=1}^{5} \frac{c}{(1+k_b)^t} + \frac{M}{(1+k_b)^5}$$

a. $300 = $70[PVIFA($k_b$, 5 yrs)] + $100[PVIF($k_b$, 5 yrs)]

<u>Try 20%</u>:

$\$300 \stackrel{?}{=} \$70(2.9906) + \$100(.4019)$

$\neq \$249.53$

20% is too high

Try 12%:

$\$300 \stackrel{?}{=} \$70(3.6048) + \$100(.5674)$

$\neq \$309.08$

12% is too low

Yield to maturity is 13 percent

b. $\$400 = \$70[PVIFA(k_b, 5 \text{ yrs})] + \$100[PVIF(k_b, 5 \text{ yrs})]$

Try 10%:

$\$400 \stackrel{?}{=} \$70(3.7908) + \$100(.6209)$

$\neq \$327.45$

10% is too high

Try 4%:

$\$400 \stackrel{?}{=} \$70(4.4518) + \$100(.8219)$

$\neq \$393.82$

4% is too high

Yield to maturity is 3.5 percent.

With finite maturity bonds, the par value is significant to the valuation. The low par value results in very low yields to maturity at the market prices given.

23.7 Consolidated Marconi Corporation has an outstanding preferred stock issue with a \$100 par value and a 12 percent dividend.
What is the price of a share of Consolidated preferred when preferred stock of the same risk class is selling to yield
a. 10%?
b. 15%?
c. 20%?

Solution:

a. $p_{ps} = \dfrac{d_{ps}}{k_{ps}} = \dfrac{\$12}{.10} = \$120$

b. $p_{ps} = \dfrac{d_{ps}}{k_{ps}} = \dfrac{\$12}{.15} = \$80$

c. $p_{ps} = \dfrac{d_{ps}}{k_{ps}} = \dfrac{\$12}{.20} = \$60$

23.8 The Dillon Company is unlevered and has total assets of $2,500,000. The firm's most recent income statement is shown below:

Sales	$4,300,000
Cost of goods sold	3,000,000
Gross profit margin	1,300,000
Other operating expenses	900,000
Net operating income (X)	400,000
Income taxes @ 40%	160,000
Net income	$ 240,000

Dillon's cost of capital, k_u, is 12 percent. Calculate the value of the firm under the following alternative growth patterns.

a. No growth.
b. Constant growth indefinitely. Dillon's investment for the period was $120,000. After-tax NOI for the preceding period was $220,800.
c. Supernormal growth of 24 percent for four years, followed by no growth.
d. Supernormal growth of 24 percent for four years, followed by constant normal growth of 8 percent per year indefinitely.

Solution:

a. No growth:

$$V_u = S = \frac{X(1-T)}{k_u} = \frac{\$400,000(.6)}{.12} = \$2,000,000$$

b. Constant normal growth:

$$V_u = \frac{X_o(1-T)(1-b)(1+g)}{k_u-g}$$

where b = ratio of net investment to after-tax NOI

$$= \frac{I}{X(1-T)}$$

$$= \frac{120,000}{400,000(.6)}$$

$$= \frac{120,000}{240,000}$$

$$= .5$$

$$r = \text{internal profitability rate of investment}$$

$$= \frac{\Delta X(1-T)}{I}$$

$$= \frac{240,000-220,800}{120,000}$$

$$= \frac{19,200}{120,000}$$

$$= .16$$

$$g = br$$

$$= .5(.16) = .08$$

$$V_u = \frac{400,000(.6)(.5)(1.08)}{.12-.08}$$

$$= \frac{129,600}{.04}$$

$$= \$3,240,000$$

c. Supernormal growth followed by no growth:

$$V_u = X_o(1-T)(1-b) \sum_{t=1}^{n} \frac{(1+g_s)^t}{(1+k_u)^t} + \frac{X_o(1-T)(1+g_s)^n}{k_u(1+k_u)^n}$$

$$= 400,000(.6)(.5) \sum_{t=1}^{n} \frac{(1.24)^t}{(1.12)^t} + \frac{400,000(.6)(1.24)^4}{.12(1.12)^4}$$

Let $\frac{1+g_s}{1+k_u} = 1+h$, then $\sum_{t=1}^{n}\left(\frac{1+g_s}{1+k_u}\right)^t = \sum_{t=1}^{n} (1+h)^t$

$$= (1+h)\text{xFVIFA}(h\%, \text{ n years})$$

Thus $\sum_{t=1}^{4}\left(\frac{1.24}{1.12}\right)^t = \sum_{t=1}^{4} (1.107)^t = 1.107\text{xFVIFA}(10.7\%, \text{ 4 yrs})$

$$\text{FVIFA} = \frac{(1+r)^n-1}{r} = \frac{(1.107)^4-1}{.107} = 4.69$$

$$V_u = 120{,}000(1.107)(4.69) + \frac{240{,}000}{.12}\left(\frac{1.24}{1.12}\right)^4$$

$$= 623{,}020 + 2{,}000{,}000(1.5025)$$

$$= 623{,}020 + 3.005{,}001$$

$$= \$3{,}628{,}021$$

d. Supernormal growth followed by constant growth:

$$V_u = X_o(1-T)(1-b)\sum_{t=1}^{n}\frac{(1+g_s)^t}{(1+k_u)^t} + \frac{X_o(1-T)(1-b)}{k_u-g}\left[\frac{(1+g_s)^n}{(1+k_u)^n}\right]$$

The first term in the valuation equation is the same as in part c above.

$$V_u = 623{,}020 + \frac{400{,}000(.6)(.5)(1.08)}{.12-.08}\left(\frac{1.24}{1.12}\right)^4$$

$$= 623{,}020 + \frac{129{,}600}{.04}(1.5025)$$

$$= 623{,}020 + 3{,}240{,}000(1.5025)$$

$$= 623{,}020 + 4{,}868{,}100$$

$$= \$5{,}491{,}120$$

23.9 The Holiday Corporation is identical to the Dillon Company (in Problem 23.8) except that the firm is levered with a target leverage ratio of debt to equity of 100 percent. The cost of debt for Holiday, k_b is 9 percent.

a. Use the Modigliani-Miller model to find the component cost of equity capital and the weighted average cost of capital for Holiday.

b through e. Find the value of Holiday under the same growth pattern assumptions used for Dillon Company in Problem 23.8.

Solution:

a. $k_s = k_u + (k_u - k_b)B/S(1-T)$

$= .12 + (.12-.09)(1)(.6)$

$= .12 + (.03)(.6)$

$= .138$

$$\text{WACC} = k = k_b(1-T)\left(\frac{B}{B+S}\right) + k_s\left(\frac{S}{B+S}\right)$$

$$= .09(.6)(.5) + .138(.5)$$

$$= .027 + .069$$

$$= .096$$

b. No growth:

$$V = \frac{X(1-T)}{k} = \frac{400{,}000(.6)}{.096} = \frac{240{,}000}{.096} = \$2{,}500{,}000$$

Recall that the value of Dillon was $2,000,000 for the no growth case. An increase of $500,000 has resulted from leverage. Since $V_L = V_u + TB$, we can infer that the value of debt is $1,250,000 and the value of equity is $1,250,000. The value of equity is $750,000 lower in the levered firm, but $1,250,000 in debt has been sold. This explains the $500,000 increase in value.

c. Constant normal growth:

$b = .5$
$g = .08$

$$V = \frac{X_o(1-T)(1-b)(1+g)}{k-g}$$

$$= \frac{400{,}000(.6)(.5)(1.08)}{.096-.08}$$

$$= \frac{129{,}600}{.016}$$

$$= \$8{,}100{,}000$$

d. Supernormal growth followed by no growth:

$$g_s = 24\%$$

$$n = 4 \text{ years}$$

$$V = X_o(1-T)(1-b) \sum_{t=1}^{n} \frac{(1+g_s)^t}{(1+k)^t} + \frac{X_o(1-T)(1+g_s)^n}{k(1+k)^n}$$

$$= 400{,}000(.6)(.5) \sum_{t=1}^{4} \left(\frac{1.24}{1.096}\right)^t + \frac{400{,}000(.6)(1.24)^4}{.096(1.096)^4}$$

$$\sum_{t=1}^{n} \left(\frac{1.24}{1.096}\right)^t = \sum_{t=1}^{n} (1.1314)^t = 1.1314 \text{ x FVIFA}(13.14\%, 4 \text{ yrs})$$

$$\text{FVIFA}(13.14\%, 4 \text{ years}) = \frac{1.1314^4-1}{.1314} = 4.8596$$

$$V = 120{,}000(1.1314)(4.8596) + \frac{240{,}000}{.096}\left(\frac{1.24}{1.096}\right)^4$$

$$= 659{,}778 + 2{,}500{,}000(1.1314)^4$$

$$= 659{,}778 + 2{,}500{,}000(1.6385)$$

$$= 659{,}778 + 4{,}096{,}323$$

$$= \$4{,}756{,}010$$

e. Supernormal growth followed by constant normal growth:

$$V = X_o(1-T)(1-b) \sum_{t=1}^{n} \frac{(1+g_s)^t}{(1+k)^t}$$

$$+ \frac{X_o(1-T)(1-b)(1+g)}{k-g}\left[\frac{(1+g_s)^n}{(1+k)^n}\right]$$

The first term in the valuation equation is the same as the first term in part d above.

$$V = 659{,}778 + \frac{129{,}600}{.016}(1.6385)$$

$$= 659{,}778 + 8{,}100{,}000(1.6385)$$

$$= 659{,}778 + 13{,}271{,}791$$

$$= \$13{,}931{,}569$$

23.10 The Tremont Company, a manufacturer of beauty supplies, was started in 1960. By 1981 Tremont dominated its business in the southern United States and was planning to go public with an offer of common stock. In order to set an appropriate price at which to offer the stock, the company has gathered data on Lowell Corporation and Hyten, Inc., two publicly traded firms similar to Tremont in size, product mix, asset composition and debt level.

Relationships	Lowell	Hyten	Tremont (Totals)
Earnings per share, 1981	$ 3.00	$ 7.50	$ 1,800,000
Average EPS, 1975-81	2.40	6.00	1,400,000
Price per share, 1981	38.00	72.50	
Dividends per share, 1981	1.50	3.00	900,000
Average dividend, 1975-81	.90	2.10	500,000
Book value per share	42.00	65.00	20,000,000

a. Calculate the per share data for Tremont assuming that 400,000 shares of stock will be sold.
b. Calculate the P/E, dividend yield, and market to book relations for Lowell and Hyten.
c. Apply the relationships in part (b) to the Tremont per share data calculated in part (a) to establish boundaries for the indicated market price for the Tremont stock.
d. Using the boundaries, and taking trend patterns into account, what is your recommendation for an issuing price for the Tremont stock?

Solution:

a. Per share data for Tremont based on 400,000 shares:

EPS, 1981	$ 4.50
Average EPS, 1975-81	3.50
Dividends per share, 1981	2.25
Average dividend, 1975-81	1.25
Book value per share	50.00

b.

	Lowell	Hyten
P/E ratio, 1981	12.7X	9.7X
Average P/E ratio, 1975-81	15.8X	12.1X
Dividend yield, 1981	3.9%	4.1%
Average dividend yield, 1975-81	2.4%	2.9%
Market to book value	90.5%	111.5%

c.

	Indicated Market Price for Tremont Stock Based on Data of	
	Lowell	Hyten
Based on earnings, 1981	$57.15	$43.65
Based on average earnings, 1975-81	55.30	42.35
Based on dividend yield, 1981	57.69	54.88
Based on average dividend yield, 1975-81	52.08	43.10
Based on book value	45.25	55.75

d. The range is from $42.35 to $57.69 per share. Factors which would suggest a price at the high end of the range include:
1. Good recent trend in sales and earnings
2. Stability of earnings
3. Favorable stock market conditions

The opposite of these factors would favor a price toward the low end of the scale. The actual price would be based on negotiations between Tremont and its underwriters, but the price would probably be around $50 per share.

This problem illustrates a technique used by investment bankers in stock valuation. This comparative approach assures that the multiples of the company whose stock is being valued will be consistent with the relationships for similar firms in its line of business.

PART SEVEN: THE TREASURER'S POINT OF VIEW: POLICY DECISIONS

CHAPTER 24

EXTERNAL FINANCING: INSTITUTIONS AND BEHAVIOR

Theme: Capital markets present a range of alternatives to a firm formulating financing decisions. This chapter will examine the broad categories of sources of funds and the relative costs of alternative methods of issuing new securities. The role of investment banking and the implications of securities laws are also discussed.

I. Sources of Funds.
   A. Internal cash flows provide an average of 73 percent of funds for business corporations.
   B. External financing has averaged 27 percent of total sources.
      1. Long-term external financing generally exceeds short-term.
      2. Short-term external financing fluctuates in response to changes in the state of the economy.
   C. External funds may be obtained privately or publicly.
      1. In private financing, funds are obtained from one or a few individuals, or more recently from institutions such as banks, insurance companies, and pension funds.
      2. Public financing is arranged through investment bankers who sell the firm's securities to a large number of public investors.

II. Direct Financing Includes Term Loans and Private Placements.
   A. Term loans are direct business loans with a maturity of more than one year but usually less than 15 years.
   B. Private placements are direct business loans with a maturity of more than 15 years--often with insurance companies or pension plans.
      1. Some private placements call for repayment of a substantial portion of principal within 5 to 10 years.
      2. The distinction between term loans and private placements is fuzzy; they represent very similar financing arrangements.
   C. Characteristics and Evaluation of Direct Financing.
      1. Repayment provisions of term loans generally provide for amortization, or systematic repayment over the life of the loan.
         a. Amortization of the loan protects both the borrower and the lender against the possibility that the borrower will not have made adequate provisions for retirement of the loan.

b. If the loan is for a piece of equipment, the amortization schedule will be geared to the productive life of the equipment, with loan payments coming from cash flows generated by the machine.

c. The amortization schedule is determined through the use of the formula:

$$a = \frac{P_{r,t}}{PVIFA}$$

where a = Amortization payment

$P_{r,t}$ = Amount of loan

PVIFA = Appropriate interest factor

2. Maturities of term loans differ depending on the liability structure of the lender:
   a. Banks tend to have shorter-term liabilities, therefore bank term loans usually run five years or less.
   b. Insurance companies have longer-term liabilities, so their term loans usually run between five and fifteen years.
   c. Commercial banks and life insurance companies sometimes combine to make loans: with, for example, the bank taking the first five years and the insurance company taking the last ten years of a fifteen-year loan.
3. Banks have required collateral on about 90 percent of the number of term loans made, while insurance companies have required collateral about one-third of the time.
   a. Stocks, bonds, machinery and equipment may be used to secure term loans from banks.
   b. Insurance companies will accept real estate to secure some of their larger loans.
4. In addition to fixed interest charges, institutional investors have increasingly taken compensation in the form of options to buy common shares. These options usually are in the form of detachable warrants permitting the purchase of the shares at stated prices over designated periods of time.
5. Because term loans represent long-term fixed commitments, restrictive provisions are generally included in the contract or agreement for the protection of the lender.
   a. The borrower must usually maintain a specified current ratio, and a specified minimum net working capital.

   b. Additional long-term borrowing, pledging of assets, assumption of contingent liabilities, and the signing of long-term leases are limited.
   c. An effort is made to insure the continuity of management.
   d. Periodic financial statements and budgets are required by the lender.
6. The costs of term loans vary with the size of the loan and the strength of the borrowing firm.
   a. On small term loans, the effective interest rate may be as high as 6 to 8 percentage points above the prime rate.
   b. On loans of $1 million and above, interest charges approximate the prime rate.
   c. The interest rate may be fixed or it may vary. It is often tied to the Fed's rediscount rate or the published prime rate of New York City banks.
7. An empirical study of risk premiums found somewhat different influences operating on private placements and public offerings.
   a. Risk premiums in public offerings depend relatively more on default risk measures of the firm.
   b. Risk premiums in private placements depend relatively more on economy-wide and market factors.
   c. The overall yield to maturity was 46 basis points higher for private placements, offsetting to some extent the economies of direct versus public financing.
8. Evaluation of direct financing.
   a. Advantages:
      (i) Avoid possible nonrenewal of short-term loans.
      (ii) Avoid public flotation costs.
      (iii) Minimal negotiation time.
      (iv) Ease of indenture modification relative to changing the terms of a public offering.
   b. Disadvantages:
      (i) May have higher interest costs.
      (ii) Large cash drain due to amortization payments.
      (iii) Restrictions and maybe required higher credit standards by lenders due to long-term exposure.
      (iv) The wide distribution of securities in a public offering enables its repurchase on favorable terms if the market price drops; direct financing does not offer this advantage.
      (v) Firm does not receive the publicity and prestige often associated with public offerings.
      (vi) Lender may require high minimum loan amount to cover high investigation costs.

9. The use of direct financing has declined in recent years and has shifted to shorter-term maturities in the face of continued high real interest rates. Some reasons include the following:
   a. Decreased participation by life insurance companies due to decreased availability of lendable funds.
   b. Increased investment by insurance companies in public securities to obtain greater liquidity.
   c. Decreased demand due to greater availability of public market funds for lower-quality issuers.
   d. Efforts by insurance companies to reduce interest rate risk by matching duration of loan portfolios to duration of guaranteed investment contracts.

III. Public financing uses investment bankers to sell securities to large numbers of individuals and financial institutions.

A. Investment banking institutions serve as financial intermediaries, making private savings available to business firms. The investment banker does this by purchasing and distributing the securities of individual companies, performing the following functions:

1. Underwriting--The investment banker purchases the new security issue, pays the issuer, and markets the securities. The banker bears the risk of price fluctuations from the time of purchase to the time that the issue is distributed.
   a. An economic function of the investment banker is to underwrite the risk of a decline in market price between the time the money is transmitted to the firm and the securities are actually distributed.
   b. For these reasons, investment bankers are sometimes called underwriters.
2. Distribution--The investment banker maintains a sales staff which performs the marketing function more efficiently and economically than if it were done by the individual firm.
3. Advice and counsel--The experience of the investment banker enables him to advise the issuer regarding the characteristics of the issue to insure successful flotation.

B. The process of floating a public issue follows these steps:

1. Preunderwriting conferences are held between the issuing firm and the investment banker to discuss alternative forms of financing and to reach the decision to float an issue.
2. An underwriting investigation is made by the underwriters into the firm's prospects. Specialists are called in to examine legal, accounting, engineering, and other aspects of the firm.

3. <u>The underwriting agreement</u> is formulated and specifies all underwriting terms except the actual price of the securities.
4. A <u>registration statement</u> is filed with the Securities and Exchange Commission. A waiting period of 20 days (which may be shortened or lengthened by the SEC) is required before clearance by the Securities and Exchange Commission is received. The underwriter can make no sales during this time but can distribute preliminary prospectuses.
5. The offering price of securities.
   a. When a company "goes public" for the first time, the investment banker and the firm negotiate the price in accordance with valuation principles.
   b. When additional offerings are involved, the underwriter agrees to buy the securities at a prescribed number of points below the closing price on the day before the offering.
   c. Generally, the investment banker prefers a low price and a high yield, while the issuer of the securities naturally wants the opposite.
   d. Competition usually forces investment bankers to price close to market-determined levels.
6. An <u>underwriting syndicate</u> is formed as a temporary association to handle the purchase and distribution of the securities issue.
   a. The underwriting syndicate is composed of the managing investment banker plus 10 to 60 other investment bankers who each have selling groups composed of other investment bankers and dealers.
   b. The managing investment banker forms an underwriting syndicate
      (1) To reduce the extent of his risk
      (2) To use the selling organizations of other investment bankers to permit economy of selling effort and encourage nationwide distribution
      (3) Because he may be unable to finance a large issue by himself
7. A selling group is formed for the purpose of distributing the securities.
   a. It may consist of as many as 300 to 400 dealers who take relatively small participations from the members of the underwriting group and act as retailers of the issue. Note the difference between a dealer and a broker.
      (1) A dealer purchases securities and holds them in inventory, gaining if the price appreciates and losing if it declines.
      (2) Brokers take orders for purchases and transmit them to the proper exchange, gaining from their commission.

b. The operations of the selling group are governed by an agreement which covers these points:
   (1) Description of the issue.
   (2) Price concession, which is the selling group's commission.
   (3) Handling of repurchased securities. The agreement provides that no member of the selling group is allowed to sell below the public offering price. The syndicate manager pegs the quotation in the market by placing continuous orders to buy at the public offering price.
   (4) The duration of the selling group is usually 30 days, but this agreement may be extended or terminated earlier.

8. After the selling group has been formed, the actual offering takes place. The formal public offering is called _opening the books_.
9. During the offering period, the price of the security is pegged by placing orders to buy at a specified price in the market. This is done to prevent a cumulative downward movement in the price.
   a. The danger of monopolistic pricing due to price pegging is mitigated by competition.
   b. The pegging operation serves a useful function since it decreases risk and therefore lowers the costs to the issuer.
10. At each level--manager, underwriting group, and members of selling groups--a commission is received. If the manager underwrites and sells the issue himself, he will receive the full amount.

C. Analysis of the costs of public flotation shows these relationships.
   1. Ranking of costs from highest to lowest:
      Common stock
      Preferred stock
      Debt
   2. This ranking can be explained by the following:
      a. The distribution job is harder for stock than for bonds because it is usually bought in smaller blocks.
      b. Underwriting risks are higher with stock because the price is more volatile.
   3. Costs as a percentage of the proceeds of the issue are greater for small than for large issues. Fixed expenses are high, and the selling job and risks are greater for the securities of small firms.
   4. The flotation costs on rights offerings are usually low, especially if the offering price is substantially below the current market price.

IV. Negotiated Underwritings are the General Practice in Most Industries.

A. A business firm develops a long-term relationship with its investment banker and works out the terms of any particular issue in direct negotiations.

B. In the public utility industry multiple-bidding underwriting is more likely, and even required by law in some cases.

1. The characteristics of public utility firms are more uniform than for industry in general.
2. Because public utilities are regulated industries, substantial amounts of relatively uniform information is publicly available.

C. Where a firm and its situation are standard, competitive bidding is facilitated; in a more complex situation or an unsettled market, the negotiated underwriting is more likely.

D. Negotiated underwritings are also competitive in the sense that the historical investment banker can be and often is replaced if its performance is not satisfactory.

E. Empirical studies of flotation costs and competitive versus negotiated underwritings are inconclusive.

1. Competitive underwritings appear to be less costly in stable markets, while negotiated may be better during unstable markets.
2. The default risk premium appears to be the most important influence on flotation costs.
   a. Higher rated bonds have lower flotation costs and vice versa.
   b. Bond rating may be a proxy for selling effort; higher rated bonds are thought to be easier to sell even taking the yield differential into account.
3. Issuer size appears to have a negative effect on flotation costs and may be a proxy for economies of scale or the hope of repeat business for the underwriter.

V. Regulation of Security Trading.

A. The financial manager should be aware of the federal laws regulating issuance and trading of securities because they influence his liability and affect financing costs.

B. The Securities Act of 1933 relates to the marketing of new issues. It seeks to provide full disclosure of information, a record of representations, and penalties for violations. The major provisions are:

1. The Act applies to public interstate offerings over a specified amount.
2. Simplified Regulation A procedures apply to offerings below $1.5 million.
3. It requires registration 20 days in advance of the offering to the public.
4. It allows purchasers who suffer loss due to misrepresentation or omission of material facts to sue for damages.

C. The Securities Exchange Act of 1934 extends the disclosure principle to the trading of existing issues. Its major provisions are:
   1. The act establishes the SEC (Securities and Exchange Commission).
   2. It requires registration and regulation of the national securities exchanges.
   3. It requires corporate insiders to file monthly reports of changes in ownership of stock of the corporation and provides legal redress for stockholders.
   4. It gives the SEC power to prohibit manipulations through wash sales, pools, and pegging operations except during stock flotations.

D. The Securities Acts Amendments of 1975 are directed toward the development of a national market system to achieve nationwide competition in securities trading. Expected benefits include the following:
   1. Broader exposure to the public of both listed and unlisted firms.
   2. Stronger secondary markets and more liquid security markets in general which will increase the willingness of investors to buy securities.

E. Recent changes in SEC rules have streamlined the securities registration process giving firms greater flexibility to act quickly in volatile markets and reducing the transactions costs of issuing securities.
   1. Abbreviated registration statements allow the issuer to refer to information disclosed in other public documents, avoiding duplication.
   2. Shelf registration allows firms to register the full amount of securities they plan to issue over a two-year period; the securities (usually bonds) can then be issued at any time within the period without further delay.

F. Appraisal of securities regulation.
   1. The objectives of regulation are to provide investors with information and to protect them from fraud and to control bank credit used in speculation within the framework of an orderly market.
   2. These objectives have been achieved to some extent at the cost of increased time and expense in new flotations.
   3. From the point of view of financial managers, regulation affects the cost of issuing securities and their risk, thus impacting the rate of return required by investors.

VI. Financing Patterns and Innovations.

A. The strong equity market of the early 1980s has increased the use of equity both by firms with publicly traded stock and firms going public for the first time.

B. 1982-83 saw a sharp increase in the use of debt financing; firms sought longer maturities on debt.

C. Financing in foreign markets, e.g. the Euromarket, is becoming more widespread.
   1. Firms can choose from a number of alternatives for the basis of floating rate debt.
   2. The Deficit Reduction Act of 1984 made U.S. investments more attractive to foreign investors.

D. Backing by commercial banks has made commercial paper more widely available.

E. Firms can improve the appearance of their balance sheets by means of "in substance defeasance".
   1. The firm creates a trust of risk-free assets with cash flows sufficient to serve a portion of its debt.
   2. The debt (and the assets in the trust) can then be removed from the balance sheet.

F. "Interest rate swaps" enable firms to exchange interest rate obligations (e.g. floating rate for fixed rate) to mutual benefits. "Currency swaps" involve swapping interest rate obligations denominated in different currencies to minimize foreign exchange risk.

G. Firms are increasingly making use of financial futures, options and forward contracts to reduce exposure to interest rate and currency value fluctuations.

VII. Emerging Trends in Financial Institutions.

A. Major legislative changes.
   1. The Depository Institutions Deregulation and Monetary Control Act of 1980 reduced restrictions and lowered reserve requirements for all commercial banks, savings banks and savings and loan associations, not just for members of the Federal Reserve System.
   2. The Garn-St. Germain Depository Institutions Act of 1982 broadened the lending power and scope of savings and loans and other thrift institutions.
   3. Competition among financial institutions has been increased by this legislation.

B. Changes in investment banking.
   1. Investment banking has moved from its traditional business of underwriting and brokerage into insurance commercial banking.
   2. The end of fixed commission schedules resulted in increased competition for large institutional accounts.
   3. Sources of income for investment bankers now include equity-based insurance policies, tax shelter programs in oil and real estate, commodity investments, as well as advice on corporate finance, cash management accounts and money market funds.
   4. Increased computerization has increased investment banking's degree of operating leverage, resulting in mergers between investment bankers to avoid bankruptcy.

C. The distinction between commercial banks and other financial institutions has been eroded.
   1. Increasingly national, commercial banks are branching

into areas such as brokerage, venture capital, insurance, and serving as underwriters in SEC shelf registration.

2. Brokerage firms, retailers, insurance companies and others are moving into traditional commercial banking areas, in many cases by means of "non-bank banks".
   a. A "non-bank bank" is stripped of either its lending or deposit functions, and does not come under the jurisdiction of the Bank Holding Company Act.
   b. The "non-bank bank" is then free to engage in all other aspects of commercial banking.

Chapter 24 - Illustrative Problems and Solutions

24.1 The Coldwell Company has just borrowed \$100,000 in the form of a 6-year term loan at 12 percent interest.

a. What is the annual payment?

b. Prepare an amortization schedule showing the breakdown between interest and principal over the life of the loan.

Solution:

a. $\text{Payment} = a = \frac{\$100,000}{\text{PVIVA}(12\%,\ 6\text{ yrs})} = \frac{\$100,000}{4.1114} = \$24,322.62$

b.

Year	Total Payment	Interest	Principal Repayment	Remaining Balance
1	\$24,322.62	\$12,000.00	\$12,322.62	\$87,677.38
2	24,322.62	10,521.29	13,801.33	73,876.05
3	24,322.62	8,865.13	15,457.49	58,418.56
4	24,322.62	7,010.23	17,312.39	41,106.17
5	24,322.62	4,932.74	19,389.88	21,716.29
6	24,322.62	2,605.95	21,716.67	(0.38)*

* Difference caused by rounding.

24.2 The Georgetown Development Company is planning a \$90 million 15-year bond issue. The market rate of interest on debt of this quality and maturity is 14 percent. Underwriting costs are expected to be 3.5 percent of gross proceeds. What is the before-tax effective cost of this debt to Georgetown Development?

Solution:
Let the coupon rate = 14%

Cash received by Georgetown on sale of bond
= \$1,000 - (.035)(\$1,000) = \$965

$$\$965 = \sum_{t=1}^{15} \frac{\$140}{(1+k_b)^t} + \frac{\$1,000}{(1+k_b)^{15}}$$

$$= \$140 \times PVIFA(k_b, 15 \text{ yrs}) + \$1,000 \times PVIF(k_b, 15 \text{ yrs})$$

Solve for k_b, the effective cost of debt.

$k_b \cong 14.6$ percent.

24.3 Martin Industries is planning a preferred stock issue of \$40 million. Total flotation costs will be 12 percent of gross proceeds. If the market rate on preferred stock of equivalent risk is 14 percent, what is the effective cost of the preferred stock?

Solution:

$$\text{Effective cost} = \frac{.14(\$40,000,000)}{\$40,000,000 - (.12)(\$40,000,000)}$$

$$= \frac{\$5,600,000}{\$40,000,000 - \$4,800,000}$$

$$= \frac{\$5,600,000}{\$35,200,000}$$

$$= 15.9\%$$

Alternatively,

$$r = \frac{.14}{1-.12} = 15.9\%$$

CHAPTER 25

COMMON STOCK FINANCING

Theme: To utilize the various forms of financing effectively, the financial manager must be aware of the ramifications of using each form. This chapter describes the characteristics of equity financing.

I. Owners of Common Stock in Business Corporations Have These General Rights.
  A. Collective rights.
    1. Make charter amendments if the changes are approved by state officials
    2. Adopt and amend the bylaws
    3. Elect the corporate directors
    4. Authorize the sale of fixed assets
    5. Ratify mergers
    6. Change the amount of authorized common stock
    7. Authorize issuance of preferred stock, debentures, bonds, and other securities
  B. Each stockholder also has specific rights as an individual owner enabling him to:
    1. Vote as prescribed by the corporate charter
    2. Transfer stock to another party
    3. Inspect the books of the corporation
    4. Share in the residual assets in case of dissolution
  C. Apportionment of income and control.
    1. Common stock is the recipient of the residual income of the corporation.
    2. Through the right to vote, holders of common stock have legal control of the corporation.
    3. Risk of equity ownership.
      a. Common equity provides a cushion for creditors if losses occur on dissolutions. The equity-to-total-assets ratio is an indicator of the degree by which the amounts realized on the liquidation may decline from stated book values before creditors suffer losses.
      b. Common stockholders have limited liability in case of loss--their loss is limited to the amount of their investment.
  D. Nature of voting rights.
    1. Each stockholder has the right to cast votes in proportion to the number of shares owned.
      a. A proxy is a temporary transfer of the right to vote.
      b. The use of proxies is supervised by the Securities and Exchange Commission to prevent:
        (1) Self-perpetuation of management
        (2) Small stockholder groups from gaining special advantages

c. Proxy contests are often initiated by former company insiders and are associated with expectations of improved corporate performance.

2. In cumulative voting the stockholder is allowed to cast multiple votes for one director. For example, 100 shares can be cast as 500 votes for one director if five directors are being elected, rather than 100 votes for each of five directors.
   a. Formula:

$$\text{req.} = \frac{\text{des.}(N)}{\# + 1} + 1$$

   where
   req. = Number of shares required to elect a desired number of directors
   des. = Number of directors desired to elect
   N = Total number of shares of common stock outstanding and entitled to be voted
   # = Total number of directors to be elected

   b. Illustration:
   des. = 2
   N = 100,000
   # = 6

$$\text{req.} = \frac{2 \times 100{,}000}{6 + 1} + 1 = 28{,}753$$

   c. See Problem 25.4.

3. The preemptive right gives the existing equity holders the option to purchase any additional issues of common stock.
   a. State laws vary with regard to the preemptive right.
      (1) In some states it is a part of every corporate charter.
      (2) In other states it must be included as a specific provision.
   b. The preemptive right is designed to protect:
      (1) The power of control of present stockholders
      (2) The pro rata share of earned surplus and earning power for the present stockholders.

4. Forms of common stock include:
   a. Classified, which consists of voting and nonvoting classes.
   b. Founders' shares, which carry sole voting rights but no right to a dividend for a number of years.

II. In Reaching a Decision to Issue Common Stock, the Financial Manager Should Consider These Factors.
   A. Advantages of common stock over other forms of financing.
      1. No continuing fixed charges are incurred
      2. No legal obligation to pay dividends
      3. No maturity date
      4. The creditworthiness of the firm is increased

5. At times may be sold more easily than debt
    a. It carries a higher expected return than does preferred stock or debt.
    b. It may provide the investor with a better hedge against inflation.
6. Returns from common stock, in the form of capital gains, are subject to lower personal income tax rates

B. Disadvantages of common stock.
1. The control of the firm is shared with the new shareholders
2. The new shares participate fully in earnings and dividends
3. Flotation costs are relatively high
4. A greater than optimal amount of equity will raise the weighted average cost of capital
5. Dividends are not deductible from income for tax purposes.

C. Empirical studies of common stock financing have found the following results.
1. Significant positive abnormal returns on new issues of 11.4 percent appear to be due to initial underpricing by underwriters for ease of selling.
2. The market takes a new issue announcement as a signal that management believes the stock to be overvalued; thus stock price falls.
3. The market interprets an announcement of stock repurchase as a message that management believes stock is undervalued; thus stock price rises.

D. From a social viewpoint common stock financing renders the firm less vulnerable to the consequences of declines in sales and earnings.

III. The Use of Rights in Financing.

A. Definitions.
1. A <u>right</u> is an option to buy a part of newly issued stock at a specified price during a designated period of time.
2. A <u>rights offering</u> involves the sale of additional stock to existing stockholders and is mandatory if the preemptive right exists for the firm in question.
3. Each stockholder is issued one right, which contains the terms of the option, for each share of stock owned.

B. Several questions face the financial manager in a rights offering.
1. How many rights will be required to purchase a share of the new stock?
2. What should be the value of each right?
3. What effect will the rights offering have on the price of existing stock?

4. What will be the subscription price of the stock?

C. To determine the number of rights required to purchase a new share of stock:

1. Calculate the number of new shares to be issued:

$$\text{Number of new shares} = \frac{(\text{Funds to be raised})}{(\text{Subscription price})}$$

2. Calculate the number of rights needed to buy a new share:

$$\text{Number of rights required} = \frac{\text{Number of old shares}}{\text{Number of new shares}}$$

D. To determine the value of each right, the following formulas may be used.

$$v_r = \frac{p_0 - p^s}{\# + 1} \quad \text{(Rights-on calculation)}$$

$$v_r = \frac{p_e - p^s}{\#} \quad \text{(Ex rights calculation)}$$

where

p_0 = The rights-on price of the stock.

p^s = The subscription price.

\# = The number of rights required to purchase a new share of stock.

p_e = The ex rights price of the stock.

v_r = The value of one right.

1. Stock is sold rights-on until a predetermined ex rights date.
2. The ex rights value of the stock differs from the rights-on value of the stock by the value of a right as determined in the above equation.
3. A right may also be viewed as a call option, and the Black-Scholes option pricing model (OPM) may be used to find its value. (See Problem 25.6.)

IV. Effects on the Position of the Stockholders.

A. If a stockholder exercises his rights, a rights offering does not affect the value of his stock.

1. A stockholder may suffer a loss if:
   a. He forgets to exercise or sell his rights.
   b. Brokerage costs of selling the rights are high.
2. The oversubscription privilege contained in most rights offerings allows stockholders to buy on a pro rata basis all shares not taken in the initial rights offering. This privilege also helps to assure a full sale of the new stock issue.
3. See Problem 25.2.

B. There are three major alternative methods of selling stock.
   1. Sell the issue through investment bankers with or without rights.
      a. This has the advantages of a wide distribution of shares and certainty of receiving funds.
      b. A disadvantage of this method is the relatively high cost of underwriters' services.
   2. Issue rights but provide only a small discount from the market price, using investment bankers to sell the unsubscribed shares.
      a. The advantages of this method include:
         (1) Small underwriting costs
         (2) Certainty of receiving funds
         (3) Increased stockholder loyalty
      b. The disadvantages include:
         (1) Narrow distribution
         (2) Losses to forgetful stockholders
   3. Issue rights allowing a large discount and do not use investment bankers.
      a. The advantages include:
         (1) No underwriting costs
         (2) Substantial decrease in unit price of shares.
         (3) Increased stockholder loyalty
      b. The disadvantages include:
         (1) Narrow distribution
         (2) Severe losses to forgetful stockholders.

C. The choice of method depends on the individual company's needs.
   1. A company may feel that a rights offering has a higher probability of raising funds without lowering the market price of stock because:
      a. If existing shareholders wish to maintain their pro rata share in the earnings and control of the firm, they will exercise their rights.
      b. Existing shareholders are most likely to have a favorable opinion of the firm.
      c. Margin requirements on rights purchases are only 25 percent, as compared to 50 percent for regular stock purchases.
   2. Some observed differences between market price and subscription price.
      a. Subscription prices have been about 15 percent lower than market prices in recent years.
      b. Generally, subscription prices are from 10 to 20 percent lower than market prices.
   3. No generalization can be made regarding the effects of a rights offering on the market price of the stock; the effect of the offering depends upon the market's evaluation of the future prospects of the issuing company.
   4. See Problem 25.3.

D. Use of rights can avoid the downward price pressure often associated with new stock issues.
  1. Existing shareholders have already evaluated the firm favorably.
  2. Cash flotation costs are lower in rights offerings.
  3. Stock split effect may bring price to a more attractive trading level.

V. Choosing Among Alternate Forms of Financing
  A. A pattern of analysis is used to evaluate the major sources of financing, including preferred stock, various forms of debt, lease financing, and financing in international markets.
  B. The analysis covers the following factors.
    1. Risk.
      a. Financial structure
      b. Fixed charge coverage
      c. Coverage of cash flow requirements
      d. Level of beta
    2. Relative costs.
      a. Effects on market value per share of common stock
      b. Effects on cost of capital
    3. Effects on control.
  C. The analysis proceeds as follows:
    1. The two forms of financing are examined with regard to the firm's risk as measured by its financial structure.
      a. Financing with debt will:
        (1) Increase debt ratios
        (2) Decrease fixed charge coverage
        (3) Decrease cash flow ratio
        (4) Increase beta level
      b. Financing with equity will:
        (1) Lower the long-term debt to net worth ratio
        (2) Increase the fixed charge coverage
        (3) Increase cash flow ratio
        (4) Decrease beta level
    2. The relative costs of the two forms of financing must then be examined.
      a. Calculate the market price per share of common stock.
        (1) The price increases as a result of expansion by debt financing--if debt ratios are low.
        (2) The price increases with equity financing--if debt ratios are too high.
      b. Calculate the effect on the cost of capital.
        (1) Expansion with debt will lower the cost of capital--if debt ratios are low.
        (2) Expansion with equity will lower the cost of capital--if debt ratios are too high.
    3. The issue of the effects on control must also be examined.

a. Debt financing does not change control.
b. Equity financing could alter the control depending on how it is done, whether rights are offered, and who buys the new issue.

D. Circumstances favoring the use of common stock.
1. The firm's sales and profits fluctuate widely.
2. Profit margins do not cover the cost of debt.
3. The firm already has a high debt ratio in relation to the prudent maximum for its line of business.
4. The firm is new, lacking access to debt financing.
5. Dilution of control is not a problem.
6. Cash flow considerations are important.
7. The relative costs of common stock financing appear favorable.
8. Available debt financing would carry onerous loan agreement restrictions.
9. Because of persistent inflation, investors may require higher interest payments on debt securities.

E. See Problem 25.5.

Chapter 25 - Illustrative Problems and Solutions

25.1 Scanlon Products' common stock is selling at $24.00 per share. Scanlon has just announced a rights offering enabling shareholders to purchase one new share at a cost of $18 for each 2 shares currently held.

a. What is the value of each right?
b. What effect will the rights offering have on the original market price of the stock?

Solution:

a. Value of a right = $v_r = \frac{p_o - p^s}{\# + 1}$

$$= \frac{\$24 - \$18}{2 + 1}$$

$$= \frac{6}{3}$$

$$= \$2.00$$

b. The market price per share will fall only to the extent of the price of one right, since this is the extent of dilution. However, the price per share may fall less than the price of one right if the funds raised in the rights offering are viewed as an indicator of prospective growth in the firm's sales and earnings.

25.2 Kenneth Solomon is a stockholder in Scanlon Products (in Problem 25.1). At the time of the rights offering, Mr. Solomon's total assets consist of 400 shares of Scanlon stock and $4,000 in cash. Prepare statements showing Solomon's position before and after the rights offering for each of the alternatives below. (Assume that the price of Scanlon's stock after the offering falls by the value of one right.)

a. He exercises all his rights.
b. He exercises 100 rights and sells the remaining rights at the value calculated in Problem 25.1.
c. He sells all his rights.
d. Through inadvertence, he failed to either exercise or sell his rights before the offering period ended.

Solution:

<u>Before rights offering</u>

Stock (400 shares @ $24)	$ 9,600
Cash	4,000
Total assets	$13,600

After rights offering

a. 400/2 = 200 shares purchased @ $18 = $3,600

Assets	
Stock (600 shares @ $22)	$13,200
Cash ($4,000-$3,600)	400
Total assets	$13,600

b. 100/2 = 50 shares purchased @ $18 $900
300 rights sold at $2 = 600

Assets	
Stock (450 shares @ $22)	$ 9,900
Cash ($4,000-$900+$600)	3,700
Total assets	$13,600

c. 400 rights sold @ $2 = $800

Assets	
Stock (400 shares @ $22)	$ 8,800
Cash ($4,000+$800)	4,800
Total assets	$13,600

d.

Assets	
Stock (400 shares @ $22)	$ 8,800
Cash	4,000
Total assets	$12,800

The stockholder's position is unchanged by a rights offering except when the rights are neither exercised nor sold, in which case a loss is suffered.

25.3 The Barent Medical Supply Company plans to raise $5,000,000 by means of a rights offering. The company's financial statements before the offering are as follows:

Balance sheet

		Debt (11%)	$10,500,000
		Common stock (400,000 shares)	2,400,000
		Retained earnings	7,100,000
Total assets	$20,000,000	Total claims	$20,000,000

Income statement (Earnings rate on total assets, before interest and taxes = 16%)

Earnings before interest and taxes	$3,200,000
Interest expense	1,155,000
EBT	$2,045,000
Taxes (40%)	818,000
Net income	$1,227,000

Earnings per share	$3.07
Dividends per share (50% payout)	$1.54
P/E ratio	12X
Market price per share	$36.84

Barent will continue to earn 16 percent on total assets after the rights offering. The P/E ratio, dividend payout and tax rate will remain as they are now. The subscription price has been set at $25 per share.

a. How many additional shares will have to be sold?
b. How many rights will be required to purchase one share?
c. What will be the new earnings per share?
d. What will be the new market price per share?
e. What will be the new dividend per share?

(Do not attempt to use the formula given in the chapter. Additional information is given here that violates the "other things constant" assumption in the formula.)

Solution:

a. $\frac{\$5,000,000}{\$25} = 200,000$ shares

b. $\frac{\text{Old shares}}{\text{New shares}} = \frac{400,000}{200,000}$ = 2 rights required to purchase 1 new share

c.

Total earnings	.16($25,000,000)	$4,000,000
Interest expense		1,155,000
EBT		$2,845,000
Taxes (40%)		1,138,000
Net income		$1,707,000

EPS = $1,707,000/600,000 = $2.85

d. P/E x EPS = 12($2.85) = $34.20
e. New dividend per share = .50($2.85) = $1.43

Note the "stock split" effect of the rights offering.

25.4 Roger Morhart has been a shareholder in the Buckman Corporation for over 20 years. Recent changes in company policy seem so ill-advised to him that he plans to run for a seat on the board of directors to be able to implement his own policy ideas. Morhart owns 110,000 shares of the 800,000 shares outstanding. Six directors will be elected at the upcoming annual meeting.

a. If voting is noncumulative, can Morhart be assured of election?
b. If voting is cumulative, can Morhart be assured of election?
c. Morhart believes that many other shareholders would vote for him if he could explain his position to them. Buckman's stock is widely held, and Morhart estimates that the cost of a campaign to contact shareholders and publicize his views will be $150,000. The current price of Buckman's stock is $21. Advise Morhart on his course of action. (Assume cumulative voting.)

Solution:

a. No. Morhart can cast only 110,000 votes for himself, while other shareholders can cast 690,000 votes. It would be possible for Morhart to be elected with the support of other shareholders, but he cannot elect himself.

b. $$\text{req.} = \frac{\text{des.}(N)}{\# + 1} + 1 = \frac{1(800,000)}{6 + 1} + 1$$

$$= 114,286$$

Morhart would require 114,286 votes in order to be assured of election to the board with cumulative voting. Since he has only 110,000 shares, he still cannot elect himself singlehandedly. Note that because of the "+ 1" term in the formula, we round the first term downward rather than upward.

c.

Shares required for election	114,286
Shares currently held	110,000
Additional shares needed	4,286
Price per share	$21
	$90,006

Morhart would have to spend $90,006 to be sure of electing himself singlehandedly versus $150,000 on the publicity campaign, which has no guarantee of success. Morhart should purchase the needed shares.

25.5 The Silverado Company needs to raise $4,000,000 for an expansion program, and must decide whether to use debt or equity financing. The financial information below has been gathered for analysis.

Silverado Company Balance Sheet as of December 31, 19X1
($ thousands)

Assets		Liabilities	
Current assets	$13,000	Notes payable (10%)	$ 5,000
Net fixed assets	9,000	Other current liabilities	1,700
		Total current liabilities	$ 6,700
		Long-term debt (10%)	4,000
		Other liabilities	1,500
		Total debt	$12,200
		Common stock ($5 par)	4,000
		Retained earnings	5,800
Total assets	$22,000	Total liabilities	$22,000

Silverado Company Income Statement
($ thousands)

	Year ended 12-31-X1	Pro forma with expansion
Total revenues	$20,000	$24,000
Net operating income	4,300	5,100
Interest expense	900	
Earnings before tax	$ 3,400	
Tax (40%)	1,360	
Net income to equity	$ 2,040	

Industry norms

Short-term debt to total assets	27%
Long-term interest bearing debt to net worth	28%
Shareholders' equity to total assets	52%
Fixed charge coverage	7.0X
Current ratio	2.6X
Return on net worth	12%

The dividend payout has averaged 50% of net income. The cost of debt is 10 percent presently, and the cost of equity is 12 percent. If the additional funds are raised by debt, the cost of debt would be 12 percent, and the cost of equity will increase to 13%. If the additional funds are raised by equity, the cost of debt will remain at 10 percent, and the cost of equity will fall to 11 percent. The reason is that the sale of equity would correct the excessive debt ratio and reduce the risk to equity holders. New equity can be sold to net $20 per share.

a. Make a financial risk analysis using financial structure ratios and the fixed charge coverage ratio.
b. Complete the pro forma income statements under the two forms of financing.
c. Calculate the market value of equity and the indicated market price per share before and after financing by the two alternative methods.
d. Calculate the value of the firm and the B/S, B/V and S/V percentages.
e. Calculate the weighted average cost of capital at present and under the two financing methods.
f. What other factors should be considered in determining which form of financing to use?
g. Recommend the best form of financing for Silverado Company.

Solution:

a. Financial risk analysis:

	Present		Pro Forma Debt		Pro Forma Equity	
	Amt.	%	Amt.	%	Amt.	%
Current debt	$ 6,700	30%	$ 6,700	26%	$ 6,700	26%
Long-term debt*	5,500	25%	9,500	36%	5,500	21%
Equity	9,800	45%	9,800	38%	13,800	53%
Total	$22,000	100%	$26,000	100%	26,000	100%

Ratio comparison:

	Norm	Present	Debt	Equity
Short-term debt to total assets**	27%	30%	26%	26%
Long-term interest-bearing debt to net worth*	28%	41%	82%	29%
Equity to total assets	52%	45%	38%	53%
Fixed charge coverage***	7 times	5 times	4 times	6 times

*"Other liabilities" and "long-term debt" are included in "long-term debt" when computing the LTD/TA ratio, since "other liabilities" are included in total claims. Only "long-term debt" is included in the ratio of long-term interest-bearing debt to net worth.

**The other (long-term) liabilities (OL) to total assets industry norm can be derived:

E/TA = .52 Let TA = 100, E = 52
LTIBD = .28(E) = .28(52) = 15
so, OL = TA - E - LTIBD - STD = 100 - 52 - 15 - 27 = 6
hence, OL/TA = 6%

***The fixed charges (interest expense) for Silverado (pro forma financing with debt) are calculated as follows: Present interest charges (interest on short-term and long-term debt) at 10 percent, plus the interest on the newly acquired debt (12 percent). (Theoretically, 12 percent should be used to compute all of the interest charges, but as a practical matter, the 'old debt' interest is paid at 10 percent, and the new at 12 percent, so that is used as the basis of our computations.)

A ratio analysis at this point reveals that at present the long-term interest-bearing debt-to-net-worth ratio is higher than the industry average, and the equity-to-total-assets ratio is lower than the norm. The fixed charge coverage is also low. Financing with debt aggravates the problems, while equity financing improves the Silverado ratios in relation to the industry standards.

b. Pro forma income statements

Component	No Expansion	Expanded by Debt	Expanded by Equity
k_b	10%	12%	10%
k_s	12%	13%	11%
B*	$9,000	$13,000	$9,000

*B = Notes payable + LTIBD

Interest calculations:			
Notes payable ($5,000 at 10%)	$500	$ 500	$500
Long-term debt ($4,000 at 10%)	400	400	400
($4,000 at 12%)	---	480	---
	$900	$1,380	$900

Income statements			
NOI	$4,300	$5,100	$5,100
Interest expense	900	1,380	900
EBT	$3,400	$3,720	$4,200
Tax (40%)	1,360	1,488	1,680
Net income to equity	$2,040	$2,232	$2,520

	No expansion	Expanded by Debt	Expanded by Equity
c. Market value of equity:			
Net income	$2,040	$2,232	$2,520
Cost of equity (k_s)	.12	.13	.11
Value of equity, $S = NI/k_s$	$17,000	$17,169	$22,909
Number of shares	800	800	1000*
Value per share	$21.25	$21.46	$22.91

*If equity is sold to net $20 per share, then $4,000,000/$20 = 200,000 new shares

d. Value of the firm:			
Value of equity (S)	$17,000	$17,169	$22,909
Value of debt (B)	9,000	13,000	9,000
Value of the firm (V)	$26,000	$30,169	$31,909
Debt/Equity (B/S)	53%	76%	39%
Debt/Value (B/V)	35%	43%	28%
Equity/Value (S/V)	65%	57%	72%

e. Weighted cost of capital:

	$k_b(1-T)(B/V)$ + $k_s(S/V)$	=	k
No expansion	.10(.6)(.35) + .12(.65)	=	9.9%
Expanded by:			
Debt	.12(.6)(.43) + .13(.57)	=	10.5%
Equity	.10(.6)(.28) + .11(.72)	=	9.6%

f. Factors to be considered in determining which form of financing should be used include:

1. Relative costs
2. Level of profit margins in relation to their cost of debt or preferred stock
3. Level of debt in relation to a prudent maximum
4. How well established the firm is
5. Dilution of control
6. Cash flow considerations
7. Stability of sales and profits
8. Restrictions in loan agreements

g. The best form of financing for Silverado Company is through equity. When equity is used, the firm's ratios are strengthened with regard to industry standards. The market value of the firm and the value of the common stock per share are increased through the use of equity financing. The cost of capital is lowest (9.6 percent) when equity financing is used. Therefore, the sale of common stock to finance the expansion is the most attractive method to achieve the expansion.

25.6 Garfield Company common stock is selling for $30 per share. The firm plans to raise $100 million in a rights offering. The subscription price is to be $25.50 per share, and 2 rights are required to buy one share.

a. What is the value of a right?
b. If the risk-free rate is 10 percent, the variance of the return on equity is 9 percent and the rights expire in 6 months, calculate the value of a right using the option pricing model.

Solution:

a. $$v_r = \frac{p^o - p^s}{\#+1} = \frac{\$30-\$25.50}{2+1} = \frac{\$4.50}{3} = \$1.50$$

b. Using the OPM,

$$C = SN(d_1) - Xe^{-R_F T}N(d_2)$$

$$\text{where } d_1 = \frac{\ln(S/X)+[R_F+(\sigma^2/2)]T}{\sigma\sqrt{T}}$$

$$d_2 = d_1 - \sigma\sqrt{T}$$

For our example,

S = stock price = \$30
X = subscription price = \$25.50
R_F = risk-free rate = .10
σ^2 = equity variance = .09
T = maturity = 6 months = .5

$$d_1 = \frac{\ln(30/25.50)+[.10+(.09/2)](.5)}{.3\sqrt{.5}}$$

$$= \frac{.1625+.0725}{.2121}$$

$$= 1.108$$

$$N(d_1) = .5 + .3661 = .8661$$

$$d_2 = 1.108 - .2121$$

$$= .8959$$

$$N(d_2) = .5 + .3148 = .8148$$

$$C = 30(.8661) - 25.50e^{-.1(.5)}(.8148)$$

$$= 25.98 - 20.78(.9512)$$

$$= 25.98 - 19.77$$

$$= 6.21$$

Since two rights are required to buy one share,
$C/2 = 6.21/2 = \$3.105$

Now we must consider the dilution factor:

= 2, therefore $q = 1/\# = 1/2 = .5$, and $1+q = 1.5$

$$\frac{C/2}{1+q} = \frac{3.105}{1.5} = \$2.07$$

Using the OPM, we obtain a value of \$2.07 per right versus \$1.50 for the formula value of a right.

CHAPTER 26

DEBT AND PREFERRED STOCK

Theme: This chapter covers the materials required to analyze debt decisions and to formulate financial policies regarding the use of alternative methods of obtaining financial leverage, in an effort to keep the cost of capital to a minimum.

I. Instruments of Long-term Debt Financing.
   A. A bond is a long-term promissory note.
   B. A mortgage is a pledge of real assets as security for a loan.
   C. A debenture is unsecured long-term debt.
   D. An indenture is a document which contains the details of the long-term contractual relationship between the issuing corporation and the bondholders. It includes:
      1. The form of the bond.
      2. A description of any pledged property.
      3. The authorized amount of the issue.
      4. Minimum current ratio requirement.
      5. Provisions for redemption or call privileges.
      6. Clauses, or covenants, which limit the borrower's actions, for the protection of bondholders. Four categories of protective covenants are recognized.
         a. Restrictions on new debt (and non-debt financing such as leases) are the most common.
         b. Restrictions on dividend payments limit the payout of corporate assets to shareholders.
         c. Mergers may be restricted unless certain conditions are met.
         d. Restrictions on production and investment policies pertain to the maintenance and disposition of assets and restrict the extent to which the firm may become a claimholder in another business; these are the most difficult covenants to monitor.
         e. Since covenants cannot eliminate all risk, investors use bond ratings which reflect the market's assessment of a firm's risk.
   E. The trustee is an agent of the bondholders, but he is appointed by the issuer before the bonds are sold.
      1. Any legal person is competent to act as a trustee, but typically the duties of the trustees are handled by a department of a commercial bank.
      2. The trustee has three main responsibilities.
         a. Certify the issue of the bonds.
         b. Police the behavior of the corporation in its performance of the responsibilities set forth by the indenture.
         c. Represent the interests of the bondholder in the event of default.

3. In the early 1930s, trustees did not act in the best interests of the bondholders, so Congress passed the Trust Indenture Act. The act provides:
   a. The trustee must be given sufficient power to act on behalf of the bondholders.
   b. The indenture must not be deceptive.
   c. The bondholders can make changes in the indenture.
   d. Prompt, protective actions must be taken by the trustee in case of default.
   e. An arm's length relationship must exist between the trustee and the issuer of the bonds.
   f. The corporation must make periodic reports to its trustee.

F. A call provision gives the issuing corporation the right to call the bond for redemption.
   1. If it is used, the company must pay a call premium over and above the par value of the bond.
   2. This provision is valuable to the firm but potentially detrimental to an investor, especially when interest rates are cyclically high.
      a. If the bond is sold when rates are high, and the rate then drops, the bond's value would rise.
      b. However, if that happened, the bond would probably be called and most likely the premium would be less than the gain in market value.
      c. Therefore, the investor would gain less than if the bond were not called.

G. A sinking fund facilitates the orderly retirement of a bond issue or preferred stock issue.
   1. Nature of sinking fund requirements.
      a. Typically, the firm is required to buy and retire a portion of the bond issue each year.
      b. The amount is sometimes related to the level of sales or earnings of the current year.
      c. Usually the requirement is a mandatory fixed amount.
      d. If it is mandatory, failure to meet a sinking fund payment usually constitutes a default on the bond issue.
   2. Alternative procedures for handling sinking funds.
      a. The sinking fund may be used to call a certain percentage of the bonds at a stipulated price, with bonds selected by lottery from serial numbers.
      b. The sinking fund payment may be used to buy bonds on the open market.
      c. The firm will choose the method that results in the required reduction of indebtedness for the smallest outlay.
   3. The call provision of the sinking fund can work to the detriment of bondholders, since the call is generally at par while the bond may have been purchased well above par.

4. Since a sinking fund provides additional protection to investors, bonds that have them are likely to carry lower yields than comparable bonds with no sinking fund provisions.

H. Funded debt is simply long-term debt.

II. Secured Long-term Debt Can Be Classified on Three Bases:

A. Priority of claims.
1. A senior mortgage has first claim on assets and earnings.
2. A junior mortgage has a subordinate lien.
3. Subordinated debt is unsecured debt, which is junior to other designated debt.

B. Right to issue additional securities.
1. A closed-end mortgage specifies that no additional bonds may be sold which have a lien on the property specified in the original mortgage.
2. An open-end mortgage exists if the bond indenture fails to mention additional bond issues. Therefore, the property can be repledged.
3. A limited open-end mortgage allows the sale of a specified amount of additional bonds.

C. Scope of the lien.
1. A specific lien specifies certain designated property.
2. A blanket mortgage pledges all real property owned by the company.

D. The factors given above have important influences on the following:
1. The degree of protection for the creditor.
2. The rate of interest paid by the firm.
3. The rating of the bond by rating agencies.

III. Unsecured Long-term Debt.

A. Debentures are unsecured bonds which are issued:
1. When the firm's property is unsuitable for a lien.
2. When the firm's finances are very strong.
3. When the firm is too weak to have alternatives; that is, all of its property may already be encumbered.

B. A subordinated debenture is an unsecured bond that has a claim on assets after unsubordinated debt in the event of liquidation. This places the debenture below present and future senior debt with regard to priorities.
1. Advantages.
   a. Subordination strengthens the position of senior creditors.
   b. Debentures have a tax advantage over preferred stock.
   c. Debentures do not restrict the ability of the borrower to obtain senior debt.
2. The use of subordinated debentures is stimulated by periods of tight money because such debentures provide an equity cushion for loans from commercial banks or other senior debt.

C. <u>Income bonds</u> are bonds which pay interest only if income is earned by the company.
   1. In the past they arose from reorganizations.
   2. In recent years, they have been used in normal financing to replace a preferred stock issue because of the tax advantage of interest payments over dividends.
   3. They typically contain:
      a. A cumulative provision
      b. A sinking fund provision
      c. A convertible provision
      d. Voting rights upon default of a specified number of interest payments
   4. Although interest is not a fixed charge, the principal must be paid when due.

D. Floating rate notes (FRNs) were developed to decrease the risks of interest rate volatility at high rates.
   1. The coupon rate varies at a given percentage above the prevailing risk-free rate (determined by either short- or long-term Treasury yields).
   2. The FRN rate is either fixed or guaranteed to exceed a stated minimum for an initial period, and then adjusted at specified intervals.
   3. Characteristics of FRNs.
      a. Convertibility: To either common stock, fixed-rate bonds or both at either the issuer's option, the holder's option or both.
      b. Put option: Allows the holder to redeem at face value under specified conditions.
      c. Minimum rate: Prevents the coupon from floating below a stated minimum.
      d. Drop-lock rate: If the coupon drops to a stated rate, it is fixed at that rate until maturity.
      e. Sinking fund provision: Permits the issuer to repay stated portions before maturity.
      f. Declining spread: The spread between the note rate and the Treasury rate decreases by given amounts at specified times.
      g. Declining minimum rate: The minimum rate declines.
      Call option: Permits the issuer to call the note at a moderate premium.
   4. Some FRN characteristics favor lenders, and others favor borrowers. Among the advantages to issuers are:
      a. Long-term funds are obtainable during tight money periods without locking into high interest rates for the life of the loan.
      b. The cost-revenue spread can be stabilized--financial institutions, whose assets bear floating rate returns, use FRNs in this way.
   5. Advantages to lenders include:
      a. Returns on investment will follow changes in Treasury rates.
      b. The market value of the FRN will remain relatively stable.
      c. Convertibility and minimum rate features provide additional assurance and flexibility.

6. The long-term costs of FRN's depends on the movement of interest rates during the life of the note.
   a. If issued when yield curves are inverted, FRNs based on short-term Treasury rates can cost more than long-term fixed-rate borrowing, but less than short-term bank loans or commercial paper.
   b. FRNs based on less variable long-term Treasury bonds may cost the borrower somewhat more for providing greater predictability of costs.

IV. Bond Values and Their Fluctuations.

A. Bond values are determined by discounting expected interest and principal payments at the discount rate appropriate for the risk of default.

B. A perpetual bond pays interest forever, but never repays the principal amount.

1. The valuation formula for a perpetual bond is

$$v_b = \frac{c}{k_b}$$

where v_b = value of the bond
c = annual coupon interest payment
k_b = appropriate interest rate

2. If the yield on bonds of similar risk rises, the value of the perpetual bond will fall (and vice versa) since the coupon payment is fixed.

3. The cost of perpetual debt is found as

$$k_b = \frac{c}{v_b}$$

In this case, v_b is the market price of the bond.

C. Term bonds pay interest annually (or semiannually), then repay the principal at the end of the term, the maturity of the bond.

1. The valuation formula for a term bond is

$$v_b = \sum_{t=1}^{n} \frac{c}{(1+k_b)^t} + \frac{M}{(1+k_b)^n}$$

where M = principal repayment
n = term of the bond

2. The value of a term bond also fluctuates inversely with the yield on bonds of similar risk.

3. The cost of a term bond is found using trial and error to find the k_b which equates the discounted cash flows with the market price of the bond.

D. Interest rate risk refers to the change in the value of a bond in response to changes in the going market rate of interest.
   1. The differential responsiveness to changes in interest rates depends on the level of required yields.
      a. In general, short-term bonds are less sensitive to changes in interest rates.
      b. However, for deep discount bonds (for which the market price is well below par value), when market yields are 10 percent or more, further declines in price for a given rise in the going rate are less for longer-maturity bonds than for shorter-term bonds.
   2. Duration is a statistical measure of interest rate risk which considers cash flow patterns rather than just the relationship between yields and maturity.
      a. Duration measures the price elasticity of bonds in response to a change in interest rates.
      b. The formula for duration weights each cash flow by a time factor, t, which gives greater weight to distant cash flows whose present value is more sensitive to interest rate changes.

$$dur_i = -\frac{\sum_{t=1}^{T} \frac{tCF_t}{(1+k_b)^t}}{v_b}$$

V. Characteristics of Long-term Debt.
   A. From the viewpoint of the holder.
      1. Debt is good with regard to risk, has limited advantages with regard to income and is weak with regard to control.
      2. Debt is favorable because it gives priority in both earnings and liquidations. It has a definite maturity and protective covenants.
      3. The bondholder generally receives a fixed return.
      4. The bondholder may exercise no control except in the case of default.
   B. From the viewpoint of the issuer.
      1. Advantages.
         a. Debt has a limited cost, and expected yield is lower than the cost of common or preferred stock.
         b. Stockholders retain voting control.
         c. Interest expense is tax deductible.
         d. Call provisions add flexibility to the financial structure.

2. Disadvantages.
    a. A fixed interest commitment is made.
    b. Higher risk may result in lowering the value of the common stock outstanding.
    c. A definite maturity date exists requiring repayment or refunding.
    d. The long-term nature involves risk of changing conditions.
    e. Stringent indenture provisions may be imposed.
    f. Financial standards limit the amount of debt in the capital structure.
3. The decision to use debt depends on many factors.
    a. The firm makes a judgement about its actual debt ratio relative to its optimal debt ratio.
    b. The use of short-term debt is more conservative than long-term fixed rate debt.
        (i) Continuously rolling over short-term debt evens out net income since both revenues and interest rates tend to be higher during favorable economic conditions and vice versa.
        (ii) Use of long-term fixed rate debt is an aggressive policy which causes greater fluctuations in income, increasing systematic risk.
    c. Variable rate debt is more conservative than fixed rate debt if revenues and interest rates are positively correlated.
    d. Secured debt is appropriate when assets can be liquidated at near market value; otherwise unsecured debentures are used.

VI. Preferred Stock.
  A. Under some circumstances, the financial manager will decide that preferred stock is a suitable source of funds because it limits cash payout and provides financial leverage.
  B. Preferred stock is by nature a hybrid security. It is classified as debt or equity depending upon the analysis being made.
    1. Preferred stock is <u>not</u> like equity (but <u>is</u> like debt) in that it does not carry voting rights.
    2. Preferred stock is <u>not</u> like debt (but <u>is</u> like equity) in that failure to pay dividends does not cause default on the obligation.
  C. The risks of preferred shareholders in relation to the risks of equity owners are reduced by these features:
    1. Preferreds have claims to earnings and to assets in liquidation prior to common stock.
    2. Occasionally, a sinking fund provides for the retirement of the issue.

3. Ordinarily, consent of the preferred shareholders must be obtained before securities with equal or prior claim on earnings can be issued.
4. Common stock dividends are restricted if the current ratio, debt ratio, or surplus account go beyond prescribed limits.

VII. Major Provisions of Preferred Stock Issues.

A. Priority in assets and earnings.
   1. Preferred stockholders must consent to a subsequent sale of securities having a prior or equal claim on earnings.
   2. A required minimum level of retained earnings before common stock dividends are allowed.

B. Par value is significant.
   1. Par value established the amount due preferred stockholders upon liquidation.
   2. Preferred dividends are usually stated as a percentage of par value.

C. Cumulative dividends.
   1. All past preferred dividends must be paid before any common dividends can be paid.
   2. No interest is paid on arrearages.
   3. Common stock is often substituted for large arrearages.

D. About 40 percent of the preferred stock issued in recent years has been convertible into common stock.

E. Summary of usual preferred stock provisions.
   1. It is nonparticipating
   2. It is nonvoting
   3. It has a prior claim on earnings and assets
   4. It is cumulative
   5. It has no maturity

F. Some infrequent provisions in preferred stock.
   1. Voting rights--preferred stockholders can vote for a minority of directors.
   2. Participating--participates with the common stock in sharing the firm's earnings.
   3. Sinking fund--purchase and retirement of a given percentage of the preferred stock each year.
   4. Maturity--date upon which it must be retired.
   5. Call provision--company must pay a call premium to call in the preferred stock for redemption.
   6. Adjustable rate--makes preferred stock more attractive to investors.

VIII. Evaluation of Preferred Stock.

A. From the viewpoint of the issuer.

1. Advantages:
   a. The obligation to make fixed payments is avoided.
   b. It obtains higher earnings for original owners if leverage is successful.
   c. It avoids provision of equal participation in earnings.
   d. It usually does not dilute existing control of the firm.
   e. Since it usually has not maturity date and no sinking fund, it is more flexible than bonds.
   f. It enables the firm to converve mortgageable assets.
2. Disadvantages:
   a. Sells at a higher yield than bonds.
   b. Dividends are not an expense for tax purposes.
   c. The cost of preferred is the full percentage amount of the preferred dividend.

B. From the viewpoint of the investor:

1. Advantages:
   a. Provides reasonably steady income.
   b. Preferred stockholders have priority over common stockholders in the event of liquidation.
   c. Corporations often like to hold preferred stock as an investment; 80 percent of the dividends received are not taxable to a corporate taxpayer.
2. Disadvantages:
   a. Returns are limited.
   b. Price fluctuations are greater than for bonds, while yields are lower.
   c. The stock has no legally enforceable right to dividends.
   d. Accrued cash dividends are seldom settled in an amount comparable to the amount of the obligation.

C. Recent trends.

1. To avoid the tax disadvantage of nondeductibility of preferred stock dividends, companies have made offers to exchange preferred stock for debentures or subordinated debentures.
   a. When preferred stock is not callable, total securities offered usually exceed the market value of the preferred.
   b. A common formula is to offer bonds equal in market value to the preferred, plus cash or common stock as an extra inducement to exchange.
2. Use of convertible preferred stock in connection with mergers.

a. Use of cash or bonds in payment to the shareholders of the acquired company would constitute realized gains from a tax standpoint.
b. If convertible preferred stock is paid to the selling stockholders, this constitutes a tax-free exchange of securities.
c. Selling stockholders thus obtain a fixed income security while postponing the capital gains taxes.

D. Since it is a hybrid security type, the use of preferred stock is favored by conditions that fall between those favoring the use of common stock and those favoring the use of debt.
1. If profit margins are adequate, the firm will gain from the additional leverage provided by preferred stock
2. Relative costs of alternative sources of financing are important.
3. When the use of debt involves excessive risk and the issuance of common stock poses control problems, preferred stock may be a good compromise.

IX. Rationale for Different Classes of Securities.
A. Different investors have different risk-return tradeoff functions.
B. In order to appeal to the widest possible market, various securities are offered.
C. Used wisely, a policy of differentiated securities can lower a firm's average cost of capital below what it would be if it issued only one class of debt and common stock.
D. The listing below ranks securities from the safest down to securities with the highest risk but also the highest return.
1. U.S. Treasury bonds
2. First mortgage bonds
3. Second mortgage bonds
4. Subordinated debentures
5. Income bonds
6. Preferred stock
7. Convertible preferred
8. Common stock

X. Refunding a Bond Issue.
A. Fluctuating interest rates create opportunities for bond refunding.
B. When interest rates fall, firms may call in outstanding bonds, issuing lower-yield bonds in their place.

C. The analysis of a refunding decision uses the NPV methodology.

$$NPV = \sum_{t=1}^{n} \frac{(1-T)(r_1-r_2)D}{[1+(1-T)k_b]^t}$$ Present value of after-tax savings on old bond issue

$$- \sum_{t=1}^{n} \frac{(1-T)r_2\Delta D}{[1+(1-T)k_b]^t}$$ Present value of interest paid on incremental (new) debt

$$- \frac{\Delta D}{[1+(1-T)k_b]^n}$$ Present value of repayment of incremental debt at maturity

$$- [(1-T)RC - \Delta D]$$ Present value of financing issued = difference between after-tax refunding costs and new financing

where r_1 = interest rate on the old issue
r_2 = interest rate on the new issue
D = face value of old debt issue
ΔD = incremental debt involved in new issue
RC = refunding costs
T = corporate tax rate
n = years to maturity on the old issue
k_b = current market rate on bonds of equivalent risk

1. Refunding costs include the following:
   a. The call premium paid on the old issue.
   b. The flotation costs involved in selling the new issue.
   c. Interest during the period when interest is accruing on both bonds.
2. If all refunding costs are financed by the new debt, $\Delta D = (1-T)RC$, and the last term above drops out.

3. The after-tax cost of new debt is the appropriate discount rate when all refunding costs are financed by the new debt.

D. When interest rates have risen substantially, a firm may simply go into the market and buy its own bonds at a discount.
   1. The difference between the value of the bonds on the firm's books and the market price at which they were purchased can be reported as realized profit on a firm's income statement.
      a. This paper profit is subject to income taxation, which can be avoided under some conditions.
      b. If this "paper" gain is taxed, cash flows are reduced.
   2. The effects of refunding when interest rates have risen are therefore unfavorable unless the tax consequences can be avoided.
   3. A better strategy would be for the firm to buy bonds of equivalent risk whose interest income would cancel out the interest expense of the outstanding discount bonds, avoiding the tax consequences of refunding.

Chapter 26 - Illustrative Problems and Solutions

26.1 Two years ago you purchased a 20-year bond at par, with a 16 percent coupon rate and a 10 percent call premium. The bond has just been called. What is your realized rate of return?

Solution:

$1,000 = $160(PVIFA,r,2 yrs) + $1,100(PVIF,r,2 yrs)

Try 20 percent:

$1,000 $\stackrel{?}{=}$ $160(1.5278) + $1,100(.6944)

$\neq$ $1,008.29

20 percent is too low. Rate of return is 20.5 percent.

26.2 The Belden Company has had several excellent investment opportunities in the past 3 years. To reduce the need for external financing, Belden has retained all of its earnings over this period. As a result, the company is 3 years in arrears on its preferred stock cumulative dividends. Belden has 100,000 shares of $6 par, 10 percent dividend preferred stock outstanding and 1,000,000 shares of $1 par common stock. This year's net income before preferred dividends is $1,000,000, and Belden would like to declare a dividend on common stock.

What is the largest dividend per common share that can be declared?

Solution:

Par value of preferred = 100,000 x $6	$600,000
Preferred dividend rate	x .10
Annual dividend	$ 60,000
Years in arrears	x 3
Dividends in arrears	$180,000
Current dividend	60,000
Total preferred dividends payable	$240,000

Net income	$1,000,000
Preferred dividends	240,000
Available to common	$ 760,000
Common shares	1,000,000
Maximum dividend per common share	$0.76

26.3 Calculate the yield to maturity of a perpetual bond with $1,000 par value and a 9 percent coupon rate when the market price is:

a. \$900
b. \$1,000
c. \$1,300

Assume interest is paid annually.

Solution:

$$k_b = \frac{c}{v_b}$$

a. $k_b = \frac{\$90}{900} = 10.0\%$

b. $k_b = \frac{\$90}{1,000} = 9.0\%$

c. $k_b = \frac{\$90}{1,300} = 6.9\%$

26.4 The following bond information was found in the Wall Street Journal in 1981:

Company	Coupon	Maturity Date	Price
BethSt	4.500%	1990	\$510.00
PGE	4.500	1990	550.00
ATT	10.375	1990	842.50
Finan	10.250	1990	760.00

a. Find the promised yield to maturity for each bond. Assume interest is paid semiannually.
b. Comment on your results.

Solution:

a. Beth St: Semiannual payment = [(.045)(1,000)]/2
= \$22.50

Compounding periods = 9 x 2 = 18

$$\$510 = \sum_{t=1}^{18} \frac{\$22.50}{(1+r)^t} + \frac{\$1,000}{(1+r)^{18}}$$

Since the bond is selling at a discount, the promised yield must be greater than the coupon rate.

Try 12 percent: (Use interest factors for 6%, 18 yrs to adjust for semiannual compounding.)

$$\$510 \stackrel{?}{=} \$22.50(10.8276) + \$1,000(.3503)$$

$$\neq \$593.92$$

12 percent is too low.

Try 15 percent:

$$\$510 \stackrel{?}{=} \$22.50(9.7060) + \$1,000(.2720)$$
$$\neq \$490.39$$

15 percent is too high.

Yield to maturity is 14.40 percent.

<u>PGE</u>: Semiannual payment = $22.50
Compounding periods = 18

Try 13 percent:

$$\$550 \stackrel{?}{=} \$22.50(10.4325) + \$1,000(.3219)$$
$$\neq \$556.63$$

13 percent is too low.

Yield to maturity is 13.20 percent.

<u>ATT</u>: Semiannual payment = [(.10375)(1,000)]/2
= $51.88
Compounding periods = 18

Try 12 percent:

$$\$842.50 \stackrel{?}{=} \$51.88(10.8276) + \$1,000(.3503)$$
$$\neq \$912.04$$

12 percent is too low.

Try 14 percent:

$$\$842.50 \stackrel{?}{=} \$51.88(10.0591) + \$1,000(.2959)$$
$$\neq \$817.77$$

14 percent is too high.

Yield to maturity is 13.45 percent.

<u>Finan</u>: Semiannual payment = [(.1025)($1,000)]/2
= $51.25
Compounding periods = 18

Try 16 percent:

$$\$760 \stackrel{?}{=} \$51.25(9.3719) + \$1,000(.2502)$$
$$\neq \$730.51$$

16 percent is too high.

Try 14 percent;

$$\$760 \stackrel{?}{=} \$51.25(10.0591) + \$1,000(.2959)$$
$$\neq \$811.43$$

14 percent is too low.

Promised yield to maturity is 15.22 percent.

b.

Company	Coupon	Promised Yield to Maturity
BethSt	4.500%	14.40%
PGE	4.500%	13.20%
ATT	10.375%	13.45%
Finan	10.250%	15.22%

All of the bonds have the same 9 years to maturity. There is a range of almost 6 percentage points in the coupon rates, but the range in the yield to maturity is just over 2 percentage points.

The BethSt and PGE bonds have the same coupon rate, but the yield to maturity required by investors, and thus the cost of debt to PGE is lower by 1.20 percentage points. In the case of the ATT and Finan bonds, there is only 1/8 of 1 percent difference in the coupon rate, but almost 2 percent difference in the yield to maturity. The disparity in promised yields reflects the market's assessment of the risk premium appropriate for each company for this maturity of bonds.

26.5 In early 1982, the Rhineman Company requested a 3-year term loan of $1,000,000 from the National Bank of Cleveland. In granting the loan, the bank required that any new debt issued by Rhineman over the 3-year loan period must be subordinated to the bank loan. In June 1982 Rhineman issued $500,000 in subordinated debentures.

Rhineman was declared bankrupt on December 31, 1982. The firm's financial structure on that date is given below.

Accounts payable	$ 800,000
Bank debt	1,000,000
Subordinated debentures	500,000
Total debt	$2,300,000
Net worth	1,000,000
Total claims on assets	$3,300,000

a. What dollar amount and percent of the bank loan will be repaid if $1,000,000 is available for claims after liquidation of Rhineman's assets?

b. What dollar amount and percent of the bank's claim will be paid if $1,500,000 is available for claims upon liquidation?

c. What is the minimum amount that must be received on liquidation before the holders of the subordinated debentures receive any payment?

Solution:

a. $1,000,000 available for claims:

Claim	Book value (a)	Percent of total debt (b)	Initial allocation (b) x $1M (c)	Actual payment (d)	Percent of original claim satisfied (e)
Accounts payable	$ 800	35%	$ 350	$ 350	44%
Bank debt	1,000	43	430	650	65
Subordinated debentures	500	22	220	0	0
	$2,300	100%	$1,000	$1,000	43%

b. $1,500,000 available for claims:

	Initial allocation (b) x $1.5M	Actual payment	% of claim satisfied
Accounts payable	$525	$525	66%
Bank debt	645	975	98
Subordinated debentures	330	0	0
	$1,500	$1,500	65%

c. The bank debt must be completely paid off before the subordinated debenture holders can begin to be repaid.

Bank debt	43% of total debt
Subordinated debentures	22% of total debt
	65%

(.65) x Amount available for claims = $1,000,000

Amount available for claims = $1,538,462.

26.6 The Hardy Tool Company, a manufacturer of garden and hand tools, is planning an expansion program which will require raising $4,000,000. Management must decide whether to use debt or equity financing. Debt can be sold at a cost of 10 percent, or new equity can be sold at $32 per share. There are currently 1,000,000 common shares outstanding. Hardy has a 40 percent corporate tax rate. The information below has been gathered for analysis:

Tool Industry Financial Ratios	
Current ratio	2.0 times
Sales to total assets	2.1 times
Current debt to total assets	36%
Long-term debt to net worth	32%
Total debt to total assets	52%
Fixed charge coverage	6.0 times
Net income to sales	4%
Return on total assets	9%
Net income to net worth	18%

Hardy Company Balance Sheet as of December 31, 1981
(thousands of dollars)

Assets		Liabilities	
Cash	$ 2,520	Current liabilities	$10,000
Accounts receivable	10,520	Long-term debt (10%)	3,600
Inventories	15,200	Total debt	$13,600
Total current assets	$28,240	Net worth	26,400
Net fixed assets	11,760		
Total assets	$40,000	Total liabilities and net worth	$40,000

Hardy Company Income Statement for Year Ended December 31, 1981
(thousands of dollars)

Revenues	$80,000
Net operating income	8,360
Interest expense	360
Earnings before tax	$8,000
Tax at 40 percent	3,200
Net income	$4,800

a. Estimate Hardy's cost of equity capital using the Security Market Line. The risk-free rate is 7 percent, the expected return on the market is 12 percent, and Hardy's β is 1.66, based on the current leverage factor.

b. What is the value of Hardy's equity? What is its indicated price per share? What is the value of the firm?

c. What is Hardy's current weighted average cost of capital? (Use 10 percent for the cost of debt, and the cost of equity calculated in part (a). Assume no short-term interest bearing debt.)

d. Calculate the new financial structure and coverage relationships for expansion with debt and equity assuming that the percentage of net operating income to total assets remains the same.

e. If debt financing is used, the cost of equity will rise to reflect the rise in β to 1.72. With equity financing, the drop in β to 1.60 lowers the cost of equity. Compare the cost of equity under debt and equity financing.
f. Calculate the total value of equity and the new value per share of common stock under each financing method.
g. Calculate the value of the firm under each alternative.
h. Compare the weighted cost of capital under each method.
i. Which form of financing should Hardy choose?

Solution:

a. $k_s = R_F + (\bar{R}_M - R_F)\beta$

$= .07 + (.12-.07)1.66$

$= 15.3\%$

b. $S = \frac{NI}{k_s}$ $\quad NI = \$4,800 \quad k_s = .153$

$S = \frac{\$4,800}{.153}$

$= \$31,373$

$p_o = \frac{S}{n} = \frac{\$31,373}{1,000} = \$31.37$

$V_L = S + B = \$31,373 + \$3,600$

$= \$34,973$

c. $k = k_b(1-T)(B/V) + k_s(S/V)$

$= .10(.6)(.103) + .153(.897)$

$= 14.34\%$

d. Hardy Company Balance Sheets

	Present		Pro forma: Debt		Pro forma: Equity	
	Amt	%	Amt	%	Amt	%
Current debt	$10,000	25%	$10,000	23%	$10,000	23%
Long-term debt	3,600	9	7,600	17	3,600	8
Net worth	26,400	66	26,400	60	30,400	69
	$40,000	100%	$44,000	100%	$44,000	100%

Hardy Company Income Statements

	Present	Pro forma Debt	Pro forma Equity
Net operating income	\$8,360	\$9,196	\$9,196
Interest expense	360	760	360
Earnings before tax	\$8,000	\$8,436	\$8,836
Tax (40%)	3,200	3,374	3,534
Net income	\$4,800	\$5,062	\$5,302

Financial structure

	Industry	Hardy Current	Hardy Debt	Hardy Equity
Short-term debt/total assets	36%	25%	23%	23%
Long-term debt/net worth	32%	14%	29%	12%
Total debt/total assets	52%	34%	40%	31%
Fixed charge coverage	6X	23X	12X	26X

DEBT FINANCING

e. $k_s = .07 + (.05)(1.72)$

$= 15.6\%$

f. $S = \frac{NI}{k_s} = \frac{\$5,062}{.156}$

$= \$32,449$

$p_o = \frac{S}{N} = \frac{\$32,449}{1,000}$

$= \$32.45$

g. $V_L = S + B$

$= \$32,449 + \$7,600$

$= \$40,049$

h. $k = k_b(1-T)(B/V) + k_s(S/V)$

At market values:

$k = .10(.6)(7,600/40,049) + .156(32,449/40,049)$

$= .0114 + .1264$

$= 13.78\%$

EQUITY FINANCING

$k_s = .07 + (.05)(1.60)$

$= 15.0\%$

$S = \frac{NI}{k_s} = \frac{\$5,302}{.15}$

$= \$35,347$

$p_o = \frac{S}{N} = \frac{\$35,347}{1,000+(4,000/32)}$

$= \$35,347/1,125$

$= \$31.42$

$V_L = S + B$

$= \$35,347 + \$3,600$

$= \$38,947$

At market values:

$k = .10(.6)(3,600/38,947) + .15(35,347/38,947)$

$= .0055 + .1361$

$= 14.16\%$

DEBT FINANCING	EQUITY FINANCING
At book values:	At book values:
k = .10(.6)(7,600/44,000) + .156(26,400/44,000)	k = .10(.6)(3,600/44,000) + .15(30,400/44,000)
= .0104 + .0936	= .0049 + .1036
= 10.40%	= 10.85%

i. Hardy is well below the industry standards for the proportions of debt in the capital structure and has a very strong coverage ratio. This remains true if the expansion is financed with debt, so the cost of debt is not increased. In comparing the use of debt versus equity financing we find that the indicated price per share of common stock is higher under debt financing than under equity financing. The value of the firm is greater under debt financing than equity financing. In addition, whether measured at market value or book value, the weighted cost of capital is lower under debt financing than under equity financing. For all of these reasons we would recommend the use of debt financing.

Indeed, the continued low debt ratio of Hardy poses the question of why it does not increase its leverage ratio further. It would appear that more debt could be added to Hardy's financial structure without adding to the risk of the company to any substantial degree. It would, therefore, be able to add more debt and still increase share price and the value of the firm and lower its weighted cost of capital. This problem is realistic in that there are a number of examples of large companies with very low debt ratios; e.g., Eastman Kodak, Kellogg Company, General Motors, etc.

26.7 The Mackin Company has a $1 million bond issue outstanding with 6 years to maturity, and a 12 percent coupon rate. Mackin now has an opportunity to refund the debt at a 10 percent coupon rate. Both the old and the new issue would pay interest annually. The refunding project would be financed exclusively with the new debt. Mackin's tax rate is 40 percent, and the after-tax cost of debt is the appropriate discount rate to be used in the analysis.

Evaluate the refunding decision based on the data on the following page.

	Old issue		New issue	
Face amount		$1,000,000		$1,063,200
Interest rate		12%		10%
Life of bond		10 years		6 years
Maturity date		August 1, 1987		August 1, 1987
Flotation costs (% of gross proceeds)	@ 2.5%	$25,000	@ 2.56%	$27,200
Net proceeds of sale		$975,000		
Date issued		August 3, 1977		August 1, 1981
Redemption date		August 1, 1981		
Call premium		6%		

Solution:

1. Call premium
   Before tax: (.06)($1,000,000) = $60,000
   After tax: $60,000(1-.4) = $36,000

2. Flotation costs on new issue
   $1,063,200(.0256) = $27,200

3. Tax savings on flotation costs of new issue

$$\frac{\$27,200}{6}(.4) \times PVIFA[(1-.4)(10\%),6\ yrs]$$

= $4,533(.4)(PVIFA,6%,6 yrs)

= $1,813(4.9173)

= $8,915

4. Tax savings on flotation costs of old issue
   Tax savings on unamortized flotation costs written off
   =$25,000(6/10)(.4) = $6,000

   PV of lost benefits
   = ($15,000/6)(.4)(PVIFA,6%,6 yrs)
   = $2,500(.4)(4.9173)
   = $4,917

5. Interest savings on new issue
   $1,000,000(.12-.10)(1-.4) = $12,000

   PV of interest savings
   = ($12,000)(PVIFA,6%,6 yrs)
   = $12,000(4.9173)
   = $59,008

Refunding Costs	Amount before tax	Amount after tax	Timing of event	Interest factor	Present value
1. Call premium	$60,000	$36,000	0	1.0	$36,000
2. Flotation costs on new issue	27,200	27,200	0	1.0	27,200
3. Tax savings on flotation costs of new issue	4,533	1,813	1-6	4.9173	(8,915)
4. Tax effects of flotation costs of old issue	15,000	6,000	0	1.0	(6,000)
	2,500	1,000	1-6	4.9173	4,917
Present value of after-tax refunding costs					$53,202
5. Interest savings on new issue	$20,000	$12,000	1-6	4.9173	$59,008

NPV of refunding = $59,008 - $53,202 = $5,806

The present value of the interest savings exceeds the after-tax refunding costs. Therefore the refunding proposal will add to the value of the firm and should be undertaken.

26.8 Three bonds were issued today, each with 4 years to maturity and a 14 percent promised yield. Bond A is a balloon payment bond, Bond B is a fully amortized bond and Bond C is a pure discount bond. The bonds' current values and annual cash flows are given in the table below.

	Bond A	Bond B	Bond C
Current value	$1,000	$1,000	$1,000
Cash flows:			
Year 1	200	343.21	--
2	200	343.21	--
3	200	343.21	--
4	905	343.21	1,688.90

a. If current market yields on bonds of equivalent risk are 14 percent, what is the duration of each bond?

b. If interest rates fall such that the rate on bonds of equivalent risk is only 10 percent, what will be the duration of each bond?

Solution:

$$dur_i = -\frac{\sum_{t=1}^{T} \frac{tCF_t}{(1+k_b)^t}}{v_b}$$

a. Bond A:

$$dur_A = -\frac{\frac{1(200)}{(1.14)^1} + \frac{2(200)}{(1.14)^2} + \frac{3(200)}{(1.14)^3} + \frac{4(905)}{(1.14)^4}}{1{,}000}$$

$$= -\frac{175.44 + 307.79 + 404.98 + 2143.33}{1000}$$

$$= -\frac{3031.54}{1000}$$

$$= -3.03154$$

Bond B:

$$dur_B = -\frac{\frac{343.21}{(1.14)^1} + \frac{2(343.21)}{(1.14)^2} + \frac{3(343.21)}{(1.14)^3} + \frac{4(343.21)}{(1.14)^4}}{1{,}000}$$

$$= -\frac{301.06 + 528.18 + 694.97 + 812.83}{1000}$$

$$= -\frac{2337.04}{1000}$$

$$= -2.33704$$

Bond C:

$$dur_C = -\frac{\frac{4(1688.90)}{(1.14)^4}}{1000} = \frac{3999.86}{1000} = 3.99986$$

RANKING BY DURATION:

Bond B	-2.33704
Bond A	-3.03154
Bond C	-3.99986

b. The first step is to calculate the new current value of the bonds.

Bond A: v_A = 200[PVIFA(10%, 3 yrs)] + 905[PVIF(10%, 4 yrs)]

= 200(2.4869) + 905(.6830)

= 497.38 + 618.12

= 1115.50

Bond B: v_B = 343.21[PVIFA(10%, 4 yrs)]

= 343.21(3.1699)

= 1087.94

Bond C: v_C = 1688.90[PVIF(10%, 4 yrs)]

= 1688.90(.6830)

= 1153.52

RANKING BY MAGNITUDE OF PRICE CHANGE:

Bond B	+ 87.94
Bond A	+115.50
Bond C	+153.52

$$dur_A = -\frac{\frac{1(200)}{(1.10)^1} + \frac{2(200)}{(1.10)^2} + \frac{3(200)}{(1.10)^3} + \frac{4(905)}{(1.10)^4}}{1115.50}$$

$$= -\frac{181.82 + 330.58 + 450.79 + 2472.51}{1115.50}$$

$$= -\frac{3435.70}{1115.50}$$

$$= -3.07996$$

$$dur_B = -\frac{\frac{1(343.21)}{(1.10)^1} + \frac{2(343.21)}{(1.10)^2} + \frac{3(343.21)}{(1.10)^3} + \frac{4(343.21)}{(1.10)^4}}{1087.94}$$

$$= -\frac{312.01 + 567.29 + 773.58 + 939.67}{1087.94}$$

$$= -\frac{2590.55}{1087.94}$$

$$= -2.38115$$

$$dur_C = -\frac{\frac{4(1688.90)}{(1.10)^4}}{1153.52} = \frac{4614.17}{1153.52} = 4.00007$$

<u>RANKING BY DURATION:</u>

Bond B	-2.38115
Bond A	-3.07996
Bond C	-4.00007

CHAPTER 27

LEASE FINANCING

Theme: Leasing has become an increasingly important method of financing--in fact virtually any kind of asset can be leased.

I. The Nature of Leasing.
   A. The use of buildings and equipment can be obtained either by buying or by leasing.
   B. Lease financing is quite similar to borrowing and is another method of providing financial leverage.
      1. Leasing differs from borrowing in that a lease is associated with specific assets.
      2. An advantage of leasing over debt is that a lessor has a better position than a creditor if the firm experiences financial difficulties, therefore riskier firms may obtain lease financing even if banks are reluctant to extend a loan.

II. Types of Leases.
   A. Sale and leaseback - a firm owning land, buildings or equipment sells the property and simultaneously executes an agreement to lease the property for a specified period under specific terms.
      1. The seller (or lessee) immediately receives the sale price of the property but retains the right to use it.
      2. Payments provided for by the lease are sufficient to return the full purchase price plus a stated return to the buyer (or lessor).
   B. Operating leases or service leases include both financing and maintenance services.
      1. Service leases involve equipment such as computers, office machines, and automobiles or trucks.
      2. The lessor usually maintains and services the equipment.
      3. The lease contract is written for less than the expected life of the leased equipment; therefore, the full cost of the equipment is not covered.
      4. Such leases typically contain a cancellation clause permitting the lessee to cancel the lease and return the equipment before the expiration of the basic lease agreement.
   C. Financial leases - do not provide for maintenance services and are not cancellable.
      1. These leases provide for full amortization of costs, plus a return on the lessor's investment.

2. The main difference between a financial lease and a sale and leaseback arrangement is that with a financial lease, the equipment is new and the lessor buys it from the manufacturer, not the user. Therefore, sale and leaseback is a special type of financial lease.

III. Annual Lease Payments are Deductible for Income Tax Purposes, Provided the Following Requirements Stated by the Internal Revenue Service are Included in the Agreement.

A. The term of the lease must be less than thirty years.
B. The rental payments must provide a reasonable rate of return to the lessor.
C. A renewal option is bona fide. A minimum requirement is that the lessee be given the first option to meet the best outside offer.
D. Any purchase option shall reflect a competitive price.

IV. Cost Comparison Between Lease and Purchase for Financial Leases.

A. From the point of view of the lessor, we can find the equilibrium lease-rental rate in a competitive market by solving a capital budgeting problem which finds the cash flow return which will earn the applicable cost of capital.
   1. The net present value of the lease rental income to the lessor (NPV_{LOR}) is set to zero in accordance with the competitive market assumption.
   2. Cash flow returns consist of lease rental payments (L_t) and the depreciation tax shelter (TDep).
   3. The appropriate discount factor is the lessor's weighted cost of capital, which is equal to the applicable rate on debt instruments of the same risk.
   4. To find the equilibrium lease-rental payment, solve for L_t:

$$NPV_{LOR} = -I_o + \sum_{t=1}^{n} \frac{L_t(1-T) + TDep_t}{(1+k_L)^t} \qquad (27.2)$$

where

I_o = Cost of the asset
n = Economic and tax depreciation life of the asset
k_L = Lessor's cost of capital

B. The lessee can have the use of the equipment either through leasing or debt financing.

1. Assume that for the user firm, debt and lease financing are perfect substitutes; for each dollar of extra tax shield provided by the lease, there is a $1 reduction in the debt tax shield.
2. The net advantage to leasing, or NPV of the lease, can be calculated as:

$$NAL = I_o - PV[L_t(1-T)] - PV(TDep_t) + PV[T\Delta(k_b B_t)] \quad (27.3)$$

$$= I_o - \sum_{t=1}^{n} \frac{L_t(1-T) - TDep_t}{[1+(1-T)k_b]^t} \quad (27.4)$$

3. The NAL is the equivalent of the cost of borrowing minus the cost of leasing:

$$\text{Cost of borrowing} = I_o - \sum_{t=1}^{n} \frac{TDep_t}{[1+(1-T)k_b]^t}$$

$$\text{Cost of leasing} = \sum_{t=1}^{n} \frac{L_t(1-T)}{[1+(1-T)k_b]^t}$$

   a. The appropriate discount rate for the lessee's analysis is the after-tax cost of debt, since both the lease payments and the foregone depreciation tax shields are risk-free and tax deductible.
   b. The NAL will be zero (the "indifference result") if two conditions are met:
      (i) Lessor and lessee have the same tax rate.
      (ii) The lessor's after-tax weighted cost of capital is equal to the lessee's after-tax cost of debt.

C. The analysis of an operating lease follows the same logic except that the value of an American put option to cancel the lease and the expected salvage value of the asset are involved in the calculation.
   1. In an operating lease, the lessor must bear the risk involved in the use of the asset.
   2. The lease and depreciation cash flows are discounted at the after-tax cost of debt. The expected salvage value is discounted at an appropriate risk-adjusted rate. The value of the American put option must be subtracted from the present values of the aforementioned cash flows.

D. A capital budgeting analysis determines whether the project which requires the use of the equipment should be undertaken.
   1. The net cash flows from the project, which are the same under leasing or owning, are capitalized at the project's risk-adjusted weighted average cost of capital.
   2. The NPV of the project will be the gross present value of the benefits less the present value of the costs (of leasing or owning); if positive, accept the project; if negative, reject.
   3. The NPV of the project is determined as a standard capital budgeting problem:

$$NPV = -I_o + \sum_{t=1}^{n} \frac{(R_t - C_t)(1-T) + TDep_t}{(1+k)^t}$$

where $(R_t - C_t)$ = project cash flows before taxes
k = project risk-adjusted discount rate

A positive net present value indicates that the project should be financed; the higher NPV indicates the method of financing that should be used.

E. If the lessor can use accelerated depreciation methods, the annual lease-rental charge will be lower than if straight line depreciation is used, because with accelerated depreciation, the tax shelter comes in larger amounts in the early years. (See Problem 27.3.)
   1. If accelerated depreciation cannot be fully utilized by the user firm, the cost of owning will be greater than the cost of leasing; therefore there is an advantage to leasing.
   2. If the user firm can fully utilize accelerated depreciation benefits, the indifference result will again obtain.

V. Alternative Computation Procedures in the Leasing Analysis.
   A. The same results achieved using compact equations can be obtained through a worksheet methodology.
      1. The alternative to leasing is assumed to be borrowing the full amount to buy the asset.
         a. An amortization schedule is prepared showing the interest paid each year.
         b. A schedule of cash inflows and outflows is then prepared to determine the present value of after-tax cash flows.

(1) Annual loan payments are outflows.
(2) Interest payments are added to depreciation and multiplied by the applicable tax rate to find the yearly tax shelter - an inflow.
(3) Inflows are subtracted from outflows to obtain cash flows after taxes, and their present value is calculated.
(4) See Problem 27.2.

B. The internal rate of return approach compares the after-tax cost of leasing with the after-tax cost of debt.
   1. The cost of leasing is the discount rate that equates the present value of leasing payments, net of their tax shields plus the present value of the tax shields for depreciation and the investment tax credit which are being foregone, to the cost of the asset.
   2. Although this method seems to avoid the problem of determining which discount rate to use, this claim is illusory; this approach is fundamentally no different from the after-tax cost of debt method used above.

VI. Additional Factors That Affect the Lease Versus Own Decision.

A. Different costs of capital for the lessor versus the user firm.
   1. If the lessor has a lower cost of capital than the user firm, leasing will be cheaper to the user than owning. But it is difficult to visualize why the risk in the use of a capital asset, and therefore the applicable cost of capital, will be different whether the asset is owned by the lessor or the user.
   2. If the user firm has a lower cost of capital than the leasing company, it would seem more profitable to buy than to lease. But such firms would also find it profitable to enter the leasing business, eliminating any divergence.

B. Interest rates are frequently assumed to be higher in leasing than in borrowing.
   1. But this may reflect higher risks to lessors considering the credit ratings of the lessees.
   2. It may be difficult to separate money costs and the cost of other specialist services provided by the lessor.

C. Leasing may seem cheaper because no explicit maintenance costs are involved.
   1. But maintenance costs may be included in the calculation of the lease-rental rate.
   2. The key point is whether maintenance can be performed more cheaply by the lessor or by the independent firm.

D. Since the lessor owns the property at the expiration of the lease, it appears that owning is less expensive than leasing, but:
   1. Obsolescence of equipment may lead to low salvage values which favor leasing such equipment.
   2. It is argued that competition will force leasing rates down to the point where potentials of high residual values are recognized in the leasing rates.
   3. Since the obsolescence factor is usually not involved in decisions concerning land, lease-purchase decisions depend on investors' expectations:
      a. Optimistic expectations may lead to overestimates of future land values, raising the current purchase price so that the rate of return on owned land will be relatively low. Here leasing will be preferable.
      b. Owning will be preferable if probable increases in land values are not reflected in current prices.

E. Leasing costs are frequently assumed to be lower due to high obsolescence costs.
   1. But when obsolescence costs are high, lease-rental rates will reflect this.
   2. Also the lessor's reconditioning and marketing activity may enable it to find users for whom older equipment is still economical. This may reduce costs of obsolescence to both lessor and lessee.

F. Leasing may enhance credit availability.
   1. To acquire the use of a specific asset, it may be possible to obtain more money for a longer period under a lease arrangement than under secured borrowing.
   2. Leasing may have less impact on future borrowing capacity. However, offsetting factors include:
      a. Most lenders are aware of the implications of leasing on a firm's leverage position.
      b. Accounting regulations require disclosure of lease obligations.

G. If the lease period is much shorter than the asset's depreciable life, the lessee would have larger tax deductions under leasing than owning. The IRS limits the deductibility of lease payments that provide for an unduly rapid write-off of the lessor's costs.

H. If the lessor's tax rate is lower than the user's tax rate, or if there are tax subsidies available to the lessor and not to the user, there is an advantage to leasing over buying.

VII. Accounting for Leases.

A. Business firms must follow the standards set forth in FASB No. 13, issued by the Financial Accounting Standards Board in November 1976.

B. A lease is classified as a capital lease if it meets one or more of the following paragraph 7 criteria.

1. The lease transfers ownership to the lessee by the end of the lease term.
2. The lessee is given the option to purchase the property at a price sufficiently below the expected fair value so that it is very likely that the option will be exercised.
3. The lease term is equal to 75 percent or more of the estimated economic life of the property.
4. The present value of the minimum lease payments exceeds 90 percent of the fair value of the property at the inception of the lease.

C. From the standpoint of the lessor there are four types of leases.

1. Sales-type leases give rise to profit or loss to the lessor - the difference between the fair value of the property at the inception of the lease and the cost of carrying. Sales-type leases meet one of the four paragraph 7 criteria and both of the following two paragraph 8 criteria.
   a. Collectibility of the minimum lease payments is reasonably predictable.
   b. There are no important uncertainties surrounding the unreimbursable costs to be incurred by the lessor.
2. Direct financing leases must meet the same criteria as sales-type leases, however, the fair value of the property at the inception of the lease is equal to its carrying cost.
3. Leveraged leases are direct financing leases where substantial financing is provided by a long-term creditor on a nonrecourse basis with respect to the general credit of the lessor.
4. Operating leases are all leases other than those discussed above.

D. From the standpoint of the lessee, there are two types of leases.

1. Operating leases
   a. Rentals are expensed
   b. Future rental obligations must be disclosed
2. Capital leases must be capitalized and shown on the balance sheet as a fixed-asset and as a noncurrent obligation.

a. Capitalization represents the present value of minimum lease payments minus that portion of lease payments representing executory costs (insurance, maintenance, etc.).
   (1) The discount factor is the lower of the implicit rate used by the lessor and the lessee's incremental borrowing rate.
   (2) The asset is amortized in a manner consistent with the lessee's depreciation policy.

b. Lease payments are allocated between:
   (1) A reduction of the lease obligation
   (2) Interest expense

Chapter 27 - Illustrative Problems and Solutions

27.1 The Pierce Company produces commercial canning machines which it sells for $45,000. The machines have a 10-year life with no expected salvage value. Pierce would like to offer its customers a lease arrangement as an alternative to purchasing, and is trying to decide on an appropriate annual lease rental rate. Pierce has a 9 percent cost of capital and a 40 percent tax rate. (Assume straight line depreciation.)

a. What is the equilibrium lease-rental rate?

b. The H.V. Packing Company needs a new canning machine and is trying to decide whether to lease the machine or to borrow to be able to buy it. The machine will produce net benefits of $18,000 per year. H.V.'s cost of debt is 15 percent, its cost of capital is 18 percent, and its tax rate is 40 percent. The firm uses straight line depreciation. Which alternative is better?

c. Green Valley Growers is also contemplating the purchase of a canning machine. Green Valley has a better credit rating than H.V. Packing and so its cost of debt is only 11.67 percent. Should Green Valley lease or purchase the machine? (Assume straight line depreciation and a 40 percent tax rate.)

Solution:

a. $$NPV_{LOR} = 0 = -I_o + \sum_{t=1}^{n} \frac{L_t(1-T)}{(1+k)^t} + \sum_{t=1}^{n} \frac{TDep_t}{(1+k)^t}$$

$$0 = -I_o + L_t(1-T)(PVIFA,k,n) + TDep_t(PVIFA,k,n)$$

$$0 = -\$45,000 + L_t(1-.4)(PVIFA,9\%,10 \text{ yrs})$$

$$+ (.4)(\$4,500)(PVIFA,9\%,10 \text{ yrs})$$

$$0 = -\$45,000 + L_t(.6)(6.4177) + (\$1,800)(6.4177)$$

$$0 = -\$45,000 + 3.85062L_t + \$11,551.86$$

$$\$33,448.14 = 3.85062L_t$$

$$L_t = \$8,686.43$$

b. $$\text{Cost of borrowing} = I_o - \sum_{t=1}^{n} \frac{TDep_t}{[1+(1-T)k_b]^t}$$

$$= \$45,000 - \sum_{t=1}^{10} \frac{(.4)(\$4,500)}{[1+(.6)(.15)]^t}$$

$$= \$45,000 - \$1,800(PVIFA,9\%,10 \text{ yrs})$$

$$= \$45,000 - \$1,800(6.4177)$$

$$= \$33,448.14$$

$$\text{Cost of leasing} = \sum_{t=1}^{10} \frac{L_t(1-T)}{[1+(1-T)k_b]^t}$$

$$= \sum_{t=1}^{10} \frac{\$8,686.43(1-.4)}{[1+(.6)(.15)]^t}$$

$$= \$8,686.43(.6)(PVIFA,9\%,10 \text{ yrs})$$

$$= \$8,686.43(.6)(6.4177)$$

$$= \$33,448.14$$

H.V. will be indifferent to owning or leasing the machine.

c. Cost of borrowing $= \$45{,}000 - \sum_{t=1}^{10} \frac{(.4)(\$4{,}500)}{[1+(.6)(.1167)]^t}$

$= \$45{,}000 - \$1{,}800(\text{PVIFA},7\%,10 \text{ yrs})$

$= \$45{,}000 - \$1{,}800(7.0236)$

$= \$32{,}357.52$

Cost of leasing $= \sum_{t=1}^{10} \frac{\$8{,}686.43(.6)}{[1+(.6)(.1167)]^t}$

$= \$5{,}211.86(7.0236)$

$= \$36{,}606.02$

Green Valley will prefer to purchase the machine rather than to lease it from Pierce. This is because Green Valley's after-tax cost of debt is lower than Pierce's cost of capital.

27.2 The Schultz Transfer Company needs a new long-distance moving van, which costs \$53,000, has an estimated life of 6 years and an estimated salvage value of \$11,000. Schultz can take out a loan for \$53,000 repayable in 6 equal payments at 10 percent interest. As an alternative, Schultz can lease the truck at an annual rate of \$15,000 per year. If owned, Schultz will have maintenance expenses of \$2,000 annually. Assume straight line depreciation and a 40 percent tax rate. Schultz's cost of capital is 16 percent.

a. What is the present value of the after-tax cost of leasing for the 6-year period?
b. What are the yearly payments required to amortize the loan? What is the present value of these payments?
c. How are the yearly loan payments divided between interest and amortization of principal? What is the present value of the interest tax shelter?
d. What is the depreciation tax shelter under the borrow-purchase arrangement?
e. What is the present value (after-tax) of the maintenance costs? (5 percent is the discount rate applicable to the risk of the maintenance costs.)
f. What is the present value of the estimated salvage value? (Assume that the cost of capital relevant to the project is the cost of capital of the firm.)
g. What is the total net after-tax cost of the borrow-purchase alternative?
h. Which method of acquisition involves the lower net outflows?
i. What effects would accelerated depreciation have had on the decision?
j. Suppose the actual salvage value turned out to be zero. Which alternative now has the lower costs?

Solution:

a. Lease: Discount rate = $k_b(1-T)$ = .10(.6)
= .06

$$\text{After-tax cost of leasing} = \sum_{t=1}^{6} \frac{L_t(1-T)}{(1.06)^t}$$

= $15,000(.6)(PVIFA,6%,6 yrs)

=$9,000(4.9173)

=$44,256

b. Annual payment:

$53,000 = a/PVIFA(10%,6 yrs)
$53,000 = a/4.3553
a = $12,169

PV of annual payments:
= $12,169(PVIFA,6%,6 yrs)
= $12,169(4.9173)
= $59,839

c. See next page.

d. $$\text{Annual depreciation} = \frac{\$53{,}000-11{,}000}{6}$$

= $7,000

PV of depreciation tax shelter
= (.4)($7,000)(PVIFA,6%,6 yrs)
= $2,800(4.9173)
= $13,768

e. After-tax maintenance costs = $2,000(.6)
= $1,200
PV of after-tax maintenance costs
= $1,200(PVIFA,5%,6 yrs) = $1,200(5.0757) = $6,091

f. PV of salvage value = $11,000(PVIF,16%,6 yrs)
= $11,000(.4104)
= $4,514

Year (1)	Balance Owed (2)	Interest .10x(2) (3)	Amortization $12,169-(3) (4)	Interest Tax Shelter .4x(3) (5)	PV Factor at 6% (6)	PV of Interest Tax Shelter (5)x(6) (7)
1	$53,000	$5,300	$ 6,869	$2,120	.9434	$2,000
2	46,131	4,613	7,556	1,845	.8900	1,642
3	38,575	3,858	8,311	1,543	.8396	1,296
4	30,264	3,026	9,143	1,210	.7921	958
5	21,121	2,112	10,057	845	.7473	631
6	11,064	1,106	11,063	442	.7050	312

PV of interest tax shelter = $6,839

g. Borrow-Purchase Outflows:

PV of loan payments	$59,839	
PV of maintenance costs	6,091	$65,930
Less:		
PV of interest tax shelter	$ 6,839	
PV of depreciation tax shelter	13,768	
PV of salvage value	4,514	25,121
Net cost of borrow-purchase arrangement		$40,809

h. After-tax cost of leasing	44,256
Advantage to owning	$ 3,447

i. Accelerated depreciation would have made owning even more attractive due to a larger depreciation tax shelter.

j. The cost of owning would be increased by the present value of the salvage value, $4,514. Depreciation would not be affected since it is based on the expected salvage value, not the actual.

Cost of owning = $40,809 + $4,514	=	$45,323
Cost of leasing	=	44,256
Advantage of leasing		$ 1,067

This illustrates the sensitivity of the lease versus purchase analysis to various inputs. Maintenance costs might also have turned out to be higher than originally estimated, similarly altering the decision after the fact. The decision to lease or purchase must be made on the basis of the best estimates available at the time, adjusted for risk. However, both the estimates and the risk-adjustment factors may be in error. The greater uncertainty attached to certain elements in the purchase analysis may make the lease alternative more attractive when the advantage to owning is slight.

27.3 The Lancaster Corporation wants to acquire an extruding machine at the lowest possible cost. Such machines cost $35,000, or they can be leased for $6,950 per year. Lancaster can borrow at a 10 percent interest rate; the company's cost of capital is 14 percent and the corporate tax rate is 40 percent. The machine has an economic life of 7 years and no salvage value. Lancaster uses straight line depreciation.

a. Which method of financing the machine is less costly?

b. If Lancaster used sum-of-years'-digits depreciation, which method of financing would be less costly?

Solution:

a. Discount rate = .10(1-.4)
= .06

$$\text{Cost of leasing} = \sum_{t=1}^{n} \frac{L_t(1-T)}{(1+k)^t}$$

= \$6,950(.6)(PVIFA,6%,7 yrs)
= \$4,170(5.5824)
= \$23,279

$$\text{Cost of owning} = \$35{,}000 - \sum_{t=1}^{n} \frac{TDep_t}{(1+k)^t}$$

= \$35,000 - (.4)(\$5,000)(5.5824)
= \$23,835

Advantage to leasing = \$23,835 - \$23,279
= \$556

b. In Appendix C, we find the present value factor for S-Y-D depreciation over 7 years at a 6 percent cost of capital is 0.844.

Cost of owning = \$35,000 - (.4)(\$35,000)(.844)
= \$23,184
Advantage to owning = \$23,279-\$23,184
= \$95

Using accelerated depreciation would change Lancaster's decision since with S-Y-D depreciation the purchase alternative has the lower cost.

CHAPTER 28

WARRANTS AND CONVERTIBLES

Theme: In general, a firm receives no benefit from transactions involving put and call options on its common stock. Warrants and convertibles are particular forms of options which do benefit the firm. Warrants are options to purchase common stock bringing additional funds to the firm. Convertible debt or preferred stock can be exchanged for common stock.

I. Warrants Are Long-Term Options Issued by the Firm.
   A. Warrants permit their holders to buy a stated number of shares of common stock at a stated exercise price for a specified period.
   B. Warrants are often sold with bonds or preferred stock to make the issue more attractive by enabling investors to share in the company's growth.
   C. Some characteristics of warrants include the following:
      1. Warrants may be nondetachable or detachable so that they can be traded separately.
      2. An antidilution clause is customary to protect the warrant in the event of a stock dividend or stock split by adjusting the exercise price.

II. Determinants of the Value of a Warrant.
   A. Formula value of a warrant:
      1. Formula value = (Market price of common stock - Exercise price) x (Number of shares each warrant entitles owner to purchase)
      2. When the stock price is less than the exercise price, the formula value is defined as zero.
   B. Warrants usually sell at a price above the formula value.
      1. The "percent premium" is calculated as

$$\frac{\text{Actual price of warrant - Formula value of warrant}}{\text{Stock price x Number of shares per warrant}}$$

      2. The actual price (and thus the percent premium) relates to the underlying determinants of any option value. Price will be higher (other things being equal) if:
         a. Stock price is higher.
         b. Exercise price is lower.
         c. Variance of stock returns is higher.
         d. Time to maturity is longer.
         e. Risk-free rate is higher.

C. Under certain assumptions, the value of a warrant can be expressed as a proportion of the value of a call option.

1. $W = \frac{1}{(1+q)} C$

   where W = value of warrant
   q = ratio of warrants to shares
   C = value of call option with the same exercise price and maturity as the warrant

2. Warrants are thus perfectly correlated with options and have the same systematic risk and required return.

III. Use of Warrants in Financing.

A. From the point of view of the issuing firm, warrants are used as sweeteners to improve financing terms.
   1. Large, strong firms may use warrants when issuing debt during a period of high interest rates.
   2. High-risk, growth firms may not be able to sell straight debt without extremely high interest rates unless they include options.

B. From the point of view of investors, warrants have the potential to increase rate of return.
   1. High-tax bracket investors can take part of their return in capital gains instead of more highly taxed interest income.
   2. Investment bankers receive additional compensation for the risk they bear in bringing out the common stock of an unestablished firm.

C. Exercise of warrants brings in additional financing to the firm.
   1. When warrants are issued the exercise price is typically set at 15 to 25 percent higher than the current stock price.
   2. As the firm grows and prospers, the stock price rises above the warrant exercise price and warrants are exercised, bringing in additional equity funding for continued growth.

IV. Convertible securities are bonds or preferred stock which are exchangeable for common stock at the holder's option. Typical terms of the conversion privilege include the following.

A. The conversion ratio - the number of shares of common stock for which the convertible may be exchanged.

B. The conversion price - the effective price paid per share of common stock upon conversion.

1. $$\text{Conversion price} = \frac{\text{Par value of convertible security}}{\text{Number of shares received on conversion}}$$

2. Usually the conversion premium is 15 to 20 percent above market price at the time the convertible is issued; that is, the conversion price exceeds the market price of the stock by 15 to 20 percent.
3. Some convertibles have decreasing ratios (increasing or stepped-up conversion prices) over time.

C. Most convertibles are callable at the option of the company. The price which must be paid when a convertible is called is called the call price. If the call price is below the conversion value, this gives the firm a means of forcing conversion.

D. Convertibles also include a clause protecting the holder against dilution due to stock splits, stock dividends, and the sale of common stock at low prices. The provision usually states that:
1. No common stock can be sold at a price below the conversion price.
2. The conversion price must be lowered by the percentage amount of any stock dividend or split.

V. Rationale for the Use of Convertibles.

A. The traditional view for using convertibles has been to obtain a lower coupon rate while the conversion price was equivalent to selling common stock at a premium over its current market price.

B. The current view is that convertible bonds are a combination of straight debt plus an option.
1. The cost and value of convertible bonds are less sensitive to the uncertainty associated with future firm or project cash flows.
2. The value of debt falls with increased risk; that is, the cost of debt rises with increased risk.
3. The value of options rises with increased risk.

C. The cost of convertible debt is a weighted average of the cost of straight debt and the cost of equity.
1. The coupon rate on convertible debt is lower than the coupon rate on comparable straight debt.
2. Convertibility reduces the coupon relatively more for higher risk firms; the convertible bondholder in high risk firms takes a greater proportion of his compensation in the value of the option.

D. Environments of high uncertainty impose greater risk on bondholders, and favor options (warrants or convertibles).
1. Low stock and bond ratings indicate an uncertain outlook.
2. Agency problems arise because shareholders can increase the risk of the firm.
    a. Options enable bondholders to participate in shareholder gains.
    b. Options are a less costly solution than bond covenant precluding adverse actions or higher interest rates to compensate for them.

3. Periods of general uncertainty in the economy hurt bondholders in two ways:
   a. Recession increases the risk of firm bankruptcy.
   b. Inflation reduces the purchasing power of bondholders' fixed return.
4. International markets impose the risk of adverse political actions by foreign governments and exchange rate risk.
5. Empirical evidence supports the thesis that the greater the uncertainty, the greater the use of convertibles.

E. Tax considerations may also favor the use of options.
   1. Interest tax shield is reduced by the lower interest payments on convertible debt.
   2. Firms with less need for interest tax shields are more likely to use convertibles.

VI. Valuation of Convertible Bonds.

A. One approach to the valuation of call options (and thus indirectly the valuation of convertible bonds) is to create a duplicating portfolio whose payoffs are identical to those of a portfolio of call options on 100 shares of stock.

1. Data to illustrate the duplicating portfolio approach to the binomial option pricing model is listed below:

   S_o = current stock price = \$32

   X = exercise price = \$30

   $1+R_F$ = 1 plus the risk-free rate = 1.08

   u = multiplicative upward movement in stock price = 1.25

   d = multiplicative downward movement in stock price = .75

   S^h = higher possible end-of-period stock price = uS_o = \$40

   S^L = lower possible end-of period stock price = dS_o = \$24

   C^h = higher possible end-of-period call value $= S^h - X = \$40 - \$30 = \$10$

   C^L = lower possible end-of-period call value $= \text{MAX}[0,\ S^L - X] = \text{MAX}[0,\ \$24-\$30] = 0$

   h = hedge ratio $= \dfrac{\text{number of stock shares}}{\text{number of calls sold}}$

   B = beginning-of-period borrowings required in addition to long position in stock (from the hedge ratio) to duplicate a 100-share call option contract

2. We first calculate the hedge ratio and required borrowings:

$$h = \frac{C^h - C^L}{S^h - S^L} = \frac{\$10-0}{\$40-\$24} = \frac{\$10}{\$16} = .625$$

$$B = \frac{100}{1+R_F}[hS^L - C^L] = \frac{100}{1.08}[(.625)(24)-0]$$
$$= 92.59(15)$$
$$= \$1,388.85$$

Thus, the duplicating portfolio consists of a long position in 62.5 shares of stock plus borrowing of $1,388.85 at the risk-free rate.

3. We then find the value of the 100 calls.

$$C = 100hS_o - B = 100(.625)(32) - 1,388.85$$
$$= \$2,000 - \$1,388.85$$
$$= \$611.15$$

4. The value of the duplicating portfolio is equivalent to the value of the 100 calls, $611.15.

Current value of 62.5 shares @ $32	$2,000.00
Less: Borrowing	1,388.85
Value of duplicating portfolio	$ 611.15

5. Next we demonstrate the equivalence of payoffs between the two portfolios
   a. <u>If high value of stock occurs</u>:

Duplicating portfolio:	
62.5 shares @ $40	$2,500
Less: Borrowing + interest $1,388.85(1.08)	1,500
Payoff	$1,000
Call option portfolio:	
100 calls @ $10	$1,000

   b. <u>If low value of stock occurs</u>:

Duplicating portfolio:	
62.5 shares @ $24	$1,500
Less: Borrowing + interest	1,500
Payoff	0
Call option portfolio:	
100 calls @ $0	0

6. The same methodology can be adapted to the valuation of a portfolio of put options, except that we have lending, not borrowing, in the duplicating portfolio.

$$P^h = MAX[0, X-S^h]$$
$$P^L = X-S^L$$
$$h^P = \frac{P^h - P^L}{S^h - S^L}$$

$$L^P = \frac{100}{1+R_F}[P^L - h^P S^L]$$

$$P = 100h^P S_o + L^P$$

B. The binomial option pricing model (BOP) builds on the duplicating portfolio approach to the valuation of call options to value straight debt and convertible debt.

1. The BOP approach involves creating a portfolio which duplicates the cash flows of the convertible (or straight debt) issue.
   a. The portfolio consists of a position in the debt and equity of the firm, plus borrowing or lending at the risk-free rate.
   b. The value of the portfolio is the same as the value of the convertible or straight debt issue.
   c. Examples are presented below.
2. Data for BOP valuation model:

   V = current market value of firm = \$20,000,000

   V_d = lower possible value, end of period = \$10,000,000

   V_u = upper possible value, end of period = \$25,000,000

   D_1 = face value of debt, end of period = \$15,000,000

   C = value of duplicating portfolio = value of contingent claim held by bondholders

   - C_u = upper possible end-of-period value
   - C_d = lower possible end-of-period value
   - C_f = present value of straight debt
   - C_{fc} = present value of convertible debt

   R_F = risk-free rate = 12 percent

   N_o = initial number of shares = 1,500,000

   CP = conversion price = \$5 per share

3. Valuation of straight debt:
   a. For straight debtholders, the best possible outcome is that they will be repaid the face value of the debt. Thus, $C_u = D_1$ = \$15,000,000.
   b. Straight debtholders receive the lower of the face value of debt or the value of the firm. Since in this case V_d is less than D_1, $C_d = V_d$ = \$10,000,000.
   c. $$h = \frac{C_u - C_d}{V_u - V_d} = \frac{15{,}000{,}000 - 10{,}000{,}000}{25{,}000{,}000 - 10{,}000{,}000} = \frac{5{,}000{,}000}{15{,}000{,}000} = .333$$

   The duplicating portfolio contains one third of the firm's debt and equity.

d. $L = \frac{1}{1+R_F}(hV_d - C_d) = \frac{1}{1.12}[.333(10,000,000)-10,000,000]$

$$= \frac{-6,667,000}{1.12}$$

$$= -\$5,953,000$$

The duplicating portfolio is completed by lending \$5,953,000 at the risk-free rate.

e. $C_f = hV-L = .333(20,000,000) - (-5,953,000)$

$$= \$12,620,000$$

The value of the straight debt is \$12.62 million. The present value of the face value of the debt discounted at the risk-free rate is \$13.39 million. The difference of \$.77 million represents the premium that must be paid to bondholders to compensate them for the risk that the lower value outcome may occur, in which case they would suffer a \$5 million loss.

4. Valuation of convertible debt:

a. ΔN = number of shares created if conversion occurs

$$= D_1/CP = 15,000,000/5 = 3,000,000$$

$\Delta N+N_o$ = total number of shares after conversion = N_1

$$= 3,000,000 + 1,500,000 = 4,500,000$$

b. If the upper firm value occurs, $V_u = \$25,000,000$;

$$CV = \text{conversion value} = \frac{V_u}{N_1} = \frac{25}{4.5} = \$5.55$$

c. The upper value for convertible debtholders will be the higher of the face value of the debt or the total conversion value. In this case, the total conversion value is calculated as

$$TCV = CV(N_o) = \$5.55(3,000,000) = \$16,650,000$$

Since the total conversion value exceeds the end-of-period face value of debt, conversion will occur. Thus, $C_u = TCV = \$16,650,000$.

d. At the lower possible outcome, V_d is less than D_1; thus, $C_d = V_d = \$10,000,000$.

e. $h = \frac{C_u - C_d}{V_u - V_d} = \frac{16,650,000-10,000,000}{25,000,000-10,000,000} = \frac{6.65}{15} = .44$

The duplicating portfolio contains 44 percent of the firm's debt and equity.

f. $L = \frac{1}{1+R_F}(hV_d - C_d) = \frac{1}{1.12}[.44(10,000,000)-10,000,000]$

$= \frac{-5,600,000}{1.12}$

$= -\$5,000,000$

The duplicating portfolio is completed by lending $5,000,000 at the risk-free rate.

g. $C_{fc} = hV - L = .44(20,000,000) - 5,000,000$

$= \$13,800,000$

The value of the convertible debt is $13,800,000.

5. Since a convertible may be considered as straight debt plus a warrant for stock, the implicit value of the warrant can be found as:

Value of warrant $= C_{fc} - C_f = 13,800,000-12,620,000$

$= \$1,180,000$

C. The cost of convertible debt is, on average, higher than the cost of straight debt.
   1. The coupon rate is typically lower than the coupon rate on straight debt.
   2. The second, riskier, component is based on the expected rise in the price of the underlying common stock.

VII. Call Policy Issues.
   A. In theory, the optimal call policy is to call a bond when its conversion value equals its call price; in practice, bonds are not called until the conversion value exceeds the call price by around 40 percent.
      1. Firms call bonds to force conversion; they do not want to redeem the bonds.
      2. Bondholders must be given 30 days notice; firms want a cushion to protect themselves against stock price fluctuations during this interval.
      3. In theory, this cushion need be only 6 to 8 percent; possible reasons for the divergence include the following.

a. If management compensation is tied to primary (undiluted) earnings per share, they may wish to delay conversion.
b. The market memory theory suggests that firms with an early (or erratic) call policy may have to pay higher rates on any subsequent convertible issues.

B. The call policy of the firm influences the rate of return received by convertible purchasers, and is the basis for a simplified convertible valuation model.

1. The conversion value of the bond at any given time is found as

$$C_t = p_o(1+g)^t q$$

where C_t = conversion value at time t
p_o = initial price of underlying stock
g = growth rate in price of stock
q = conversion ratio
q = face value of debt/conversion price

2. The _ex post_ return on a convertible bond is a function of the price paid for the bond, the coupon rate and the call policy of the firm.

$$B_{co} = \sum_{t=1}^{n} \frac{c}{(1+k_c)^t} + \frac{C_n}{(1+k_c)^n}$$

where B_{co} = price paid for the convertible
c = coupon interest payments
n = time of conversion
C_n = terminal value received on conversion
k_c = return on the convertible bond

3. The _ex ante_ yield is dependent on a number of random variables and may be estimated using expectations of the firm's growth rate and call policy.

C. Convertible calls are associated with a decline in stock prices. Possible explanations include the following:

1. Interest tax shelter is reduced by reduction in debt.
2. The call conveys negative information about the firm's future prospects.

Chapter 28 - Illustrative Problems and Solutions

28.1 At the time of issue, what price relationship generally exists between the subscription price on warrants and the market price of common stock?

Solution:
The subscription price of warrants is generally above the market price of the stock; that of rights is set below the stock price.

28.2 True or False? Warrants generally sell above their formula value.

Solution:
True. This is always true unless arbitrageurs fail to fulfill their function.

28.3 In which of the following cases would current financing by means of debt with warrants be inappropriate?

a. External funds needed now but no additional requirement expected for many years.
b. External funds needed now with a continuing requirement for additional funds.
c. A large amount of external funds needed now with diminishing requirements expected for next several years.
d. Some external funds needed now with an expected increase in funds required for next several years.

Solution:
a.

28.4 Where is the conversion price on a convertible bond usually set?

Solution:
Above the price of the stock.

28.5 True or False? The coupon rate on a convertible bond is usually higher than on an equivalent straight bond.

Solution:
False. It is typically lower because of the advantage to the investor of the conversion privilege. So, the coupon rate is usually lower than k_b.

28.6 A firm can sell convertible debentures with a 6 percent coupon rate when the conversion price is set 20 percent above the current market price. If the firm wishes to lower the coupon rate to 5 percent, it will probably have to:

a. Increase the conversion price.
b. Decrease the conversion price.
c. Increase the conversion ratio.
d. Decrease the conversion ratio.

Solution:
b and c. In order to compensate for the lower coupon rate, the conversion price should be decreased. And a decrease in the conversion price entails an increase in the conversion ratio.

28.7 Weatherell Corporation's bonds have warrants attached enabling bondholders to purchase 1 share of stock at $25 per share. Compute the formula value of a warrant if:

a. The current market price of Weatherell stock is $23.50 per share.
b. The current market price is $27 per share.
c. The current market price is $30 per share.
d. Each warrant entitles you to purchase 3 shares at $25 each and the current stock price is $30 per share.

Solution:

a. Formula Value = (Market price - Option price)(number of shares)

= ($23.50 - 25) (1)

= -$1.50

Price would be slightly higher than zero.

b. ($27 - 25) (1) = $2.00
c. ($30 - 25) (1) = $5.00
d. ($30 - 25) (3) = $15.00

28.8 A convertible bond with a face value of $1,000 and a 12 percent coupon rate is convertible to stock at $50; that is, each bond can be exchanged for 20 shares of common stock. The current stock price is $36 per share.

a. If the price per share grows at 8 percent per year for the next five years, what will be the approximate conversion value at the end of five years?
b. If dividends on the stock are presently $2.50 per share, and if these also grow at 8 percent per year, will the bondholders convert after five years? Explain.
c. If the bonds are callable at a 5 percent premium, how much would you lose per bond if the bonds were called at the end of five years?

Solution:

a. $p_5 = p_0$[FVIF(8%,5 yrs)]
= \$36(1.4693)
= \$52.89

Conversion value at end of 5 years = 20 x \$52.89
= \$1,057.80

b. $d_5 = d_0$[FVIF(8%,5 yrs)]
=\$2.50(1.4693)
= \$3.67

Dividend income = 20 x \$3.67
= \$73.40

Bondholders would prefer not to convert because the dividend income would be lower than the coupon interest.

c. Loss per bond = \$1,057.80 - \$1,050.00
= \$7.80

28.9 Foothill Ford Company needs financing of \$250,000, and is trying to decide whether to issue convertible debentures or debentures with warrants. Foothill's present balance sheet is shown below:

Balance Sheet 1

Current assets	\$200,000	Current debt	\$250,000
Net fixed assets	300,000	Common stock, \$10 par	100,000
		Retained earnings	150,000
Total assets	\$500,000	Total claims	\$500,000

With spontaneous financing and retained earnings, next year's balance sheet is projected below:

Balance Sheet 2

Current assets	\$350,000	Current debt	\$250,000
Net fixed assets	450,000	Debentures	250,000
		Common stock, \$10 par	100,000
		Retained earnings	200,000
Total assets	\$800,000	Total claims	\$800,000

The convertible debentures will pay 8 percent interest and will be convertible into 50 shares of common stock for each \$1,000 debenture. The debentures with warrants will carry a 10 percent coupon and entitle each holder of a \$1,000 debenture to buy 20 shares of common stock at \$50. Foothill's earnings before interest and taxes are 18 percent of total assets, its P/E ratio is 12, and the corporate tax rate is 40 percent.

a. Assuming that convertible debentures are issued and that all are later converted, prepare a new balance sheet and the corresponding income statement for Foothill Ford.

b. Assuming instead that debentures with warrants are issued and that all are exercised, prepare a new balance sheet and the corresponding income statement.
c. Compute the EPS and the market price per share for each alternative.
d. Should Foothill Ford issue convertible debentures or debentures with warrants?

Solution:

a. Addition to common stock = 50 shares x 250 debentures x $10 par value
= $125,000

Paid-in capital = $250,000 - $125,000
= $125,000

Balance Sheet

		Current debt	$250,000
		Common stock, $10 par	225,000
		Paid-in capital	125,000
		Retained earnings	200,000
Total assets	$800,000	Total claims	$800,000

Income Statement

EBIT (18% of total assets)	$144,000
Interest expense	0
Taxable income	$144,000
Tax (at 40%)	57,600
Net income	$ 86,400

b. Addition to common stock = 20 shares x 250 debentures x $10 par value
= $50,000

Total option price = $50 option price x 5,000 new shares
= $250,000

Paid-in capital = $250,000 - $50,000
= $200,000

Balance Sheet

		Current debt	$ 250,000
		Debentures (10%)	250,000
		Common stock, $10 par	150,000
		Paid-in capital	200,000
		Retained earnings	200,000
Total assets	$1,050,000	Total claims	$1,050,000

Income Statement

EBIT (18% of total assets)	$189,000
Interest expense	25,000
Taxable income	$164,000
Tax (at 40%)	65,600
Net income	$ 98,400

c. Convertible debentures:
EPS = $86,400/(10,000+12,500) = $3.84
Share price = $3.84 x 12 = $46.08

Debentures with warrants:
EPS = $98,400/(10,000+5,000) = $6.56
Share price = $6.56 x 12 = $78.72

d. Foothill Ford should choose the debentures with warrants attached. It results in a higher share price. The reason is that the problem assumed a profitability rate higher than the cost of both debt and equity. The debentures with warrants result in more leverage and more total financing and investment.

28.10 Jay Arnold has purchased a callable 20-year convertible bond recently issued by the Ramsay Corporation. The coupon rate on the bond is 12 percent. Each bond is convertible into 80 shares of Ramsay common stock. The price of the underlying stock at issue date is $10.40. The stock price is expected to grow at a rate of 7 percent per year. Based on past experience, Arnold expects Ramsay to call the bond as soon as its conversion value rises 40 percent above the call price. The initial call premium is $50, declining by $5 per year; beyond 10 years, the bond is callable at par.

a. If Arnold paid $1,058 for the bond, what is his _ex ante_ expected rate of return?
b. After reading several financial journal articles on convertible bonds, the chief financial officer of Ramsay Corporation has decided that the call should be made as soon as the conversion value rises 6 percent above the call price. If this policy is followed, what will Arnold's _ex post_ rate of return be?

Solution:

a.

Year	Conversion Value $p_o(1+g)^t q = C_t$		Call Price	Call Price x 1.40
1	$10.4(1.07)^1(80)$	= \$890	\$1050	\$1470
2	$832(1.07)^2$	= 953	1045	1463
3	$832(1.07)^3$	= 1019	1040	1456
4	$832(1.07)^4$	= 1090	1035	1449
5	$832(1.07)^5$	= 1167	1030	1442
6	$832(1.07)^6$	= 1249	1025	1435
7	$832(1.07)^7$	= 1336	1020	1428
8	$832(1.07)^8$	= 1429	1015	1421

The above tabulation shows that the call and forced conversion are expected after approximately 8 years.

Arnold's *ex ante* expected rate of return is found by solving the equation below for k_c.

$$B_{co} = \sum_{t=1}^{n} \frac{c}{(1+k_c)^t} + \frac{C_n}{(1+k_c)^n}$$

where B_{co} = price paid for the stock = \$1058
c = interest payments = \$120
n = time of conversion = 8
C_n = conversion value = \$1429

$$1058 = \sum_{t=1}^{8} \frac{120}{(1+k_c)^t} + \frac{1429}{(1+k_c)^8}$$

$$1058 = 120[\text{PVIFA}(k_c, 8 \text{ years})] + 1429[\text{PVIF}(k_c, 8 \text{ years}]$$

Using trial and error, we find that Arnold's *ex ante* expected rate of return is 14 percent.

b.

Year	Conversion Price	Call Price x 1.06
1	$ 890	$1113
2	953	1108
3	1019	1102
4	1090	1097

The conversion price is approximately 6 percent above the call price after about 4 years. Arnold's <u>ex post</u> return is thus solved as

$$1058 = \sum_{t=1}^{4} \frac{120}{(1+k_c)^t} + \frac{1090}{(1+k_c)^4}$$

Using trial and error, we find that the <u>ex post</u> rate of return is approximately 12 percent. This is 2 percentage points below the <u>ex ante</u> expected return. It is likely that Ramsay might have to pay a higher return on any subsequent issues of convertible bonds to compensate investors against the possibility of early forced conversion.

28.11 The Karrol Corporation has a current market value of $50 million with 4 million shares of common stock outstanding. If the firm's current investment policy is successful, its value at the end of one period is expected to be $75 million; if unsuccessful, end-of-period value is expected to be $20 million. The firm has debt outstanding on which the face value of $25 million must be repaid at the end of the period. The risk-free rate is 10 percent.

a. Use the BOP model to find the present value of Karrol's debt if the debt is non-convertible.
b. If the debt is convertible with a conversion price of $4.50 per share, what is the present value of the convertible debt.

Solution:

Using BOP notation, the data of the problem is represented below:

V = current value of the firm = $50 million

V_u = upper possible end-of-period value = $75 million

V_d = lower possible end-of-period value = $20 million

D_1 = end-of-period face value of debt = $25 million

R_F = risk-free rate = 10 percent

N_o = initial number of shares = 4 million

CP = conversion price = $4.50

a. For straight debt: $C_u = D_1 = \$25$ million.

$V_d < D_1$, thus $C_d = V_d = \$20$ million

$$h = \frac{C_u - C_d}{V_u - V_d} = \frac{25-20}{75-20} = \frac{5}{55} = .091$$

$$L = \frac{1}{1+R_F}(hV_d - C_d) = \frac{1}{1.10}[.091(20)-20]$$

$$= \frac{-18.18}{1.10}$$

$$= -\$16.53 \text{ million}$$

The duplicating portfolio consists of 9.1 percent of Karrol's debt and equity, plus lending \$16.53 million at the risk-free rate.

The value of the duplicating portfolio (and of Karrol's straight debt) is

$$C_f = hV - L = .091(50)-(-16.53)$$

$$= 4.55 + 16.53$$

$$= \$21.08 \text{ million}$$

The present value of the face value of debt discounted at the risk-free rate is

$$\frac{\$25}{1.10} = \$22.73 \text{ million}$$

The difference is \$1.65 million; this represents the premium over the risk-free rate demanded by bondholders to compensate them for the risk that the lower value outcome might occur.

b. For convertbile debtholders:

If the upper value outcome occurs, $V_u = \$75{,}000{,}000$

ΔN = number of shares created by conversion

$$= \frac{D_1}{CP} = \frac{25 \text{ million}}{4.50} = 5.6 \text{ million shares}$$

$\Delta N + N_o$ = total number of shares after conversion = N_1 = 5.6 + 4 = 9.6 million shares

$$CV = \text{conversion value} = \frac{V_u}{N_1} = \frac{75}{9.6} = \$7.81$$

$$TCV = \text{total conversion value} = CV(N_o) = 7.81(5.6)$$

$$= \$43.74 \text{ million}$$

Since the total conversion value exceeds the end-of-period face value of debt, bondholders will convert. Thus C_u = total conversion value = \$43.74 million.

Since V_d is less than D_1, $C_d = V_d$ = \$20 million

$$h = \frac{C_u - C_d}{V_u - V_d} = \frac{43.74-20}{75-20} = \frac{23.74}{55} = .432$$

$$L = \frac{1}{1+R_F}(h\,V_d - C_d) = \frac{1}{1.10}[.432(20)-20]$$

$$= \frac{-11.36}{1.10} = -\$10.33 \text{ million}$$

The duplicating portfolio consists of 43.2 percent of Karrol's debt and equity, plus lending \$10.33 million at the risk-free rate.

$$C_{fc} = h\,V - L = .432(50) - (-10.33)$$

$$= 21.6 + 10.33$$

$$= \$31.93 \text{ million} = \text{value of convertible}$$

The value of the warrant to buy common stock implicit in the convertible debt is the difference between the value of convertible debt and the value of straight debt; in this case,

$$C_{fc} - C_f = 31.93 - 21.08$$

$$= \$10.85 \text{ million}$$

28.12 Cassell Company had net income in 19X1 of $1,000,000. 200,000 shares of common stock are outstanding and 70,000 warrants, each good for buying 3 shares of common stock at $12 each. The warrants are protected against dilution. On August 1, 19X2, Cassell issued rights to purchase 1 new share for $10 for each 2 shares owned. The market price of Cassell stock on August 1 was $20 per share.

a. Calculate primary and fully-diluted EPS for 19X1.
b. What is the theoretical value of the rights before the stock sells ex rights?
c. What is the adjusted exercise price of the warrants after the rights offering?
d. Net income for 19X2 is $1,200,000. All of the rights and none of the warrants have been exercised. Calculate primary and fully-diluted EPS for 19X2.

Solution:

a. $$\text{EPS} = \frac{\text{Net income}}{\text{No. of shares}}$$

Primary EPS: $$\text{EPS} = \frac{\$1,000,000}{200,000} = \$5$$

Fully-diluted EPS: Number of shares = 200,000 + 70,000(3)
= 200,000 + 210,000
= 410,000

$$\text{EPS} = \frac{\$1,000,000}{410,000} = \$2.44$$

The fully-diluted EPS is less than one half of primary EPS.

b. Value of a right = v_r

$$v_r = \frac{p_o - p^s}{\#+1} = \frac{20-10}{2+1} = \frac{10}{3} = \$3.33$$

c. We find the formula value of the warrants before the rights offering, then adjust the exercise price so that the formula value will be the same after the rights offering.

Formula value before rights offering = (Market price of common stock minus Option price) x (Number of shares each warrant holder may purchase)
= ($20-$12)(3)
= $24

Market price of stock after rights offering
= $20 - $3.33 = $16.67

$24 = ($16.67 - X)(3)
$24 = 50-3X
3X = 26
X = $8.67 = adjusted exercise price of warrants after rights offering

d. 200,000/2 = 100,000 new shares as a result of the rights offering

$$\text{Primary EPS} = \frac{\$1,200,000}{300,000} = \$4$$

$$\text{Fully-diluted EPS} = \frac{\$1,200,000}{300,000 + 210,000} = \$2.35$$

CHAPTER 29

PENSION FUND MANAGEMENT

Theme: A pension plan represents a promise by an employer to provide retirement benefits to employees. Corporate pension plans have grown rapidly over the past three decades to encompass 30 percent of the workforce with pension fund assets of over $700 billion. This chapter discusses pension plan management, regulation and evaluation.

I. A Pension Plan is Established for the Benefit of Employees and Managed by a Trustee.
   A. Duties of the trustee include the following:
      1. Collect contributions from the firm and employees.
      2. Manage the assets of the pension fund.
      3. Disburse pension benefits to retirees.
   B. Taxes play an important role in the growth of pension plans.
      1. Pension funds pay no taxes on their earnings.
      2. Corporate contributions are tax deductible.
      3. Retirement benefits, taxed at the beneficiaries' personal tax rates, are deferred compensation.
   C. The pension fund income statement contains cash inflows and outflows.
      1. Cash inflows include:
         a. Corporate contributions.
         b. Employee contributions.
         c. Dividends, interest and capital gains earned by the fund.
      2. Cash outflows include:
         a. Management fees and brokerage expenses.
         b. Disbursements to beneficiaries.
         c. Capital losses.
   D. The pension fund balance sheet has the following elements:
      1. Assets.
         a. Marketable securities (money market accounts, bonds, stocks) are carried at their market value.
         b. The present value of future contributions to the fund including cash contributions and the earnings on fund assets. The earnings rate on fund assets and the discount rate assumed for the present value calculation impact the required level of corporate contribution.
      2. Liabilities include the present value of benefits for past and future service.
         a. The present value of benefits for past service can be calculated in either of two ways.
            (i) Vested benefits are those which would have to be paid if all employees left the firm immediately.

(ii) Accrued benefits represent all benefits accrued regardless of whether employees are fully vested.

b. The present value of benefits for future service depends on actuarial assumptions as to employee turnover, age and seniority of retirees, life expectancy and the discount rate.

c. Total liabilities are unaffected by the choice of method for past service since the difference would be offset in the calculation of future service benefits.

3. A deficit or surplus results from the difference between pension fund assets and liabilities.

a. An unfunded deficit is an asset of the pension fund and a liability for the firm.

b. Pension fund liabilities are disclosed in a footnote to the firm's financial statements.

E. Firms may either manage their own pension funds through the trustee, or make contributions to insurance companies which guarantee benefits.

F. The two main types of pension plans are defined contribution and defined benefit plans.

1. In a defined contribution plan, the corporation contributes a fixed percentage of each employee's wages into the fund; upon retirement, the employee receives a portion of the current value of the fund based on his own contributions and the corporate contributions on his behalf.

2. The more typical plan is a defined benefit plan in which the corporation is committed to pay a predetermined contractual benefit upon retirement.

II. Pension Funds are Regulated by the Employment Retirement Income Security Act (ERISA) of 1974.

A. ERISA mandates eligibility, vesting, funding, reporting and disclosure, fiduciary responsibility, plan termination and insurance requirements.

B. Eligibility--no employee over 25 years old with more than 1 year of service and hired more than 5 years before normal retirement age can be excluded from a pension plan.

C. Vesting--a pension plan must conform to one of three vesting schedules with respect to corporate contributions. (Employee contributions and their returns are fully vested from the start.)

1. 10-year vesting--100 percent vesting after 10 years of service.

2. Graded vesting--25 percent vesting after 5 years, with an additional 5 percent per year for the next 5 years, followed by 10 percent per year for the next 5 years. Fully vested after 15 years.

3. Rule of 45--50 percent vesting when the employee's age plus years of service sum to 45, then 10 percent per year for the next 5 years.

D. ERISA mandates minimum funding. (Because contributions are tax-deductible, the IRS mandates maximum funding.) Required funding includes:
   1. Normal costs--costs attributable to benefit claims from employee services in a given year must be paid in that year.
   2. Experience losses result from decline in the value of the fund, unexpected change in employee turnover or changes in the actuarial assumption of the discount rate.
      a. ERISA requires that experience losses be amortized over not more than 15 years.
      b. IRS requires experience losses be amortized over not less than 10 years.
   3. Supplemental liabilities arise from increased benefits or unfunded past service costs.
      a. ERISA requires amortization over not more than 30 years.
      b. IRS requires amortization over not less than 10 years.

E. The Pension Benefit Guarantee Corporation (PBGC) was created by ERISA to insure pension plans.
   1. A plan may be terminated voluntarily by the firm or involuntarily by PBGC under the following circumstances:
      a. Plan does not meet minimum funding standards.
      b. Plan is unable to pay benefits when due.
      c. Plan is improperly administered.
      d. Liability of PBGC is likely to increase unreasonably.
   2. In termination for underfunding, the firm is liable for 100 percent of the deficit up to 30 percent of net worth; PBGC can place a lien on firm assets with the same priority as a federal tax lien.
   3. PBGC premiums are a fixed annual amount per employee, not based on the firm's risk.
   4. There is some doubt as to whether PBGC has sufficient resources to insure benefits in the event of a major corporate bankruptcy.

F. ERISA mandates techniques for computing projected pension fund benefits.
   1. The accrued benefit method must be used when computing the liabilities of the plan.
   2. Other methods accelerate the rate of corporate contributions; unlike accelerated depreciation, pension fund contributions are cash flows.

G. Accounting regulations A.P.B. 8 and F.A.S.B. 36 govern pension plan disclosure requirements, including the following:
   1. Actuarial present value of vested benefits.
   2. Actuarial present value of non-vested benefits.
   3. The plan's net assets available for benefits.
      a. Positive if contributions accumulate more rapidly than expenses.
      b. Negative if expenses accumulate more rapidly than contributions.
   4. The assumed actuarial rates of return used in calculating the present values.

5. The date as of which benefit information was determined.

III. Pension Fund Management Decisions Affect Shareholder Wealth.
   A. Increasing the actuarial assumption of the discount rate to reduce required corporate contributions and increase reported corporate profits is meaningless from the point of view of the shareholders.
      1. Shareholder wealth is impacted by the market value of pension fund assets and liabilities, not their accounting book values.
      2. Cash flow effects are likely to be negative.
         a. Funds generated from the change must be used for some other tax-deductible expense.
         b. If funds are not used for a tax-deductible expense, taxable income is raised, reducing after-tax cash flows to shareholders.
   B. In the post-ERISA world, with taxes, shareholder wealth is maximized by investing all pension fund assets in bonds.
      1. Before ERISA, in a world without taxes, shareholders are in the position of having a call option on a levered firm, while pension beneficiaries have the equivalent of a risky debt claim.
         a. Shareholders could increase the value of their call option at the expense of pension beneficiaries by increasing the risk of pension fund assets.
         b. Employees might be able to mitigate their risk by demanding higher wages or requiring pension fund insurance.
      2. With ERISA and PBGC, but still without taxes, a very high-risk pension fund strategy would be best for shareholders of a firm facing bankruptcy.
         a. PBGC premiums are not based on risk, therefore risky firms pay relatively too little.
         b. A successful high-risk strategy could result in large gains to shareholders and an overfunded pension fund.
         c. In bankruptcy, shareholders receive nothing, but the PBGC claim on 30 percent of net worth is also worthless, and PBGC pays pension beneficiaries.
      3. With taxes and ERISA, pension fund assets should be invested in securities with the highest pre-tax returns, that is, bonds.
         a. Since pension fund earnings are not taxed, it would not be appropriate to invest in securities for which tax benefits are a major component of return.
         b. The high pre-tax bond return is passed through the firm (via the overfunded pension plan which is a firm asset) to the shareholders in the form of higher share prices which are taxed at the lower capital gains rate.
         c. Shareholders may also benefit from a gain to leverage.
            (i) A pension fund completely invested in bonds

reduces shareholder risk.

(ii) Risk is restored to the original level by additional borrowing, thus increasing the interest tax shelter.

C. Pension plan portfolio performance evaluation should be based on a time-weighted, risk-adjusted measure.

1. A time-weighted return takes into account all contributions and disbursements. The methodology is as follows:
   a. The initial fund is divided into hypothetical equal shares.
   b. If fund value declines, share value declines, and vice versa.
   c. When cash is contributed, this results in new shares; the number of new shares depends on the share value at the time of the contribution. (And vice versa when cash is disbursed.)
   d. The time-weighted return is calculated as

$$\frac{\text{(end-of-period share price)} - \text{(beginning share price)}}{\text{beginning share price}}$$

2. Use the CAPM methodology to assess risk-adjusted returns.
   a. Find the pension fund portfolio beta and the predicted return based on risk.
   b. The risk-adjusted abnormal return is the difference between the actual return and the return predicted by the CAPM.
3. Rules for managing and evaluating pension funds include the following:
   a. Keep bond and stock portfolios separate.
   b. Calculate time-weighted returns.
   c. Evaluate managers' performance by subtracting management and brokerage fees from gross returns, and then comparing the net return to the risk-adjusted return expected for the level of risk.
   d. Give fund managers guidelines for the mix of portfolio assets; keep in mind the effect of decisions on pension fund risk and after-tax shareholder wealth.

D. Firms can voluntarily terminate overfunded pension plans.

1. Employees receive lump-sum payments covering their vested benefits.
2. Excess assets revert to the firm if very specific ERISA and PBGC regulations are followed.
3. Underfunded plans are rarely terminated voluntarily because of potential PBGC claims against 30 percent of net worth.
   a. PBGC can look beyond book value to determine net worth of going concern.
   b. PBGC will look to the net worth of the parent corporation in the event of a subsidiary pension plan termination.
4. Many companies replace defined benefit plans with defined

contribution plans shifting the uncertainties of pension fund portfolio performance from the firm to the employees.

E. Insurance company contracts cover about 39 percent of all non-government pension plans.
   1. Insurance companies generally guarantee a specific return for a fixed period.
      a. Contributions are invested in government bonds of the specified return and maturity.
      b. Firms cannot withdraw their funds before the end of the period.
   2. Firms which handle their own pension funds can follow the same strategy as the insurance companies, or can immunize risk by buying bonds which mature with the same pattern as expected employee retirements.

Chapter 29 - Illustrative Problems and Solutions

29.1 Howard Eberhard is fully vested in Faber Corporation's pension plan with 25 years of service. Eberhard is 50 years old and earned $40,000 last year. His salary is expected to increase at a rate of 8 percent per year, and he is expected to take early retirement at age 60.

The formula used to calculate annual pensions is

Annual pension = (.20 + .015n)[MAX S]

where n = years of service
MAX S = maximum salary earned

If Eberhard's life expectancy is 80 years old, what will Faber's normal pension costs be for the next 10 years if benefits are discounted at 10 percent? (The present value of Eberhard's accumulated benefits was $75,494 last year.)

Solution:

Year (1)	N (2)	Expected Salary (3)	Annual Pension Starting at End of Year 10 (4)	PV of Benefits at End of Year 10 (5)	PV of Accumulated Benefits (6)	Normal Cost (7)
1	26	$43,200	$25,488	$216,995	$ 92,028	$16,534
2	27	46,656	28,227	240,313	112,106	20,078
3	28	50,388	31,241	265,973	136,497	24,391
4	29	54,420	34,557	294,204	166,078	29,581
5	30	58,773	38,202	325,237	201,940	35,862
6	31	63,475	42,211	359,368	245,453	43,513
7	32	68,553	46,616	396,870	298,174	52,721
8	33	74,037	51,456	438,076	362,046	63,872
9	34	79,960	56,772	483,334	439,395	77,349
10	35	86,357	62,609	533,028	533,028	93,633

Column (2) Years of service = n

Column (3) Expected salary growth at 8 percent per year.
For example, Year 1: $40,000(1.08) = $43,200

Year 2: $\$40,000(1.08)^2 = \$46,656$
etc.

Column (4) The annual pension based on the salary calculated in Column (3), based on n years of service.
For example,
Year 1: [.20 + .015(26)]43,200 = $25,488
Year 2: [.20 + .015(27)]46,656 = $28,227
etc.

Column (5) The present value at expected retirement date of the assumed 20 years of pension benefits discounted at 10 percent. PVIFA(10%, 20 years) = 8.5136.
For example, Year 1: 8.5136(25,488) = $216,995
Year 2: 8.5136(28,227) = $240,313
etc.

Column (6) Present value in year n of the amount in Column (5) discounted at 10 percent = present value of accumulated benefits. For example,

Year 1: $\$216,995(1/(1.10)^9) = \$92,028$

Year 2: $\$240,313(1/(1.10)^8) = \$112,106$

Year 3: $\$265,973(1/(1.10)^7) = \$136,497$
etc.

Column (7) Normal costs; this represents the amount by which the present value of accumulated benefits has increased because Eberhard has worked an additional year. This represents normal costs which are the minimum amount that Faber must contribute into the pension fund. For example,
Year 1: $92,028 - 75,494 = $16,534
Year 2: $112,106 - 92,028 = $20,078
etc.

29.2 Arrange the following accounts to form a pension fund balance sheet and income statement. Does the pension fund balance show a deficit or a surplus?

Employer contributions	$ 500
Stocks	2,000
Interest income	250
PV of future contributions	7,000
Employee contributions	425
Disbursements to beneficiaries	1,500
Cash	1,000
Brokerage fees	75
PV of benefits for future service	10,000
Dividend income	75
Bonds	4,000
Management costs	25
PV of benefits for past service	6,000
Capital gains income	(25)

Solution:

Income statement

Funds received:		
From employer	$500	
From employees	425	
From dividends, interest capital gains	300	
		$1,225
Funds expended:		
Management fees and brokerage costs	100	
Disbursements to beneficiaries	1,400	
		$1,500
Change in net fund balance		($ 275)

Balance Sheet

ASSETS		LIABILITIES	
Marketable securities			
Cash	$ 1,000	PV of benefits for past service	$ 6,000
Stocks	2,000		
Bonds	4,000		
PV of future contributions	7,000	PV of benefits for future service	10,000
	14,000		
Deficit	2,000		
Total	$16,000	Total	$16,000

29.3 The table below shows the cash positions and transactions of the Coreblock Company's pension fund over the past 8 years, and the returns on the S&P 500 and 90-day T-bills (annualized) over the same period. (Dollar amounts are in millions.

Year	S&P 500 Returns	T-bill Returns	Beginning Cash	Beginning of Year Deposit	Ending Cash
1	11.7%	8.1%	$30	--	$20
2	21.3	7.9	20	+5	28
3	2.8	7.3	28	-3	30
4	3.1	8.4	30	-4	32
5	12.7	8.6	32	+5	39
6	10.1	9.0	39	+6	49
7	-3.1	9.2	49	-5	43
8	13.4	9.1	43	+4	45

a. Calculate the dollar-weighted and time-weighted returns for each year.

b. On the basis of the S&P 500 and T-bill returns, evaluate Coreblock's pension fund investment strategy.

Solution:

a.

	Beginning of Year			Beginning Deposit		End of Year		
Year	Cash	No. of shares	Price per share	Cash	No. of shares	Cash	No. of shares	Price per share
1	$30	30.00	$1.00	--	--	$20	30.00	$0.67
2	$20	30.00	$0.67	+$5	7.46	$28	37.46	$0.75
3	$28	37.46	$0.75	-$3	-4.00	$30	33.46	$0.90
4	$30	33.46	$0.90	-$4	-4.44	$32	29.02	$1.10
5	$32	29.02	$1.10	+$5	4.55	$39	33.57	$1.16
6	$39	33.57	$1.16	+$6	5.17	$49	38.74	$1.26
7	$49	38.74	$1.26	-$5	-3.97	$43	34.77	$1.24
8	$43	34.77	$1.24	+$4	3.23	$45	38.00	$1.18

	Dollar-weighted Return	Time-weighted Return
Year 1:	(20-30)/30 = -33.0%	(.67-1)/1 = -33.0%
Year 2:	(28-20)/20 = 40.0%	(.75-.67)/.67 = 11.9%
Year 3:	(30-28)/28 = 7.1%	(.9-.75)/.75 = 20.0%
Year 4:	(32-30)/30 = 6.7%	(1.10-.9)/.9 = 22.2%
Year 5:	(39-32)/32 = 21.9%	(1.16-1.10)/1.10 = 5.5%
Year 6:	(49-39)/39 = 25.6%	(1.26-1.16)/1.16 = 8.6%
Year 7:	(43-49)/49 = -12.2%	(1.24-1.26)/1.26 = - 1.6%
Year 8:	(45-43)/43 = 4.7%	(1.18-1.24)/1.24 = - 4.8%

b. Let R_C = Coreblock pension fund return

R_M = S&P 500 return, proxy for market return

R_F = T-bill return, proxy for risk-free rate

Year	R_C	$R_C-\bar{R}_C$	$(R_C-\bar{R}_C)^2$	R_M	$R_M-\bar{R}_M$	$(R_M-\bar{R}_M)^2$	R_F
1	-33.0	-36.6	1339.56	11.7	2.7	7.29	8.1
2	11.9	8.3	68.89	21.3	12.3	151.29	7.9
3	20.0	16.4	268.96	2.8	-6.2	38.44	7.3
4	22.2	18.6	345.96	3.1	-5.9	34.81	8.4
5	5.5	1.9	3.61	12.7	3.7	13.69	8.6
6	8.6	5.0	25.00	10.1	6.4	40.96	9.0
7	-1.6	-5.2	27.04	-3.1	-12.1	146.41	9.2
8	-4.8	-8.4	70.56	13.4	4.4	19.36	9.1
	28.8		2149.58	72.0		452.25	67.6

$\bar{R}_C = 28.8/8 = 3.6\%$ $\qquad \bar{R}_M = 72/8 = 9\%$ $\qquad R_F = 67.6/8 = 8.45\%$

$\sigma_C^2 = 2149.58/7 = 307.08$ $\qquad \sigma_M^2 = 452.25/7 = 64.61$

$\sigma_C = 17.52$ $\qquad \sigma_M = 8.04$

$(R_C-\bar{R}_C)(R_M-\bar{R}_M)$
-98.82
102.09
-101.68
-109.74
7.03
32.00
62.92
-36.96
-143.16

$COV(R_C,R_M) = -143.16/7 = -20.45$

The average return for Coreblock is only 3.6 percent, as opposed to a return on the market of 9 percent and a risk-free rate of 8.45 percent. At first glance, it would appear that Coreblock's investment strategy has not been particularly successful.

Using the calculations above we can calculate Coreblock's beta and use the SML to find the predicted risk-adjusted rate of return.

$$\beta_C = \frac{COV(R_C,R_M)}{\sigma_M^2} = \frac{-20.45}{64.61} = -.32$$

$$\begin{aligned} \text{Predicted return} = \hat{R}_C &= R_F + (\overline{R}_M - R_F)\beta_C \\ &= 8.45 + (9-8.45)(-.32) \\ &= 8.45 + (-.176) \\ &= 8.27 \end{aligned}$$

In spite of the fact that pension fund returns are negatively correlated with the market returns, its actual returns are still 4.67 percentage points below its risk-adjusted predicted return. Thus its strategy has not been successful.

(Even without the above calculations, it is obvious that Coreblock underperformed the risk-free rate. Since their strategy presumably could not be less risky than the risk-free rate, a negative evaluation would be appropriate. The pension fund would be better off abandoning its current strategy in favor of investing pension fund assets in the S&P 500.)

Dollar-weighted returns are completely irrelevant to this analysis, since only time-weighted returns are appropriate for pension fund portfolio performance evaluation.

PART EIGHT. INTEGRATED TOPICS IN MANAGERIAL FINANCE

CHAPTER 30

MERGERS AND CORPORATE CONTROL

Theme: Mergers and corporate control issues play important roles in the growth of firms. Since financial managers are required to participate in appraising the desirability of a prospective merger and in the evaluation of companies involved in the merger, these materials are a necessary part of their background.

I. Mergers and Acquisitions.
   A. The two basic forms of combination are mergers and acquisitions.
   B. Any transaction that forms one economic unit from two or more previous ones is a merger.
   C. An acquisition generally refers to the purchase of a smaller entity which is absorbed into the acquiring firm.

II. Tender Offers.
   A. Definition.
      1. A group seeking a controlling interest in another corporation invites the stockholders of the firm it is seeking to control to submit, or tender, their shares in exchange for a specified price.
      2. A tender is a direct appeal to stockholders, so it is not necessary to receive approval of the board of directors of the acquired firm.
      3. Often acquiring firms will initially propose an offer to buy stock to the board of directors of a company with an indication that if the offer is turned down, it will then go directly to the shareholders with a tender offer.
   B. Advantages.
      1. No prior approval is required
      2. The percentage of shares to be acquired can be specified in advance.
   C. Disadvantages.
      1. Conflict and dissension may develop between firms that are joined.
      2. A bidding war may result in very high purchase prices.
   D. Increased legal controls.
      1. Congressional controls enacted July 1968 (Williams Act):
         a. The acquiring firm must give 30 days' notice both to management of the acquired firm and to the Securities and Exchange Commission.

b. When substantial blocks of stocks are purchased through tender offers, the beneficial owner must be disclosed as well as the party providing the funds.

2. Another federal law, effective as of July 1978, requires pre-merger notification to the FTC of large mergers.
   a. This results in competition among bidders in takeover efforts.
   b. Consequently, the acquisition price rises well above the market price of the stock before the initial tender offer.
3. Individual states have passed laws regulating tender offers.

III. Types of Business Combinations and Restructurings.

A. Firms expand in various ways.
   1. In a merger, firms come together by mutual agreement.
   2. In a tender offer, one firm takes the initiative in acquiring the other, with or without the other's consent.
   3. Joint ventures involve only a small portion of each firm's activities, and for a limited duration.

B. Business combinations come apart in various types of sell-offs.
   1. In a divestiture, part of the firm's assets are sold.
   2. A spin-off involves the creation of a subsidiary whose shares are distributed pro rata to parent company shareholders; subsidiary shares can then be publicly traded.
   3. A split-off is a type of spin-off.
      a. The subsidiary's stock is distributed to only some of the parent company shareholders in exchange for their parent company stock; alternatively, the parent may make a public offering of a portion of the subsidiary's stock.
      b. The parent company generally retains a controlling interest in the subsidiary.
   4. In a split-up, the parent firm ceases to exist; it is split into 2 or more parts with shares distributed to the original shareholders.

C. Corporate control events involve takeover attempts and efforts by incumbent management to thwart takeovers.
   1. Premium buy-backs consist of the repurchase, at a premium, of a substantial shareholder's interest.
   2. In a standstill agreement, a substantial shareholder agrees not to increase his ownership interest; often used in conjunction with premium buy-backs.
   3. Firms may amend corporate bylaws to make takeovers more difficult; antitakeover amendments include:
      a. Requiring a supermajority (e.g. 80%) of shareholder approval for a merger.

b. Staggered terms for the board of directors to delay ultimate change in control.
c. "Golden parachutes" which award high severance pay to terminated management.
4. Proxy contests are used by dissidents to gain representation on boards of directors.

D. Firms may rearrange their ownership structure to change the control position, even in the absence of a takeover attempt.
1. Share repurchase, if substantial, may be used to change the control position.
2. A public firm may go private, selling all its equity to a small group of investors.
a. The investor group is generally controlled by incumbent management.
b. If the investor group borrows substantially to purchase the equity, the transaction is called a leveraged buy-out.

IV. Potential Gains to Merger-Type Activity are Explained by a Number of Theories.

A. Merger theories also apply to other types of acquisitions.
1. The efficiency theory focuses on the synergy (2+2=5) issue. Three types of synergy are identified:
a. Operating synergy results from economies of scale, complementary resources, or better coordination among stages of production.
b. Financial synergy suggests that mergers may lower the cost of capital by increasing debt capacity or by achieving economies of scale in flotation costs on new financing.
c. Synergy may be realized in a long-range strategic planning framework by enabling firms to expand into new markets more rapidly by merger in response to environmental changes.
2. The information, or signaling, hypothesis posits that revaluation is caused by new information generated during the merger or tender offer bidding process.
a. The information may be seen as a "kick-in-pants" stimulating incumbent management.
b. The market's assumption that bidders have superior information may lead to the "sitting-on-a-gold mine" interpretation with subsequent revaluation.
c. Another form of undervaluation results when the replacement cost of a firm's assets is much higher than the book value, or the price of stock required to control the assets.
(i) The q-ratio is defined as the market value of stock divided by the replacement cost of firm assets.
(ii) If a target firm's q-ratio is less than 1

the acquiring firm can increase capacity more cheaply by buying the target firm than by building "bricks and mortar."

3. The threat of takeover may be a partial solution to the agency problem.
   a. Incumbent management becomes self-monitoring if the market for takeovers assures that inefficient or incompetent management will be replaced.
   b. The managerialism theory suggests that management compensation is tied to firm size and that mergers are a manifestation of the agency problem rather than a solution; this view is not supported by evidence which shows compensation to be tied to profit rate rather than firm size.
4. The market power hypothesis suggests that undue concentration in an industry could lead to monopoly profits.
   a. Former Justice Department guidelines raised concern whenever 4 or fewer firms accounted for 40 percent or more of industry sales.
   b. New merger guidelines utilize the Herfindahl (H) index which considers the market shares of every firm in an industry:

$$H = \sum_{j=1}^{n} (MS_j)^2$$

where n = number of firms in industry
MS = market share of each firm

   c. The economic basis for concern over undue concentration has not been established; many contend that concentration is the result of competition and that tacit collusion is generally not feasible.
5. Tax effects may explain gains in many combinations and sales.
   a. A firm may acquire a non-dividend paying growth firm and sell it after the growth period, realizing capital gains not dividend income.
   b. A firm whose growth has slowed cannot justify earnings retention to the IRS; selling out to another firm is a way to capitalize future earnings.
   c. Benefits may be realized by purchasing a firm with accumulated tax losses.
   d. An acquisition results in a stepped-up basis for depreciable assets, increasing the depreciation tax shelter.
   e. Uncertainty as to the valuation of a closely-held firm for estate taxes may encourage its sale before the owner's death.

B. Restructuring a firm may also result in value increase.
   1. Reverse synergy (5-1=7) may mean gains to both parties in divestiture if assets are transferred to a higher valued use and/or were ill-fitted to their original owner.
   2. Other restructurings can improve management incentives and accountability.
      a. Spin-offs may enhance decision-making authority.
      b. The market is able to evaluate managment performance through the public trading of subsidiary stock.

C. Empirical studies of mergers and other corporate control events use the empirical market line to determine whether the events impact stock prices.
   1. Value increases result from most of these events due to a combination of efficiency, information effects, reduced agency costs and tax benefits.
      a. In mergers acquired firms achieved positive abnormal returns of 20 percent, while acquiring firms did not have negative returns.
      b. Most other events resulted in significant positive returns for all parties.
      c. Only premium buy-backs and standstill agreements associated with thwarting a corporate raider resulted in negative returns.
   2. Value increases in corporate control events are ascribed to organizational aspects of running large firms, and improvement in management incentives and compensation plans.

V. Arriving at the Terms of a Merger.

A. Quantitative factors to be considered on the basis of their trends and variability.
   1. <u>Present earnings and expected future earnings</u> after the merger are the most important determinants of the price that will be paid for a firm that is being acquired.
      a. The critical variables are:
         (1) Respective rates of growth of earnings of the two firms
         (2) Their relative sizes measured by net income
         (3) The firms' P/E ratios
         (4) The merger exchange ratio
      b. These variables influence the negotiations in which the terms of the merger are determined.
   2. <u>Dividends</u> paid are likely to have little influence on the market price of companies with a record of high growth and profitability.

3. <u>Market prices</u> clearly influence the price that must be paid in an acquisition, but the acquisition price is likely to exceed the current market price because:
   a. A low current market price may be reflective of industry-wide conditions rather than of the true value of the firm.
   b. The acquired company may be worth more to an informed purchaser than it is in the general market.
   c. Control may enable the acquirer to make changes that an individual investor is unable to bring about. For example, if the acquired firm has a very low debt ratio, more debt may be issued after the merger.
   d. Higher prices will be offered to current stockholders as an inducement to sell.
   e. The price paid for the acquired firm averages about 20 percent above the market price before the merger announcement.
4. <u>Book value</u>. Historical book values and current replacement costs of assets may influence the value placed on the firm because they indicate the cost to the acquiring firm of buying the physical assets instead of a total company.
5. <u>Net current assets</u>. Net current assets are an indication of the amount of liquidity being purchased.
   a. Acquiring a company with high net current assets may place the acquiring company in a position for further mergers.
   b. If it is debt-free, the acquired firm's assets and earning power may be used as security for the purchase loan.

B. Qualitative factors to be considered.
   1. Synergistic, or 2 + 2 = 5, effects represent reinforcement of capabilities in a very broad sense.
   2. Management experience.
   3. Technical competence of its staff.
   4. Abilities of the sales organization.
   5. Possible economies through cost savings.
   6. Degree to which one firm complements the operations of the other.

VI. A Holding Company is Formed for the Purpose of Owning the Stock of Other Companies, Which Operate as Separate Legal Entities.

A. Advantages of holding companies.
   1. In general, advantages of the holding company may include any which accrue to large scale operations.
   2. Advantages specific to the holding company form.
      a. Control with fractional ownership is possible with widely distributed stock.
         (1) A firm in a declining industry may use funds to buy a position in a growth industry.
         (2) Greater leverage is obtainable through fractional ownership.
      b. Isolation of risks - Each firm in a holding company is a separate legal identity, and the obligations of any one unit are largely separate from the obligations of the other units.

B. Disadvantages of holding companies.
   1. <u>Partial multiple taxation</u> - If the holding company owns less than 80 percent of the subsidiary's stock, returns may not be consolidated. However, it is taxable on only 15 percent of the dividends received from the subsidiary.
   2. <u>Risks from excessive pyramiding</u> - The leverage effects possible in holding companies result in magnification of both potential profits as well as losses.

VII. Leveraged Buy-outs are Going-Private Transactions Financed by Substantial Borrowing.

A. In a leveraged buy-out, all the equity of a publicly-held firm is bought by a small group of investors.
   1. Incumbent management controls most (or all) of the equity under the new ownership structure.
   2. The group may include some outside equity investors.
   3. Substantial borrowing is arranged to finance buying up the stock; initial debt/equity ratios may be as high as 900 percent.

B. Several conditions contribute to the success of a leveraged buy-out.
   1. Earnings should be predictable and sufficient to cover interest and rapid loan amortization.
   2. Cash flow growth should exceed inflation.
   3. The firm should have a strong market position.
   4. A large asset base suitable for collateral is typical.
   5. The balance sheet should exhibit high liquidity, little debt, few encumbered assets.
   6. Future resaleability is critical--typically the investor group plans to sell out or go public again after about five years.

C. Leveraged buy-outs typically result in significant value increases for a number of reasons.
   1. Managers have records as highly successful executives, and are motivated by the opportunity for substantial personal wealth gains.

2. The firm avoids the government constraints of a publicly-held firm.
3. Tax advantages result from increased depreciation on assets written up in the buy-out, and from increased interest tax shelter.

VIII. Effects of Mergers on Earnings per Share.

A. Illustrative examples.

1. Assume the following facts for two companies:

	Company A	Company B
Total earnings	$20,000	$50,000
Number of shares of common stock	5,000	10,000
Earnings per share of stock	$ 4.00	$ 5.00
Price/earnings ratio per share	15X	12X
Market price per share	$ 60.00	$ 60.00

2. The firms agree to merge, with B, the surviving firm, acquiring the shares of A by a 1-for-1 exchange of stock. The exchange ratio here is based on their respective market prices.
3. Assuming no immediate increase in earnings, the effects on earnings per share are shown in the following tabulations:

	Shares of Company B Owned After Merger	Earnings per Share Before Merger	Earnings per Share After Merger
A stockholders	5,000	$4.00	$4.67
B stockholders	10,000	5.00	4.67
Total	15,000		

4. Earnings will <u>increase</u> by 67 cents for A's stockholders, but they will <u>decline</u> by 33 cents per share for B's.
5. The effects on market value are less certain Will A's or B's P/E ratio prevail after the merger?
6. If the merger takes place on the basis of earnings rather than market prices, neither earnings dilution nor earnings appreciation will take place.

	Shares of Company B Owned After Merger	Earnings per Old Share Before Merger	Earnings per Old Share After Merger
A stockholders	4,000	$4	$4
B stockholders	10,000	5	5
Total	14,000		

B. Generalizations on initial effects on earnings per share.

1. If the exchange terms are based on market prices and the prevailing price/earnings ratios differ, the company with the higher P/E ratio will attain initial earnings accretion while the company with the lower P/E ratio will suffer initial earnings dilution.
2. If the merger takes place on the basis of earnings, no earnings accretion or dilution will occur.
3. Any initial earnings dilution or accretion may be offset by a new growth rate in the merged company as compared with what the growth rates of the individual companies would have been without the merger.
4. If synergy is present in a merger, future earnings per share for stockholders of both companies may be greater than earnings per share would have been for the companies without the merger.

IX. Managerial Policies in a Valuation Framework.

A. Merger analysis involves projecting firm values that might occur under alternative merger combinations.

B. A framework for merger analysis suggests the following steps:

1. Select alternative merger candidates.
2. Estimate the prospective returns and risk of alternative combinations based on historical data and forecasts.
3. Analyze product markets to assess potential synergy.
4. Estimate beta for each combination.
    a. Estimate cost of equity, cost of debt.
    b. Estimate target leverage, cost of capital.
5. Apply valuation formulas.
    a. Deduct initial value of acquiring firm.
    b. Compare remainder to cost of acquiring merger candidate.
    c. Excess may indicate ability to pay premium and still realize gains from the merger.

X. Accounting Policies in Mergers - Guidelines of the APB of the AICPA, in APB 16 and APB 17, Effective October 31, 1970.

A. Pooling of interests.

1. Six conditions - if met, pooling of interest <u>can</u> be used.
    a. Acquired firm's stockholders continue ownership.
    b. Basis for accounting for the assets of acquired entity is unchanged.
    c. Each entity must have been autonomous; no more than 10 percent common ownership before the merger.

d. The merger must be effected in a single transaction. The contingent payouts permitted in a purchase are not allowed in a pooling.
e. Payment by acquiring company in common stock for substantially all of the voting common stock of company acquired; substantially defined at 90 percent.
f. No intention to dispose of a significant portion of assets within two years after the merger.

2. If these conditions are met, then the combination is a merger among equals, and pooling of interests can be employed.

B. Purchase involves:
   1. New owners
   2. New basis for accounting for assets of acquired companies
   3. Possibility of consideration paid greater than the book value of entity purchased

C. Accounting treatment of pooling of interests and purchases.
   1. Pooling of interests.
      a. The total assets of the surviving firm are equal to the sum of the assets of the two independent companies.
      b. No goodwill is involved.
      c. The excess of market value paid over book value is charged first against capital surplus and then against retained earnings.
      d. See Problem 30.6.
   2. Purchases.
      a. When payment is greater than acquired net worth, the excess is associated with either tangible depreciable assets or with goodwill.
      b. Total assets after the purchase may exceed the sum of the total assets of the individual companies.
      c. Goodwill is depreciable over a reasonable period, no longer than 40 years, but it is not tax deductible.
      d. See Problem 30.5.

Chapter 30 - Illustrative Problems and Solutions

30.1 The Commoner Company has agreed to merge with the Pauley Company. The following is information about the two companies prior to the merger:

	Commoner	Pauley
Earnings	$2,500,000	$1,300,000
Shares outstanding	1,000,000	500,000
P/E ratio	8	39

The Commoner Company will buy the Pauley Company with a 3-for-1 exchange of stock. Combined earnings will remain at the pre-merger level.

a. What will be the effect of the merger on EPS for current Commoner shareholders?

b. What will be the effect of the merger on EPS for the pre-merger Pauley shareholders?

Solution:

a.

Earnings, Commoner	$2,500,000
Earnings, Pauley	1,300,000
Total earnings	$3,800,000

Pre-merger shares, Commoner	1,000,000
New share created (3x500,000)	1,500,000
Total post-merger shares	2,500,000

$$\text{Post-merger EPS} = \frac{\$3{,}800{,}000}{2{,}500{,}000} = \$1.52$$

$$\text{Commoner EPS before merger} = \frac{\$2{,}500{,}000}{1{,}000{,}000} = \$2.50$$

1.52

$0.98 decline

$$\frac{\$.98}{\$2.50} = 39.2\%\ \text{dilution}$$

b. Adjusted post-merger EPS for Pauley = 3 x $1.52 = $4.56

$$\text{Pauley EPS before merger} = \frac{\$1{,}300{,}000}{500{,}000} = 2.60$$

$1.96 increase

$$\frac{\$1.96}{\$2.60} = 75.4\%\ \text{accretion}$$

30.2 The Murdock Company has agreed to merge with the Tishman Company. Tishman shareholders have agreed to accept 1/4 share of Murdock for each Tishman share currently held. The new company will have a P/E ratio of 28. Following is additional information about the two companies.

	Murdock	Tishman
P/E ratio	35	5
Shares outstanding	2,500,000	500,000
Earnings	$2,000,000	$625,000

a. What are the current market prices of Murdock and Tishman stock?
b. What will be the market price of stock following the merger?
c. Calculate the dollar and percentage accretion or dilution in EPS for each firm.
d. What is the effect of the merger on the market price of stock for each company?
e. Assume that Murdock has been growing at a 26 percent annual rate, and that Tishman has been growing at 6 percent. What is the expected growth rate for the merged firm if there are no synergistic effects of the merger?
f. How long will it take before Tishman's EPS recovers from the dilution caused by the merger? Illustrate by means of a graph showing pre-merger and post-merger EPS.

Solution:

a.

Murdock:	EPS = $2,000,000/2,500,000	=	$ 0.80
	P/E ratio	=	35
	Share price	=	$28.00
Tishman:	EPS = $625,000/500,000	=	$ 1.25
	P/E ratio	=	5
	Share price	=	$ 6.25

b. Total number of shares in merged firm:

2,500,000	from Murdock
125,000	1/4 share of new Murdock for each old Tishman
2,625,000	Total post-merger shares

$$EPS = \frac{\text{Post-merger earnings}}{\text{Post-merger shares}} = \frac{\$2,625,000}{2,625,000} = \$1.00$$

Share price = (P/E)(EPS) = 28($1.00) = $28.00

c. Murdock: Pre-merger EPS = \$0.80
Post-merger EPS = 1.00
\$0.20 accretion

$$\frac{0.20}{0.80} = 25\% \text{ accretion}$$

Tishman: Adjusted post-merger EPS =
= 1/4 x \$1.00 = \$0.25
Pre-merger EPS = 1.25
\$1.00 dilution

$$\frac{\$1.00}{1.25} = 80\% \text{ dilution}$$

d. Murdock: Pre-merger share price = \$28.00
Post-merger share price = 28.00
\$ 0 no change

Tishman: Adjusted post-merger share price
= 1/4 x \$28.00 = \$7.00
Pre-merger share price 6.25
\$ .75 increase

A firm may suffer an EPS decline from a merger, but have its market price rise because of a higher price/earnings ratio than it experienced before.

e. Weighted by respective pre-merger earnings:

Murdock: $\frac{\$2,000,000}{\$2,625,000} \times .26 = .198$

Tishman: $\frac{\$625,000}{\$2,625,000} \times .06 = \underline{.014}$

Combined growth rate = .212 ≅ 21%

f. Tishman: Pre-merger EPS \$1.25
Pre-merger growth rate .06

Post-merger adjusted EPS = \$0.25
Post-merger growth rate = .21

Solve for n to find the number of years required to recover from dilution:

$$(\$1.25)(1.06)^n = (\$0.25)(1.21)^n$$

$$\frac{\$1.25}{\$0.25} = \left(\frac{1.21}{1.06}\right)^n$$

$$5 = (1.14)^n$$

From Table A.1, the FVIF at 14 percent is 4.8179 for 12 years and 5.4924 for 13 years. Therefore approximately 12 1/2 years are required to overcome the EPS dilution effects of the merger.

Year		0	1	5	8	10	15
Pre-merger EPS growth:							
	EPS	$1.25	$1.33	$1.67	$1.99	$2.24	$3.00
Post-merger adjusted EPS growth:							
	EPS	$0.25	$0.30	$0.65	$1.15	$1.68	$4.36

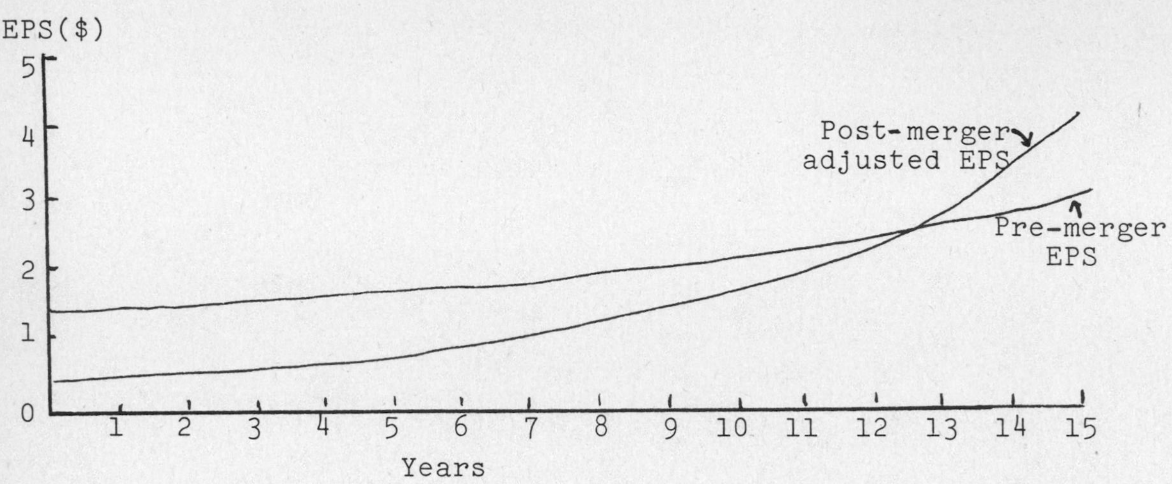

30.3 The merger of Dictron Company with Ledyard Corporation is to be carried out through the use of convertible debentures. In exchange for 75 shares of Ledyard stock, Dictron will give one debenture with a maturity value of $1,000 and a 12 percent coupon, convertible into 15 shares of Dictron stock. Prior to the merger, both firms were unlevered. The merged firm will have a 40 percent tax rate. Following are more data:

	Dictron	Ledyard
Earnings before taxes	$6,000,000	$300,000
Net income available to common	$3,900,000	$180,000
Common shares outstanding	1,300,000	72,000
Expected growth rate in earnings	25%	6%
Dividends per share	$0.96	$2.10
P/E ratio	32X	7X
Dividend yield	.01	.12

a. What is the total annual dollar return to the former Ledyard shareholders before and after the merger?
b. What are the new EPS and market price of Dictron if the P/E ratio remains at 32 times on a primary and fully diluted basis?
c. Why might Ledyard shareholders agree to the merger?

Solution:

a. Pre-merger dividend return = 72,000 x $2.10 = $151,200
Post-merger: 960 debentures x $1,000 x .12 = 115,200

Ledyard shareholders would lose $36,000 annually as a result of the merger in the first year.

b.

	Primary	Fully Diluted
Earnings before interest and taxes	$6,300,000	$6,300,000
Debenture interest	115,200	0
Earnings before tax	$6,184,800	$6,300,000
Taxes (40%)	2,473,920	2,520,000
Net income available to common	$3,710,880	$3,780,000
Common shares	1,300,000	1,314,400*
EPS	$2.85	$2.88
Market price = 32 x EPS	$91.20	$92.16

*960 debentures x 15 = 14,400 shares from conversion
1,300,000 original Dictron shares
1,314,400 shares after conversion

c. While the dollar returns to Ledyard's shareholders are reduced in terms of interest versus dividend income, the initial conversion value of the Dictron debentures is $96 x 15 = $1,440, which exceeds the market value of the Ledyard shares surrendered ($17.50 x 75 = $1,312.50). And if the Dictron pre-merger P/E ratio persists, the conversion value will rise even more. Thus Ledyard shareholders will have given up dividend income for the possibility of large capital gains.

30.4 Midsouth Enterprises is a holding company which owns the entire common stock of two operating companies, Atlanta Beverage Company and Biloxi Bottling Company. The balance sheets of the two subsidiaries are identical to the one below.

Balance Sheet as of December 31, 1984 (thousands of dollars)

Assets		Liabilities	
Current assets	$11,500	Current liabilities	$ 3,000
Net fixed assets	17,000	Long-term debt (9%)	8,500
		Preferred stock (13%)	4,200
		Common stock ($1 par)	8,500
		Retained earnings	4,300
Total assets	$28,500	Total claims	$28,500

Each operating company earns 14 percent annually on total assets before interest, taxes and preferred dividends. Assume a 40 percent tax rate for all three companies.

a. What is the annual rate of return on each subsidiary's shareholders' equity?

b. Construct a balance sheet for Midsouth Enterprises based on the following assumptions:
   (1) The only asset of the holding company is the common stock of the subsidiaries, carried at par value.
   (2) The holding company has $3,600,000 of 10 percent coupon long-term debt and $5,500,000 of 12 percent preferred stock.

c. What is the rate of return on shareholders' equity for the holding company?

d. How could the rate of return in part (c) be increased?

e. What investment is necessary to control the three companies?

f. If the subsidiaries' return on total assets falls from 14 percent to 8.5 percent, what will be the effect on Midsouth Enterprises?

Solution:

a.

EBIT (14%)	$3,990
Interest expense	765
EBT	$3,225
Tax (40%)	1,290
Earnings after tax	$1,935
Preferred dividends	546
Net income available to common	$1,389

Earnings/Shareholders' equity = $1,389/$12,800 = 10.9%

b.

Midsouth Enterprises Balance Sheet (thousands of dollars)

Assets		Liabilities	
Atlanta common stock	$ 8,500	Long-term debt (10%)	$ 3,600
Biloxi common stock	8,500	Preferred stock (12%)	5,500
		Shareholders' equity	7,900
Total assets	$17,000	Total claims	$17,000

c. Since each of the operating companies has net income available to common stock of $1,389, total gross receipts for Midsouth are $2,778(=$1,389x2).

Income	$2,778
Interest expense	360
Income after interest	$2,418
Preferred dividends	660
Net income available to common	$1,758

Earnings/Shareholders' equity = $1,758/$7,900 = 22.3%

Note that no tax is deducted here since Midsouth owns 100 percent of its subsidiaries' stock and may therefore exclude this dividend income from taxable income.

d. More leverage by the subsidiaries and/or the holding company could increase the rate of return on equity.

e. It depends on how widely the holding company's stock is held. For example, a small percentage of the stock in General Motors would permit control. On the other hand, a greater percentage of Ford stock would be necessary to gain control.

f.

	Subdidiary Income Statement	Midsouth Enterprises Income Statement
Income	$2,423	$898
Interest expense	765	360
Income after interest	$1,658	$538
Tax (40%)	663	0
Income after tax	$ 995	$538
Preferred dividends	546	660
Net income available to common	$ 449	-$122
Return on shareholders' equity	3.5%	-1.5%

When the subsidiaries earned 14 percent on assets, the return on equity to the holding company was magnified to over 22 percent. However, a drop to 8.5 percent results in a loss for the holding company even though the subsidiaries continue to earn a profit.

30.5 The Matlock Company has just purchased the Vigor Company, paying a 25 percent premium over the market price of Vigor stock. Data on the two companies is given below.

a. Fill in the blanks, complete the adjustments and the pro forma balance sheet columns, treating the transaction as a purchase for merger accounting.
b. Assuming that total earnings remain the same, calculate whether earnings dilution or accretion occurs for either company.
c. Calculate each company's dilution or accretion on the assumption that earnings available to common stock rise to $1,000,000.

	Matlock	Vigor	Adjustments Debit	Adjustments Credit	Pro forma Balance Sheet
1. Current assets	$1,300,000	$ 32,000			
2. Other assets	300,000	2,000			
3. Fixed assets	1,400,000	76,000			
4. Intangibles					
Total assets	$3,000,000	$110,000			
5. Current liabilities	$ 500,000	$ 25,000			
6. Long-term debt	600,000	- - -			
7. Common stock	600,000	50,000			
8. Capital surplus	450,000	- - -			
9. Retained earnings	850,000	35,000			
Total claims	$3,000,000	$110,000			

	Matlock	Vigor	Adjustments Debit Credit	Pro forma Balance sheet
Par value	$2.00	$1.00		
Number of shares				
Earnings available to common stock	$750,000	$62,500		
Book value per share				
Earnings per share				
Price/earnings ratio	20X	32X		
Market price per share				

Solution:

a. See next page.

b. New EPS = $\dfrac{\text{Total earnings}}{\text{Total shares}} = \dfrac{\$812,500}{300,000 + 50,000} = \$2.32$

Matlock:	Pre-merger EPS	$2.50
	Post-merger EPS	2.32
		$ .18 dilution
Vigor:	Pre-merger EPS	$1.25
	Post-merger EPS	2.32
		$1.07 accretion

c. New EPS = $\dfrac{\$1,000,000}{350,000} = \$2.86$

Matlock:	Pre-merger EPS	$2.50
	Post-merger EPS	2.86
		$ .36 accretion
Vigor:	Pre-merger EPS	$1.25
	Post-merger EPS	2.86
		$1.61 accretion

30.6 Company A and Company B have agreed to merge in a transaction which accountants would refer to as a pooling of interests. The following data is provided.

	Company A	Company B
Current assets	$149,000	$149,000
Fixed assets	101,000	101,000
Total assets	$250,000	$250,000

30.5 (Solution)

a.

	Matlock	Vigor	Adjustments Debit	Adjustments Credit	Pro forma Balance Sheet
1. Current assets	$1,300,000	$ 32,000			$1,332,000
2. Other assets	300,000	2,000			302,000
3. Fixed assets	1,400,000	76,000			1,476,000
4. Intangibles			2,415,000[5]		2,415,000
Total assets	$3,000,000	$110,000			$5,525,000
5. Current liabilities	$ 500,000	$ 25,000			$525,000
6. Long-term debt	600,000	- - -			600,000
7. Common stock	600,000	50,000	50,000[1]	100,000[3]	700,000
8. Capital surplus	450,000	- - -		2,400,000[4]	2,850,000
9. Retained earnings	850,000	35,000	35,000[2]		850,000
Total claims	$3,000,000	$110,000			$5,525,000
Par value	$2.00	1.00			
Number of shares	300,000	50,000			
Earnings available to common stock	$750,000	$62,500			
Book value per share	$6.33	$1.70			
Earnings per share	$2.50	$1.25			
Price/earnings ratio	20X	32X			
Market price per share	$50	$40			

Explanation of adjustments:

Vigor stock price + 25% premium = $40(1.25) = $50
Matlock will give one share of Matlock stock (market value $50)for each share of Vigor stock.

Adjustments 1 and 2 ($50,000 and $35,000 debits) eliminate the common stock and retained earnings accounts of Vigor Company.

Adjustment 3 ($100,000 credit to common stock) represents the 50,000 new shares of Matlock stock at their $2.00 par value.

Adjustment 4 ($2,400,000 credit to capital surplus) represents the excess over par value which was given in exchange for the Vigor stock [($50-$2)(50,000) = $2,400,000].

Adjustment 5 ($2,415,000 debit to intangibles) is the goodwill arising from the excess paid over the book value of Vigor.

	Company A	Company B
Current liabilities	$ 70,000	$ 70,000
Long-term debt	43,000	43,000
Total debt (10%)[a]	$113,000	$113,000
Common stock ($3 par)	60,000	60,000
Capital surplus	62,000	62,000
Retained earnings	15,000	15,000
Total claims	$250,000	$250,000

[a]Average interest rate on total debt.

1. Number of shares	20,000	20,000
2. Book value per share		
3. Earnings before interest and taxes (Tax rate = 40%)	$55,650	$29,000
4. Earnings per share		
5. P/E ratio	15X	12.5X
6. Market price of stock		
7. Working capital per share		
8. Dividends per share (50% payout)		
9. Exchange ratio		
10. Equivalent earnings per old share		

a. What would be a reasonable basis for determining the terms at which shares in Companies A and B would be exchanged for shares in Company C? Find the ratio of A to B for: (1) Book value per share; (2) earnings per share; (3) market price of stock; (4) dividends per share; (5) working capital per share; (6) return on total assets, and (7) return on equity.

b. Use the market price of stock as the basis of the terms of exchange of stock in the old company for stock in the new company (three shares of C for one share of A and one share of C for one share of B). Complete all adjustments and prepare the consolidated balance sheet for Company C.

Solution:

a.

	Company A	Company B
Earnings before interest and taxes	$55,650	$29,000
Interest expense	11,300	11,300
Earnings before tax	$44,350	$17,700
Tax at 40 percent	17,740	7,080
Net income to common stock	$26,610	$10,620
Less: 50 percent dividend	13,305	5,310
To retained earnings	$13,305	$ 5,310
Net income to common stock	$26,610	$10,620
Add: Interest(1-T)	6,780	6,780
	$33,390	$17,400
Rate of return on total assets	13.4%	7.0%
Rate of return on equity	19.4%	7.8%

		Ratio A/B
Book value per share		1.0
Earnings per share	$1.33/$0.53	2.5
Market price of stock	$19.95/$6.63	3.0
Dividends per share	$0.67/$0.27	2.5
Working capital per share		1.0
Average of above ratios		2.0
Return on total assets	13.4%/7.0%	1.9
Return on equity	19.4%/7.8%	2.5
Average of:		
Earnings per share		2.5
Market price per share		3.0
Average		2.8

The exact exchange rate is established by the relative function of management ability, technical skills, production know-how, sales organization, market knowledge, research capabilities and many other qualitative factors.

It is clear, however, that the range within which such bargainings will occur is set by the underlying assets and earnings. The five ratios that influence the terms of the merger average 2.0, which is above the 1.9 ratio of the return on total assets of the companies. The return on total assets is fundamental, and provides a check on the other ratios. Earnings per share and market price are two factors of great importance to common stock investors. These ratios average 2.8. Thus the bargaining range will be approximately 1.9 to 2.8. This range provides only a guideline. In part (b) of this problem, the ratio of market values is used, which is typical of many mergers, but in this case the value falls outside the range.

b.

	Company A	Company B	Adjustments	Consolidated Balance Sheet Company C
Current assets	$149,000	$149,000		$298,000
Fixed assets	101,000	101,000		202,000
Total assets	$250,000	$250,000		$500,000
Current liabilities	$ 70,000	$ 70,000		$140,000
Long-term debt	43,000	43,000		86,000
Total debt (10%)	$113,000	$113,000		$226,000
Common stock ($3 par)	60,000	60,000	Cr. $120,000	240,000
Capital surplus	62,000	62,000	Dr. $120,000	4,000
Retained earnings	15,000	15,000		30,000
Total claims	$250,000	$250,000		$500,000

	Company A	Company B	Ratio A to B	Company C
1. Number of shares	20,000	20,000	1.0	80,000
2. Book value per share	$6.85	$6.85	1.0	$3.43
3. Earnings before interest and taxes (Tax rate=40%)	$55,650	$29,000	1.9	$84,650
4. Earnings per share	$1.33	$0.53	2.5	$0.47
5. P/E ratio	15X	12.5X		
6. Market price of stock	$19.95	$6.63	3.0	
7. Working capital per share	$3.95	$3.95	1.0	$1.98
8. Dividends per share, 50% payout	$0.67	$0.27	2.5	$0.24
9. Exchange ratio	3/1	1/1	3.0	
10. Equivalent earnings per old share ($0.47 x Line 9)	$1.41	$0.47		

30.7 Watrous Construction Company is considering merger to achieve better growth and profitability. It has narrowed potential merger candidates to two firms: The Albercan Company, a southern California swimming pool builder has a strong marketing department and a good record of internal profitability. The Save-U Corporation operates a chain of drug and discount stores in the Pacific Northwest, and has a very high profitability rate. Data on all three firms is given below:

	Watrous	Albercan	Save-U
Book value per share	$6	$6	$6
Price/earnings ratio	4X	15X	10X
# of shares (millions)	5	2.5	2.5
Debt/Equity ratio	1	1	1
Beta for existing leverage	1.3	1.2	1.5
Internal profitability rate, r	.09	.14	.18
Investment rate, b	.5	1.5	1.0
Growth rate, g = br	.045	.21	.18

The risk-free rate is 8 percent and the expected return on the market is 12 percent. Each firm pays 10 percent interest on its debt and has a 40 percent tax rate. Ten years of supernormal growth are forecasted, followed by no growth.

a. Prepare accounting balance sheets for each firm.
b. If each company earns the before-tax r on total assets in the current year, what is each company's NOI?
c. What is the indicated market price per share for each firm, and the indicated market value of equity?
d. What will be the immediate effect on Watrous' EPS of an acquisition of Albercan or Save-U at its current market price by an exchange of stock based on each firm's current market price?
e. Compare Watrous' new beta and required return on equity if it merges with Albercan and if it merges with Save-U.
f. Calculate the new required cost of capital for a Watrous-Albercan combination and for a Watrous-Save-U combination.
g. Compare Watrous' increase in value as a result of merger at market value with the cost of acquiring Albercan or Save-U if the combined firms have the following financial parameters.

	Watrous-Albercan	Watrous-Save-U
Net operating income	$16	$17
Internal profitability rate, r	.18	.14
WACC	10%	9.8%
Investment rate, b	0.8	0.8
Growth rate, g = br	.144	.112

Solution:

a.

WATROUS	Assets	Claims on Assets	
		Debt	$30
		Equity	30
	Total assets $60	Total claims	$60
ALBERCAN		Debt	$15
		Equity	15
	Total assets $30	Total claims	$30
SAVE-U		Debt	$15
		Equity	15
	Total assets $30	Total claims	$30

b.

	Watrous	Albercan	Save-U
After-tax r	.09	.14	.18
Before-tax r = r/(1-T)	.15	.23	.30
NOI = before-tax r(TA)	$9.00	$6.90	$9.00

c.

	Watrous	Albercan	Save-U
NOI	$9.00	$6.90	$9.00
Less interest on debt	3.00	1.50	1.50
EBT	6.00	5.40	7.50
Tax @ 40%	2.40	2.16	3.00
Net income	3.60	3.24	4.50
Divided by # of shares	5	2.5	2.5
EPS	$0.72	$1.30	$1.20
Times P/E ratio	4	15	10
Market price per share	$2.88	$19.50	$12.00
Times # of shares	5	2.5	2.5
Total market value of equity	$14.40	$48.75	$30.00

d.

Watrous merges with:	Albercan	Save-U
1. $\frac{\text{Share price of A or S}}{\text{Share price of W}}$	6.77X	4.17X
2. # of acquired firm shares	2.5	2.5
3. # of new shares	16.9	10.4
4. # of old W shares	5	5
5. Total shares	21.9	15.4
6. NI of W + NI of A or S	$6.84	$8.10
7. New EPS	$0.31	$0.53
8. W's original EPS	$0.72	$0.72
9. Dilution $\left[\frac{\text{Row 8 - Row 7}}{\text{Row 8}}\right]100$	57%	26%

e. Because betas are additive, we simply weight the betas of each firm according to the market value of its equity as calculated in part c. The total market value of equity for the proposed merged firms would be:

Watrous-Albercan: $14.40 + $48.75 = $63.15
Watrous-Save-U: $14.40 + $30.00 = $44.40

$$\text{Beta}_{WA} = \frac{14.40}{63.15}(1.3) + \frac{48.75}{63.15}(1.2) = .296 + .926 = 1.222$$

$$\text{Beta}_{WS} = \frac{14.40}{44.40}(1.3) + \frac{30.00}{44.40}(1.5) = .422 + 1.014 = 1.436$$

To find the required return on equity, we use the SML:

$$E(R_j) = R_F + [E(R_M)-R_F]\beta_j$$

$$E(R_{WA}) = .08 + (.12-108)1.222 = .08 + .04888 = .12888$$

$$E(R_{WS}) = .08 + (.12-.08)1.436 = .08 + .05744 = .13744$$

f. Use the merged firms' market values of debt and equity to determine the weights for the cost of capital calculation. (We assume that the market value of debt is equal to its book value.)

	Watrous-Albercan	Watrous-Save-U
Debt	$45.00	$45.00
Equity	63.15	44.40
Value of firm	$108.15	$89.40

$$\text{WACC} = k = k_b(1-T)(B/V) + k_s(S/V)$$

$$\begin{aligned} k_{WA} &= .10(.6)(45/108.15) + .12888(63.15/108.15) \\ &= .025 + .075 \\ &= .10 \end{aligned}$$

$$\begin{aligned} k_{WS} &= .10(.6)(45/89.40) + .13744(44.4/89.4) \\ &= .030 + .068 \\ &= .098 \end{aligned}$$

g. Using Equation 23.14 we have:

$$V = X_o(1-T)(1-b)\sum_{t=1}^{n}\frac{(1+g_s)^t}{(1+k)^t} + \frac{X_o(1-T)(1+g_s)^n}{k(1+k)^n}$$

$$V_{WA} = 16(.6)(.2) \sum_{t=1}^{10} \frac{(1.144)^t}{(1.10)^t} + \frac{16(.6)(1.144)^{10}}{.10(1.10)^{10}}$$

$$= 1.92(1+h)[FVIFA(h\%, 10 \text{ yrs})] + 96[FVIF(h\%, 10 \text{ yrs})]$$

$$\text{where } \frac{1.144}{1.10} = 1+h = 1.04$$

$$= 1.92(1.04)(12.006) + 96(1.4802)$$

$$= 23.97 + 142.10$$

$$= \$166.07 \text{ million}$$

$$V_{WS} = 17(.6)(.2) \sum_{t=1}^{10} \frac{(1.112)^t}{(1.098)^t} + \frac{17(.6)(1.112)^{10}}{.098(1.098)^{10}}$$

$$= 2.04(1+h)[FVIFA(h\%, 10 \text{ yrs})] + 104.08[FVIF(h\%, 10 \text{ yrs})]$$

$$\text{where } \frac{1.112}{1.098} = 1+h = 1.013$$

$$= 2.04(1.013)(10.606) + 104.08(1.1379)$$

$$= 21.92 + 118.43$$

$$= \$140.35 \text{ million}$$

	Watrous-Albercan	Watrous-Save-U
Firm value	\$166.07	\$140.35
Less debt	45.00	45.00
Value of equity	121.07	95.35
Less W's pre-merger value of equity	14.40	14.40
Gain in equity value	106.67	80.95
Cost of acquisition (A or S value of equity)	48.75	30.00
Gain in value	57.92	50.95

A merger with Albercan will result in a larger gain to Watrous shareholders than a merger with Save-U. Watrous could pay a premium to Albercan's shareholders and still have a positive NPV. This result follows from the forecasted NOI and internal profitability rates which reflect greater potential synergy in a merger of the construction firm with the pool builder than with the retail drugstore chain.

CHAPTER 31

REORGANIZATION AND BANKRUPTCY

Theme: The financial manager has a double responsibility in relation to financial difficulties. If it is his own firm that has financial problems, the financial manager's ability may make the difference between loss of ownership of the firm and the rehabilitation of the firm as a going enterprise. When other firms fall into financial difficulties, knowledge of the rights of creditors may make the difference between large losses and small or no losses.

I. Bankruptcies Affect All Types of Firms.
   A. Major bankruptcies can involve billions of dollars in assets and debts.
   B. Some bankruptcies involve impropriety or fraud.
   C. Financial enterprises (commercial banks) have recently been plagued by bankruptcies.
      1. Among the causes are the following:
         a. Unstable economic environment
         b. Fraud
         c. Excessive debt-to-equity ratios
         d. Too rapid expansion
         e. Loans to impoverished developing countries
      2. Bank failures have raised concerns over Federal deposit insurance.
         a. The FDIC tries to find merger partners rather than let large banks fail; this may reduce management incentive to manage well.
         b. A proposal has been made to base insurance premiums on the risk of the banks rather than a flat percentage of deposits.

II. Failure.
   A. Economic--A firm's revenues do not cover costs.
   B. Financial--Financial failure signifies insolvency.
      1. Technical insolvency: A firm cannot meet its current obligations as they come due (even though its total assets may exceed its total liabilities).
      2. In bankruptcy sense, if a firm's total liabilities exceed its total assets, the net worth of the firm is negative.

C. Cause of failure.
   1. Neglect
   2. Fraud
   3. Disaster
   4. Management inexperience or incompetence--the major cause
D. In recent years, less than .5 percent of all business firms failed.
   1. Failure rate rises in recession periods
   2 Mergers and government intervention help to avoid bankruptcy for some firms
E. Government and industry try to prevent large firms from going bankrupt.
   1. To help the firm reestablish its viability
   2. To maintain a viable supplier
   3. To avoid disrupting a local community

III. Informal Remedies Allow for Two Possible Outcomes.
   A. The firm continues to exist.
      1. Extension involves the postponement of the due date of an obligation.
         a. Debtor buys current purchases on a cash basis and pays off the past due balance over an extended time.
         b. Creditors must have faith the debtor will solve the problems.
         c. Creditors will want to exercise control over the debtor:
            (1) Assignment of assets to be held in escrow in case of default.
            (2) Stockholders transfer stock in escrow until the repayment has been completed.
            (3) Designate a representative to countersign all checks.
            (4) Obtain security notes, mortgages.
      2. Composition is a voluntary reduction of creditor claims. A pro rata cash settlement is paid to the creditors.
         a. Creditors receive a uniform percentage of the obligations from the debtor.
         b. The cash received is taken as full settlement of the debt.
      3. A combination settlement is a mixture of extension and composition.
   B. The firm is liquidated in a common-law assignment.
      1. A trustee is selected to liquidate the assets and distribute the proceeds among creditors on a pro rata basis.
      2. Checks to creditors contain a statement that endorsement represents acceptance of the check as full payment of the obligation.

IV. Procedures and Assessment of Informal Reorganization

A. Procedures.

1. An adjustment bureau normally arranges and conducts meetings between the debtor and his creditors.
2. The creditors are represented by a committee composed of the largest four or five creditors and one or two representatives of the smaller creditors.
3. The bureau receives the facts of the case and sends investigators to examine the firm.
4. The bureau and the creditors' committee prepare an adjustment plan.
5. Meetings are held between the debtor and the creditors' committee to reach a final agreement. An agreement is feasible under the following conditions:
    a. Debtor is a good moral risk.
    b. Debtor has the ability to recover.
    c. General business conditions are favorable.

B. Advantages.

1. Bankruptcy costs are avoided.
2. Debtor is kept in business and avoids stigma of bankruptcy.
3. Creditors absorb a temporary loss but have better chance of greater recovery.

C. Appraisal of voluntary settlements.

1. Advantages include its simplicity, minimum costs, and maximum benefits to creditors.
2. Disadvantages include the fact that control of the business stays with the debtor. Also, one has to contend with the nuisance of small creditors who demand full payment.
3. An extension is preferred by creditors because it provides payment in full.

V. Federal Bankruptcy Law Has Recently Undergone Major Changes.

A. Chapter X proceedings under the old law applied to large public corporations.
1. A trustee was placed in charge of the debtor's business.
2. The trustee often did not have the technical knowledge necessary to run the firm successfully resulting in losses to creditors.

B. Former Chapter XI proceedings applied to small corporations and business without public participation.
1. The debtor remained in possession under court supervision.
2. Chapter XI was less time-consuming and more flexible, and was favored by creditors.

C. The new law provides Chapter 7 for liquidations and Chapter 11 for reorganizations.
1. The debtor is allowed to remain in possession.
2. A trustee with very broad powers and discretion may also be appointed to augment or replace management.

D. Potential advantages of the new law include the following.
   1. Greater flexibility, resulting in reduced time and cost of bankruptcy proceedings.
   2. Facilitation of informal negotiations with creditors.
   3. Relaxation of absolute priority rule, giving unsecured claimants an increased possibility of recovery.

E. Potential disadvantages of the new law include:
   1. Debtor and large creditors may dominate a reorganization to detriment of smaller creditors.
   2. Role of SEC may be weakened.

VI. Formal Legal Proceedings Provide for Three Possible Outcomes.

A. The firm continues in existence.
   1. A Chapter 11 reorganization under the 1978 Bankruptcy Reform Act represents court-supervised procedures for scaling down creditors' claims.
   2. This is the formal equivalent of composition.

B. The firm merges into another firm, continuing as a subsidiary or being completely absorbed, as an alternative to bankruptcy.

C. The firm is liquidated.
   1. In statutory assignment, an assignee liquidates the firm's assets in accordance with strict legal requirements.
   2. Liquidation under Chapter 7 of the new bankruptcy law involves greater court supervision of the liquidation process.

D. Benefits of formal legal proceedings include the following.
   1. Safeguard against fraud by the debtor.
   2. Equitable distribution of assets to creditors.
   3. Debtor may start anew unhampered by prior debt.

VII. Evaluation of Formal Reorganization.

A. A firm is reorganized if it is determined that the net value of the rehabilitated firm will be greater than the value of the sum of the parts if dismembered.

B. Formal reorganization may take several forms, all of which have these features in common:
   1. The firm is either insolvent or bankrupt.
   2. New funds are needed for working capital or property improvement.
   3. Management must be improved.

C. A sound reorganization plan meets the tests of fairness and feasibility.
   1. The basic doctrine of fairness is met if claims are scaled down in order of their contractual priority and if junior claimants are included only when they make an additional cash contribution to the firm. This requires an estimate of total value, based on the following steps:
      a. An estimate of future sales.
      b. Analyze operating conditions in order to estimate future earnings on sales.

c. Determine the capitalization rate to apply to the future earnings.
d. Capitalize earnings to obtain a total value figure.
e. Provide for distribution of estimated value available to the claimants.

2. A reorganization plan is <u>feasible</u> if it will not result in subsequent default.
a. Fixed charges on the income of the corporation after reorganization should be covered by earnings.
b. Necessary steps to prevent another default.
(1) Extend debt maturity or convert to stock.
(2) Improve management.
(3) Reduce inventories.
(4) Modernize plant and equipment.
(5) Improve operations in sales and finance.
(6) Revamp product policies.

D. Both the courts and the SEC review reorganization plans to determine their fairness and feasibility.

E. The priority of expenses and claims in bankruptcy is as follows:
1. Secured creditors receive proceeds of sale of security assets.
2. Trustee's costs in bankruptcy proceedings.
3. Other bankruptcy costs incurred before appointment of trustee.
4. Wages due workers, up to a limit with #5 below.
5. Unpaid pension plan contributions.
6. Unsecured claims for customer deposits.
7. Taxes.
8. Unfunded pension up to 30% of common and preferred equity.
9. General or unsecured creditors.
10. Preferred stockholders up to par value.
11. Common stockholders.

F. The priority of claims of general creditors is scaled down as follows:
1. The ratio of available funds to creditors' claims is calculated.
2. The ratio is applied to the amounts claimed.
3. Allocations to subordinated creditors are transferred to senior creditors until their claims are satisfied.
4. The balance, if any, is allocated to stockholders.
5. See Problems 31.1 and 31.4.

VIII. Reorganization is Sometimes Used to Break Labor Contracts.

A. Firms with labor contracts may be at a disadvantage with competitors using non-union labor.

B. The courts have recognized that burdensome labor contracts can be a threat to a reorganized firm's financial health.

C. The traditional approach is to compensate labor with equity participation in the reorganized firm.
1. The equity compensates labor for the lower wages.
2. Equity participation provides incentives for labor to work for renewed profitability.

IX. Liquidation Occurs When Reorganization or Merger is Not Appropriate.
   A. Assignment is a technique for liquidating assets to yield more to the creditors than is likely in bankruptcy.
      1. Common-law assignment is the most informal liquidation.
      2. Statutory assignments are carried out through the courts.
      3. Assignment plus settlement refers to the fact that creditors agree beforehand that payments received will be accepted as full settlement of claims.
   B. Formal liquidation under Chapter 7 follows specified legal rules with respect to priority of claims and distribution of assets.

X. Quantitative Models Have Been Developed to Predict Bankruptcy.
   A. Multiple discriminant analysis (MDA) of financial ratios has been successfully used to predict firms with high and low probabilities of bankruptcy.
   B. Altman's Z-ratio MDA model is able to predict bankruptcy with a high degree of accuracy.
   C. MDA is also used in credit analysis and portfolio management.

Chapter 31 - Illustrative Problems and Solutions

31.1 The final balance sheet of the bankrupt Reilly Company is shown below:

Assets		Liabilities	
Current assets	$2,000,000	Accounts payable	$ 950,000
Fixed assets	2,250,000	Notes payable (bank)	220,000
		Accrued wages	90,000
		Taxes payable	230,000
		Current liabilities	$1,490,000
		Mortgage	$ 315,000
		Subordinated debentures[a]	300,000
		Long-term debt	$ 615,000
		Preferred stock	$ 250,000
		Common stock	1,500,000
		Retained earnings	395,000
		Net Worth	$2,145,000
Total assets	$4,250,000	Total claims	$4,250,000

[a]Subordinated to $220,000 notes payable to bank.

Total legal fees and administrative expenses of the bankruptcy proceedings were $350,000. Upon liquidation of the firm's assets, only $1,500,000 was realized, as shown:

Current assets	$1,200,000
Net property	300,000
	$1,500,000

Prepare a schedule showing the distribution of the liquidation proceeds.

Solution:

Cash received from sale of current assets		$1,200,000
Less priority claims:		
1. Fees and expenses of bankruptcy proceedings	$350,000	
2. Wages due workers	90,000	
3. Taxes due	230,000	$ 670,000
Available for general claims		$ 530,000

Cash received from sale of property	$300,000
Mortgage claim	315,000
Unsatisfied portion of mortgage claim	$ 15,000

Claims of general creditors	Amount	Application of 35.7%*	After subordination	% of original claim received
Unsatisfied portion of mortgage	$ 15,000	$ 5,355	$ 5,355	96.9%***
Bank notes payable	220,000	78,540	185,640	84.4
Accounts payable	950,000	339,150	339,150	35.7
Subordinated debentures	300,000	107,100	0	0
	$1,485,000	$530,000**	$530,000**	46.5%****

*$530,000/$1,485,000 = 35.7%

**Does not add to total because of rounding.

***($5,355 + $300,000)/$315,000 = 96.9%

****($530,000 + $300,000)/($1,485,000 + $300,000) = 46.5%

31.2 The financial statements of the Sayres Corporation for 1984 were as shown on the following page.

A recapitalization plan is proposed in which each share of the $9 preferred will be exchanged for one share of $1.75 preferred (stated value, $40) plus $70 of stated principal in 10 percent subordinated debentures with a par value of $1,000. The $10 preferred stock is retired by calling it at $110 and drawing down the cash account of current assets by $11.0 million.

a. Show the pro forma balance sheet (in millions of dollars) giving effect to the recapitalization plan, showing the new preferred at its stated value and the common stock at its par value.
b. Adjust the income statement to show the effect of the recapitalization.
c. How much does the firm increase income to common stock by the recapitalization?
d. How much less are the required pre-tax earnings after recapitalization compared to those before the change? "Required earnings" is that amount which is just enough to meet fixed charges, debenture interest, and/or preferred dividends.
e. If you were a holder of the $9 preferred stock, would you favor the recapitalization plan?

Sayres Corporation Balance Sheet as of Dec. 31, 1984 (millions of dollars)

Assets		Liabilities	
Current assets	$180	Current liabilities	$190
Net fixed assets	240	Reserves	20
Goodwill	55	$9 preferred stock, $100 par	190
		$10 preferred stock, no par, 100,000 shares callable at $110	10
		Common stock, $4 par	20
		Retained earnings	45
Total assets	$475	Total claims	$475

Sayres Corporation Income Statement for year ended Dec. 31, 1984 (millions of dollars)

Operating income		$240.0
Operating expenses		214.0
Earnings before tax		$ 26.0
Income tax (40%)		10.4
Income after taxes		$ 15.6
Dividends on $9 preferred stock	$17.1	
Dividends on $10 preferred stock	1.0	18.1
Income available to common stock		-$ 2.5

Solution:

a.

Assets		Liabilities	
Current assets	$169	Current liabilities	$190
Net fixed assets	240	Reserves	
Goodwill	55	10% subordinated debentures, $1,000 par*	133
		$1.75 preferred stock 1,900,000 shares, $40 par	76
		Common stock, $4 par	20
		Retained earnings	45
Total assets	$464	Total claims	$464

*Calculation of new subordinated debentures:
Old $9 preferred $190 million/$100 par = 1.9 million shares
1.9 million x $70 stated principal = $133 million in subordinated debentures

b. Pro Forma Income Statement

Operating income	$240.00
Operating expenses	214.00
Earnings before interest and taxes	$ 26.00
Interest expense	13.30
Earnings before tax	$ 12.70
Tax at 40 percent	5.08
Income after taxes	$ 7.62
Dividends on $1.75 preferred stock	3.33
Income available to common stock	$ 4.29

c. Earnings available to common stock are increased by $4.29 - (-$2.5) = $6.79 million.

d. Preferred dividends had been $18.1 million. To pay these, Sayres had to earn $18.1/(1-T) = $30.17 million before tax. After recapitalization, Sayres must earn only the debenture interest of $13.3 million plus the preferred dividend of $3.33 million divided by (1-T) = $5.55 million, a total of $18.85 million, representing a reduction of $11.32 million in required earnings before interest and taxes.

e. Former dividend was $9. New income will be $1.75 in preferred stock dividends plus (.10)($70) = $7.00 in interest income for a total of $8.75.

The former holders of the $9 preferred stock would not favor the recapitalization plan since their income would be reduced. Although the firm's earnings position is improved, this will benefit common stock shareholders, not holders of fixed-income securities.

If, on the other hand, the alternative to recapitalization were bankruptcy, the $9 preferred stockholders would probably accept the plan.

31.3 The Beatty Corporation develops and manufactures computer components. High research costs on two products which proved unsuccessful led to a large deficit at the end of 1981. See the balance sheet and income data below.

Beatty Corporation Balance Sheet as of Dec. 31, 1981
(millions of dollars)

Assets		Liabilities	
Current assets	$38	Current liabilities	$36
Net fixed assets	22	Long-term debt	18
		Common stock	12
		Retained earnings (deficit)	(6)
Total assets	$60	Total claims	$60

Beatty Corporation Sales and Profits 1977-1981
(millions of dollars)

Year	Sales	Net Profit After Tax Before Fixed Charges
1977	$210	$ 20
1978	190	17
1979	195	13
1980	110	- 7
1981	100	-12

The liquidation value of the firm has been assessed at approximately $40 million. However, Beatty's management believes that a reorganization is possible with the investment of an additional $25 million. Management is negotiating with its lenders to obtain these funds. Several of the major computer manufacturers have expressed great interest in a new product Beatty has developed, and management feels that earnings can be restored to $8 million per year after taxes and before fixed charges. The planned reorganization would give half the common stock in the reorganized firm to the current creditors in place of their unsecured debt claims.

a. If the appropriate earnings multiplier for Beatty is 9, should the creditors approve the plan?

b. If the appropriate earnings multiplier is 7, should the plan be approved?

Solution:

a. Liquidation value = \$40 million
   Going-concern value with added investment:
   \$8 million x 9 = \$72 million
   Net value of reorganization:
   \$72 million - \$25 million = \$47 million.

   At an earnings multiplier of 9, creditors should approve the plan since the value of the reorganization exceeds the liquidation value by \$7 million.

b. Going-concern value with added investment:
   \$8 million x 7 = \$56 million

   Net value of reorganization:
   \$56 million - \$25 million = \$31 million

   At an earnings multiplier of 7, the creditors would be better off by \$9 million in a liquidation rather than a reorganization.

31.4 The 1984 balance sheet and income statements for the Fawlty Company are shown below before financial readjustment.

Balance Sheet as of Dec. 31, 1984
(thousands of dollars) Before Financial Readjustment

Current assets	\$165	
Net fixed assets	250	
Total assets		\$415
Accounts payable	\$ 70	
Taxes payable	14	
Notes payable to banks (10%)	70	
Notes payable to trade creditors (12%)	70	
Accrued wages	14	
Total current liabilities		\$238
14% mortgage bonds, due 2000	\$ 70	
15% subordinated debentures, due 1995	140	
Total long-term debt		\$210
Common stock (\$1 par)	\$ 14	
Paid-in capital	60	
Retained earnings	(107)	
Net worth		(33)
Total liabilities and capital		\$415

Income Statement for year ended Dec. 31, 1984
(thousands of dollars) Before Financial Readjustment

Earnings before depreciation, interest and taxes	$ 54.0
Depreciation (5% of $550)	27.5
EBIT	$ 26.5
Interest expense	46.2
Earnings before tax	$(19.7)
Taxes	---
Earnings after tax	$(19.7)
Memo:	
Number of shares	14,000
Earnings per share	$(1.41)

Before financial readjustment, the Fawlty Company earns $54,000 before depreciation, interest and taxes. Depreciation is 5 percent of the gross value of fixed assets of $550,000, or $27,500. EBIT is $26,500. The interest expense is calculated as follows:

Notes payable to banks (10%x$70)	= $ 7.0
Notes payable, trade (12%x$70)	= 8.4
Mortgage bonds (14%x$70)	= 9.8
Subordinated debentures (15%x$140)	= 21.0
Total interest expense	$46.2

Therefore, the earnings before taxes before financial readjustment represent a loss of $19,700. It is assumed that the firm has been suffering losses for a long period of time, so that there are no longer any tax credits from previous profits to include in the current income statement. The firm has a small number of supplier firms which hold most obligations due to trade creditors. After meeting with the two banks which have been lenders to Fawlty and with the four insurance companies who own all of the 15 percent subordinated debentures, all parties agree on a financial readjustment plan for Fawlty.

a. Develop a readjustment plan of the type that the banks and insurance companies would find acceptable.
b. If a voluntary adjustment is not possible, a formal reorganization may be required. In the somewhat more formal reorganization procedure, the company first files a petition for reorganization with a federal court. The court, in accordance with the law, appoints a disinterested trustee. Subsequently, the trustee files a plan of reorganization with the court which obtains an advisory opinion from the Securities and Exchange Commission. In this case the trustee found that the company could not be rehabilitated by management changes, so concluded that the only feasible program would be to

combine Fawlty with Excell, an established producer of a similar line of product whose characteristics would make the combination of the operations more efficient. Excell then made a formal proposal:

(1) To assume the obligation of the 14% mortgage bonds;

(2) To pay Fawlty's $28,000 in back wages and back taxes;

(3) To offer 3,500 shares of Excell stock which has a current market value of $5 per share.

c. As a final alternative, assume that bankruptcy and liquidation are found to be necessary. Set out the priority of claims on the cash that is realized in liquidation of the assets of the Fawlty Company. Bankruptcy fees are $7,000. The following amounts are realized on liquidation:

Current assets	$ 82,500
Net property	55,500
Total	$138,000

Solution:

a. The following adjustments are made to the balance sheet. Inventories are written down by $79,000 and fixed assets are written down by $140,000. Thus total assets become $415,000 - ($79,000+$140,000) = $196,000. The banks are persuaded to forego interest on the notes payable for five years as part of their contribution to the hoped-for revitalization of the firm. Beginning in the sixth year, the banks are to receive 20 percent of the firm's cash flow as loan repayments. In return for their claims, the subordinated debenture holders and the trade creditors are each given 7,000 shares of stock; therefore, together they own shares of the company that are equal to those held by the existing shareholders before the financial readjustments. The total liabilities and capital, therefore, become $196,000, equal to the adjusted total assets. (See adjusted balance sheet on next page.)

The adjustments to the income statement include a reduction in depreciation expense to 5 percent of $400,000. For the first five years, interest expense is reduced to the $9,800 due on the mortgage bonds. Hence the net income of Fawlty Company will be $14,500 per year during the first five years, with earnings of $.52 per share. (See adjusted income statement on next page.)

Thus, by the write-down of the depreciable fixed assets, and by changing the nature of some of the liability claims, the Fawlty Company has been turned from an unprofitable company into a profitable one. The expectation is, of course, that the previous management errors still must be corrected so that the underlying earning power of Fawlty will also be improved.

Balance Sheet (thousands of dollars) After Financial Readjustment

Current assets	$ 86	
Net fixed assets	110	
Total assets		$196
Accounts payable	$ 0	
Taxes payable	14	
Notes payable to banks (10%)	70	
Notes payable to trade creditors (12%)	0	
Accrued wages	14	
Total current liabilities		$ 98
14% mortgage bonds (due 2000)	$ 70	
15% subordinated debentures (due 1995)	0	
Total long-term debt		$ 70
Common stock ($1 par)	$ 28	
Paid-in capital	0	
Retained earnings	0	
Net worth		$ 28
Total liabilities and capital		$196

Income Statement (thousands of dollars) After Financial Readjustment

EBDIT	$54.0
Depreciation (5% of $400)	20.0
EBIT	$34.0
Interest expense	9.8
EBT	$24.2
Taxes at 40%	9.7
Earnings after tax	$14.5

Memo:

Number of shares	28,000
Earnings per share	$ 0.52

b. Excell has offered an amount equivalent to the following:

Mortgage bond assumed	$ 70,000
Payment of wages	14,000
Payment of taxes	14,000
Value of common shares	17,500
	$115,500

The trustee's plan allocated the claims of the unsecured creditors as set forth in Table 31.1. The Securities and Exchange Commission made an evaluation from the standpoint of fairness. On the basis of estimates set forth in Table 31.2, the SEC arrived at an evaluation of net value. First, sales estimates based on the underlying properties of Fawlty Co. were made. These ranged from $380,000 to $460,000. The earning power of companies in this line of business is 4-5 percent of sales. Applying the 4 percent to the $380,000 of sales gives an earnings estimate of $15,200; applying the 5 percent estimate to $460,000 of sales gives earnings of $23,000. It was agreed that a 6 times price/earnings ratio was reasonable. Utilizing the 6 times price/earnings ratio, they arrived at a total value less the $98,000 mortgage assumed plus the cash paid ranging from a negative $6,800 to a positive $40,000. Although the amount paid by Excell is at the low end of the range of the indicated value of the Fawlty Company, the SEC recommended the approval of the trustee's plan for reorganization as meeting the test of fairness.

Table 31.1 Trustee's Plan for Fawlty Company

Prior Claims	Amount	Receives
Wages	$14,000	Cash paid by Excell
Taxes	14,000	Cash paid by Excell
First mortgage, 14%, 2000	70,000	Assumed by Excell
	$98,000	

Trustee's Plan for Remainder of Claims--Valuation based on 3,500 shares at $5 = $17,500, or 5 percent of $350,000 liabilities

Claims	Amount	5 Percent x Amount of Claim	Claim After Subordination	Number of Shares of Common Stock
1. Notes payable to banks	$ 70,000	$ 3,500	$10,500	2,100
2. Notes payable to trade	70,000	3,500	3,500	700
3. General unsecured creditors	70,000	3,500	3,500	700
4. Subordinated debentures	140,000	7,000	0	0
	$350,000	$17,500	$17,500	3,500

Table 31.2 Fawlty Company, SEC Evaluation of Fairness Valuation

Estimated sales of Fawlty Co. properties	$ 380,000 ---$ 460,000	per year
Earnings at 4-5% of sales	$ 15,200 ---$ 23,000	
P/E ratio of 6 times earnings	$ 91,200 ---$ 138,000	
Less cash paid and mortgage assumed	$(98,000)---$(98,000)	
Net value	$(6,800)---$ 40,000	

c.

Table 31.3 Order of Priority of Claims for the Fawlty Co.

Cash received from sale of current assets		$82,500
1. Fees and expenses of bankruptcy proceedings	$ 7,000	
2. Wages due workers earned 3 months prior to filing of bankruptcy petition	14,000	
3. Unpaid taxes	14,000	
Total of priority claims from current assets		35,000
Available to general claims		$47,500
Cash received from sale of net property	$55,500	
First mortgage claim	70,000	
Unsatisfied portion of first mortgage claim	$14,500	

Claims of general creditors	Claim (1)	Application of 13 percent (2)	After subordination (3)	% of original claim received (4)
Unsatisfied portion of first mortgage	$ 14,500	$ 1,885	$ 1,885	82%
Notes payable to bank	70,000	9,100	27,300	39
Notes payable to trade	70,000	9,100	9,100	13
Accounts payable	70,000	9,100	9,100	13
Subordinated debentures	140,000	18,200	0	0
	$364,500	$47,500*	$47,500*	25%

*Does not add to total because of rounding.

In Table 31.3 we see that the amount available to general creditors is $47,500. The total general claims are $364,500. Thus, only 13 percent of the total claims can be met. Since the debentures are subordinated to the bank notes payable, the full amount of the claim of the subordinated debentures must be transferred to the claim of the notes payable to banks. The total amount realized on liquidation is the first mortgage claim of $55,500 plus the $47,500 available to the general creditors, a total of $103,000. This represents, of course, the $138,000 proceeds less the prior claims of $35,000 representing bankruptcy fees, wages owed and taxes owed. Thus, the creditors on total claims of $364,500 plus the $55,500 first mortgage claim satisfied, have total claims of $420,000. For these total claims of $420,000, a net of $103,000 is available. Thus the creditors as a group receive $.25 on the dollar on liquidation.

But the percentages realized vary among the individual claimants: ranging from 82 percent for the first mortgage holders and 39 percent for the banks, down to 13 percent for the other general creditors, and nothing for the subordinated debenture holders. This illustrates the value of the mortgage security as well as the subordination agreement. It also illustrates the generally unfavorable position of the general creditors on liquidation. It is for this reason that they are often willing to work out some informal financial readjustment as described earlier, in hopes that they may do better than the average of 15-20 percent on the dollar received by general creditors.

CHAPTER 32

INTERNATIONAL BUSINESS FINANCE

Theme: Increasingly, we are all affected by international business finance. This chapter will discuss factors which impact the international firm, including exchange rates, international financing and translation of financial statements.

I. Changes in Relative Monetary Values in Recent Years.
   A. In August 1971, the major countries of the world departed from a policy of fixed exchange rates.
   B. Changes in currency values in relation to the dollar have been very substantial in both directions.

II. Foreign Exchange Rate Relationships.
   A. Terminology.
      1. E = Dollars ($) per foreign, or local, currency unit = $/FC; dollar value of a foreign currency amount.
      2. X = foreign currency units per dollar = FC/$; foreign currency value of one dollar.
      3. The subscript "o" refers to the spot exchange rate, for example E_o. The subscript "f" indicates the forward rate at the present time, E_f. The subscript "1" indicates the expected future spot rate, E_1 corresponding to E_f.
      4. D = Percentage change after a devaluation or revaluation.
         a. D_{fd} = the change in value in terms of FC/$

$$= \frac{E_o - E_1}{E_1}$$

         b. D_{df} = the change in value in terms of $/FC

$$= \frac{X_1 - X_o}{X_1}$$

      5. See Problem 32.1.
   B. Consistent foreign exchange rates (consistent cross rates) - The same foreign exchange rate relationships must obtain in all locations (assuming minimal transportation costs). (See Problem 32.2.)
   C. The Fisher effect states that nominal interest rates rise to reflect the anticipated rate of inflation.

$$r = \left[(1+R_n)\frac{P_o}{P_1}\right] - 1$$

$$R_n = \left[(1+r)\frac{P_1}{P_o}\right] - 1$$

where

r = Real rate of interest

R_n = Nominal rate of interest

P_o = Initial price level

P_1 = Subsequent price level

$\frac{P_o}{P_1}$ = Relative purchasing power of the currency unit

$\frac{P_1}{P_o}$ = Rate of inflation

D. The interest rate parity theorem extends the Fisher effect to international markets, stating that the ratio of forward and spot exchange rates will equal the ratio of foreign and domestic gross interest rates.

$$\frac{X_f}{X_o} = \frac{1 + R_{fo}}{1 + R_{do}} = \frac{E_o}{E_f}$$

where

R_{fo} = Current foreign interest rate

R_{do} = Current domestic interest rate

(See Problem 32.3.)

E. The purchasing power parity theorem relates exchange rates to the purchasing power of currencies as measured by the ratio of inflation rates.

$$CX = \frac{X_1}{X_o} = \frac{P_{f1}/P_{fo}}{P_{d1}/P_{do}} = RPC$$

where CX = change in exchange rate

P_{fo} and P_{f1} = initial and subsequent price level in foreign country

P_{do} and P_{d1} = initial and subsequent domestic price level

RPC = change in relative prices

(See Problem 32.12.)

III. Impact of Exchange Rate Fluctuations.

A. Foreign exchange markets enable the buyer to pay in one currency and the seller to receive payment in another.

B. The two currencies are linked in the foreign exchange market by an exchange rate. Fluctuations in the relative values of the currencies, and hence in the exchange rate are an added risk with which international firms must contend.

C. If a firm has assets denominated in a foreign currency in excess of liabilities in the same currency, it is said to be in a long position in that foreign currency, and will benefit from a rise in the value of the foreign currency. A short position means the firm gains if the value of the foreign currency declines.

D. Firms can protect against exchange rate fluctuations by hedging in the forward market. The cost of hedging is the premium or discount of the forward rate relative to the spot rate.

E. The forward market is used as protection against unexpected changes in the foreign exchange value of a currency.

IV. Alternative Methods of Dealing with the Risk of Changes in Foreign Currency Values.

A. Hedge in the forward market.

1. Hedge a foreign currency receivable by selling the foreign currency forward. When collected, use the receivable to pay the forward sale.
2. Hedge a foreign currency payable by buying the foreign currency forward. Use the proceeds from the forward contract to pay the liability.

B. Cover in the capital markets to achieve net monetary balance.

1. Protect a receivable by borrowing foreign and converting to dollars immediately. Use the receivable to pay the loan.
2. Protect a payable by borrowing domestic and converting immediately to foreign currency. Invest and use the proceeds to pay the liability. Pay the domestic loan with dollars.

C. Do not cover the exposed position, and collect the receivable or pay the liability at the future spot rate.

D. The choice of which method to use is based on considerations of both cost and risk.

E. See Problems 32.6 through 32.9.

V. Monetary Balance.

A. Monetary assets and liabilities are items whose value, expressed in local currency units, does not change with devaluation or revaluation.

B. Firms can avoid exchange risk by maintaining monetary balance in local currency units.

C. Firms' balance sheet:
Monetary assets (MA) + Real assets = Monetary liabilities (ML) + Net worth.

D. Net monetary position.
1. MA > ML is a net monetary creditor.
2. MA < ML is a net monetary debtor.

E. In countries where relative currency values are likely to fall, firms should attempt to reduce MA and increase ML.

F. In countries where relative currency values are likely to rise, they should attempt to increase MA and reduce ML.

G. See Problem 32.4.

VI. Translation of Financial Statements.

A. A foreign subsidiary's financial statements must be translated from the foreign currency into the currency of the parent firm in order to prepare consolidated financial statements for the firm as a whole.

B. Three principles of translation have been developed.
1. The current-noncurrent approach translates current assets and liabilities at current exchange rates and all other assets and liabilities at the appropriate historical exchange rates.
2. The monetary-nonmonetary approach translates monetary items at current exchange rates and nonmonetary items at historical rates.
3. The temporal method modifies the monetary-nonmonetary approach by considering the valuation basis of assets and liabilities (for example, inventory).

C. Financial Accounting Standards Board (FASB) Statement No. 8 issued in 1976 recommended the use of the temporal method of translation.

D. FASB No. 52 issued in 1981 superseded FASB No. 8.
1. Provisions of FASB 52 include the following:
a. All balance sheet items except for common stock are to be translated at the current exchange rate.
b. All income statement items except for cost of goods sold and depreciation expense are to be translated at the average rate for the period.
c. The temporal method is to be used for subsidiaries operating in highly inflationary environments.
d. Net income as translated is reflected in the balance sheet retained earnings account; any discrepancy is reflected in a translation adjustment account which assures a balanced balance sheet.

2. FASB No. 52 preserves the same financial ratios in the translated financial statements; however, the underlying economic factors may indicate a change in ratios.

E. The temporal method better captures economic reality in which exchange risk is measured not by accounting numbers, but patterns of real cash flows.

VII. Financing International Operations.

A. Overdrafts permit customers to draw checks up to some specified maximum limit.
   1. They are used widely in Europe.
   2. They are provided for in a previous loan agreement.

B. The discounting of trade bills is used both in domestic and forcign transactions.

C. Commercial banks provide medium- to long-term lending.
   1. European banks are more active than American banks in this activity because of legal requirements.

D. Arbi-loans (international interest arbitrage financing).
   1. The borrower obtains loans in a country where the supply of funds is relatively abundant.
   2. He then converts them into the required local currency.
   3. Simultaneously, he enters into a forward exchange contract to protect himself on the conversion of the local currency into the foreign currency that will be required at the time the loan must be repaid.

D. Link financing is generally short term.
   1. A lender in a foreign country deposits funds with a bank in the borrower's country where interest rates are higher.
   2. This deposit may be ear-marked for a specific borrower.
   3. Or it may be channeled through a money broker to borrowers of good credit standing.
   4. The lender would probably hedge his position in the foreign exchange markets, since he will be repaid in the currency of the country in which the bank deposit was made.

F. Financing subsidiaries are often established to serve as a conduit in international financing.
   1. To avoid a withholding tax at the source in the country in which financing takes place.
   2. To supplement the thin equity basis of the subsidiary, with the parent company acting as guarantor.

VIII. Expanding Role of U.S. Commercial Banks and Investment Bankers.

A. U.S. commercial banks have expanded internationally in a number of ways.
   1. Increased number of foreign branches.
   2. Increased participation in international financing consortiums with foreign banks.
   3. Substantial lending to foreign borrowers, including less-developed countries.

B. Edge Act subsidiaries provide means for commercial banks to:
   1. Make equity investments
   2. Issue or confirm letters of credit
   3. Finance foreign trade
   4. Engage in spot and foreign exchange transactions, etc.

C. U.S. investment banking firms
   1. Arrange Eurocurrency financing
   2. Develop joint participation activities with foreign merchant banks and investment banking houses
   3. Establish offices in foreign countries
   4. Participate in international underwriting groups

D. International project financing. International projects are
   1. Generally large and are financed both from international and government sources
   2. Characterized by developmental activity
   3. Normally have more than one equity owner
   4. Have relatively high debt leverage

IX. Eurodollar System.

A. The Eurodollar system operates as an international money market.
   1. It is a worldwide system and includes many different currencies.
   2. The leakages out of the Eurodollar system are larger than those out of the national demand deposit systems, since Eurodollars do not circulate as a medium of exchange.
   3. Eurobanks include the foreign branches of U.S. banks and foreign banks that deposit and loan Eurocurrencies.
   4. Eurodollar loans are typically in multiples of $1 million with maturities ranging from thirty days to five to seven years, generally unsecured.
   5. The rate on the loan is quoted as a percentage above the London interbank offer rate (LIBOR).
   6. The Eurocurrency system contributes toward increasing and redistributing the world supply of international reserves or liquid resources. This can:
      a. Cause exchange rate movements
      b. Offset the actions of the central banks.

B. Eurobonds are offered for sale in more than one country through international syndicates of underwriting and selling banks.
   1. They are typically denominated in a strong currency.
   2. Convertible Eurobonds have the advantage for the foreign investor of:
      a. Fixed rate of interest higher than dividend yield
      b. Potential capital gains

X. Working Capital Management in International Enterprise.

A. International cash management involves the minimizing of exposure of foreign located funds to:
   1. Foreign exchange rate risk
   2. The avoidance of prohibitions on the movements of funds from one country to another

B. Exposure is decreased by:
   1. Speeding up collection of cash by having bank accounts in the banking system of each country
   2. Using telegraphic transfer
   3. Using international banks with many branches and correspondent banks
   4. Requiring payment in dollars
   5. Concentration banking which makes use of cash centers for cash transfers

C. Problems with international float.
   1. Loss of income of funds while they are in the transfer process
   2. Exposure to foreign exchange rate risk during the transfer period
   3. May take two to three weeks whereas domestic transfers only require two to three days
   4. See Problem 32.5.

D. Services provided by international banks.
   1. Speed up transfer of funds
   2. Can provide consulting service to establish efficient cash flow systems
   3. Provide additional funds through the elimination of float

E. Finance functions take on increased significance for the multinational business enterprise.
   1. Decisions become more centralized
   2. Management information systems take on increased importance
   3. Cash management becomes more important

Chapter 32 - Illustrative Problems and Solutions

32.1 On July 13, 1981, the Swiss franc was worth \$.4811. The 180-day forward rate was \$.4992.

   a. What is X_o? What is X_f?
   b. If the actual future spot rate, E_1, is \$.5114, what is the percentage devaluation or revaluation of the Swiss franc in terms of the U.S. dollar?
   c. What is the percentage devaluation or revaluation of the U.S. dollar in terms of the Swiss franc under the assumption that E_1 = \$.5114?

   (For b and c, start with the value of the reference currency in terms of the other and use the initial value as the base.)

Solution:

a. E_o = the spot exchange rate expressed as the number of dollars per foreign currency unit
= $.4811

$X_o = 1/E_o$

= 1/$.4811

= 2.0786 Swiss francs

= the spot exchange rate expressed as the number of foreign currency units per dollar

E_f = the forward exchange rate = $.4992

$X_f = 1/E_f$ = 1/$.4992

= 2.0032 Swiss francs

b. The Swiss franc has been revalued in terms of the dollar:

% change = $(E_1 - E_o)/E_o$

= (.5114-.4811)/.4811

= .063 = D_{df}

There has been a 6.3 percent increase in the value of the Swiss franc in terms of the U.S. dollar.

c. The dollar has been devalued in terms of the Swiss franc:

$X_1 = 1/E_1$ = 1/.5114 = 1.9554

% change = $(X_o - X_1)/X_o$

= (2.0786-1.9554)/2.0786

= .059 = D_{fd}

There has been a 5.9 percent decrease in the value of the U.S. dollar in terms of the Swiss franc.

32.2 If the exchange rate between dollars and Mexican pesos is 24.56 pesos = $1, and between dollars and West German Deutschemarks is 1DM = $.4119, what is the exchange rate between Mexican pesos and West German Deutschemarks?

Solution:

$1 = 24.56 pesos
1DM = $.4119
1 peso = ?DM

By the principle of consistent cross rates, the product of the right-hand sides of the relations must equal 1.

$$(24.56)(.4119)(X) = 1$$
$$10.116X = 1$$
$$X = .09885\text{DM} = 1 \text{ peso}$$

Also, 1DM = 1/.09885 = 10.116 pesos

32.3 The *Wall Street Journal* for July 14, 1981 listed the following information on the exchange rates between the Japanese yen and the U.S. dollar:

$$X_o = 228.45 \text{ yen per dollar}$$

$$E_o = \$.004377 \text{ per yen}$$

$$X_f(180 \text{ day}) = 217.45 \text{ yen per dollar}$$

$$E_f(180 \text{ day}) = \$.004599 \text{ per yen}$$

The prime interest rate on that day was 20 1/2 percent.

a. What can be inferred about the Japanese interest rate? What is the Japanese interest rate?
b. If the forward exchange rate was $.0042 per yen, what would be the Japanese interest rate?
c. If the Japanese interest rate was 15 percent, what would be the 180-day forward rate on yen per dollar?

Solution:

a. The Japanese interest rate is lower than the U.S. interest rate. By the interest rate parity theorem (IRPT):

$$\frac{X_f}{X_o} = \frac{1 + R_{fo}}{1 + R_{do}}$$

$$\frac{217.45}{228.45} = \frac{1 + R_{fo}/2}{1 + .205/2}$$

$$.95185 = \frac{1 + R_{fo}/2}{1.1025}$$

$$1.0494 = 1 + R_{fo}/2$$

$$R_{fo}/2 = .0494$$

$$R_{fo} = .0988 = 9.88 \text{ percent}$$

b. The Japanese rate would be higher than the U.S. rate.

$$\frac{1 + R_{fo}}{1 + R_{do}} = \frac{E_o}{E_f}$$

$$\frac{1 + R_{fo}/2}{1.1025} = \frac{.004377}{.0042}$$

$$1 + R_{fo}/2 = 1.1490$$

$$R_{fo} = .298 = 29.8 \text{ percent}$$

c. $$\frac{X_f}{X_o} = \frac{1 + R_{fo}}{1 + R_{do}}$$

$$\frac{X_f}{228.45} = \frac{1 + .15/2}{1 + .205/2}$$

$$\frac{X_f}{228.45} = \frac{1.075}{1.1025}$$

$$X_f = (.975)(228.45)$$

$$= 222.74 \text{ yen per dollar}$$

32.4 The Brazilian subsidiary of Andersen International Corporation has monetary assets of FC450,000 and monetary liabilities of FC700,000. Andersen's British subsidiary has monetary assets of FC350,000 and monetary liabilities of FC185,000.

a. Calculate the gain or loss to Andersen if Brazil devalues its currency from FC90 per dollar to FC98 per dollar.
b. Calculate the gain or loss if Britain revalues its currency from FC0.5 per dollar to FC0.4 per dollar.
c. Recalculate the gain or loss in part (b) if Britain devalues its currency from FC0.5 per dollar to FC0.7 per dollar.

Solution:

a.

ML	FC700,000
MA	FC450,000
Net monetary liabilities	FC250,000

$ value at FC90 per $1 before devaluation	$2,778
$ value at FC98 per $1 after devaluation	2,551
Gain on devaluation	$ 227

b.

MA	FC350,000
ML	FC185,000
Net monetary assets	FC165,000

$ value at FC0.5 per $1 before revaluation	$330,000
$ value at FC0.4 per $1 after revaluation	412,500
Gain on revaluation	$ 82,500

c.

$ value at FC0.5 per $1 before devaluation	$330,000
$ value at FC0.7 per $1 after devaluation	235,714
Loss on devaluation	$ 94,286

A devaluation will mean a loss for a company with net monetary assets. For a company with net monetary liabilities, a devaluation means that the firm's liabilities will be repaid in units of lesser value, resulting in a gain.

32.5 Trans-Ocean Industries has subsidiaries in Europe, Asia and Africa. These subsidiaries transfer a total of $1 million monthly to the company's cash center in Zurich. The average transfer time for the funds is 5 days. What is the maximum amount Trans-Ocean should pay for a service which would guarantee a transfer time of not more than two days if Trans-Ocean's opportunity cost is 16 percent?

Solution:

$1,000,000 per month = $12,000,000 per year

Time saved: 5-2 = 3 days funds are freed for other uses

Invest $12,000,000 at 16% for 3 days:

($12,000,000)(.16)(3/360) = $16,000

Trans-Ocean should pay a maximum of $16,000 per year, or 0.133 percent of funds transferred for this service. However, the reduction in transfer time does reduce the exposure of the funds to risk, and this may induce Trans-Ocean to value the service at more than the maximum calculated above.

32.6 A U.S. department store chain has ordered clothing from a French manufacturer at a price of 900,000 francs. The goods will be delivered and paid for in 90 days. For planning purposes the U.S. firm wants to establish its dollar cost now, and on the basis of the information below is considering three alternative courses of action:

Spot exchange rate ($/franc)	$.1728
90-day forward rate ($/franc)	$.1700
Expected future spot rate ($/franc)	$.1715

1. To enter the forward market buying francs at the 90-day forward rate for delivery in 90 days.
2. To lend in France (i.e., to buy French government securities) an amount that with interest will equal 900,000 francs in 90 days. The annual interest rate on French government bonds is 15.2 percent.
3. To make no attempt to cover the exchange rate risk involved in waiting and merely convert dollars to francs at whatever spot rate prevails at the time payment is due.

Which alternative will result in the lowest dollar cost? (Ignore taxes)

Solution:
Alternative 1:
Buy 900,000 francs at $.1700 per franc = $153,000
Total cost = $153,000
Alternative 2:
900,000 fr = (Amount loaned) x (1+.152/4)
900,000 fr = (Amount loaned)(1.038)
Amount loaned = 867,052 fr

To get the francs to purchase this amount of French government securities, the American company must convert dollars to francs at the current spot rate, $.1728/fr
Total cost = (867,052)($.1728) = $149,827

Alternative 3:
Convert dollars to francs at whatever spot rate prevails in 90 days.
Total cost = (900,000)($.1715) = $154,350

The fact that the 90-day forward rate ($/franc) is lower than the current spot rate indicates that the franc is expected to decline in value, which will be advantageous to the American company buying French goods. The exchange rate risk which the American firm must guard against is that the franc will rise in value, or that it will not decline in value as much as anticipated at the current time. In this example, the illustrative future spot rate at the end of 90 days ($.1715/fr) in Alternative 3 represents a decline from the current spot rate, but not as great a decline as predicted by the 90-day forward rate.

For the data given in this example, Alternative 2 has the lowest dollar cost.

32.7 Recalculate the dollar cost of Alternative 3 in Problem 32.6, assuming that the actual future spot rate turns out to be $.165/fr.

Solution:

Total cost = (900,000)($.165) = $148,500
Under these conditions, Alternative 3 would have the lowest dollar cost. However, Alternative 3 is also the riskiest, and has the highest dollar cost under the perhaps equally possible future spot rate of $.1715 assumed in Problem 32.6.

32.8 On January 1, 1982, the Kramer Company sells industrial machinery to a foreign company. Kramer will receive FC5,000,000 on June 30, 1982 when the machinery is delivered. All of Kramer's expenses are in dollars, and the company needs to know the definite dollar amount that it will receive on June 30. The corporate tax rate in both countries is 40 percent, and the expected future spot rate is 6 FC per dollar. The treasurer of Kramer is considering three options to deal with the exchange rate risk:

1. To enter the forward market to sell FC5,000,000 for dollars at the 180-day forward rate quoted on January 1, 1982 which is 4FC per dollar.
2. To borrow on January 1, 1982, from a foreign bank an amount in the foreign currency that with interest will equal the FC5,000,000 that Kramer will be receiving on June 30, 1982. The interest rate on the loan would be 22 percent. By borrowing, Kramer will receive FCs on January 1 which it can immediately convert to dollars at the January 1 spot rate which is 3.125 FC per dollar. The dollars received can be invested in the U.S. at a 16 percent interest rate. When Kramer receives the FC5,000,000 on June 30, it can liquidate the foreign currency loan.
3. To make no attempt to cover the exchange rate risk involved in the 6-month wait, Kramer will merely convert the FC5,000,000 received on June 30 at the 6 FC per dollar spot rate expected to prevail on that date.

Which alternative should be chosen?

Solution:
For a company which expects to receive foreign currency in the future, the risk is that the foreign currency will decline in value during the interim.

Alternative 1:

FC5,000,000 ÷ 180-day forward rate quoted on January 1, 1982
= FC5,000,000 ÷ 4
= $1,250,000

Computation of loss for tax shelter:
FC5,000,000 ÷ January 1 spot rate
= FC5,000,000 ÷ 3.125
= $1,600,000

$1,600,000	
- 1,250,000	
$ 350,000	loss
x.40	tax rate
$ 140,000	tax shelter

Net proceeds with tax shelter = $1,250,000 + $140,000
= $1,390,000

Alternative 2:
On June 30, 1982 Kramer will receive FC5,000,000.

Borrow FC for 180 days:

$$\text{FC5,000,000} = \text{Loan principal}\left[1 + \frac{R_F}{2}(1-T_f)\right]$$

$$= \text{Loan principal}\ [1 + .11(.6)]$$

$$= \text{Loan principal}\ (1.066)$$

FC4,690,432 = Loan principal

Convert the FC loan to $ at January 1 spot rate:
= FC4,690,432 ÷ 3.125
= $1,500,938

Invest proceeds in U.S.:

$$\$1{,}500{,}938\left[1 + \frac{r_{us}}{2}(1-T_{us})\right]$$

$$= \$1{,}500{,}938[1+.08(.6)]$$

$$= \$1{,}500{,}938(1.048)$$

$$= \$1{,}572{,}983$$

Net proceeds = $1,572,983

Alternative 3:
FC5,000,000 ÷ expected spot rate June 30, 1982
= FC5,000,000 ÷ 6
= $833,333
Computation of loss for tax shelter:
FC5,000,000 ÷ January 1 spot rate
= FC5,000,000 ÷ 3.125
= $1,600,000

$1,600,000	
833,333	
$ 766,667	loss
x.40	tax rate
$ 306,667	tax shelter

Net proceeds = $833,333 + $306,667
= $1,140,000

Alternative 2 yields the highest net proceeds.

32.9 Recalculate Alternative 2 in Problem 32.8 assuming a foreign interest rate of 75 percent. Which alternative is most attractive now? Explain.

Solution:
Alternative 2:
Borrow FC for 180 days
FC5,000,000 = Loan principal [1+.75/2(1-.4)]

FC5,000,000 = Loan principal (1.225)
FC4,081,633 = Loan principal

Convert the FC loan to $ at the January 1 spot rate:
FC4,081,633 ÷ 3.125
= $1,306,123

Invest proceeds in the U.S.:
$1,306,123[1+.16/2(1-.4)]

= $1,306,123(1.048)
= $1,368,817
Net proceeds = $1,368,817

Alternative number 1 (with net proceeds at $1,390,000) is the most attractive.

The expected decline in the value of the foreign currency indicated by a January 1 spot rate of 3.125FC/$ and a January 1 180-day forward rate of 4 FC/$ is 28 percent in six months or 56 percent annually. The interest rate in the U.S. is 16 percent annually, so adding the differential change in the foreign exchange rate gets us to a rough foreign interest figure of 72 percent. The equilibrating interest rate implied by the exchange rate in the problem can be calculated using the IRPT.

$$\frac{X_f}{X_o} = \frac{1 + R_{fo}/2}{1 + R_{do}/2}$$

$$\frac{4}{3.125} = \frac{1 + R_{fo}/2}{1 + .16/2}$$

$$1.28 = \frac{1 + R_{fo}/2}{1.08}$$

$$1.3824 = 1 + R_{fo}/2$$

$$.3824 = R_{fo}/2$$

$$.7648 = R_{fo}$$

32.10 The Consalvo Company of Brazil borrowed $10,000 in dollars at a 10 percent interest rate when the exchange rate was 4,000 Brazilian cruzeiros per dollar. One year later, when the loan was repaid, the exchange rate was 4,300 cruzeiros per dollar.

a. What was the effective interest rate based on cruzeiros received and cruzeiros repaid?
b. Verify your result in part a using the interest rate parity theorem.

Solution:

a.

Cruzeiros repaid	$10,000 x 1.10 x 4,300	= 47,300,000
Cruzeiros received	$10,000 x 4,000	= 40,000,000
		7,300,000

$$\text{Effective interest rate} = \frac{7,300,000}{40,000,000} = 18.25\%$$

b. The interest rate parity theorem states that interest rates will reflect expected forward rates.

$$\frac{1+R_{fo}}{1+R_{do}} = \frac{X_f}{X_o}$$

$$\frac{1+R_{fo}}{1.10} = \frac{4,300}{4,000}$$

$$1.10(1.075) = 1+R_{fo}$$

$$1.1825 = 1+R_{fo}$$

$$.1825 = R_{fo}$$

By the interest rate parity theorem, the effective rate of borrowing in dollars must equal the borrowing rate in cruzeiros. According to the IRPT, the interest rate in Brazil at the time of the loan should have been 18.25 percent. If the Brazilian rate was higher than 18.25 percent, then Consalvo benefitted from borrowing in dollars, and vice versa if the Brazilian rate was lower than 18.25 percent.

32.11 New York-based Semblance Corporation requires $50,000 for 3 months. The funds can be borrowed in the U.S. at a 22.5 percent interest rate, or in the United Kingdom for 8 percent. The spot rate for British pounds is $1.40; the forward rate for a 90-day contract is $1.45. Is there an advantage to borrowing in the United Kingdom at the lower rate?

Solution:

$$\text{Cost of UK borrowing} = \frac{E_1}{E_o}\left(1+\frac{R_{fo}}{4}\right) = \frac{1.45}{1.40}(1.02)$$

$$= 1.0357(1.02)$$

$$= 1.0564$$

$$= 5.64 \text{ percent}$$

The effective cost of borrowing in the UK is practically the same as the U.S. interest rate of 22.5/4 = 5.625 percent, in spite of the apparently much lower rate. This is as predicted by the IRPT. There is no advantage to borrowing at the "lower" rate, since all the "savings" are consumed by the change in exchange rates.

32.12 The spot exchange rate of Silesian korbogs to the U.S. dollar on April 15, 1985 was KB5 = $1. It was expected that inflation in the United States would be 5 percent over the following year, and that inflation in Silesia would be at a 20 percent rate. The real rate of interest in both countries is 5 percent.

a. What is the expected future spot rate of KB per dollar on April 15, 1985? (Use the purchasing power parity theorem.)
b. Use the Fisher relation to estimate the nominal interest rates in Silesia and the United States which will enable investments in each country to earn the real rate of interest.
c. Use the interest rate parity theorem to estimate the current forward rate of KB per dollar. How does your estimate compare with the expected future spot rate predicted in part a?

Solution:

a. Using the PPPT we have:

$$\frac{X_1}{X_o} = \frac{P_{f1}/P_{fo}}{P_{d1}/P_{do}}$$

where d represents the U.S.
f represents Silesia

$X_o = 5$

$P_{f1}/P_{fo} = 1.2$

$P_{d1}/P_{do} = 1.05$

$$\frac{X_1}{5} = \frac{1.2}{1.05}$$

$$X_1 = 5(1.1429)$$

$$X_1 = 5.7 \text{ KB/\$}$$

b. The Fisher relation states:

$$\frac{1+r}{1+R_n} = \frac{P_o}{P_1} \quad \text{or } 1+R_n = (1+r)(P_1/P_o)$$

where r = real rate of interest
R_n = nominal rate
P_1/P_o = inflation rate

Solving for Silesia:

$$1+R_n = 1.05(1.2) = 1.26$$

$$R_n = 26 \text{ percent}$$

Solving for the United States:

$$1+R_n = 1.05(1.05) = 1.1025$$

$$R_n = 10.25 \text{ percent}$$

c. The IRPT states:

$$\frac{X_f}{X_o} = \frac{1+R_{fo}}{1+R_{do}}$$

where R_{fo} = nominal rate in Silesia

R_{do} = nominal rate in U.S.

$$\frac{X_f}{5} = \frac{1.26}{1.1025}$$

$$X_f = 5(1.1429)$$

$$X_f = 5.7 \text{ KB/\$}$$

This result is exactly the same as above, illustrating the internal consistency of the PPPT, the Fisher relation, and the IRPT.

APPENDIX TABLES

APPENDIX A

INTEREST TABLES

Table A.1 Future Value of $1 at the End of n Periods: $FVIF_{r,n} = (1 + r)^n$

Period	1%	2%	3%	4%	5%	6%	7%	8%	9%	10%	12%	14%	15%	16%	18%	20%	24%	28%	32%	36%
1	1.0100	1.0200	1.0300	1.0400	1.0500	1.0600	1.0700	1.0800	1.0900	1.1000	1.1200	1.1400	1.1500	1.1600	1.1800	1.2000	1.2400	1.2800	1.3200	1.3600
2	1.0201	1.0404	1.0609	1.0816	1.1025	1.1236	1.1449	1.1664	1.1881	1.2100	1.2544	1.2996	1.3225	1.3456	1.3924	1.4400	1.5376	1.6384	1.7424	1.8496
3	1.0303	1.0612	1.0927	1.1249	1.1576	1.1910	1.2250	1.2597	1.2950	1.3310	1.4049	1.4815	1.5209	1.5609	1.6430	1.7280	1.9066	2.0972	2.3000	2.5155
4	1.0406	1.0824	1.1255	1.1699	1.2155	1.2625	1.3108	1.3605	1.4116	1.4641	1.5735	1.6890	1.7490	1.8106	1.9388	2.0736	2.3642	2.6844	3.0360	3.4210
5	1.0510	1.1041	1.1593	1.2167	1.2763	1.3382	1.4026	1.4693	1.5386	1.6105	1.7623	1.9254	2.0114	2.1003	2.2878	2.4883	2.9316	3.4360	4.0075	4.6526
6	1.0615	1.1262	1.1941	1.2653	1.3401	1.4185	1.5007	1.5869	1.6771	1.7716	1.9738	2.1950	2.3131	2.4364	2.6996	2.9860	3.6352	4.3980	5.2899	6.3275
7	1.0721	1.1487	1.2299	1.3159	1.4071	1.5036	1.6058	1.7138	1.8280	1.9487	2.2107	2.5023	2.6600	2.8262	3.1855	3.5832	4.5077	5.6295	6.9826	8.6054
8	1.0829	1.1717	1.2668	1.3686	1.4775	1.5938	1.7182	1.8509	1.9926	2.1436	2.4760	2.8526	3.0590	3.2784	3.7589	4.2998	5.5895	7.2058	9.2170	11.703
9	1.0937	1.1951	1.3048	1.4233	1.5513	1.6895	1.8385	1.9990	2.1719	2.3579	2.7731	3.2519	3.5179	3.8030	4.4355	5.1598	6.9310	9.2234	12.166	15.916
10	1.1046	1.2190	1.3439	1.4802	1.6289	1.7908	1.9672	2.1589	2.3674	2.5937	3.1058	3.7072	4.0456	4.4114	5.2338	6.1917	8.5944	11.805	16.059	21.646
11	1.1157	1.2434	1.3842	1.5395	1.7103	1.8983	2.1049	2.3316	2.5804	2.8531	3.4785	4.2262	4.6524	5.1173	6.1759	7.4301	10.657	15.111	21.198	29.439
12	1.1268	1.2682	1.4258	1.6010	1.7959	2.0122	2.2522	2.5182	2.8127	3.1384	3.8960	4.8179	5.3502	5.9360	7.2876	8.9161	13.214	19.342	27.982	40.037
13	1.1381	1.2936	1.4685	1.6651	1.8856	2.1329	2.4098	2.7196	3.0658	3.4523	4.3635	5.4924	6.1528	6.8858	8.5994	10.699	16.386	24.758	36.937	54.451
14	1.1495	1.3195	1.5126	1.7317	1.9799	2.2609	2.5785	2.9372	3.3417	3.7975	4.8871	6.2613	7.0757	7.9875	10.147	12.839	20.319	31.691	48.756	74.053
15	1.1610	1.3459	1.5580	1.8009	2.0789	2.3966	2.7590	3.1722	3.6425	4.1772	5.4736	7.1379	8.1371	9.2655	11.973	15.407	25.195	40.564	64.358	100.71
16	1.1726	1.3728	1.6047	1.8730	2.1829	2.5404	2.9522	3.4259	3.9703	4.5950	6.1304	8.1372	9.3576	10.748	14.129	18.488	31.242	51.923	84.953	136.96
17	1.1843	1.4002	1.6528	1.9479	2.2920	2.6928	3.1588	3.7000	4.3276	5.0545	6.8660	9.2765	10.761	12.467	16.672	22.186	38.740	66.461	112.13	186.27
18	1.1961	1.4282	1.7024	2.0258	2.4066	2.8543	3.3799	3.9960	4.7171	5.5599	7.6900	10.575	12.375	14.462	19.673	26.623	48.038	85.070	148.02	253.33
19	1.2081	1.4568	1.7535	2.1068	2.5270	3.0256	3.6165	4.3157	5.1417	6.1159	8.6128	12.055	14.231	16.776	23.214	31.948	59.567	108.89	195.39	344.53
20	1.2202	1.4859	1.8061	2.1911	2.6533	3.2071	3.8697	4.6610	5.6044	6.7275	9.6463	13.743	16.366	19.460	27.393	38.337	73.864	139.37	257.91	468.57
21	1.2324	1.5157	1.8603	2.2788	2.7860	3.3996	4.1406	5.0338	6.1088	7.4002	10.803	15.667	18.821	22.574	32.323	46.005	91.591	178.40	340.44	637.26
22	1.2447	1.5460	1.9161	2.3699	2.9253	3.6035	4.4304	5.4365	6.6586	8.1403	12.100	17.861	21.644	26.186	38.142	55.206	113.57	228.35	449.39	866.67
23	1.2572	1.5769	1.9736	2.4647	3.0715	3.8197	4.7405	5.8715	7.2579	8.9543	13.552	20.361	24.891	30.376	45.007	66.247	140.83	292.30	593.19	1178.6
24	1.2697	1.6084	2.0328	2.5633	3.2251	4.0489	5.0724	6.3412	7.9111	9.8497	15.178	23.212	28.625	35.236	53.108	79.496	174.63	374.14	783.02	1602.9
25	1.2824	1.6406	2.0938	2.6658	3.3864	4.2919	5.4274	6.8485	8.6231	10.834	17.000	26.461	32.918	40.874	62.668	95.396	216.54	478.90	1033.5	2180.0
26	1.2953	1.6734	2.1566	2.7725	3.5557	4.5494	5.8074	7.3964	9.3992	11.918	19.040	30.166	37.856	47.414	73.948	114.47	268.51	612.99	1364.3	2964.9
27	1.3082	1.7069	2.2213	2.8834	3.7335	4.8223	6.2139	7.9881	10.245	13.110	21.324	34.389	43.535	55.000	87.259	137.37	332.95	784.63	1800.9	4032.2
28	1.3213	1.7410	2.2879	2.9987	3.9201	5.1117	6.6488	8.6271	11.167	14.421	23.883	39.204	50.065	63.800	102.96	164.84	412.86	1004.3	2377.2	5483.8
29	1.3345	1.7758	2.3566	3.1187	4.1161	5.4184	7.1143	9.3173	12.172	15.863	26.749	44.693	57.575	74.008	121.50	197.81	511.95	1285.5	3137.9	7458.0
30	1.3478	1.8114	2.4273	3.2434	4.3219	5.7435	7.6123	10.062	13.267	17.449	29.959	50.950	66.211	85.849	143.37	237.37	634.81	1645.5	4142.0	10143.
40	1.4889	2.2080	3.2620	4.8010	7.0400	10.285	14.974	21.724	31.409	45.259	93.050	188.88	267.86	378.72	750.37	1469.7	5455.9	19426.	66520.	*
50	1.6446	2.6916	4.3839	7.1067	11.467	18.420	29.457	46.901	74.357	117.39	289.00	700.23	1083.6	1670.7	3927.3	9100.4	46890.	*	*	*
60	1.8167	3.2810	5.8916	10.519	18.679	32.987	57.946	101.25	176.03	304.48	897.59	2595.9	4383.9	7370.1	20555.	56347.	*	*	*	*

*FVIF > 99,999

Table A.2 Present Value of $1 Received at the End of n Periods: $PVIF_{r,n} = 1/(1 + r)^n = (1 + r)^{-n}$

Period	1%	2%	3%	4%	5%	6%	7%	8%	9%	10%	12%	14%	15%	16%	18%	20%	24%	28%	32%	36%
1	.9901	.9804	.9709	.9615	.9524	.9434	.9346	.9259	.9174	.9091	.8929	.8772	.8696	.8621	.8475	.8333	.8065	.7813	.7576	.7353
2	.9803	.9612	.9426	.9246	.9070	.8900	.8734	.8573	.8417	.8264	.7972	.7695	.7561	.7432	.7182	.6944	.6504	.6104	.5739	.5407
3	.9706	.9423	.9151	.8890	.8638	.8396	.8163	.7938	.7722	.7513	.7118	.6750	.6575	.6407	.6086	.5787	.5245	.4768	.4348	.3975
4	.9610	.9238	.8885	.8548	.8227	.7921	.7629	.7350	.7084	.6830	.6355	.5921	.5718	.5523	.5158	.4823	.4230	.3725	.3294	.2923
5	.9515	.9057	.8626	.8219	.7835	.7473	.7130	.6806	.6499	.6209	.5674	.5194	.4972	.4761	.4371	.4019	.3411	.2910	.2495	.2149
6	.9420	.8880	.8375	.7903	.7462	.7050	.6663	.6302	.5963	.5645	.5066	.4556	.4323	.4104	.3704	.3349	.2751	.2274	.1890	.1580
7	.9327	.8706	.8131	.7599	.7107	.6651	.6227	.5835	.5470	.5132	.4523	.3996	.3759	.3538	.3139	.2791	.2218	.1776	.1432	.1162
8	.9235	.8535	.7894	.7307	.6768	.6274	.5820	.5403	.5019	.4665	.4039	.3506	.3269	.3050	.2660	.2326	.1789	.1388	.1085	.0854
9	.9143	.8368	.7664	.7026	.6446	.5919	.5439	.5002	.4604	.4241	.3606	.3075	.2843	.2630	.2255	.1938	.1443	.1084	.0822	.0628
10	.9053	.8203	.7441	.6756	.6139	.5584	.5083	.4632	.4224	.3855	.3220	.2697	.2472	.2267	.1911	.1615	.1164	.0847	.0623	.0462
11	.8963	.8043	.7224	.6496	.5847	.5268	.4751	.4289	.3875	.3505	.2875	.2366	.2149	.1954	.1619	.1346	.0938	.0662	.0472	.0340
12	.8874	.7885	.7014	.6246	.5568	.4970	.4440	.3971	.3555	.3186	.2567	.2076	.1869	.1685	.1372	.1122	.0757	.0517	.0357	.0250
13	.8787	.7730	.6810	.6006	.5303	.4688	.4150	.3677	.3262	.2897	.2292	.1821	.1625	.1452	.1163	.0935	.0610	.0404	.0271	.0184
14	.8700	.7579	.6611	.5775	.5051	.4423	.3878	.3405	.2992	.2633	.2046	.1597	.1413	.1252	.0985	.0779	.0492	.0316	.0205	.0135
15	.8613	.7430	.6419	.5553	.4810	.4173	.3624	.3152	.2745	.2394	.1827	.1401	.1229	.1079	.0835	.0649	.0397	.0247	.0155	.0099
16	.8528	.7284	.6232	.5339	.4581	.3936	.3387	.2919	.2519	.2176	.1631	.1229	.1069	.0930	.0708	.0541	.0320	.0193	.0118	.0073
17	.8444	.7142	.6050	.5134	.4363	.3714	.3166	.2703	.2311	.1978	.1456	.1078	.0929	.0802	.0600	.0451	.0258	.0150	.0089	.0054
18	.8360	.7002	.5874	.4936	.4155	.3503	.2959	.2502	.2120	.1799	.1300	.0946	.0808	.0691	.0508	.0376	.0208	.0118	.0068	.0039
19	.8277	.6864	.5703	.4746	.3957	.3305	.2765	.2317	.1945	.1635	.1161	.0829	.0703	.0596	.0431	.0313	.0168	.0092	.0051	.0029
20	.8195	.6730	.5537	.4564	.3769	.3118	.2584	.2145	.1784	.1486	.1037	.0728	.0611	.0514	.0365	.0261	.0135	.0072	.0039	.0021
25	.7798	.6095	.4776	.3751	.2953	.2330	.1842	.1460	.1160	.0923	.0588	.0378	.0304	.0245	.0160	.0105	.0046	.0021	.0010	.0005
30	.7419	.5521	.4120	.3083	.2314	.1741	.1314	.0994	.0754	.0573	.0334	.0196	.0151	.0116	.0070	.0042	.0016	.0006	.0002	.0001
40	.6717	.4529	.3066	.2083	.1420	.0972	.0668	.0460	.0318	.0221	.0107	.0053	.0037	.0026	.0013	.0007	.0002	.0001	*	*
50	.6080	.3715	.2281	.1407	.0872	.0543	.0339	.0213	.0134	.0085	.0035	.0014	.0009	.0006	.0003	.0001	*	*	*	*
60	.5504	.3048	.1697	.0951	.0535	.0303	.0173	.0099	.0057	.0033	.0011	.0004	.0002	.0001	*	*	*	*	*	*

*The factor is zero to four decimal places.

Table A.3 Sum on an Annuity of $1 Per Period for n Periods:

$$FVIFA_{r,t} = \sum_{t=1}^{n} (1 + r)^{t-1} = \frac{(1 + r)^n - 1}{r}$$

Number of Periods	1%	2%	3%	4%	5%	6%	7%	8%	9%	10%	12%	14%	15%	16%	18%	20%	24%	28%	32%	36%
1	1.0000	1.0000	1.0000	1.0000	1.0000	1.0000	1.0000	1.0000	1.0000	1.0000	1.0000	1.0000	1.0000	1.0000	1.0000	1.0000	1.0000	1.0000	1.0000	1.0000
2	2.0100	2.0200	2.0300	2.0400	2.0500	2.0600	2.0700	2.0800	2.0900	2.1000	2.1200	2.1400	2.1500	2.1600	2.1800	2.2000	2.2400	2.2800	2.3200	2.3600
3	3.0301	3.0604	3.0909	3.1216	3.1525	3.1836	3.2149	3.2464	3.2781	3.3100	3.3744	3.4396	3.4725	3.5056	3.5724	3.6400	3.7776	3.9184	4.0624	4.2096
4	4.0604	4.1216	4.1836	4.2465	4.3101	4.3746	4.4399	4.5061	4.5731	4.6410	4.7793	4.9211	4.9934	5.0665	5.2154	5.3680	5.6842	6.0156	6.3624	6.7251
5	5.1010	5.2040	5.3091	5.4163	5.5256	5.6371	5.7507	5.8666	5.9847	6.1051	6.3528	6.6101	6.7424	6.8771	7.1542	7.4416	8.0484	8.6999	9.3983	10.146
6	6.1520	6.3081	6.4684	6.6330	6.8019	6.9753	7.1533	7.3359	7.5233	7.7156	8.1152	8.5355	8.7537	8.9775	9.4420	9.9299	10.980	12.135	13.405	14.798
7	7.2135	7.4343	7.6625	7.8983	8.1420	8.3938	8.6540	8.9228	9.2004	9.4872	10.089	10.730	11.066	11.413	12.141	12.915	14.615	16.533	18.695	21.126
8	8.2857	8.5830	8.8923	9.2142	9.5491	9.8975	10.259	10.636	11.028	11.435	12.299	13.232	13.726	14.240	15.327	16.499	19.122	22.163	25.678	29.731
9	9.3685	9.7546	10.159	10.582	11.026	11.491	11.978	12.487	13.021	13.579	14.775	16.085	16.785	17.518	19.085	20.798	24.712	29.369	34.895	41.435
10	10.462	10.949	11.463	12.006	12.577	13.180	13.816	14.486	15.192	15.937	17.548	19.337	20.303	21.321	23.521	25.958	31.643	38.592	47.061	57.351
11	11.566	12.168	12.807	13.486	14.206	14.971	15.783	16.645	17.560	18.531	20.654	23.044	24.349	25.732	28.755	32.150	40.237	50.398	63.121	78.998
12	12.682	13.412	14.192	15.025	15.917	16.869	17.888	18.977	20.140	21.384	24.133	27.270	29.001	30.850	34.931	39.580	50.894	65.510	84.320	108.43
13	13.809	14.680	15.617	16.626	17.713	18.882	20.140	21.495	22.953	24.522	28.029	32.088	34.351	36.786	42.218	48.496	64.109	84.852	112.30	148.47
14	14.947	15.973	17.086	18.291	19.598	21.015	22.550	24.214	26.019	27.975	32.392	37.581	40.504	43.672	50.818	59.195	80.496	109.61	149.23	202.92
15	16.096	17.293	18.598	20.023	21.578	23.276	25.129	27.152	29.360	31.772	37.279	43.842	47.580	51.659	60.965	72.035	100.81	141.30	197.99	276.97
16	17.257	18.639	20.156	21.824	23.657	25.672	27.888	30.324	33.003	35.949	42.753	50.980	55.717	60.925	72.939	87.442	126.01	181.86	262.35	377.69
17	18.430	20.012	21.761	23.697	25.840	28.212	30.840	33.750	36.973	40.544	48.883	59.117	65.075	71.673	87.068	105.93	157.25	233.79	347.30	514.66
18	19.614	21.412	23.414	25.645	28.132	30.905	33.999	37.450	41.301	45.599	55.749	68.394	75.836	84.140	103.74	128.11	195.99	300.25	459.44	700.93
19	20.810	22.840	25.116	27.671	30.539	33.760	37.379	41.446	46.018	51.159	63.439	78.969	88.211	98.603	123.41	154.74	244.03	385.32	607.47	954.27
20	22.019	24.297	26.870	29.778	33.066	36.785	40.995	45.762	51.160	57.275	72.052	91.024	102.44	115.37	146.62	186.68	303.60	494.21	802.86	1298.8
21	23.239	25.783	28.676	31.969	35.719	39.992	44.865	50.422	56.764	64.002	81.698	104.76	118.81	134.84	174.02	225.02	377.46	633.59	1060.7	1767.3
22	24.471	27.299	30.536	34.248	38.505	43.392	49.005	55.456	62.873	71.402	92.502	120.43	137.63	157.41	206.34	271.03	469.05	811.99	1401.2	2404.6
23	25.716	28.845	32.452	36.617	41.430	46.995	53.436	60.893	69.531	79.543	104.60	138.29	159.27	183.60	244.48	326.23	582.62	1040.3	1850.6	3271.3
24	26.973	30.421	34.426	39.082	44.502	50.815	58.176	66.764	76.789	88.497	118.15	158.65	164.16	213.97	289.49	392.48	723.46	1332.6	2443.8	4449.9
25	28.243	32.030	36.459	41.645	47.727	54.864	63.249	73.105	84.700	98.347	133.33	181.87	212.79	249.21	342.60	471.98	898.09	1706.8	3226.8	6052.9
26	29.525	33.670	38.553	44.311	51.113	59.156	68.676	79.954	93.323	109.18	150.33	208.33	245.71	290.08	405.27	567.37	1114.6	2185.7	4260.4	8233.0
27	30.820	35.344	40.709	47.084	54.669	63.705	74.483	87.350	102.72	121.09	169.37	238.49	283.56	337.50	479.22	681.85	1383.1	2798.7	5624.7	11197.9
28	32.129	37.051	42.930	49.967	58.402	68.528	80.697	95.338	112.96	134.20	190.69	272.88	327.10	392.50	566.48	819.22	1716.0	3583.3	7425.6	15230.2
29	33.450	38.792	45.218	52.966	62.322	73.639	87.346	103.96	124.13	148.63	214.58	312.09	377.16	456.30	669.44	984.06	2128.9	4587.6	9802.9	20714.1
30	34.784	40.568	47.575	56.084	66.438	79.058	94.460	113.28	136.30	164.49	241.33	356.78	434.74	530.31	790.94	1181.8	2640.9	5873.2	12940.	28172.2
40	48.886	60.402	75.401	95.025	120.79	154.76	199.63	259.05	337.88	442.59	767.09	1342.0	1779.0	2360.7	4163.2	7343.8	22728.	69377.	*	*
50	64.463	84.579	112.79	152.66	209.34	290.33	406.52	573.76	815.08	1163.9	2400.0	4994.5	7217.7	10435.	21813.	45497.	*	*	*	*
60	81.669	114.05	163.05	237.99	353.58	533.12	813.52	1253.2	1944.7	3034.8	7471.6	18535.	29219.	46057.	*	*	*	*	*	*

*FVIFA > 99,999

Table A.4 Present Value of an Annuity of $1 Per Period for n Periods:

$$PVIFA_{r,t} = \sum_{t=1}^{n} \frac{1}{(1 + r)^t} = \frac{1 - \frac{1}{(1 + r)^n}}{r}$$

Number of payments	1%	2%	3%	4%	5%	6%	7%	8%	9%	10%	12%	14%	15%	16%	18%	20%	24%	28%	32%
1	0.9901	0.9804	0.9709	0.9615	0.9524	0.9434	0.9346	0.9259	0.9174	0.9091	0.8929	0.8772	0.8696	0.8621	0.8475	0.8333	0.8065	0.7813	0.7576
2	1.9704	1.9416	1.9135	1.8861	1.8594	1.8334	1.8080	1.7833	1.7591	1.7355	1.6901	1.6467	1.6257	1.6052	1.5656	1.5278	1.4568	1.3916	1.3315
3	2.9410	2.8839	2.8286	2.7751	2.7232	2.6730	2.6243	2.5771	2.5313	2.4869	2.4018	2.3216	2.2832	2.2459	2.1743	2.1065	1.9813	1.8684	1.7663
4	3.9020	3.8077	3.7171	3.6299	3.5460	3.4651	3.3872	3.3121	3.2397	3.1699	3.0373	2.9137	2.8550	2.7982	2.6901	2.5887	2.4043	2.2410	2.0957
5	4.8534	4.7135	4.5797	4.4518	4.3295	4.2124	4.1002	3.9927	3.8897	3.7908	3.6048	3.4331	3.3522	3.2743	3.1272	2.9906	2.7454	2.5320	2.3452
6	5.7955	5.6014	5.4172	5.2421	5.0757	4.9173	4.7665	4.6229	4.4859	4.3553	4.1114	3.8887	3.7845	3.6847	3.4976	3.3255	3.0205	2.7594	2.5342
7	6.7282	6.4720	6.2303	6.0021	5.7864	5.5824	5.3893	5.2064	5.0330	4.8684	4.5638	4.2883	4.1604	4.0386	3.8115	3.6046	3.2423	2.9370	2.6775
8	7.6517	7.3255	7.0197	6.7327	6.4632	6.2098	5.9713	5.7466	5.5348	5.3349	4.9676	4.6389	4.4873	4.3436	4.0776	3.8372	3.4212	3.0758	2.7860
9	8.5660	8.1622	7.7861	7.4353	7.1078	6.8017	6.5152	6.2469	5.9952	5.7590	5.3282	4.9464	4.7716	4.6065	4.3030	4.0310	3.5655	3.1842	2.8681
10	9.4713	8.9826	8.5302	8.1109	7.7217	7.3601	7.0236	6.7101	6.4177	6.1446	5.6502	5.2161	5.0188	4.8332	4.4941	4.1925	3.6819	3.2689	2.9304
11	10.3676	9.7868	9.2526	8.7605	8.3064	7.8869	7.4987	7.1390	6.8052	6.4951	5.9377	5.4527	5.2337	5.0286	4.6560	4.3271	3.7757	3.3351	2.9776
12	11.2551	10.5753	9.9540	9.3851	8.8633	8.3838	7.9427	7.5361	7.1607	6.8137	6.1944	5.6603	5.4206	5.1971	4.7932	4.4392	3.8514	3.3868	3.0133
13	12.1337	11.3484	10.6350	9.9856	9.3936	8.8527	8.3577	7.9038	7.4869	7.1034	6.4235	5.8424	5.5831	5.3423	4.9095	4.5327	3.9124	3.4272	3.0404
14	13.0037	12.1062	11.2961	10.5631	9.8986	9.2950	8.7455	8.2442	7.7862	7.3667	6.6282	6.0021	5.7245	5.4675	5.0081	4.6106	3.9616	3.4587	3.0609
15	13.8651	12.8493	11.9379	11.1184	10.3797	9.7122	9.1079	8.5595	8.0607	7.6061	6.8109	6.1422	5.8474	5.5755	5.0916	4.6755	4.0013	3.4834	3.0764
16	14.7179	13.5777	12.5611	11.6523	10.8378	10.1059	9.4466	8.8514	8.3126	7.8237	6.9740	6.2651	5.9542	5.6685	5.1624	4.7296	4.0333	3.5026	3.0882
17	15.5623	14.2919	13.1661	12.1657	11.2741	10.4773	9.7632	9.1216	8.5436	8.0216	7.1196	6.3729	6.0472	5.7487	5.2223	4.7746	4.0591	3.5177	3.0971
18	16.3983	14.9920	13.7535	12.6593	11.6896	10.8276	10.0591	9.3719	8.7556	8.2014	7.2497	6.4674	6.1280	5.8178	5.2732	4.8122	4.0799	3.5294	3.1039
19	17.2260	15.6785	14.3238	13.1339	12.0853	11.1581	10.3356	9.6036	8.9501	8.3649	7.3658	6.5504	6.1982	5.8775	5.3162	4.8435	4.0967	3.5386	3.1090
20	18.0456	16.3514	14.8775	13.5903	12.4622	11.4699	10.5940	9.8181	9.1285	8.5136	7.4694	6.6231	6.2593	5.9288	5.3527	4.8696	4.1103	3.5458	3.1129
25	22.0232	19.5235	17.4131	15.6221	14.0939	12.7834	11.6536	10.6748	9.8226	9.0770	7.8431	6.8729	6.4641	6.0971	5.4669	4.9476	4.1474	3.5640	3.1220
30	25.8077	22.3965	19.6004	17.2920	15.3725	13.7648	12.4090	11.2578	10.2737	9.4269	8.0552	7.0027	6.5660	6.1772	5.5168	4.9789	4.1601	3.5693	3.1242
40	32.8347	27.3555	23.1148	19.7928	17.1591	15.0463	13.3317	11.9246	10.7574	9.7791	8.2438	7.1050	6.6418	6.2335	5.5482	4.9966	4.1659	3.5712	3.1250
50	39.1961	31.4236	25.7298	21.4822	18.2559	15.7619	13.8007	12.2335	10.9617	9.9148	8.3045	7.1327	6.6605	6.2463	5.5541	4.9995	4.1666	3.5714	3.1250
60	44.9550	34.7609	27.6756	22.6235	18.9293	16.1614	14.0392	12.3766	11.0480	9.9672	8.3240	7.1401	6.6651	6.2492	5.5553	4.9999	4.1667	3.5714	3.1250

APPENDIX B

TABLE OF NATURAL LOGARITHMS

Natural Logarithms of Numbers between 1.0 and 4.99

N	0	1	2	3	4	5	6	7	8	9
1.0	0.00000	.00995	.01980	.02956	.03922	.04879	.05827	.06766	.07696	.08618
.1	.09531	.10436	.11333	.12222	.13103	.13976	.14842	.15700	.16551	.17395
.2	.18232	.19062	.19885	.20701	.21511	.22314	.23111	.23902	.24686	.25464
.3	.26236	.27003	.27763	.28518	.29267	.30010	.30748	.31481	.32208	.32930
.4	.33647	.34359	.35066	.35767	.36464	.37156	.37844	.38526	.39204	.39878
.5	.40547	.41211	.41871	.42527	.43178	.43825	.44469	.45108	.45742	.46373
.6	.47000	.47623	.48243	.48858	.49470	.50078	.50682	.51282	.51879	.52473
.7	.53063	.53649	.54232	.54812	.55389	.55962	.56531	.57098	.57661	.58222
.8	.58779	.59333	.59884	.60432	.60977	.61519	.62058	.62594	.63127	.63658
.9	.64185	.64710	.65233	.65752	.66269	.66783	.67294	.67803	.68310	.68813
2.0	0.69315	.69813	.70310	.70804	.71295	.71784	.72271	.72755	.73237	.73716
.1	.74194	.74669	.75142	.75612	.76081	.76547	.77011	.77473	.77932	.78390
.2	.78846	.79299	.79751	.80200	.80648	.81093	.81536	.81978	.82418	.82855
.3	.83291	.83725	.84157	.84587	.85015	.85422	85866	.86289	.86710	.87129
.4	87547	.87963	88377	.88789	.89200	.09609	.90016	.90422	.90826	.91228
.5	.91629	.92028	.92426	.92822	.93216	.93609	.94001	.04391	.94779	.95166
.6	95551	.95935	.96317	.96698	.97078	.97456	.97833	.98208	.98582	.98954
.7	.99325	.99695	.00063[a]	.00430[a]	.00796[a]	.01160[a]	.01523[a]	.01885[a]	.02245[a]	.02604[a]
.8	1.02962	.03318[a]	.03674	.04028	.04380	.04732	.05082	.05431	.05779	.06126
.9	.06471	.06815	.07158	.07500	.07841	.08181	.08519	.08856	.09192	.09527
3.0	1.09861	.10194	.10526	.10856	.11186	.11514	.11841	.12168	.12493	.12817
.1	.13140	.13462	.13783	.14103	.14422	.14740	.15057	.15373	.15688	.16002
.2	.16315	16627	.16938	.17248	.17557	.17865	.18173	18479	.18784	.19089
.3	.19392	.19695	.19996	20297	.20597	.20896	.21194	.21491	.21788	.22083
.4	.22378	.22671	.22964	.23256	.23547	.23837	.24127	.24415	.24703	.24990
.5	.25276	.25562	.25846	.26130	.26413	.26695	.26976	.27257	.27536	.27815
.6	.28093	.28371	.28647	.28923	.29198	.29473	.29746	.30019	.30291	.30563
.7	.30833	.31103	.31372	.31641	.31909	.32176	.32442	.32708	.32972	.33237
.8	.33500	.33763	34025	.34286	.34547	.34807	.35067	.35325	.35584	.35841
.9	.36098	.36354	36609	36864	.37118	.37372	.37024	.37877	.38128	.38379
4.0	1.38629	.38879	.39128	.39377	.39624	.39872	.40118	.40364	.40610	.40854
.1	.41099	.41342	.41585	.41828	.42070	.42311	.42552	.42792	.43031	.43270
.2	.43508	.43746	.43984	.44220	.44456	.44692	.44927	.45161	.45395	.45629
.3	.45862	46094	.46326	46557	.46787	.47018	47247	.47476	.47705	.47933
.4	.48160	.48387	.48614	48840	.49065	.40200	.49515	.49739	.49962	.50185
.5	.50408	.50630	.50851	.51072	.51293	.51513	.51732	.51951	.52170	.52388
.6	.52606	.52823	.53039	.53256	.53471	.53687	.53902	.54116	.54330	.54543
.7	.54756	.54969	.55181	.55393	.55604	.55814	.56025	.56235	.56444	.56653
.8	.56862	.57070	.57277	.57485	.57691	.57898	.58104	.58309	.58515	.58719
.9	.58924	.59127	.59331	.59534	.59737	.59939	.60141	.60342	.60543	.60744

a. Add 1.0 to indicated figure.

APPENDIX C

TABLES OF ACCELERATED DEPRECIATION FACTORS

Sum-of-Years'-Digits Method (SYD) at Different Costs of Capital

Period	6%	8%	10%	12%	14%	15%	16%
1	—	—	—	—	—	—	—
2	—	—	—	—	—	—	—
3	0.908	0.881	0.855	0.831	0.808	0.796	0.786
4	0.891	0.860	0.830	0.802	0.776	0.763	0.751
5	0.875	0.839	0.806	0.775	0.746	0.732	0.719
6	0.859	0.820	0.783	0.749	0.718	0.703	0.689
7	0.844	0.801	0.761	0.725	0.692	0.676	0.661
8	0.829	0.782	0.740	0.702	0.667	0.650	0.635
9	0.814	0.765	0.720	0.680	0.643	0.626	0.610
10	0.800	0.748	0.701	0.659	0.621	0.604	0.587
11	0.786	0.731	0.683	0.639	0.600	0.582	0.565
12	0.773	0.715	0.665	0.620	0.581	0.562	0.545
13	0.760	0.700	0.648	0.602	0.562	0.543	0.526
14	0.747	0.685	0.632	0.585	0.544	0.525	0.508
15	0.734	0.671	0.616	0.569	0.527	0.508	0.491
16	0.722	0.657	0.601	0.553	0.511	0.492	0.475
17	0.711	0.644	0.587	0.538	0.496	0.477	0.460
18	0.699	0.631	0.573	0.524	0.482	0.463	0.445
19	0.688	0.618	0.560	0.510	0.468	0.449	0.432
20	0.677	0.606	0.547	0.497	0.455	0.436	0.419

Double Declining Balance Method (DDB) at Different Costs of Capital

Period	6%	8%	10%	12%	14%	15%	16%
1	—	—	—	—	—	—	—
2	—	—	—	—	—	—	—
3	0.920	0.896	0.873	0.851	0.831	0.821	0.811
4	0.898	0.868	0.840	0.814	0.789	0.777	0.766
5	0.878	0.843	0.811	0.781	0.753	0.739	0.727
6	0.858	0.819	0.783	0.749	0.718	0.704	0.689
7	0.840	0.796	0.756	0.720	0.687	0.671	0.656
8	0.821	0.774	0.731	0.692	0.657	0.641	0.625
9	0.804	0.753	0.708	0.667	0.630	0.614	0.597
10	0.787	0.733	0.685	0.643	0.605	0.588	0.571
11	0.771	0.714	0.664	0.620	0.582	0.564	0.547
12	0.755	0.696	0.644	0.599	0.559	0.541	0.524
13	0.740	0.678	0.625	0.579	0.539	0.521	0.504
14	0.725	0.661	0.607	0.560	0.520	0.501	0.484
15	0.711	0.645	0.590	0.542	0.502	0.483	0.466
16	0.697	0.630	0.573	0.526	0.485	0.466	0.450
17	0.684	0.615	0.558	0.510	0.469	0.451	0.434
18	0.671	0.601	0.543	0.495	0.454	0.436	0.419
19	0.659	0.587	0.529	0.480	0.440	0.422	0.405
20	0.647	0.574	0.515	0.467	0.427	0.409	0.392

APPENDIX D

TABLE OF AREAS UNDER THE NORMAL CURVE

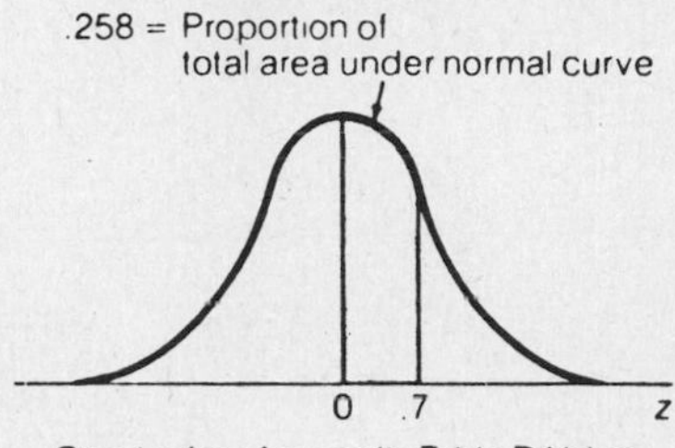

Graph of an Appendix Table D Value

z	.00	.01	.02	.03	.04	.05	.06	.07	.08	.09
0.0	.0000	.0040	.0080	.0120	.0160	.0199	.0239	.0279	.0319	.0359
0.1	.0398	.0438	.0478	.0517	.0557	.0596	.0636	.0675	.0714	.0753
0.2	.0793	.0832	.0871	.0910	.0948	.0987	.1026	.1064	.1103	.1141
0.3	.1179	.1217	.1255	.1293	.1331	.1368	.1406	.1443	.1480	.1517
0.4	.1554	.1591	.1628	.1664	.1700	.1736	.1772	.1808	.1844	.1879
0.5	.1915	.1950	.1985	.2019	.2054	.2088	.2123	.2157	.2190	.2224
0.6	.2257	.2291	.2324	.2357	.2389	.2422	.2454	.2486	.2517	.2549
0.7	.2580	.2611	.2642	.2673	.2704	.2734	.2764	.2794	.2823	.2852
0.8	.2881	.2910	.2939	.2967	.2995	.3023	.3051	.3078	.3106	.3133
0.9	.3159	.3186	.3212	.3238	.3264	.3289	.3315	.3340	.3365	.3389
1.0	.3413	.3438	.3461	.3485	.3508	.3531	.3554	.3577	.3599	.3621
1.1	.3643	.3665	.3686	.3708	.3729	.3749	.3770	.3790	.3810	.3830
1.2	.3849	.3869	.3888	.3907	.3925	.3944	.3962	.3980	.3997	.4015
1.3	.4032	.4049	.4066	.4082	.4099	.4115	.4131	.4147	.4162	.4177
1.4	.4192	.4207	.4222	.4236	.4251	.4265	.4279	.4292	.4306	.4319
1.5	.4332	.4345	.4357	.4370	.4382	.4394	.4406	.4418	.4429	.4441
1.6	.4452	.4463	.4474	.4484	.4495	.4505	.4515	.4525	.4535	.4545
1.7	.4554	.4564	.4573	.4582	.4591	.4599	.4608	.4616	.4625	.4633
1.8	.4641	.4649	.4656	.4664	.4671	.4678	.4686	.4693	.4699	.4706
1.9	.4713	.4719	.4726	.4732	.4738	.4744	.4750	.4756	.4761	.4767
2.0	.4772	.4778	.4783	.4788	.4793	.4798	.4803	.4808	.4812	.4817
2.1	.4821	.4826	.4830	.4834	.4838	.4842	.4846	.4850	.4854	.4857
2.2	.4861	.4864	.4868	.4871	.4875	.4878	.4881	.4884	.4887	.4890
2.3	.4893	.4896	.4898	.4901	.4904	.4906	.4909	.4911	.4913	.4916
2.4	.4918	.4920	.4922	.4925	.4927	.4929	.4931	.4932	.4934	.4936
2.5	.4938	.4940	.4941	.4943	.4945	.4946	.4948	.4949	.4951	.4952
2.6	.4953	.4955	.4956	.4957	.4959	.4960	.4961	.4962	.4963	.4964
2.7	.4965	.4966	.4967	.4968	.4969	.4970	.4971	.4972	.4973	.4974
2.8	.4974	.4975	.4976	.4977	.4977	.4978	.4979	.4979	.4980	.4981
2.9	.4981	.4982	.4982	.4983	.4984	.4984	.4985	.4985	.4986	.4986
3.0	.4987	.4987	.4987	.4988	.4988	.4989	.4989	.4989	.4990	.4990